AGRARIAN ELITES AND ITALIAN FASCISM

AGRARIAN ELITES AND ITALIAN FASCISM

The Province of Bologna, 1901-1926

ANTHONY L. CARDOZA

PRINCETON UNIVERSITY PRESS

Published by Princeton University Press, 41 William Street,
Princeton, New Jersey
In the United Kingdom: Princeton University Press, Guildford, Surrey

Library of Congress Cataloging in Publication Data will be found on the last printed page of this book

Publication of this book has been aided by a grant from the Paul Mellon Fund of Princeton University Press

This book has been composed in Linotron Aldus
Designed by Barbara Werden
Clothbound editions of Princeton University Press books are printed on acid-free paper, and binding materials are chosen for strength and durability

Printed in the United States of America by Princeton University Press, Princeton, New Jersey

To My Parents
LENUS JOHN AND KATHERINE CARDOZA

Contents

List of Maps

Acknowledgments

This work has been made possible by the assistance of many individuals and institutions, whose help I gratefully acknowledge. My former mentor, Professor Arno J. Mayer of Princeton University, first inspired me to study the role of agrarians in the rise of Italian fascism. Without his support, prodding, and humor, this project might never have been undertaken, let alone completed. Professors Carlo Poni, Salvatore Sechi, and the late Giorgio Porisini of the University of Bologna provided me with helpful interpretive and research suggestions during my first stay in Italy. Doctor Silvio Fronzoni aided me immensely in tracking down sources and was a loyal comrade throughout the long months of work in the libraries and archives of Bologna. The advice, criticism, and friendship of Professor Alexander De Grand of Roosevelt University have been of inestimable value to me in the period of writing and revision. In addition my warmest thanks are due to the following individuals who read earlier drafts of the manuscript: Professor Charles S. Maier of Harvard University, Professor Victoria de Grazia of Rutgers University, Professor Alice Kelikian of Brandeis University, Professor Adrian Lyttelton of the Johns Hopkins University Bologna Center, Dr. Paul Corner of the University of Reading, and Professor Marion Miller of the University of Illinois Chicago Circle.

A number of institutions have been most cooperative. First and foremost, I must thank Dr. Isabella Zanni Rosiello and her staff at the Archivio di Stato of Bologna for their knowledge, patience, and good will. My thanks are also due to the staffs of the Biblioteca Comunale and the Biblioteca Universitaria of Bologna as well as to the personnel of the Archivio Centrale dello Stato, the Istituto Nazionale di Economia Agraria, the Biblioteca di Storia Contemporanea, and the Biblioteca della FAO, all in Rome. I must record my gratitude for financial support from Princeton University, the American Academy in Rome, and the National Endowment for the Humanities. Finally, I owe thanks to Mrs. Arlene Ranalli, who masterfully typed the draft of the manuscript, and to the Department of History of Loyola University of Chicago, which gave me the opportunity to complete this book.

A special word of appreciation goes to my friend Beth M. Spekter, who shared many of the sacrifices and burdens through years of research and writing.

Abbreviations

AAB	Bolognese Agrarian Association (Associazone Agraria Bolognese)
ACS	Archivio Centrale dello Stato
AP	*Atti Parlamentari*
APA	Provincial Association of Agriculturalists (Associazione Provinciale di Agricoltori)
ASB	Archivio di Stato di Bologna
CGA	General Confederation of Agriculture (Confederazione Generale di Agricoltura)
CGII	General Confederation of Italian Industry (Confederazione Generale dell'Industria Italiana)
CGL	General Confederation of Labor (Confederazione Generale di Lavoro)
CNA	National Agrarian Confederation (Confederazione Nazionale Agraria)
Edile	Federation of Building Contractors (Federazione Edile)
Federconsorzi	Italian Federation of Agrarian Consortia (Federazione Italiana di Consorzi Agrari)
Federterra	National Federation of Agricultural Laborers (Federazione Nazionale di Lavoratori della Terra)

FISA	Italian Federation of Farmers Syndicates (Federazione Italiana Sindacati Agricoltori)
FPSA	Provincial Federation of Farmers Syndicates (Federazione Provinciale dei Sindacati Agrari)
FPSFA	Provincial Federation of Fascist Farmers Syndicates (Federazione Provinciale Sindacati Fascisti Agricoltori)
GdB	*Giornale di Bologna*
GdE	*Giornale dell'Emilia*
Interprovinciale	Interprovincial Agrarian Federation (Federazione Interprovinciale Agraria)
MAIC	Ministry of Agriculture, Industry and Commerce (Ministero di Agricoltura, Industria e Commercio)
PNF	National Fascist Party (Partito Nazionale Fascista)
PPI	Italian Popular Party (Partito Popolare Italiano)
PSI	Italian Socialist Party (Partito Socialista Italiano)
RdC	*Il Resto del Carlino*
SAN	National Agricultural Secretariat (Segretariato Agricolo Nazionale)

Archival Terms:

B	*Busta*
C	*Categoria*
Cart.	*Carteggio*
Cart. Ris.	*Carteggio Riservato*
F	*Fascicolo*
SF	*Sottofascicolo*

AGRARIAN ELITES AND ITALIAN FASCISM

INTRODUCTION

Political commentators and scholars alike have long recognized the central importance of the countryside in the rise of fascist movements throughout Europe. Indeed, both electoral analyses and studies of party membership have underscored the massive involvement of rural folk in these movements, while the most cursory glance at fascist ideology reveals a striking emphasis on the values and virtues of the country life.[1] Italian fascism is certainly no exception. Although Mussolini originally claimed that his movement could not spread beyond the towns, it was the sudden expansion of rural-based fascism in the winter of 1920-21 that saved his urban *fasci* from extinction. Already in the spring of 1921, contemporary observers began to link the dramatic revival of the fascist movement to a broader reaction of the propertied classes in the countryside against the landless day laborers and the socialist movement.[2] This link has remained a cardinal feature of

[1] On the importance of the countryside in fascist movements, see Juan J. Linz, "Some Notes Toward a Comparative Study of Fascism in Sociological Historical Perspective," in Walter Laqueur, ed., *Fascism, A Reader's Guide* (Berkeley, 1976), pp. 3-121.

[2] See the collection of essays written by representatives of all the major parties between 1921 and 1923 under the editorship of R. Mondolfo and republished in a single volume edited by Renzo De Felice, *Il fascismo e i partiti politici italiani* (Bologna, 1966). For Gramsci's early analysis of the agrarian movement, see Enzo Santarelli, ed., *Gramsci sul fascismo* (Rome, 1973).

subsequent scholarship. Luigi Preti, for instance, has argued that the agrarians of Emilia were the first to discover fascism, "rescuing it from a path leading nowhere and setting it on the high road to success." More recently, Renzo De Felice has shown how agrarian fascism provided Mussolini's movement with its initial mass support, broadened its social appeal, and enlarged its territorial base.[3]

The prominent role played by agrarian elements in the various fascist movements has led a number of scholars to view fascism as an essentially reactionary revolt against modern industrial capitalist society and an attempt to return to an idealized rural past.[4] Even those political theorists who have portrayed fascist regimes as agents of modernization have tended to see agrarian involvement as part of a rear-guard defense of vanishing privileges and prerogatives by an archaic and backward elite. Thus, A.F.K. Organski has argued that fascism rested upon an economic and social compromise between an industrial elite and a traditional agrarian elite, in which the latter attempted to halt the further deterioration of its own position by slowing the pace of industrialization and controlling its consequences. Similarly, Barrington Moore has depicted fascism as the product of an authoritarian modernization process spearheaded by a declining landed upper class that sought "to make reaction and conservatism popular and plebeian."[5]

In the case of Italy, the standard picture of agrarian fascism has been that of a white guard of social reaction which aimed to turn the clock back by eliminating the peasant leagues and restoring the power and prestige of the older rural elites. According to this view, the *fasci* in the countryside were the product of a unique

[3] Luigi Preti, *Le lotte agrarie nella valle padana* (Turin, 1955), p. 449; R. De Felice, *Mussolini il fascista,* Vol. I, *La conquista del potere 1921-1925* (Turin, 1966), pp. 5-12. This link is also stressed in two classical studies of Italian fascism: Angelo Tasca, *The Rise of Italian Fascism, 1918-1922* (London 1938) and Gaetano Salvemini, *Le origini del fascismo in Italia* (Milan, 1966).

[4] For a recent statement of this view, see Henry A. Turner Jr., "Fascism and Modernization," *World Politics,* XXIV (July 1972), pp. 547-564.

[5] A.F.K. Organski, *The Stages of Political Development* (New York, 1965), pp. 122-155; Barrington Moore Jr., *Social Origins of Dictatorship and Democracy* (Boston, 1966), pp. 433-452.

postwar crisis characterized by bitter class conflict and fear of bolshevik revolution. Despite their activism and systematic use of violence, they were only the temporary expression of immediate and localized class interests. Once they had completed their primary task, the destruction of the socialist labor organizations, the agrarian fascists lost any independent momentum and were absorbed into the institutions of the national party and later the Italian state.[6] While such an interpretation is basically correct as far as it goes, its narrow emphasis on the postwar situation leads to a neglect of the profound structural problems and prewar conflicts that predisposed certain sectors of the rural population toward fascism. Also by concentrating on the violence of the squads and the belligerent rhetoric of the fascist warlords, it sheds little light on the movement's mass support or the subsequent growth of the Fascist party's labor syndicates. Finally, this interpretation reduces the actions of the propertied classes to a purely reactive response to socialist excesses, and thereby ignores the internal divisions, larger aspirations, and enduring influence of fascism's wealthy patrons.

An alternative approach has viewed agrarian fascism as the end result of certain longterm trends in the Italian economy and society. Beginning with Gaetano Salvemini and Antonio Gramsci, many historians have attributed the political weaknesses of the liberal state and the deformations in the economy after 1861 to an alliance between northern entrepreneurs and southern semifeudal landowners. The resultant agrarian-industrial bloc found expression in the systems of political transformism and economic protectionism that corrupted parliamentary life and distorted industrial growth. Scholars like Emilio Sereni have argued that the alliance reached its fullest development under the Fascist regime, which sacrificed industrial growth and the interests of capitalist agriculture to ensure social stability and defend the position of

[6] R. De Felice, *Mussolini il fascista*, vol. I, pp. 12-20; Frank M. Snowden, "On the Social Origins of Agrarian Fascism in Italy," *European Journal of Sociology*, XIII (1972), pp. 271-275; Marco Bernabei, "La base di massa del fascismo agrario," *Storia Contemporanea*, VI, no. 1, p. 123.

backward southern *latifondisti*. Sereni has gone so far as to speak of "the transformation of Italian society in an agrarian direction" during the fascist period.[7]

The following study of the transformation of an influential agrarian elite in the province of Bologna, however, suggests a substantial revision of both these standard approaches. For developments in Bologna indicate that agrarian fascism was not simply the expression of the most economically regressive and "anti-modern" elements in the countryside. On the contrary, it must be understood in relation to a particular form of agrarian capitalist development and, more specifically, to the longterm tendencies of a new group of big commercial farmers who gradually rose to prominence after 1900. In this respect, the case of Bologna supports and supplements a body of revisionist scholarship that has recently challenged the view of fascism as a regime of economic stagnation and reasserted the fundamental relationship between fascism and capitalist development in Italy. Scholars like Nicos Poulantzas and Ester Fano Damascelli have stressed the considerable industrial expansion that took place between 1922 and 1929 as well as the rapid resurgence of industrial production after 1934. Moreover, they have noted important qualitative changes in the structure and financing of industry, the consolidation of heavy industry, and the massive intervention of the state in the private sector during the fascist period.[8] Paul Corner and others have extended the revisionist critique to the fascist political economy in the countryside. Corner,

[7] For Gramsci's views on the agrarian-industrial bloc, see *Selections from the Prison Notebooks* (New York, 1971), pp. 55-113. On the importance attributed to this bloc in the development of liberal Italy, see among others Christopher Seton-Watson, *Italy from Liberalism to Fascism* (London, 1967), pp. 82-84; Emilio Sereni, *Il capitalismo nelle campagne* (Turin, 1947); Idomeneo Barbadoro, *Storia del sindacalismo italiano*, Vol. I, *La Federterra* (Florence, 1974), p. xlvi. On the role of the bloc under fascism, see E. Sereni, "La politica agraria del regime fascista," in Comitato promotore, *Fascismo e antifascismo (1918-1936). Lezioni e testimonianze* (Milan, 1972), pp. 298-304.

[8] Nicos Poulantzas, *Fascismo e dittatura. La terza internazionale di fronte al fascismo* (Milan, 1971); Ester Fano Damascelli, "La 'restaurazione antifascista liberista': ristagno e sviluppo economico durante il fascismo," *Il Movimento di Liberazione in Italia*, June-September 1971, pp. 47-99.

in particular, has pointed to fascist initiatives to encourage the movement of property toward large farms, the penetration of finance capitalism into the countryside, and the integration of commercial interests in agriculture and industry.[9]

As the title suggests, this book aspires to be more than simply another local history of the origins of fascism. While most provincial-level studies have focused primarily on the postwar crisis, I have chosen a considerably longer time-frame, one that extends from the late nineteenth century deep into the fascist era. Such a periodization has allowed me to explore the links between fascism and certain fundamental changes in the patterns of landownership, agricultural enterprise, and labor relations that already gave rise to a new agrarian leadership and strategy in the northern Italian countryside before World War I. The province of Bologna is well suited to this exploration. During the first three decades of the twentieth century, the situation there reflected the larger stresses and strains of rapid but uneven industrialization and political democratization on the Italian peninsula. By 1900 the province and the surrounding region of Emilia constituted one of Italy's most advanced agricultural areas. Its farm labor unions were the largest and most powerful in the entire country and made the province an early stronghold of the socialist movement. Bologna's elite of large landowners and commercial farmers took the lead in founding strong employer associations and provided both the personnel and ideas for the agrarian interest-group organizations that arose at the regional and national levels after 1901. As a consequence of the confrontation between the propertied classes and organized labor, the province became a focal point of social and political struggle in Italy prior to 1914. But perhaps most importantly, Bologna was the cradle of the rural-based fascism that elevated Mussolini's marginal extremist movement into a dominant force on the Italian political scene after the war.

[9] Paul Corner, "Fascist Agrarian Policy and the Italian Economy in the inter-war Years" in John A. Davis, ed., *Gramsci and Italy's Passive Revolution* (London, 1979), pp. 239-274; Ester Fano, "Problemi e vicende dell'agricoltura italiana tra le due guerre," *Quaderni Storici*, x, no. 29-30 (May-December 1975), pp. 468-496.

In the decade and a half prior to World War I, the propertied classes of Bologna faced a host of new problems and challenges. Rapid industrial growth after 1896 eroded the relative position of the agricultural sector within the national economy and hastened the transfer of political power and influence from the countryside to new business interests in Milan, Turin, and Genoa. At the provincial level, the Bolognese elite confronted an exceptionally strong socialist labor movement that began to threaten its privileges and prerogatives in virtually all areas of public life. To make matters worse the liberal reform governments of Giovanni Giolitti seemed to encourage the challenge from below by pursuing more enlightened labor policies and by extending suffrage rights to the mass of the Italian population.

These circumstances not only inflamed the struggle between capital and labor in the Bolognese countryside; they also sharpened divisions within the heterogeneous local elite. An old guard of agrarian notables, for the most part aristocratic absentee landowners, proposed to slow the pace of economic and social change in the hope of restoring an idealized rural society where their own paternalism and the deference of the peasants had once appeared to provide peace and stability. Their approach to the problems of social control and political power encountered stiff resistance from a younger group of commercial farmers and leaseholders who sought higher profits through intensified exploitation of labor, the development of industrial crops, and the use of more modern methods of cultivation. My own work explores the interplay between these internal divisions and external challenges as they were manifested in the various business cycles, strikes, electoral contests, and interest-group initiatives.

The evolution of the agricultural economy, elite politics, and labor relations in Bologna and nearby provinces reveals important continuities between prewar and postwar developments on the Italian peninsula. Despite recurrent conflicts and tensions, the trend toward increasing interpenetration of manufacturing, financial, and agrarian interests, which characterized the fascist era, was already becoming evident in the years after 1900. The growth of agrarian consortia and industrial cartels, and the establishment of local agreements between commercial farmers and their industrial suppliers laid the foundations for the postwar national contracts between agrarian marketing organizations and the industrial monopolies. Similarly, early efforts by sugar beet and hemp growers to form syndicates and standardize their relations with refiners and processors prefigured the great agrarian-industrial cartels of the interwar period that would regulate production and set market quotas. Indeed, by 1914 an informal system of interest representation and economic bargaining between major agrarian and industrial groups had begun to take shape, a system that fascism would subsequently institutionalize in the corporative state.

The prewar years also witnessed the beginnings of a crucial shift in the style and structure of elite politics. Throughout the second half of the nineteenth century, limited suffrage and personal prestige had allowed landed gentlemen to dominate public office in Bologna and advance agrarian interests in the capital effectively. Only in the late 1890s did such informal interest representation begin to break down under the stress of changing social and political circumstances. Above all, the growing power of organized labor on the municipal level and in Rome forced agrarians to seek out a new role for themselves in the Italian political system. While the liberal notables remained influential, the balance of power within the propertied classes had shifted by 1910, both in the province and at the regional level, to spokesmen for a younger group of commercial farmers who favored disciplined corporative organization and rejected the old paternalist methods of dealing with peasants and laborers. Recurrent recessions and worker unrest led these growers to adopt a strategy of intransigent resistance to the socialist leagues, and drew them toward coercive solutions to the problems of production, labor control, and interest representation on the eve of World War I. At the same time, employer militancy resulted in serious friction between agrarian interest groups and Italy's liberal political class. Mounting frustration with the difficulties of expressing their economic interests or halting the advance of the left within the fragmented Italian parliamentary system predisposed commercial farmers in Bologna and the Po Valley toward new authoritarian movements: nationalism before 1914, fascism after the war.

The argument for continuity should not be oversimplified, however. The convergence of the rural propertied classes with the fascist movement in late 1920 resulted not only from their authoritarian susceptibilities, but also from a short-term crisis that magnified their sense of weakness and vulnerability. Already prior to the war, militant agrarians who rejected the tutelage of the old parties of order had little success in finding a replacement for them that could represent their interests and mobilize mass support required for political survival. On the contrary, their strategy of confrontation sharpened divisions within the elite and increased the general isolation of the propertied classes in the countryside. War and revolution abroad greatly intensified these problems by temporarily strengthening and radicalizing the left. Socialist electoral landslides and massive strikes in 1919 and 1920 threatened to undermine permanently the authority and property rights of the elite. In this context, the inability of agrarian interest groups to resist labor demands or develop their own viable alternative to the antiquated liberal cliques finally pushed them to merge with fascism.

While big commercial farmers initially constituted just one component of a broad antisocialist reaction that involved all the propertied classes as well as more plebeian elements in the countryside, they quickly assumed a dominant role in the Bolognese fascist movement. From the outset, they were the chief beneficiaries of fascism's violent offensive against the peasant leagues. Moreover, through their powerful positions in the private sector and in the party's political and economic organizations, they were able to shape and influence the turbulent process of fascist institutional consolidation after the March on Rome. The years of transition from movement to regime saw commercial farming interests gain the regimentation of labor and strengthen their hold over the agricultural sector locally and nationally. The situation in Bologna by 1927 clearly illustrates Paul Corner's observation that if fascism generally favored the large proprietors against the little man, "within the dominant group some gained more than others."[10] For the new power structure in the province marked less a return to the past than a major advance for the most technologically modern and commercially advanced, but politically reactionary elements of the local agrarian elite.

[10] P. Corner, "Fascist Agrarian Policy," p. 253.

Map 1 *The Communes of Bologna.*

I. THE PROVINCE OF BOLOGNA IN THE NINETEENTH CENTURY

A benign conspiracy of geography, climate, soil, and cultural heritage had elevated the province of Bologna and its major city to the rank of acknowledged, if unofficial, capital of agricultural Italy by the beginning of the twentieth century. Nestling at the foot of the Apennine Mountains in the southeastern zone of the fertile Po Valley, the city of Bologna commanded the main route to Florence and the south, linked the Adriatic with the Mediterranean, and provided a point of convergence for both the railroad lines and highways of northern Italy. The soil and climate of the province, as local boosters never failed to point out, encouraged cultivation of virtually all important crops of Italian agriculture; its university was the first and most famous in Italy and placed Bologna securely in the forefront of the nation's cultural life. All these factors combined to make Bologna a hub of commercial, administrative, and political activity between the regions of northern and central Italy.[1]

[1] Both in population and territory, Bologna constituted the largest province in the north central region of Emilia. The commercial, agricultural, and cultural importance of the province and its capital city are amply testified to in a variety of sources; see in particular, Camera di Commercio e Industria della Provincia di Bologna, *Cenno storico sulla Camera di Commercio e Industria di Bologna e caratteristiche del distretto camerale* (Bologna, 1924), p. 9 and 41; Marion I. Newbigin, *Southern Europe: A Regional and Economic Geography of the Mediterranean Lands* (New York, 1932), pp. 171-172; Consiglio Provinciale dell'Economia Corporativa, *La Provincia di Bologna nell'anno decimo. Monografia statistica-*

Agriculture, Bologna's chief industry, left its imprint on all areas of local life, for as the Chamber of Commerce proudly affirmed, the province drew "its principal riches . . . from the cultivation of the fields."[2] Bologna had long been the center of Italian hemp cultivation and, together with four neighboring provinces, accounted for over half the country's production of this important crop. In the years after 1900, she also had the fifth largest wheat harvests in Italy, while her rice production was twice that of any other province in Emilia and ranked fourth nationally.[3] Not surprisingly, most of the local populace earned their livelihood directly or indirectly from agriculture. At the beginning of this century, over two-thirds of the population lived in rural communes of the province, with the remainder concentrated in the urban centers of Bologna and Imola. In 1901 64 percent of the active population worked in agriculture, less than a quarter in manufacturing; two decades later farming still provided jobs for over half the work force.[4] Even these figures do not reveal the full extent to which agriculture influenced the occupational structure in the province. Many urban workers depended indirectly on the countryside, since the largest industrial employers were those who processed agri-

---

economica (Bologna, 1932); *La città e provincia di Bologna descritta ne'suoi rapporti storici, statistici, topografici e commerciali* (Bologna, 1889), pp. 3-5.

[2] Camera di Commercio, *Cenno storico*, p. 15.

[3] On industrial crops in Bologna, see Vittorio Peglion, *Piante industriali. Produzione, commercio, regime doganale* (Rome, 1917), p. 39; Giovanni Proni, *La canapicoltura italiana nell'economia corporativa* (Rome, 1938), p. 49; and Consiglio Provinciale, *La provincia di Bologna*, pp. 632-635. The long history of hemp cultivation in the province is discussed in Roberto Roversi, *Canapa ed autarchia* (Rome, 1939), pp. 12-16. For wheat production in Bologna, see Giorgio Porisini, "Produzione e produttività del frumento in Italia durante l'età giolittiana," *Quaderni Storici*, v, no. 14 (May-August 1970), p. 518; on statistics of rice production, see MAIC, Direzione Generale della Statistica, *Annuario Statistico Italiano, 1900* (Rome, 1901), pp. 394-397.

[4] For the distribution of the population in the province, see Giuseppe Puppini, *Le bonifiche in Emilia e Romagna nell'ultimo secolo* (Bologna, 1951), p. 66. Population and employment statistics are from MAIC, *Censimento della popolazione del Regno d'Italia 1901* Vol. III (Rome, 1902), pp. 216-217 and G. Medici and G. Orlando, *Agricoltura e disoccupazione*, Vol. I, *I braccianti della bassa pianura padana* (Bologna, 1952), p. 107.

cultural products or built farm machines. Moreover, the majority of people classified by the census as "nonprofessionals" were women employed in the fields during certain periods of the year. Similarly, a substantial number of professional people in the city were tied to the agricultural sector that required lawyers to facilitate transfers of land or other property in the countryside and engineers to design and implement the various land reclamation projects which helped make "Bolognese agriculture . . . one of the most progressive in the nation."[5]

In comparison with the thriving agricultural sector, manufacturing played only a marginal role in the provincial economy. Several factors militated against industrial growth in the province: the torrential river system could not generate adequate hydroelectric power, the distance of the province from good ports made it difficult to procure raw materials, and mineral resources in the subsoil were not sufficiently abundant. Yet perhaps the most important factor in discouraging the advance of industry was the very strength of the agricultural sector that drew capital away from more risky investments in manufacturing.[6] In the last decades of the nineteenth century, Bologna registered a modest rate of industrialization, but even this development was limited to refiners and processors of agricultural products such as hemp and sugar beets and, to a lesser extent, to those mechanical and chemical enterprises that provided farm machinery and fertilizers. Significantly, in 1898 only three Bolognese firms employed more than one hundred fifty workers; one was a hemp mill, the other two were machine manufacturers.[7] Agriculture also stimulated and sus-

[5] Camera di Commercio, *Cenno storico*, pp. 36-38; Franco Cavazza, *Le agitazioni agrarie in provincia di Bologna dal 1910 al 1920* (Bologna, 1940), p. 40.

[6] Camera di Commercio, *Cenno storico*, p. 23; Augusto Calzoni, "L'evoluzione dell'industria bolognese," *La Mercanzia*, XXIII, no. 6 (1968), p. 522. On the impact of agriculture on industrial growth in the nineteenth century, see Luigi Dal Pane, *Economia e società a Bologna nell'età del Risorgimento* (Bologna, 1969), chaps. 5 and 6 and Enzo Piscitelli, "Aspetti di vita economica bolognese dal 1815 al 1859," in *Convegno di studi sul Risorgimento a Bologna e nell'Emilia* (Bologna, 1960), p. 738.

[7] Camera di Commercio, *Statistica industriale, Provincia di Bologna* (Bologna,

tained most of the commercial activity that revolved around the importation of seed, fertilizers, and other farm supplies and the exportation of local crops. As a result of its strategic location in the Po Valley, Bologna became one of the most important wheat markets in the country, while its hemp market assumed "not only a national, but an international prominence" in the years after 1900.[8]

1. *The Topography and Structure of Rural Society in Bologna*

Much as in other provinces of the Po Valley, the agricultural sector in Bologna during the period between 1900 and 1930 incorporated a range of disparate forms of land tenure and methods of cultivation roughly corresponding to the major topographical divisions of the province. Then as now, the province contained three major topographical zones: mountains, foothills, and plains (Map 2). In the Apennines bordering on Tuscany, the mountainous zone covered an area of approximately 470 square miles of marginal farmland, meadows, and forests. The second zone, that of the foothills, measured some 428 square miles and was itself divided into smaller subzones of high and low foothills. The largest and agriculturally most important zone, the plains extended over an area of 546 square miles with a high plateau around the commune of Anzola and three subzones of low plains to the east and west of the Reno Rivers and the Idice and Sillaro Rivers (Map 3).[9]

Low soil fertility, small crop yields, and general economic backwardness prevailed in the twenty-one mountainous communes of the province. Well over half the land surface consisted of forests and pastures; less than 40 percent of the land was devoted to crop

1898), pp. 24-53; Camera di Commercio, *Appunti per gli studi sulle industrie locali nei riguardi del 'dopoguerra'* (Bologna, 1918), pp. 1-15.

[8] Giorgio Roletto, "Le basi geografiche dell'economia bolognese" *Il comune di Bologna*, 1929, no. 6-7, pp. 52-63.

[9] Franco Cavazza, *Le agitazioni agrarie*, pp. 5-8.

Map 2
Bologna's Topographical Divisions.

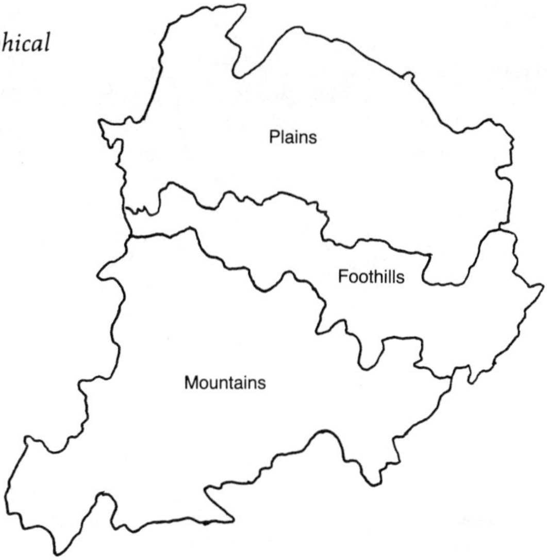

cultivation. Given the rugged terrain and infertility of the soil, sheep, chestnuts, and wood from the forests constituted the traditional economic bases of the local inhabitants.[10] Small peasant property represented the most characteristic form of land tenure. The majority of proprietors in the province who worked their own land—over ten thousand people in 1901—were concentrated in the mountainous communes. Nearly two-thirds of these peasant cultivators owned only one plot of land; 80 percent of the plots measured less than twenty-five acres.[11] Living close to the margins of subsistence, they tended to cultivate those crops suitable for direct consumption: corn, potatoes, beans, and chickpeas. To supplement the meager earnings from their tiny plots, they often took additional employment for themselves and their families outside the zone, the men finding jobs in public works projects and on the

[10] Consiglio Provinciale, *La provincia di Bologna*, pp. 385, 392.

[11] *Ibid.*, p. 471; Aldo Pagani, *Rapporti fra proprietà, impresa e mano d'opera nell'agricoltura italiana*, Vol. XIII, *Emilia*, (Milan-Rome, 1932), pp. 65-71; MAIC, *Censimento 1901*, p. 217.

Map 3
Bologna's Agricultural Zones.

large estates, the women working as domestic servants.[12] As in other mountainous areas that ringed the Po Valley, these peasant cultivators were geographically and culturally isolated from the mainstream of economic and political life in Bologna.

Below this zone of forests and pasture lay the Bolognese foothills with its own distinctive methods of cultivation and forms of land tenure. Unlike in the mountains, forests covered less than 15 percent of the territory so that from 60 to 90 percent of the land was under crop cultivation. Richer soils, larger farms, and more efficient methods of cultivation afforded a much wider range of agricultural products that included wheat, corn, wine grapes, fruit, and livestock. The peasant proprietor, the mainstay of agriculture in the mountains, accounted for a mere tenth of the property. In his place appeared the more substantial property holder who owned two or more farms, the average dimensions of which were slightly

[12] A. Pagani, *Rapporti fra proprietà*, Vol. XIII, pp. 111-112.

larger than those found in the mountainous communes.[13] The dominant form of land tenure in the foothills was the *mezzadria*, a type of share tenancy in which the peasant had a fixed plot and divided his crop with the landlord on the basis of a predetermined ratio. As a rule, local custom dictated that the *mezzadro* or sharecropper furnish all the labor, tools, livestock, and half the seed, while the landlord provided the land, housing and stables, and half the seed. Ordinarily, after the harvest the two contracting parties divided the products equally. Traditionally, the tenant was also expected to bring the products to the manor house or market, to pay a specified rent for his housing, and to give the landlord gifts of capons, chickens, and eggs on designated holidays. Agreements between the landowners and sharecroppers were supposed to be renewed annually.[14]

Slightly less than half the sharecroppers, the largest single peasant class in the Bolognese countryside in 1901 (Map 4), lived in the communes of the foothills, where the *mezzadria* covered four-fifths of the land devoted to agriculture.[15] The family represented the basic productive unit of the sharecropping economy. With seven to nine members on the average, it had a rigid, hierarchical structure. The *reggitore* or head of the family assigned the work duties and handled all contractual matters, purchasing, and marketing. The female head of the family or *reggitrice* ruled over domestic matters, distributing the various household tasks among the other women. At harvest, however, all able-bodied men, women,

[13] On land utilization in the foothills, see Consiglio Provinciale, *La provincia di Bologna*, p. 578; for the farm dimensions and crops grown, see A. Pagani, *Rapporti fra proprietà*, vol. XIII, pp. 65-71.

[14] See Museo civiltà contadina, *Bozze stampa museo civiltà contadina San Marino in Bentivoglio* (Bologna, no date), p. 7; Osvaldo Passerini, *Inchiesta sulla piccola proprietà coltivatrice formatasi nel dopoguerra*, Vol. VII, *Emilia e Marche* (Milan, 1932), pp. 7-20; A. Pagani, *Rapporti fra proprietà*, vol. XIII, pp. 52-53. For an example of a late nineteenth-century sharecropping contract in Bologna, see Carlo Poni, *Gli aratri e l'economia agraria nel Bolognese dal XVII al XIX secolo* (Bologna, 1963), app. 6, "Module e scritte coloniche," pp. 231-237.

[15] MAIC, *Censimento 1901*, p. 217; Consiglio Provinciale, *La provincia di Bologna*, p. 471; A. Pagani, *Rapporti fra proprietà*, vol. XIII, pp. 65-71.

Map 4
Population Distribution of Sharecroppers in Bologna.

and children went to work in the fields.[16] The more prosperous or fortunate peasant families lived in *case coloniche* or farm houses, separated from the stables. Typically such houses were two-story edifices with a kitchen, cellar, and two rooms on the ground floor, four rooms and a granary on the second. Yet no less common were smaller, less sanitary dwellings that combined living quarters and stables in the same building.[17] Living in relative isolation on his small but stable farm, the *mezzadro* represented a central figure in the old rural order of Bologna. Generations of peasant families often worked the same plot of land under the direction of the same

[16] Museo civiltà contadina, *Bozze stampa*, pp. 13-14; Comizio Agrario di Bologna, *Monografia del podere bolognese* (Bologna, 1881), p. viii; Consiglio Provinciale, *La provincia di Bologna*, p. 481; A. Pagani, "La distribuzione del lavoro umano nell'azienda agraria," in *Annali dell'Osservatorio di Economia Agraria di Bologna* (Piacenza, 1932), p. 396.

[17] Museo civiltà contadina, *Bozze stampa*, p. 12; Comizio Agrario, *Podere bolognese*, p. vii.

family of landlords. Such continuity in tenure, where it continued to exist after 1900, helped to maintain the sharecropper's attachment to certain traditional values and customs: deference to social superiors, a lingering devotion to the church and village priest, and a distrust of change and innovation.[18]

Because of his position in the local agricultural economy, the Bolognese sharecropper incorporated features of both the dependent laborer and the small-scale entrepreneur. Under contract to a specific landlord, he was essentially a laboring employee whose interests did not always coincide with those of his employer. Friction between the peasant tenant and the landlord became especially sharp during the periods of contractual negotiation and over the centuries the two had engaged in bitter conflicts over issues of crop selection, methods of cultivation, rents, and the distribution of shares in the harvest.[19] At the same time, the sharecropper was himself an agricultural employer in the summer months when he had to hire outside laborers for the harvest. As an employer with limited resources, the sharecropper had an obvious interest in keeping wages low and work hours long that diverged from and often clashed with the interests of the laborers.[20] Moreover, unlike the day laborers', the sharecropper's annual income and the survival of his family enterprise depended entirely on the success of the harvest. Consequently, he tended to oppose any disruptive labor actions such as strikes, since as one agricultural expert noted in 1911, they endangered "not only the landlord's share of the product, but also the portion that [he himself] expected as repayment for [his] labor."[21] Both his psychology and his economic position

[18] For a discussion of the traditionalism of the sharecroppers, see Frank M. Snowden, "On the Social Origins of Agrarian Fascism in Italy," *European Journal of Sociology*, XIII (1972), pp. 276-277.

[19] For the history of such conflicts, see C. Poni, *Gli aratri*, chaps. 5-10.

[20] On the average dimensions of the sharecropper farms in the province, see Comizio Agrario, *Podere bolognese*, p. viii and A. Pagani, "La distribuzione del lavoro," p. 396; on statistics for the employment of day laborers on the farms of sharecroppers, see the same article of Pagani's, p. 400.

[21] *Commissione d'inchiesta sui conflitti in Romagna del 1911* cited in Franco Cavazza, *Le agitazioni agrarie*, p. 55.

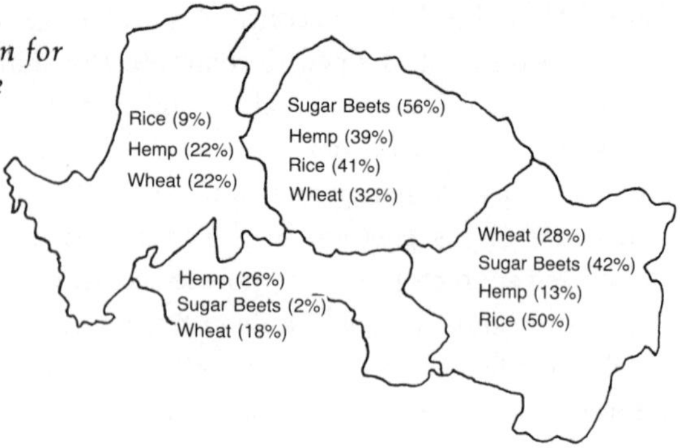

Map 5
Acreage Distribution for Major Crops on the Bolognese Plains.

helped to make the sharecropper's relations with other rural classes extremely unstable. For depending on the circumstances, he could be an ally or a tenacious adversary of either the landlords or the day laborers.

With the descent from the foothills to the vast Bolognese plains, the *mezzadria* became less prevalent. In place of the small peasant plots, there appeared large commercial farms extending over the richest and most fertile lands of the province. Virtually all the farms in this zone measured over fifty hectares; in the thirteen largest communes, farms larger than one hundred hectares comprised two-thirds of the arable land.[22] In the decades after 1890, these farms made extensive use of machines, chemical fertilizers, and high yield seed in order to produce an impressive range of crops: wheat, sugar beets, hemp, forage, potatoes, tobacco, rice, maize, and trefoil. On the plains, there was a certain degree of territorial crop specialization (Map 5). Rice cultivation, for instance, was restricted to some fifty or sixty farms in the low plains of the Idice and Sillaro Rivers and to the east of the Reno River.

[22] Statistics on large landowners in the plains were compiled from the Catasto dei terreni. Registro delle partite of 1924-25 for the communes of San Pietro in Casale, Sant'Agata Bolognese, Baricella, Bentivoglio, Budrio, Galliera, Malalbergo, Medicina, Molinella, Sala Bolognese, San Giovanni in Persiceto, Crevalcore, and Minerbio. For the average size of the farms in this zone, see A. Pagani, *Rapporti fra proprietà*, vol. XIII, pp. 65-71.

The same subzone also developed into an increasingly important area of sugar beet cultivation after 1900, its large and efficient farms being particularly well suited to a crop that required substantial capital investments, abundant fertilizers, and careful cultivation. Hemp figured less in the low plains of the Idice and Sillaro and was concentrated instead in the other three subzones of the plains which furnished nearly 90 percent of the total output in the province.[23] Apart from the rice areas, dry crop cultivation prevailed throughout the plains. The most common form of crop rotation followed a four-year cycle. In the first year, the so-called plants of renewal—hemp, sugar beets, tomatoes or tobacco—were grown. The second year farmers would plant wheat with trefoil, the following year, solely trefoil. Finally in the last year of the cycle, the fields would be devoted exclusively to wheat.[24]

Already prior to World War I, many of the biggest farms in the plains had become "factories in the fields." In addition to their carefully tended fields, they contained buildings where the work of cleaning, refining, and selecting of crops took place, enormous warehouses and silos for the storage of agricultural products, spacious stables often housing several hundred farm animals, and big garages where an assortment of motor-powered threshers, harvesters, and seeding machines were kept.[25] Enterprises of these dimensions maintained a full-time staff of several hundred people and had a fairly sophisticated division of labor. At the top of the farm hierarchy stood the landowner. In 1900 a comparatively small group of two or three hundred landowners possessed the bulk of

[23] *Ibid.*, p. 112; Consiglio Provinciale, *La provincia di Bologna*, p. 397, pp. 600-636; Luigi Perdisa, *Monografia economico-agraria dell'Emilia* (Faenza, 1937), pp. 221-223; O. Passerini, *Inchiesta piccola proprietà*, vol. VII, pp. 7-20.

[24] Federazione Provinciale Fascista degli Agricoltori, *Relazione della presidenza 1932* (Bologna, 1932), p. 25.

[25] The description of the large commercial farms of the plains represents a composite picture drawn from a series of articles by the local agricultural expert Luigi Zerbini which appeared in the monthly journal, *L'Agricoltura Bolognese* between 1909 and 1911 on the most modern and efficient farms in the provinces. These articles were then republished as a book, *Illustrazione delle principali aziende agrarie del Bolognese* (Bologna, 1913).

private property in the plains. Their ranks included prominent families of the Bolognese, Roman, and more recent Napoleonic aristocracies as well as a significant number of untitled proprietors. With few exceptions, they were absentee landlords who lived either in the city of Bologna or else outside the province in Rome, Vienna, and Paris.[26] During the first decades of this century, effective management of many large farms shifted increasingly to a group of enterprising leaseholders. With longterm leases that ran for nine years or more, these rural entrepreneurs had a relatively free hand in the organization of the farms and were the chief agents in the industrializing of agricultural production in the province.[27] Below the leaseholder or the manager appointed by the landowner were a number of technical experts and peasant specialists responsible for superintending the various activities of the farm. Some big estates of the lower plains employed an engineer on a full-time basis to direct the work of land reclamation and to regulate the irrigation systems. Separate agents, assisted by subagents and labor foremen, cared for the dry and wet crops, while other personnel handled winemaking, threshing, milling, and storage operations. At the bottom of the permanent staff were the fixed-salary laborers or *salariati* who cared for the horses, cattle, oxen, and other farm animals. As a rule, they received free housing on the estate and a one-year contract and were paid half in cash and half in shares of the harvest.[28]

[26] See Catasto dei terreni 1924-25 and Archivio di Stato di Bologna, C6 F2, (1902), "Elenco dei detentori di terreno nel mandamento di Minerbio" (hereafter cited as ASB).

[27] A. Pagani, *Rapporti fra proprietà*, vol. XIII, pp. 65-71 furnishes statistics on the extent of leaseholding in the low plains. For the general features of the contracts, see Comizio Agrario, *Podere bolognese* and O. Passerini, *Inchiesta piccola proprietà*, vol. VII, pp. 7-20. On the advantageous features of the Bolognese leases, see Giorgio Giorgetti, *Contadini e proprietari nell'Italia moderna. Rapporti di produzione e contratti agrari dal secolo XVI a oggi* (Turin, 1974), p. 402 and A. Pagani, "Illustrazione statistica ed economica dell'Emilia e Romagna" in *Annali dell'Osservatorio di Economia Agraria di Bologna*, vol. I, 1927, pp. 140-141.

[28] L. Zerbini, *Illustrazione aziende agrarie; Archivio Centrale dello Stato*, Presidenza del Consiglio dei Ministri, F3, 1924 (hereafter cited as ACS); Calisto Paglia, *Donazione Pizzardi. Relazione sul modo gestire la tenuta del Bentivoglio* (Bologna, 1923), vol. II, p. 5; L. Perdisa, *Monografia economico-agrario*, p. 205.

Map 6
Distribution of Agricultural Day Laborers in Bologna.

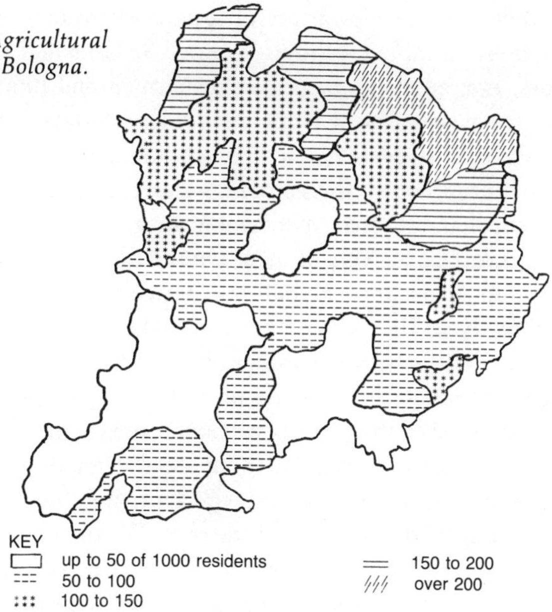

The organization and crops of these commercial farms demanded vast numbers of casual day laborers or *braccianti* to work in the fields, above all at harvest time. In the first decades of this century, two-thirds of all the landless rural workers in the province were located in the communes of the plains, over half in the three subzones of low plains where they made up the majority of the local population (Map 6).[29] While seasonal migration outside the province did take place, ordinarily laborers and their families resided in make-shift "agro-towns" along the roadways of the plains. As early as the 1880s, these settlements caught the eye of investigators for the *Inchiesta Agraria Jacini* who reported that "the concentration of families of day laborers is sometimes dreadful; in a few hovels perhaps a hundred families live heaped together."[30]

[29] A. Pagani, *I braccianti della valle padana* (Rome, 1932), pp. 35-36; Consiglio Provinciale, *La provincia di Bologna*, table 128.

[30] *Atti della Giunta per la inchiesta agraria e sulle condizioni della classe agricola*, Vol. II, *Relazione del commissario Marchese Luigi Tanari* (Rome, 1881), p. 20; hereafter cited as L. Tanari, *Inchiesta agraria*. On the agro-towns, see Idomeneo

People from a wide variety of social backgrounds were to be found in these humble dwellings—ruined artisans and peasant proprietors, evicted sharecroppers, exfishermen and hunters—all drawn by the possibility of work on the large estates. At harvest their ranks were swelled by a temporary influx of marginal leaseholders, small proprietors, sharecroppers and even urban workers anxious to supplement their modest incomes. Nor was this work force composed exclusively of men. On the contrary, in some communes women made up over half the agricultural labor force, working primarily in the rice and sugar beet fields.[31]

Instability was the dominant feature of the landless day laborers, characterizing their relations with the landowners, their work schedules, and their incomes. Government officials described them as a "fluctuating mass" without steady employment or individual contracts who sold "their own labor, now here and now there, according to the season and the crop."[32] Hired by the day or week, they moved from one farm to the next as the demand for labor required and were paid either an hourly wage or a piece rate. The irregular seasonal distribution of agricultural employment meant that the laborers might work for as few as ninety days each year. Generally they had to rely on their earnings from the peak summer months, supplemented by temporary jobs in the agricultural processing industries and on the public work projects, to sustain themselves and their families through the long winter months of enforced idleness.[33]

Housing patterns, work conditions, and economic circumstances all coincided to give the day laborers of the plains a group consciousness that sharply distinguished them from the sharecroppers and other kinds of rural workers in the province. Unlike the share-

Barbadoro, *Storia del sindacalismo italiano dalla nascita al fascismo*, vol. I, *La Federterra* (Florence, 1973), p. 52 and Thomas Sykes, "Capitalist Agriculture in Italy. The Mobilization of Day Laborers in the Po Valley: 1901-1915" (typescript, 1976), p. 14.

[31] L. Perdisa, *Monografia economico-agraria*, pp. 206-207; A. Pagani, *I braccianti*, pp. 36-37; Emilio Sereni, *Il capitalismo nelle campagne* (Turin, 1968), pp. 315-341.

[32] ASB, C7 F1, Prefect to Ministry of Interior, no date 1914.

[33] A. Pagani, *I braccianti*, pp. 10-12.

cropper who lived in isolation on his family plot, their concentration in the "agro-towns" encouraged them to develop communal habits of cooperation and collective action. The uniformity of field work, their common poverty, and their shared interest in jobs and wages served to reinforce these habits. Without any permanent ties to the land or continuous relations with a specific employer, they lacked the *mezzadro's* economic and psychological stability or his deference toward the landowners. Indeed, by 1900 this army of *braccianti* no longer consisted of "peasants without land" who dreamed of returning to some lost paradise of the soil, but rather of rural proletarians who viewed their employers as a "ferocious and gloomy enemy that speculated in misery and brutishness."[34]

As the growing militancy of the day laborers suggests, social structure and economic relations in rural Bologna during the first three decades of this century were considerably less static than this brief and schematic survey might indicate. For much as in other provinces of Emilia, the gradual and uneven penetration of capitalism into the Bolognese countryside, a process "which sought to industrialize production and refine the relations between producers in the interests of greater profits," injected a new dynamism and instability that affected all areas of provincial life.[35] Already in the nineteenth century, the juxtaposition of new and old agricultural systems began to generate stresses and strains that steadily undermined and transformed the traditional, hierarchical, and paternalistic foundations of rural society.

2. *The Evolution of the Agrarian Elite in the Nineteenth Century*

On the eve of the French Revolution, a small circle of aristocrats—headed by the Hercolani, Tanari, Malvezzi, and Isolani

[34] *Bollettino dell'Associazione Agraria Parmense*, August 24, 1907 as quoted in T. Sykes, "Capitalist Agriculture," p. 15. For additional information on the distinctive mentality of the day laborers, see Giuliano Procacci, *La lotta di classe in Italia agli inizi del secolo XX* (Rome, 1970), pp. 47-48; A. Pagani, *I braccianti*, p. 11; G. Medici and G. Orlando, *Agricoltura e disoccupazione*, vol. I, p. 74.

[35] Paul Corner, *Fascism in Ferrara 1915-1925* (London, 1975), p. 1.

families—dominated social and economic life in Bologna much as they had for centuries. As one contemporary observer wrote in 1780, the population of the province could be divided into "60 or 70 tyrants and 260,000 slaves."[36] Descendants of city dwellers who had built up their patrimonies more by commercial acquisitions than feudal concessions, these great families and their fellow nobles possessed over three-quarters of the private property; from their ranks came the overwhelming majority of local notables and administrators who shared power with the high church officials of the Papal States.[37] Despite its political influence, the church hierarchy played only a marginal role in the provincial property system, owning less than 10 percent of the land. Untitled proprietors held slightly under a quarter of the private property, but the average value of their possessions was one-tenth that of the typical noble holding. Urban merchants, contractors, or successful professional men, these landowners did not aim at ever increasing profits nor were they interested in technological innovation. They tended to constitute a "landed bourgeoisie," involved chiefly in trade and business in the city rather than in the development of their properties.[38]

The rural world over which the aristocratic families presided in 1789 was one of social stability and relative economic stagnation. Entrenched behind their privileges and special exemptions, the local nobility had few incentives to change the existing methods of cultivation or to invest in land improvements. The large proprietors clung tenaciously to the *mezzadria* for the cultivation of their estates which were often dispersed throughout the province. This system not only provided them with a steady and secure income,

[36] Letter from Boncompagni to Pallavicini, May 20, 1780 quoted in Renato Zangheri, *La proprietà terriera e le origini del Risorgimento nel Bolognese*, Vol. I (Bologna, 1960), p. 93.

[37] *Ibid.*, pp. 93-94; R. Zangheri, *Prime ricerche sulla distribuzione della proprietà fondiaria nella pianura bolognese 1789-1835* (Bologna, no date), pp. 43-45. The other major families of the time included the Segni, Spada, Marsigli, and Bentivoglio.

[38] R. Zangheri, *La proprietà terriera*, vol. I, pp. 94-97.

but also helped maintain the traditional social order in the countryside by tying the peasants to the land and to a fixed hierarchical relationship with the landlords. The price of privilege and stability, however, was high: a sluggish land market, paralyzed investments, and the retarded development of agricultural technology.[39]

This placid and seemingly static agrarian community with its well-established patterns of wealth, power, and prestige received a powerful jolt when Napoleon and his armies invaded the region in 1796. In Bologna the new regime imposed by the French forces immediately carried out a number of reforms that, in a brief span of years, swept away old juridical bonds, rendered alienable all forms of property, and guaranteed mortgage credits.[40] The extraordinarily active land market created by these reforms, together with rising agricultural prices, led to a rapid redistribution of property in the province during the following decade, largely to the benefit of new men from the bourgeoisie. By 1804, untitled proprietors accounted for 42 percent of all the private property in the province. Significantly, the largest and most prosperous of these landowners—those who owned estates of more than one hundred hectares—were the chief beneficiaries, doubling their share of the land holdings between 1789 and 1804, while the portion held by small proprietors, with holdings of less than ten hectares, actually declined.[41] The advance of this new group of proprietors was achieved, in large measure, at the expense of the old noble families whose share of the private property fell from 77 percent in 1789 to 65 percent in 1804 to 51 percent by 1835.[42]

The Napoleonic period also witnessed the increasing commercialization of agriculture in the Bolognese plains. Encouraged by

[39] *Ibid.*, p. 104.

[40] R. Zangheri, *Prime ricerche*, pp. 1-5.

[41] Although there is a lack of precise information on the subject, it would appear that these new landowners were ambitious urban merchants and professional people as well as certain favorites of the Napoleonic government. For statistics on the formation of these new properties, see R. Zangheri, *La proprietà terriera*, vol. I, p. 144 and Claudio Rotelli, *I catasti imolesi dei secoli XIX and XX* (Milan, 1967), pp. 62-63.

[42] R. Zangheri, *Prime ricerche*, pp. 55-63.

steadily rising agricultural prices and the elimination of old crop restrictions, local agrarians began to expand their cultivation of such cash crops as rice and hemp. In the span of a decade and a half, the area devoted to rice in the low plains more than quadrupled as enterprising farmers rushed to grow a crop that often provided in the first year alone profits that exceeded the original value of the land. Far from being a temporary phenomenon, rice cultivation continued to grow in importance in subsequent decades; between 1819 and 1860, the annual production of rice more than doubled.[43] Favorable market conditions also pushed growers to increase their production of hemp which rose from thirty-six thousand quintals at the end of the eighteenth century to well over eighty thousand quintals by 1860.[44] Significant changes in the systems of cultivation and land tenure accompanied the rapid proliferation of these crops. In particular, rice cultivation, which required large-scale operations, substantial capital investments, and ample supplies of unskilled labor, favored the development of large, consolidated farms and the replacement of sharecroppers by landless day laborers. The spread of forage crops in the first half of the nineteenth century produced a similar result, since it was more advantageous to cultivate them when the landowner directly farmed the land with hired labor.[45]

The redistribution of property and the accelerated commercialization of agriculture, however, did not betoken any revolutionary transformation of Bolognese society. In the decades after 1815, the leading aristocratic families still controlled over half the land in the province and continued to exercise a prominent, if somewhat diminished, role in local political and social life. Moreover, while

[43] *Ibid.*, pp. 11-12, and by the same author, "Un dibattito sulle risaie bolognesi agli inizi della Ristorazione," in *Convegno di studi sul Risorgimento*. On the growing output of rice, see Camera di Commercio, *Cenno storico*, p. 17.

[44] C. Poni, *Gli aratri*, p. 85; Consiglio Provinciale, *La provincia di Bologna*, p. 632.

[45] C. Poni, *Gli aratri*, pp. 102-105, and by the same author, "Carlo Berti-Pichat e i problemi economici e sociali delle campagne bolognesi dal 1840 al 1848," in *Bollettino del Museo del Risorgimento*, v, pt. 2 (1960), p. 762.

the new landowners introduced a novel spirit of enterprise into the province that clearly influenced some aristocratic proprietors, they tended to embrace the lifestyle and many of the values of the old nobility.[46] Whatever tensions and conflicts might have existed between the two groups of large landowners during the Napoleonic occupation, they were largely overcome through a gradual process of compromise and integration that bred a new hybrid elite of aristocratic notables and untitled proprietors with the restoration of Papal authority in the region.

The more dynamic elements of this elite found their most concrete institutional expression in the Agrarian Society of Bologna. Founded in 1807, the Agrarian Society initially aspired to "improve agriculture in general and that of Bologna in particular by means of the dissemination of useful agronomical information and the promotion of new methods of cultivation."[47] During the Restoration, the organization became much more than a technical body or a mere gentlemen's debating society, for it also provided a setting in which the "best and the brightest" from diverse backgrounds could gather, exchange ideas, establish contacts, and develop a common outlook on the problems of the day. Beginning with discussions of the latest agricultural advances and more efficient methods of cultivation, the society evolved into an increasingly powerful and vocal pressure group to advance the interests of commercial agriculture within the Papal States.[48] By the 1850s the organization had shifted from economic lobbying to more direct political action. Much as in other areas of the Po Valley, concern over narrow markets and local tariff barriers that stifled economic development drew the enterprising landowners of Bologna into the struggles for national unification. Indeed, in the 1850s men like

[46] R. Zangheri, *Prime ricerche*, p. 66.

[47] *Statuto della Società Agraria di Bologna*, Article 1, quoted in Francesco Coletti, *Le associazioni agrarie in Italia dalla metà del secolo XVIII alla fine del XIX* (Rome, 1901), p. 21.

[48] See Mirella Bartolotti, "La Società Agraria di Bologna dalla sua fondazione al 1860," in R. Zangheri, ed. *Le campagne emiliane nell'epoca moderna* (Milan, 1957), p. 87.

Marco Minghetti, Carlo Berti-Pichat, and Marchese Luigi Tanari began to take charge of the organization and to use it as a forum for the preparation, discussion, and propagation of political and economic reforms. By the summer of 1857, when local landed interests had lost all hope of winning any significant concessions from Pius IX, the Agrarian Society became one of the most important organized centers of political opposition to the papal government in the region, providing most of the personnel for the Bolognese committee of the National Society. The nomination of Count Camillo Benso di Cavour as an honorary member and the election of Minghetti as president in 1858 dramatically testified to the growing politicization of the society.[49]

The Bolognese agrarians' support for national unification reflected a particular blend of idealism and economic self-interest. Like influential propertied interests elsewhere in northern and central Italy, they identified with Count Cavour's liberal party, the so-called moderates, and its constitutional, monarchical solution to the problem of national unification. Inspired by the institutions of the British political system, they saw this form of government as uniquely capable of reconciling "liberty with order" and of developing an infrastructure for economic growth on the peninsula.[50] Thus, they envisioned a unified national state that would not only give a political voice to respectable men of property, but would also open new markets for agricultural products, expand the transportation systems, enlarge credit facilities, and encourage land

[49] On the political activity of the Agrarian Society, see A. Bertelli, "Movimenti politici a Bologna dal 1815 al 1860," *Bollettino del Museo del Risorgimento*, v, pt. 1 (1960), pp. 242-247; Carlo Zanolini, Giuseppe Boraggine, and Dino Zucchini, *Sunto storico-monografico della Società Agraria di Bologna dall'anno 1807 all'anno 1938* (Bologna, 1939), p. 21; G. Grabinski and D. Zucchini, "Cenni storici della Società Agraria di Bologna dal 1807 al 1930" in Accademia dei Georgofili, *Accademie e società agrarie italiane* (Florence, 1931), pp. 179-192.

[50] Richard Hostetter, *The Italian Socialist Movement*, Vol. I (Princeton, 1958), pp. 6-11; Dennis Mack Smith, *Italy, A Modern History* (Ann Arbor, 1969), p. 23. For the Bolognese agrarians, see G. Grabinski and D. Zucchini, "Cenni storici," pp. 179-192; E. Passerin D'Entreves, "Piemonte e Romagna nel 1859-60" in *Il Risorgimento e Luigi Carlo Farini*, Vol. II (Bologna, 1960), pp. 213ff.

improvements. At the same time, their vision of political change was tempered by a concern with the maintenance of the social order in the city and countryside and, above all, the avoidance of any repetition of "the horrors of 1848."[51] One local notable perhaps expressed the limits of the moderates' program best when he affirmed that "the primary and most important protection that agriculture can receive from governments is the defense of private property."[52]

With both clerical conservatives and radical democratic forces in a state of disarray, the Bolognese agrarian moderates' substantial financial resources, superior organization, and precise objectives enabled them to pose as the most authoritative spokesmen for the entire population and to take charge of the insurrection that overthrew the papal authorities in June 1859. In the immediate wake of the insurrection, Enrico Sassoli, the president of the Agrarian Society from 1855 to 1859, and other leading moderates set up the first provisional government, over which another prominent landowner, Marchese Gioacchino Napoleone Pepoli, presided. The same group of moderates was equally successful in dominating the election of deputies to the Assembly of Romagna in July, in part because of voting restrictions that excluded both urban and rural workers as well as sharecroppers who did not own real estate.[53] The following months saw the moderate provisional government move swiftly to extend its control over the press, crush the marginal dissident movements of clericals and radicals in the region, and prepare a quick and unconditional unification with Piedmont. Significantly, yet another former president of the Agrarian Society, Antonio Alessandrini was the first person in the Assembly of

[51] Marco Minghetti to a "dear friend" no date, 1860, in Biblioteca Comunale di Bologna, "Manoscritti Minghetti," 140, cart. VIII, F44.

[52] Quoted in C. Zanolini, *Sunto storico-monografico*, p. 141; see also M. Bartolotti, "La Società Agraria," pp. 92-93.

[53] G. Grabinski and D. Zucchini, "Cenni storici," pp. 179-192; Isabella Zanni Rosiello, "Aspetti del movimento democratico Bolognese," in *Bollettino del Museo del Risorgimento di Bologna*, VI (1961), p. 99n. Other local landowners in the Constituent Assembly included Count Agostino Salina, Count Giovanni Malvezzi, Count Francesco Isolani, and Luigi Pizzardi.

Romagna to vote for the downfall of the papal regime and the annexation of Bologna to the House of Savoy, a decision that received formal confirmation through a well-orchestrated plebescite in March 1860.[54]

Bolognese agrarian moderates went on to play an influential role in the new Italian state during the ensuing decade and a half. Indeed, Bologna gave the country one of its first prime ministers, Marco Minghetti, who served from 1863 to 1864 and again from 1873 to 1876.[55] In the same period, the large landed interests, who had led the local moderate forces in 1859-60, consolidated their positions on the municipal and provincial levels. The province where they came to monopolize wealth, power, and prestige after 1860 consisted of sixty-two communes or municipalities grouped together in three main districts: Bologna, Imola, and Vergato. Each commune had an elected mayor and municipal council with important responsibilities in the areas of education, poor relief, public works, and taxation. The activities of the municipal councils, in turn, were subject to the supervision of the provincial administrative committee that was composed of the prefect, two government functionaries, and four members elected by the provincial council. Under the highly centralized administrative system imposed by the House of Savoy, tremendous power was vested in the office of the prefect who controlled the police in the province and had wide discretionary authority over the elective administrative councils. The prefect and his subordinates received their orders from the Ministry of Interior that was invariably headed by the prime minister. As a result, the ostensibly neutral prefecture tended to become a potent weapon of the ruling political coalitions

[54] *Ibid.*, pp. 99-112; I. Zanni Rosiello, "Note intorno al giornalismo politico bolognese degli anni 1859-1860," *Bollettino del Museo del Risorgimento di Bologna*, v (1960), pp. 1-31.

[55] The governing coalitions of the *destra* or right were dominated by large landed interests of the north and center. See Giampiero Carocci, *Giolitti e l'età giolittiana* (Turin, 1971), p. 9; Paolo Farneti, *Sistema politico e società civile* (Turin, 1971), pp. 169-185.

in Rome.[56] For purposes of political representation, the province was divided into eight electoral colleges, each a single-member constituency with one deputy to represent it in the Chamber of Deputies.

Throughout the second half of the nineteenth century, this political and administrative system provided the framework for agrarian supremacy in virtually every area of provincial life. Invariably, large landowners like Count Felice Cavazza, Antonio Bonora, Count Nerio Malvezzi, and Giuliano Cacciaguerra headed the roster of the richest men in the city of Bologna.[57] As a rule, the same agrarian notables also presided over the boards of the major local financial institutions: the Banca Cavazza, the Cassa di Risparmio, the Banca Popolare, and the Monte di Pietà. While this propertied elite derived most of its wealth from agriculture, it did not neglect the urban commercial scene; in the 1890s, for instance, the presidency of the Bolognese Chamber of Commerce was held by such prominent landowners as Count Felice Cavazza, Francesco Bernaroli, and Cesare Zucchini.[58] Many local notables gained additional distinction as the chief patrons of Bolognese social and cultural life. In their elegant palaces took place the costume balls, sumptuous dinner parties, and concerts of provincial high society; their salons attracted the foremost intellectual luminaries of the day and provided settings for discussions of the latest artistic, literary, and scientific questions. Some old line landowners were themselves cultivated and erudite men who wrote extensively on

[56] For a more extensive discussion of the Italian administrative system, see Robert C. Fried, *The Italian Prefects: A Study in Administrative Politics* (New Haven, 1963); A. Pellicani, "Il prefetto nell'Italia unita," *Studi Storici*, 1968, no. 2, pp. 438-443; Massimo Severo Giannini, "Autonomie comunali e controlli statali" in I. Zanni Rosiello, ed., *Gli apparati statali dall'Unità al Fascismo* (Bologna, 1976), pp. 103-122. On municipal government at the beginning of this century, see Bolton King and Thomas Okey, *Italy To-Day* (London, 1901), pp. 263-276.

[57] See for example the tax information in *Il Resto del Carlino*, July 5-6, 1906. Hereafter cited as *RdC*.

[58] On Chamber of Commerce, see *ibid.*, January 17, 1893. For the banks, see Cassa di Risparmio, *La Cassa di Risparmio in Bologna nei suoi primi cento anni* (Bologna, 1937), and Mario Maragi, *I cinquecento anni del Monte di Pietà* (Bologna, 1972).

the artistic and architectural heritage of Bologna.[59] With wealth and economic power also came the prizes and rewards of public life. An electoral system, in which property and tax qualifications limited the vote to less than 2 percent of the population in 1870, guaranteed the agrarian elite's political dominance in the province. Under the leadership of Minghetti, the political club of the Bolognese moderates, the Constitutional Association, captured nearly every election in the decades after 1860. Reflecting the close identity between the economic elite and the political class, Bologna's representatives were typically landed gentlemen like Count Malvezzi, Minghetti, Marchese Augusto Mazzacorati, and Enrico Pini. In a similar fashion, suffrage restrictions assured agrarian moderates virtually unchallenged control over most of the municipal councils as well as the provincial administrative committee.[60]

The biographies of the more distinguished members of this provincial ruling class indicate both the extent of its power and influence and the diversity of its social make-up. Count Agostino Salina, scion of an old Bolognese family, served as a municipal and provincial councilor, mayor of the commune of Malalbergo, and president of the Cassa di Risparmio and the Monte di Pietà in the years between 1860 and 1906. Count Francesco Isolani, descendant of another old aristocratic family, was at various times a municipal and provincial councilor, mayor of the commune of Ozzano, and president of the Banca Popolare; his brother, Count Procolo Isolani, served as president of the Cassa di Risparmio. Other influential families had acquired their wealth and position only in the nineteenth century. Coming from a banking family "ennobled in recognition of its work and charity," Count Francesco Cavazza was

[59] See *RdC*, January 4, 1923 for publication of excerpts from a manuscript of Count Francesco Rangone on high society in Bologna. On the cultural activity of the local elite, see, for example, Silvio Fronzoni, "Francesco Cavazza," (typescript, 1976), p. 1.

[60] *RdC*, October 27-28, 1904 provides a brief chronological history of political elections in the province between 1874 and 1900. In addition, see *Clero e partiti a Bologna dopo l'Unità* (Bologna, 1968). On the size of the electorate, see M. S. Giannini, "Autonomie comunali," p. 118.

the self-appointed protector of the city's artistic patrimony, a leading organizer of local charitable activities, and during his long career of public service occupied the posts of municipal and provincial councilor, mayor of Minerbio, parliamentary deputy, and the leading national agrarian spokesman. Enrico Pini, an untitled proprietor of a vast estate in the foothills, had an equally lengthy and impressive career, serving as a director on the boards of a number of joint-stock companies, municipal and provincial councilor, parliamentary deputy, and in the last years of his life senator.[61]

While agriculture and landed wealth predominated, the inner circles of the Bolognese elite also comprehended the principal industrialists like Frank De Morsier and the Calzoni family, whose firms specialized in the construction of farm machinery. De Morsier, for example, not only managed his family business, but was also a leading figure in the Agrarian Society and the Constitutional Association, and at one time served as personal secretary to Baron Sidney Sonnino, one of Italy's most powerful politicians.[62] On the fringes of this inner circle were clustered a host of lawyers, engineers, merchants, and various financial middlemen whose numbers and importance increased with the growing commercialization of Bolognese agriculture in the late nineteenth century. Much as in other provinces of the Po Delta, a clear symbiosis between these groups had taken place by 1900 so that well-heeled attorneys and engineers often owned sizeable tracts of property in the countryside while many sons of old landed families pursued professional or academic careers in the city.[63]

[61] For biographical information on these landed notables, see Agostino Bignardi, *Dizionario biografico dei liberali bolognesi 1860-1914* (Bologna, 1956), pp. 10-11, 22-23, 44. Additional information on Cavazza can be found in S. Fronzoni, "Francesco Cavazza" and *RdC*, April 2-3, 1901; on Enrico Pini, L. Zerbini, *Illustrazione aziende agrarie*, pp. 104-110.

[62] On the Bolognese manufacturers, see Camera di Commercio, *Notizie sulle condizioni industriali e commerciali della provincia di Bologna* (Bologna, 1888), p. 29; on De Morsier, see *RdC*, August 11, 1923; on Calzoni family, see Silvio Fronzoni, "Alessandro Calzoni" (typescript, 1976).

[63] For a similar situation in Ferrara, see P. Corner, *Fascism in Ferrara*, pp. 7-8.

During the first two decades after unification, social and political relations within the elite were not altogether free of tensions and conflicts. Above all, the battle between church and state created sharp divisions within the propertied classes of Bologna. One faction of the Agrarian Society that had supported the papal government in the 1850s was harassed by the new authorities and excluded from power after 1860; certain families of the high aristocracy with close ties to the Vatican withdrew completely from public life.[64] Minghetti had a notorious reputation among intransigent Catholics for his supposedly anticlerical policies. To challenge the moderate leadership, another local notable, Count Giovanni Acquaderni, who according to the prefect exercised an "enormous influence over the richest patrician class of the city," founded the Universal Catholic League to work for the restoration of the pope's temporal power and in the 1870s a small number of wealthy aristocratic families supported a clerical party in the province through various lay Catholic associations. By the following decade, however, divisive religious questions had given way to a shared concern with social unrest that found political expression in new clerical-moderate electoral coalitions.[65] Even after religious tensions had dissipated, the very ascendancy of the moderates served to encourage factional infighting that typically reflected personal animosities, municipal rivalries, and petty struggles for office or favor.

Despite their differences on church-state relations and their factional fights, most members of Bologna's ruling elite shared similar economic interests and were united by a common world view that combined an enthusiasm for technical innovation and free-market liberalism with a sense of *noblesse oblige* and the glorification of

[64] See G. Grabinski and D. Zucchini, "Cenni storici," pp. 179-192.

[65] On the clerical political movement in Bologna, see N. O. Alvisi, "I partiti politici a Bologna dopo l'avvento della Sinistra al potere 1876-1882" in *Clero e partiti*, pp. 76-85; on their convergence with the moderates, see Giovanna Straziota, "I partiti a Bologna nell'età del trasformismo 1883-1887," pp. 113-144 in the above cited volume. For additional information on the activities of Acquaderni, see Giovanni Spadolini, *L'opposizione cattolica da Porta Pia al 1898* (Florence, 1961), pp. 57-58.

the traditional rural hierarchy. Both before and after national unification, the speeches and discussions in the Agrarian Society testified eloquently to the agrarians' interest in the technical modernization of agriculture. They consistently called for more efficient methods of cultivation, greater mechanization on the farms, increased agricultural credits, and larger investments in land reclamation. Similarly, prominent landowners like Marchese Luigi Tanari and Enrico Pini took part actively in the initiatives sponsored by the government for crop experimentation, popular technical education, and the promotion of chemical fertilizers. Moreover, they extolled the virtues of the new economic liberty gained with the political unification of the peninsula and the consequent free exchange of goods and capital in the expanded national market.[66]

Their enthusiasm for agricultural modernization coexisted with a pronounced distrust of rapid industrialization and its accompanying social dislocations and depersonalized market relations. For the nineteenth-century Bolognese landowner tended to be an ardent defender of the traditional, hierarchical social order in the countryside, a world where the peasant's deference and obedience harmonized with the paternalistic concern of the landlord. Thus, a man like Count Nerio Malvezzi, the head of one of Bologna's oldest aristocratic families and an influential figure in moderate political circles, insisted proudly that he had "always been a friend of the peasants and field workers with whom [he] lived . . . in close contact."[67] Both stalwart defenders of risorgimental liberalism and intransigent clericals idealized the old agricultural community where the employer and the laborer cooperated in the achievement of "common religious, moral, civil, and economic

[66] The speeches given in the Agrarian Society are collected in *Annali della Società Agraria Provinciale di Bologna*. For a discussion of the role of agrarian leaders in the modernizing activity of the Agrarian Committee see *Annali della Cattedra Provinciale di Agricoltura di Bologna*, 1893, p. 5. A more general account of agrarian interest in technical innovation can be found in Giuseppe Carlo Marino, *La formazione dello spirito borghese in Italia* (Florence, 1974), p. 215.

[67] ASB, Archivio Privato Malvezzi de' Medici, Titolo 28, interview given by Nerio Malvezzi in 1906.

ends."[68] Few local agrarian notables would have disagreed with the judgment of Count Giuseppe Grabinski that "harmony among the social classes" rested upon the "prosperity of the wealthy and the progressive amelioration of our less fortunate brothers."[69]

A similar blend of conservative stability and "liberal progress" marked the elite's conception of politics. As practiced by the Bolognese moderates, politics was not an occupation but rather an avocation and an "honorific" pursuit of landed gentlemen whose financial independence and cultural refinement made them uniquely suited to the task of ensuring the general welfare of the society. Count Giovanni Codronchi, a parliamentary deputy and Minghetti's successor at the head of the Constitutional Association, perhaps captured this sentiment best in a letter to the young Count Nerio Malvezzi in 1884: "It seems to me that the upper classes have the duty of involving themselves in public life in order to prevent society from falling into the hands of the worst elements; I always look with envy upon the aristocracy of old England which, whether liberal or conservative, victorious or defeated, never loses heart and always stands firm. You have an illustrious name and I must invoke *noblesse oblige* to induce you to accept an office that will acquire authority and decorum from your name."[70] Condronchi, Malvezzi, and the other moderate notables believed firmly in constitutional, parliamentary government, but they saw little

[68] *Atti e documenti del VII Congresso Cattolico Italiano* (Bologna, 1888), cited in G. Spadolini, *L'opposizione cattolica*, p. 245. The same ideas and values permeate Tanari's volume of the *Inchiesta Agraria Jacini* as well as many of the speeches to the Agrarian Society.

[69] G. Grabinski, *Lo sciopero e la questione sociale nelle campagne* (Bologna, 1888), p. 39; G. C. Marino, *Spirito borghese*, p. 182. For the views of Marco Minghetti, in particular, see Federico Chabod, *Storia della politica estera italiana dal 1870 al 1896*, Vol. I (Bari, 1971), p. 469.

[70] ASB Archivio Malvezzi, letter from Count Giovanni Codronchi, September 16, 1884. For biographical information on Codronchi, see N. O. Alvisi, "I partiti politici," p. 74n. For a more general discussion of moderate politics, see F. Chabod, *Politica estera*, p. 377. In many respects, the Bolognese moderates fit into the traditional model formulated by Max Weber in his classical essay, "Politics as a Vocation," reprinted in *From Max Weber: Essays in Sociology*, ed. and trans. H. Gerth and C. W. Mills (New York, 1965), pp. 84-86.

need for the participation of the ignorant masses in the political process and felt most comfortable in the system of limited suffrage that prevailed in Italy throughout most of the late nineteenth century.[71] Since they did not have to mobilize huge numbers of voters, they did not develop any permanent, disciplined party structures, preferring instead to operate through a network of loosely organized local clubs and associations, in which a select group of grand electors met at election time to negotiate the choice of candidates. Once elected, moderate deputies and their colleagues from other provinces shaped public policy and mediated their constituents' interests by means of informal understandings and personal contacts made in the corridors of power in Rome.[72]

In the decades after 1860, Bologna's landed notables justified their claims to such exclusive moral and ideological leadership in terms of their role as architects of the Risorgimento and founders of a new national state. Yet by the 1880s the old concerns with unification and state building had been largely supplanted by new problems associated with poverty and mass discontent, for which the moderates had few solutions. While they frequently expressed concern for the welfare of the peasant classes, economic self-interest and a commitment to individual initiative and the free interplay of supply and demand in the labor market prevented them from developing a coherent program of social amelioration in the countryside. They opposed government intervention to relieve economic distress and poverty, viewing their own charitable efforts as sufficient remedies since, as Count Francesco Cavazza expressed it, the deserving poor would always receive assistance while "those miserable individuals who want to remain so for love of idleness and the lazy life" had to be "abandoned to their own fate."[73]

This limited vision of social reform only highlighted a more basic contradiction in their world view. Like England's improving

[71] F. Chabod, "Rapporti fra eletti ed elettori nei primi decenni unitari," in I. Zanni Rosiello, ed., *Gli apparati statali*, pp. 301-308.

[72] On the moderates and suffrage, see P. Farneti, "La classe politica della Destra e della Sinistra" in *ibid.*, pp. 285-289.

[73] Quoted in S. Fronzoni, "Francesco Cavazza," p. 2.

landlords a half century earlier, they "advocated an economy which implied mutually antagonistic classes, but did not want to disrupt a society of ordered ranks."[74] For precisely those forces that had enhanced the prosperity and power of the provincial elite also destabilized the traditional rural community it wished to preserve. Above all, the increasing commercialization of agriculture in the nineteenth century undermined the old forms of land tenure, transformed relations between landlord and peasant, and introduced a host of new stresses and strains into provincial society. Instead of peace and harmony, the elite faced mounting mass unrest as the century came to a close.

3. *Commercial Agriculture and Social Change in the Bolognese Countryside*

The circumstances that made the province of Bologna a focal point of social conflict in the 1890s had their origins in developments in the first half of the century. Beginning during the period of the Napoleonic occupation and continuing into the Restoration, the lure of profits and the pressures of competition induced a growing number of landowners to dismiss their sharecroppers, consolidate their farms, and employ vast quantities of landless day laborers for the cultivation of rice and forage crops. These changes in crops and systems of cultivation had a dramatic impact on the *mezzadri* of the plains. After decades, if not centuries, of working the same plot of land, many peasant families were deprived of their traditional homes and livelihood and suddenly found themselves forced to sell their labor in the market place. Often with the mere stroke of a pen, ties that had bound the sharecropper to the land and the proprietor for generations were brutally severed. Although the dimensions of this social transformation cannot be measured exactly, they must have been considerable; the changes did not escape the attention of local

[74] See Eric Hobsbawm and George Rude, *Captain Swing* (Middlesex, England, 1969), p. 27.

agrarian leaders like Carlo Berti-Pichat who in the 1840s lamented "the growing transformation of the peasant population into a class of day laborers." According to Berti-Pichat, there existed in the communes of the low plains "clear and all too numerous examples . . . of stables without livestock and of peasant farm houses inhabited not by a single sharecropping family but by two or three families of day laborers." During the same decade, Minghetti expressed a similar concern for the plight of the sharecroppers that he attributed to the excessive expansion of artificial meadow land and the deterioration of the *mezzadria* contracts.[75]

Such laments reflected not simply a nostalgia for the *mezzadria*, but also the recognition that a large mass of landless day laborers, subject to seasonal unemployment and pauperism, constituted a serious threat to law and order in the countryside. Indeed, as early as 1828 one prominent agronomist warned: "One of the greatest evils of agriculture in the territory of Bologna is the multitude of so-called *braccianti* who, dispersed in the countryside with their families and living in the most miserable huts, . . . dissipate their small earnings . . . and wind up each winter without any of the necessities of food, clothing, and heat. And from here they are driven to thievery and begging."[76] This view found confirmation in the reports of government authorities who stressed that "the great number of these people, abandoned to idleness and deprived of food, represent a substantial danger to public . . . safety." The warnings and proposed remedies of Berti-Pichat and Minghetti, however, did not appear to have a noticeable effect on the behavior of local landowners. On the contrary, the expansion of rice and forage crops and the gradual proletarianization of the sharecroppers

[75] Carlo Berti-Pichat, "Della tutela dei prodotti campestri" in *Memorie lette nelle adunanze ordinarie della Società Agraria della provincia di Bologna negli anni accademici 1845-1846*, Vol. III (Bologna, 1847), p. 182. On the activities and accomplishments of Berti-Pichat, see G. Grabinski, "Cenni storici," pp. 179-192. For Minghetti's views, see "Della proprietà rurale e dei patti fra il padrone ed il lavoratore" in *Memorie*, Vol. II (Bologna, 1845), p. 166.

[76] Quoted in C. Poni, "Berti-Pichat," pp. 751-752.

in the low plains continued unabated throughout the 1840s and 1850s.[77]

The consolidation of a unified Italian state and the creation of a national market served only to accelerate the commercialization of Bolognese agriculture after 1861. Under the direction of the government in Rome, local tariff barriers disappeared and the means of communication and transportation were expanded and improved so that both total railroad mileage and the quantity of goods transported on the peninsula more than quadrupled between 1870 and 1895.[78] These changes and improvements greatly facilitated the participation of enterprising farmers in the enormous growth of world trade in agricultural produce that had been stimulated by the seemingly insatiable demand of the industrial economies for foodstuffs and raw materials during the third quarter of the nineteenth century. The first decade and a half after unification witnessed an economic boom in Bologna as local landowners responded to the new market conditions by increasing their production of all major crops: wheat harvests, which had averaged 557,086 quintals in the decade before 1861, rose to 967,228 quintals by 1870-74; rice production climbed from 113, 165 to 209, 916 quintals, while the annual hemp yields went from 85,000 to over 266,000.[79]

The expansion and prosperity of the early 1870s, however, was followed by an unprecedented world agricultural depression in the 1880s that proved to be the most powerful solvent of the old rural order in Bologna. Already in 1875 the competition of cheaper grains from the North American plains, the Argentinian pampas, and the Russian steppes began to drive down agricultural prices on the markets of central Europe. By 1880, the full impact of foreign competition, overproduction, and collapsing prices hit the

[77] On the reform proposals of Berti-Pichat and their lack of success, see *ibid.*, pp. 763-770.

[78] On improved transportation and expanded trade, see E. Sereni, *Il capitalismo*, p. 9; for information on land reclamation, see G. Puppini, *Le bonifiche*, pp. 5-6; G. Medici and G. Orlando, *Agricoltura e disoccupazione*, vol. I, p. 79; I. Barbadoro, *Storia del sindacalismo*, vol. I, p. 42.

[79] For production statistics, see Consiglio Provinciale, *La provincia di Bologna*, pp. 589, 600, and 632. On the general expansion in this period, see E. Hobsbawm, *The Age of Capital 1848-1875* (New York, 1975), pp. 174-181.

Italian peninsula; that year wheat prices fell some 23 percent, setting a trend for the other principal crops of the country.[80] Among the first to feel the effects of the depression were the landowners of Bologna and the Po Delta who had embraced a large-scale, commercialized pattern of agriculture and adapted their production to the demands of the national and international markets. After having risen continually in the 1860s and 1870s, prices for their main cash crops—wheat, rice, and hemp—fell steadily throughout the following decade and a half, sharply reducing landed incomes as well as property values, which dropped 20 percent.[81] They did not delay in sharing their difficulties with the less affluent sectors of the rural population.

In response to the crisis, landowners withdrew land from cultivation, shifted to less intensive crops, and cut their labor costs to a minimum; all measures worked decisively to the disadvantage of both sharecroppers and day laborers, since they transferred many of the burdens of the depression on to their shoulders. With the drop in prices, Marchese Tanari noted as early as 1881 the growing tendency of landlords to intensify their exploitation of the sharecroppers by altering the *mezzadria* contracts in ways that made the peasant "more a subject than a partner."[82] Other landowners found it more economical simply to eliminate the *mezzadria* altogether and to rely instead on systems that used hired hands and allowed for the rapid introduction of new techniques and methods of cultivation. Conversely, in those areas where landowners replaced wheat and hemp with forage crops that required little labor, it became increasingly difficult for entire sharecropping families to make a living from their small plots.[83] The deteriorating conditions of the sharecroppers and marginal peasant proprietors

[80] See E. Sereni, *Il capitalismo*, pp. 238-239, and C. J. Robertson, "Agricultural Regions of the North Italian Plain" *The Geographical Review*, XXVIII, no. 4 (October 1938), p. 573.

[81] For the drop in prices and its consequences in Bologna, see G. Porisini, *Bonifiche e agricoltura nella bassa valle padana* (Milan, 1978), pp. 41-43.

[82] L. Tanari, *Inchiesta agraria*, pp. 434, 443, and 447.

[83] G. Porisini, *Bonifiche e agricoltura*, p. 49; C. Goretti, *Sulla crisi agraria nell'agro bolognese* (Bologna, 1884), pp. 43ff.

aggravated in turn the plight of the landless day laborers by swelling their ranks precisely at a time when agrarian employers were doing everything possible to limit their demand for hired hands. With Bologna's small and backward industrial sector unable to absorb the excess manpower in the countryside, employers were in a position to dominate the labor market. As a result, the 1880s and 1890s saw a disastrous decline in employment, wages, and living standards of rural workers. While there is no precise information for Bologna, in the neighboring province of Ravenna the average laborer, who had worked 200-220 days a year in 1880, found a mere 86 days of employment in 1902; as late as 1901, the wages of many agricultural workers remained well below the levels of the 1870s.[84] Two foreign observers provided a graphic picture of their living and working conditions after nearly two decades of depression: "Everywhere the life of the casual laborer is a cruel struggle for survival and in the large-farm districts there are few laborers of any class who rise above the level of abject poverty. Their wages, low enough at best, are interrupted by bad weather or want of work and are often partly paid in pellegra-breeding maize, charged to them above its real value. Their food is insufficient, their houses disgrace a civilized country."[85]

The accelerated erosion of the *mezzadria* and the increased exploitation of the laborers, however, were just two aspects of a more general transformation of agriculture in the Po Valley, to which the crisis gave a decisive impetus. For market conditions in the 1880s not only wiped out many marginal and less efficient producers, but they also gradually forced the stronger farmers to limit production to the best suited lands, intensify their methods of cultivation, and develop specialized fodder and industrial crops.[86]

[84] See I. Barbadoro, *Storia del sindacalismo*, vol. I, pp. 46-47.

[85] B. King and T. Okey, *Italy To-Day*, pp. 175-176.

[86] C. J. Robertson, "Agricultural Regions," p. 573. G. Carocci, *Agostino Depretis e la politica interna italiana dal 1876 al 1887* (Turin, 1956), p. 416n cites prefectoral reports from the province of Bologna which asserted that even in the midst of the crisis there were significant improvements made through the introduction of new methods of mechanized cultivation.

More importantly, the crisis brought about a major shift in the economic policies of the Italian state. Under mounting pressure from northern agrarian interests, the governments of the 1880s began to intervene actively in the troubled agricultural sector. Already in 1882, the demands of moderate deputies from the Po Delta led to the passage of the Baccarini Law that provided substantial state subsidies and favorable credit arrangements for projects of land reclamation. The measure placed the landowners from the low plains of Bologna and neighboring provinces in an especially advantageous position, since they now had to sustain a mere quarter of the expenses for reclamation, but received all the benefits of the resultant increases in production and property values.[87] In 1885, Bolognese landowners allied with agrarian interests from other areas of the Po Valley in the Agrarian League, an improvised pressure group that successfully lobbied for protective legislation. The new agricultural tariffs imposed in 1887 protected cereal crops, sugar beets, and hemp, largely at the expense of such prevalently southern products as olive oil, wines, and citrus fruits.[88] Duties on imported wheat quadrupled, and rice and oats received comparable protection. In particular, the extremely high duty on sugar provided a powerful stimulus to the cultivation of sugar beets, which had previously been a marginal and unprofitable crop, by virtually excluding foreign competition and giving growers and refiners a virtual monopoly of the domestic market.[89]

Beginning in the 1880s, the government encouraged the growth

[87] See G. Porisini, *Bonifiche e agricoltura*, pp. 50-51, 62-75.

[88] The wheat duty, which had remained fixed at 1.4 lire during the previous seventeen years was increased to 5 lire in 1888 and to 7.5 lire six years later. See Mario Bandini, "Consequenze e problemi della politica doganale per l'agricoltura italiana" in Ministero per la Costituente, *Rapporto della Commissione economica*, Vol. I, *Agricoltura* (Rome, 1946), p. 393; L. Preti, *Le lotte agrarie nella valle padana* (Turin, 1955), pp. 106-110; G. Carocci, *Agostino Depretis*, pp. 415-460. On the beneficial effects of the tariff on northern commercial farmers, see G. Porisini, "Produzione e produttività" and G. Orlando, "Progressi e difficoltà dell'agricoltura" in Giorgio Fuà, ed., *Lo sviluppo economico in Italia*, Vol. III (Milan, 1975), p. 28.

[89] L. Perdisa, *La bietola da zucchero nella economia italiana* (Rome, 1938), pp. 18-23.

and modernization of the agricultural sector in other less dramatic ways. Property taxes, for instance, fell steadily from the mid-1880s until 1910, freeing capital for investments and improvements on the farms of the northern plains.[90] During the same period, the budget of the Ministry of Agriculture nearly tripled, allowing the government to ease farm credit terms and establish experimental stations, technical schools, and *cattedre ambulanti* or traveling chairs of agriculture. After the founding of the first one in the province of Rovigo in 1886, the chairs spread throughout the Po Valley where they offered a wide range of services to enterprising farmers: public conferences and private consultations; laboratories to evaluate soils, seeds, and fertilizers; experimental fields to determine the most productive combination of factors for local agricultural conditions.[91]

As a consequence of the crisis and the government's responses to it, the preexisting dualism of Italian agriculture, with its primitive southern sector and modern capitalist sector in the north, became even more pronounced. From the outset, the enterprising mentality and superior organization and capital resources of the large market-oriented farmers of the Po Valley enabled them to adapt more quickly to the imperatives of commercial competition by adopting more efficient methods of cultivation, mechanization, fertilizers, and crop specialization. The new protective regime accentuated their natural advantages. In contrast to the apathetic *latifondisti* of the south, they were able to gain a substantially higher level of profits from the grain duties, since for them alone the tariff provided a powerful incentive to elevate their production through new capital investments and the employment of more rational farming methods. Indeed, in the following decades they managed to raise the monetary value of their products well above

[90] Property taxes, which had been over 125 million lire in the mid-1880s, fell to 106 by 1900 and to 84 million in 1910. See G. Orlando, "Progressi e difficoltà," p. 29.

[91] On the operations of the traveling chairs of agriculture, see for example, *Annali dell'Ufficio Provinciale per l'agricoltura ed Atti del Comizio Agrario di Bologna*, IX, 1901-1902, p. 17.

the levels achieved prior to the crisis.[92] In a similar fashion, sugar protection benefitted producers from the Po Delta almost exclusively since they had the soil, climate, capital, and technical expertise required to grow the crop.[93]

Within the province of Bologna, the crisis combined with the tariffs and reclamation legislation to favor the advance of a new group of ambitious rural entrepreneurs. As early as 1881, Marchese Tanari noted, not altogether happily, their presence in the plains. Alongside of the traditional landowners like himself who maintained the "old patriarchal spirit," appeared a different breed of farmers "characterized by a greedy industrial spirit which they are injecting into the management of the farms," men whose "principal infatuations are experimental adventures, rents, and profits."[94] Sons of wealthy urban merchants or manufacturers, officials from the land reclamation projects, or in other cases enterprising stewards on the large estates—they tended to be big leaseholders rather than property holders. As a rule, they shared few of the gentlemanly pretensions and paternal sentiments of the agrarian old guard; they were essentially "agricultural industrialists" in the business of maximizing profits by increasing production, lowering costs, and selling their crops in the most lucrative markets.[95] Running business enterprises rather than peasant households, they began to apply systematic economic calculation to farming and to introduce new crop rotations, machines, and chemical fertilizers on an unprecedented scale.

Beginning in the 1880s, hard-pressed landowners turned in-

[92] See Valerio Castronovo, *Storia d'Italia*, Vol. IV Bk. I (Turin, 1975), pp. 140-141; G. Porisini, "Produzione e produttività," pp. 513-515; G. Valenti, "L'Italia agricola dal 1861 al 1911" in *Cinquanta anni di storia italiana*, Vol. II (Milan, 1911), p. 133.

[93] L. Perdisa, *La bietola da zucchero*, pp. 10-16; C. J. Robertson, "The Italian Beet-Sugar Industry," *Economic Geography*, XIV (January 1938), pp. 1-13; *L'Italia Agricola*, April 1927, pp. 206-210.

[94] L. Tanari, *Inchiesta agraria*, pp. 229-230.

[95] Tomaso Crispolti, "Della partecipazione del lavoro al prodotto della terra" in *Annali della Società Agraria Provinciale di Bologna*, Vol. XXXIV, February 18, 1894, pp. 137-138. On their social origins, see E. Sereni, *Il capitalismo*, p. 264.

creasingly to these leaseholders whose large-scale operations, market orientation, and greater efficiency assured them the maximum rents for their estates. Numbering fewer than forty in 1881, the large leaseholders grew steadily in size and importance, and by the end of the succeeding decade they had emerged as the most dynamic and innovative economic force in the Bolognese countryside. While few of their names appeared among the provincial political leadership or on the rolls of the Agrarian Society, they were managing many of the largest estates in the plains in the first years of this century. In the commune of Minerbio, for example, over half the big farms were in their hands; in the commune of Molinella, they directed five of the eight most important rice farms.[96]

Some of the more prominent leaseholders like Annibale Certani and Antonio Bonora came from established Bolognese families. Born in the city of Bologna in 1829, Certani attended the university and received his degree in engineering. In 1854 he leased the enormous properties of the Bonaparte family in Budrio and in the following fifteen years carried out an extensive project of land reclamation that transformed over a thousand acres of marshes and swamps into fields suitable for rational cultivation. Certani also distinguished himself as a pioneer of technical innovation: he invented a new and more efficient iron plow, was the first farmer to use high-yield seed and chemical fertilizers in the province, and became an early promoter of the agricultural processing industry.[97] Antonio Bonora was the son of a noted landowner and agricultural innovator who received his initial training and experience on his family's farm in Galliera. In 1895 he leased the Ducato di Galliera, an estate of over two thousand hectares in the low plains, where he won fame and fortune for his reclamation work, his use of

[96] The estimate of the number of large leaseholders in 1881 is derived from questionnaire responses sent to Tanari's committee from the communes of Galliera, S. Giorgio di Piano, S. Maria in Duno, San Pietro in Casale, Castel S. Pietro, Crespellano, and Crevalcore. See ASB Archivio della Camera di Commercio, B65, F2 (XF). On the role of the leaseholders at the beginning of this century, see ASB C6 F2, "Elenco dei detentori di terreno nel mandamento di Minerbio," 1902 and *ibid.*, Mayor of Molinella to Prefect, May 9, 1903.

[97] For information on Certani, see *RdC*, June 6, 1914, *L'Agricoltura Bolognese*, v, no. 4 (April 1911), pp. 49-52; C. Poni, *Gli aratri*, p. 156.

steam-powered machines, and his cultivation of sugar beets, tobacco, and rice. Apart from his agricultural activities, Bonora also founded a chemical fertilizer factory as well as one of the first sugar refineries in the region.[98]

Men from humbler social backgrounds such as Alfredo Benni and Ignazio Benelli were perhaps more representative of this new breed of commercial farmer. Born into a modest family of farm stewards in Budrio, Benni held various leases in his native commune during the last decades of the nineteenth century and, much like Bonora, achieved wealth and distinction for his land reclamation and rice cultivation. First as an associate of Certani and subsequently as a sole leaseholder of the estate of the former empress of France, he introduced sugar beets, potatoes, and tobacco, obtaining what local agricultural experts described as "extremely high levels of production." Moreover, he constructed an internal network of rail tracks to transport products from the fields to the processing areas and was an earlier user of motorized threshers and harvesters. By 1905 even his harshest critics had to concede that Benni was "a man skilled in agricultural matters."[99] Ignazio Benelli came from a family of small peasant cultivators and worked as a leaseholder until 1894 when he purchased a vast but largely undeveloped estate of some twenty-four hundred hectares in the commune of Medicina. Within the span of a decade, he succeeded in completely transforming the property, bringing nearly one thousand hectares of marsh land under cultivation. During the same period, he tripled the wheat yield of the estate, increased the production of rice eight-fold, and introduced such industrial crops as sugar beets and hemp.[100]

As the careers of these men indicate, the large leaseholders had

[98] *RdC*, October 12, 1922, obituary notice written by Enrico Pini. For a more detailed account of Bonora's accomplishments, see L. Zerbini, *Illustrazione aziende agrarie*, pp. 17-18.

[99] A. Bignardi, *Costruttori di terra* (Bologna, 1958), pp. 9-11; *RdC*, June 6, 1914; L. Zerbini, *Illustrazione aziende agrarie*, pp. 4-10. For a judgment of Benni's critics, see the weekly paper of the Socialist party in Bologna, *La Squilla*, July 3, 1905.

[100] On Benelli, see *RdC*, June 9-10, 1904; *L'Agricoltura Bolognese*, IV, no. 2 (February 1910), pp. 17-23.

become the main protagonists in the accelerated development of commercial agricultural relations in Bologna by the end of the nineteenth century. Tailoring their investment and labor policies to take full advantage of government subsidies and incentives, they brought in machines, fertilizers, and new crops and had begun to build the large and efficient farms that would enable them to reap huge profits in the more favorable economic climate of the new century. Even the most skeptical of the agrarian old guard had to recognize that the new rural entrepreneurs were making significant technical and organizational improvements. While insisting that they "contribute greatly to the absenteeism of the landowners," Marchese Tomaso Crispolti for one conceded in an address to the Agrarian Society in 1894 that the leaseholders were chiefly responsible for the tangible progress of agriculture in the province. Similarly, Count Francesco Massei, another prominent old landowner, admitted that "the work of the leaseholders has been and is far from detrimental."[101]

At the same time, the principal spokesmen of the provincial elite tended to blame the leaseholders for the undesirable social ramifications of commercial agricultural development. Virtually all contemporary observers noted the propensity of the leaseholders to eliminate most of their dependent workers and to hire instead the more disposable day laborers. Already in 1881, Marchese Tanari warned that the big commercial farms were gradually supplanting the *mezzadria*, a system which in his view constituted a "guarantee of a certain social stability in the countryside."[102] A decade later, Agostino Ramponi, another influential member of the Agrarian Society, reported that "this pernicious tendency has become increasingly accentuated in the last five years" largely as a result of the leaseholders who treated agriculture as a "speculative adventure" and introduced "too many innovations solely to augment

[101] T. Crispolti, "Della partecipazione," pp. 140-141. For the views of Count Massei, see in the same volume, "Verbali dell'adunanza," p. 144.

[102] L. Tanari, *Inchiesta agraria*, p. 224. For the similar views of the Tuscan landowners, see G. C. Marino, *Spirito borghese*, pp. 180-183.

the value of the harvests."[103] Men like Tanari and Ramponi were equally disturbed by the parallel growth of a vast army of impoverished day laborers, without stable ties to the land or the proprietors, who had been drawn in steadily increasing numbers to the low plains by the prospects of work in the reclamation projects and in the expanding hemp and rice farms. Indeed, by 1901 a number of communes in this zone of the province had twice as many *braccianti* as sharecroppers.[104] Above all, the agrarian old guard was alarmed by the new depersonalized relationship between employers and laborers that accompanied the spread of the large commercial leases in the Bolognese countryside. While the established landed families aspired to maintain their traditional, hierarchical ties with their dependent peasants, the leaseholders were reducing their connection to the laborers to one of a simple cash nexus. For Marchese Tanari, the leaseholders, with "their greedy industrial spirit and the so-called progress that they have brought to agriculture" were chiefly to blame for the "deteriorating social relations" and the disappearance of "the old harmony" in the countryside.[105] Echoing these sentiments, Count Giuseppe Grabinski denounced in 1892 "the abuses of capital, abuses that too often lead to physical and moral sufferings for the people."[106] Such criticisms seemed particularly appropriate in the newly reclaimed lands of the low plains where the relative absence of the Church, a resident class of traditional landlords, and a stable population of peasant cultivators had given social relations a distinctive form in the late nineteenth century; a raw and unmediated class struggle prevailed that pitted a small number of rich leaseholders against a mass of desperate day laborers who had little to lose by revolting against their situation.

Clearly some of the old landowning notables had certain doubts

[103] Agostino Ramponi, "La mezzadria e la coltura intensiva," in *Annali della Società Agraria Provinciale di Bologna*, Vol. xxxii, April 24, 1892, p. 97.

[104] L. Tanari, *Inchiesta agraria*, pp. 428-429; on the growing population of day laborers, see G. Procacci, *La lotta di classe*, p. 112.

[105] L. Tanari, *Inchiesta agraria*, pp. 229-230, 443.

[106] G. Grabinski, *Lo sciopero e la questione sociale*, pp. 7, 29-30, 36.

about the unlimited benefits of commercial agriculture; a few even attempted to improve the conditions of their dependent laborers and sharecroppers. But on the whole, neither the established landowners nor the large leaseholders were prepared to make the slightest economic or social sacrifice for the sake of the rural poor. On the contrary, the irresistible lure of higher rents or in other cases the competition of industrialized agriculture led more and more landowners to follow the example of the leaseholders by investing in new methods of cultivation and intensifying their exploitation of the sharecroppers. Despite the periodic warnings voiced in the Agrarian Society, farming in the Bolognese plains, and to a lesser extent in the foothills, increasingly became an industry like any other, in which sound business principles took precedence over the uneconomical considerations of status, prestige, and social responsibility. As Marchese Tanari had feared, the chief victim of this process was the traditional rural order with its stable relationships and fixed patterns of deference. For the new class of landless laborers that accompanied the growth of the big commercial farms in the plains had little of the older peasants' affection for the land or their submissiveness toward the landlords. Faced with living and working conditions that nearly all contemporary observers characterized as intolerable, they responded to their employers with mounting hostility and resistance. Initially undisciplined and spontaneous, their discontent gradually assumed more organized forms and in the 1890s began to be mobilized by a nascent socialist movement to challenge the economic supremacy and political hegemony of the agrarian moderates within the province.

4. The Challenge from Below: The Socialist Labor Movement in the Countryside

After describing the appalling conditions of the rural laborers, Marchese Tanari went on in his report of 1881 to note what he defined as the "propagation of subversive ideas" in the communes of the low plains. Three years later, his Bolognese colleague, Count Giovanni Codronchi warned the Chamber of Deputies that the "popular classes" were falling under the sway of agitators who advocated the "collective ownership of the land and equipment."[107] In fact, as the decade of the 1880s unfolded, a small but persistent group of propagandists and organizers began to find a receptive audience for their socialist ideas among the rice workers in the province. Several factors made the rice workers ripe for these new appeals. Concentrated in rural ghettoes in the newly reclaimed lands, they lived in an environment that cut them off from the landowners and the institutions of the older municipal centers, but which facilitated the circulation of ideas and the development of a group consciousness. The nature of their work, which involved little internal stratification and entailed long hours of labor up to their knees in water in the hottest days of the summer, sharpened their sense of a common fate and reinforced this group consciousness.[108] More immediately, the crisis of the 1880s and the gradual shift from permanent rice cultivation to systems of crop rotation by greatly reducing available employment and driving down their already miserable wages provided a powerful impetus for them to adopt new methods of collective action and resistance.[109]

While the actual process whereby this "fluctuating mass" was transformed into a disciplined and militant force remains obscure, it appears that the early socialist organizers initially benefited from the relative absence of established political and cultural institutions in the new lands of the low plains. Apart from occasional speeches

[107] L. Tanari, *Inchiesta agraria*, p. 443; for Count Codronchi's statement, see *Atti Parlamentari, Camera dei Deputatai*, Legislatura xv, Discussioni, June 26, 1884, p. 9243; hereafter cited as *AP*. For popular protests in the 1860s, see R. Zangheri, "I moti del macinato nel Bolognese" in *Le campagne emiliane*.

[108] On the importance of their living conditions, see I. Barbadoro, *Storia del sindacalismo*, vol. I, p. 52; on the working conditions of the rice workers, see: B. King and T. Okey, *Italy To-Day*, p. 176; Pietro Puglioli, *La coltivazione del riso nei rapporti della disoccupazione operaia e della malaria nella pianura bolognese* (Rome, 1906), p. 30; Luigi Faccini, "I lavoratori della risaia fra '700 e '800," *Studi Storici*, xv, no. 3 (1974), pp. 545-588.

[109] See I. Barbadoro, *Storia del sindacalismo*, vol. I, p. 38.

in the Agrarian Society, most absentee landlords, as Agostino Ramponi sadly observed in 1892, "occupied themselves with the pleasant and mundane life of the city" and "neglected their land, forgetting the path that led them to their position of dominance."[110] For their part, the local church hierarchy and the Catholic lay associations displayed little missionary zeal in the reclaimed lands, preferring instead to concentrate their efforts on the older classes of small peasant cultivators and sharecroppers.[111] In what amounted to a raw and comparatively unformed frontier society, socialist theories of class conflict and mass organization had an immediate attraction for workers who had few attachments to traditional values and whose daily existence seemed to be living proof of capitalist exploitation.

Socialist organizers carefully geared their initiatives to the concrete conditions they encountered. Thus, the first unions or "leagues of resistance" were organized exclusively on the local level, bringing together laborers who lived in the same ghettoes and who worked the same estates in pursuit of immediate and tangible demands for higher wages and better working conditions. From the outset, however, the leagues constituted far more than simple economic organizations. Indeed, they provided the institutional framework for a completely new subculture with its own distinctive values, customs, and social relations. On a day-to-day basis, the league offices came to serve as the social center of the villages in the low plains, a place where laborers met to discuss their problems, exchange ideas and experiences, or simply to gossip and play cards. Through the continual propaganda, debates, and rallies of the leagues, the rank and file gradually acquired a sense of their collective strength and learned to channel their explosive discontent into disciplined acts of resistance to the employers. At the same time, the leagues taught the laborers to read and write and instilled in them an almost messianic vision of a juster society. In such an atmosphere of new hopes and expectations, league bosses like Giu-

[110] A. Ramponi, "La mezzadria," pp. 109-110.

[111] I. Barbadoro, *Storia del sindacalismo*, vol. I, pp. 62-65.

seppe Massarenti of Molinella became folk heroes who exercised enormous influence over the laborers and were treated with a veneration that in earlier centuries would have been reserved for saints and religious leaders.[112]

Above all, it was the experience of struggle, and its accompanying sacrifices, setbacks, and satisfactions, that shaped the development of the leagues in the last two decades of the nineteenth century. Beginning in June 1886 when the rice workers of Molinella went out on strike for higher wages, rural labor agitation became an annual phenomenon in the low plains. By 1893, some fourteen leagues existed in the province; in February of that year, they united for the first time in support of a platform of demands for an eight-hour day, differential pay scales, and the right to elect their field foremen.[113] This initial unity proved to be fragile, for although the strike of 1893 spread to twenty communes in the plains, it ended in failure, ushering in a three-year period of setbacks and disarray. But in the summer of 1897, the leagues re-emerged after a victorious strike by some two hundred field hands against three big rice growers triggered walkouts throughout the low plains and finally involved not only rice workers but laborers employed in the wheat harvest. Even these strikes were slight by comparison with the agitation of August 1900 in which over six thousand laborers participated, the largest single agricultural strike in Italy during that year.[114]

[112] *Ibid.*, pp. 66-70, 145-146; R. Zangheri, *Lotte agrarie in Italia. La Federazione Nationale dei Lavoratori della Terra, 1901-1926* (Milan, 1960), pp. xxiv-xxv, xxxv-xxxviii. On Massarenti, see Lucilla Antonelli, *Il santo della palude. Biografia di Giuseppe Massarenti* (Milan, 1955) and Enrico Bassi, *Giuseppe Massarenti. Apostolato e opera* (Bologna, 1951).

[113] See Angelo Bertolini, "Lo sciopero di Molinella," *Giornale degli Economisti*, xxi (1900), pp. 387-389; *RdC*, February 28, 1893; Ministero di Agricoltura, *Statistica degli scioperi avvenuti nell'industria e nell'agricoltura durante gli anni dal 1884 al 1891*, selectively reprinted in Sergio Zaninelli, *Le lotte nelle campagne dalla grande crisi agricola al primo dopoguerra 1880-1921* (Milan, 1971), pp. 143-164.

[114] On the strikes of these years, see A. Bertolini, "Lo sciopero," p. 388, 393; Luigi Arbizzani, *Sguardi sull'ultimo secolo. Bologna e la sua provincia 1859-1961* (Bologna, 1961), p. 88.

To a certain extent, the organizational instability and erratic growth of the leagues in the 1890s resulted from the policies of the agrarian employers. Accustomed to the passivity and submissiveness of the laborers, virtually all factions of the provincial elite reacted with horror and outrage to the emergence of the leagues and the upsurge in strikes. Despite their differing interests and values, both the old landlords and the new commercial farmers denounced the strikes as acts of "economic repression and violence" that violated the fundamental "norms of reason, custom, [and] law" and viewed the leagues as the work of dangerous outside agitators who were deceiving the laborers, exciting their greed, and "making them dream of some unrealizable Eldorado."[115] Agrarians responded accordingly to this perceived menace by refusing to recognize or negotiate with league representatives, rejecting outside mediation, importing strikebreakers, and in the most extreme cases by abandoning their crops in the fields.[116] While socialist leaders claimed that the landowners and leaseholders fought the leagues because "their conservative instincts and interests drive them to obstruct the development of anything that endangers their privileges,"[117] their intransigence also reflected the peculiar character of strikes in the agricultural sector. Throughout most of the year, the limited demand for labor deprived rural laborers of any effective bargaining power. But in the harvest season, strikes suddenly acquired an awesome potency. Unlike industrial strikes that involved the loss of production for a relatively brief period when the factories were actually closed, work stoppages during the harvest threatened agrarian employers with

[115] Giovanni Enrico Sturani, *Ancora del decimo sciopero di Molinella* (Bologna, 1900), pp. 13-15; G. Urtoller, "I movimenti agrari in ordine al diritto e all'economia sociale," in *Annali della Società Agraria Provinciale di Bologna*, Vol. XXXVIII, May 29, 1898, pp. 225-226; G. Grabinski, *Lo sciopero e la questione sociale*, pp. 5-7; *RdC*, March 31, April 22, 1898.

[116] For agrarian responses to the leagues, see A. Bertolini, "Scioperi in Italia nel 1898 e 1899 e all'estero nel 1898, 1899, 1900," *Giornale degli Economisti*, XXIV (1902), pp. 530-553; S. Zaninelli, *Le lotte nelle campagne*, pp. 143-164; *RdC*, March 31, April 3, 4, 1898 and August 22, 1900.

[117] See *AP Camera*, Leg. XVIII, Discussioni, May 3, 1893, p. 3125.

the loss of an entire year's investments and production, since the crops rotted if they remained uncollected. At the same time, a harvest strike entailed enormous risks for the laborers who derived most of their annual income from the field work in the summer months. The arrival of large numbers of strikebreakers or even a prolonged strike meant not only immediate suffering for the laborers, but also possible starvation for themselves and their families during the long winter months of enforced idleness. With so much at stake for both parties, it was scarcely surprising that harvest strikes made the clash between agricultural employers and laborers exceptionally bitter and violent.[118]

Bolognese agrarian spokesmen used the frequent conflicts that took place when striking laborers attempted to prevent blacklegs from entering the fields to portray the strikes as violent revolts against the established order and to demand the intervention of the police.[119] In the last decade of the century conservative political leaders in Rome tended to share the perceptions and concerns of Bologna's propertied classes. Already in 1893 governmental authorities clearly demonstrated their receptiveness to appeals from local employers. Following publication of the leagues' demands in February of that year, the prefect immediately dispatched troops to Molinella "for the maintenance of public order"; in the ensuing weeks the police compiled lists of subversives and repeatedly searched the offices of the leagues and the homes of strike leaders in what Socialist party representatives denounced as a systematic campaign of "intimidation."[120] Responding to these charges, the minister of interior, Giovanni Giolitti spelled out what was to be the basic policy of the central government in agricultural strikes for the remainder of the decade: "The laborer is perfectly free to work or

[118] For an interesting discussion of the unique features of strikes in agriculture, see Edward E. Malefakis, *Agrarian Reform and Peasant Revolution* (New Haven, 1970), pp. 108-109.

[119] See, for example, G. Grabinski, *Lo sciopero e la questione sociale*, pp. 5-7, and G. Urtoller, "I movimenti agrari," pp. 225-226.

[120] *RdC*, February 28, 1893; *AP Camera*, Leg. XVIII, Discussioni, May 3, 1893, p. 3125.

not, to accept or not accept the wages that are offered to him, but he does not have the right to prevent other laborers from working. . . . He who wishes to accept the wages that are offered to him has the right not to be disturbed . . . and government authorities have intervened and will intervene to protect the right to work for all laborers."[121]

In practice such a policy translated into increasingly open collusion between agrarian employers and police in the breaking of strikes and the persecution of the leagues. After the workers had won major concessions from the landowners in the spring of 1897, the prefect closed the labor organizations and the Socialist Electoral Union in the commune of Budrio; in the summer this order was extended to all the socialist circles in the province.[122] The following year, police jailed striking women rice workers in mass, while the prefect closed the Resistance League of Molinella and procured the arrest of Massarenti on charges of inciting "hatred between the social classes, rebellion, and crimes against the right-to-work laws."[123] Moreover, in the aftermath of the strikes of 1898, the minister of interior informed the Bolognese prefect of plans for a "company of soldier-harvesters" that could be used in the event of renewed labor agitation to "increase the supply of labor and render strikes more difficult." Two years later, these contingency plans were actually put into effect; when strikes broke out in August 1900, troops were sent into the plains, lodged on the estate of a large landowner, and put to work harvesting the crops in the deserted fields.[124]

Such partisan intervention reinforced the intransigence of the landowners and commercial farmers. Assured of the energetic support of government officials, agrarian employers had few incentives to organize themselves, modify their labor policies, or compromise with the leagues. The Agrarian Society continued to be a prestigious institution of the agrarian old guard, but by the 1890s it had

121 *Ibid.*, p. 3123.

122 See L. Arbizzani, *Sguardi sull'ultimo secolo*, p. 88.

123 *RdC*, March 23-30, April 2, 5, 1898.

124 ASB, C6 F2, 1900, Minister of Interior to Prefect, June 14, 1898.

become little more than a gentlemen's club, while the *ad hoc* committees set up by employers during strikes represented only emergency expedients that invariably ceased to function once the unrest had subsided.[125] For their part, the large leaseholders steadfastly denied both the legitimacy of the strikes and the need for labor unions in the countryside. Taking a leaf from the pages of De Tocqueville, their foremost spokesman, Giovanni Enrico Sturani attributed the chronic unrest in Molinella, for instance, to the relative prosperity of the laborers that, in his view, "favored their organization and resistance."[126] Older landlords like Count Grabinski were more likely to recognize the existence of poverty and exploitation in the countryside, but they preferred to blame the unrest on a few troublemakers and declining moral standards, and looked to religion rather than reform as the means of helping the laborers become once again "resigned to their humble conditions."[127]

In the face of agrarian intransigence and government repression, the leagues displayed a remarkable resilience during the difficult period of the 1890s. Their capacity for reconstituting themselves after defeats and setbacks stemmed in part from the broad territorial base and decentralized structure of the early rural labor movement. Far from being an isolated phenomenon, the Bolognese leagues were part of a more general upsurge in labor organizing and agitation throughout the region of Emilia as well as in the plains of the southern Veneto, Lombardy, and Piedmont where commercial agriculture and large concentrations of day laborers predominated.[128] Chiefly the product of innumerable local initiatives, this movement had a highly decentralized structure that proved quite resistant to simple repression. For no sooner had the police and landowners managed to break a strike or crush the

[125] On the exclusiveness of the Agrarian Society, see *Annali della Società Provinciale di Bologna*, Vol. LXIII, 1913, pp. 79-88 for a list of all the members and the dates of their admission into the Società.

[126] G. E. Sturani, *Ancora del decimo sciopero*, p. 6.

[127] G. Grabinski, *Lo sciopero e la questione sociale*, pp. 7, 29-30, 36.

[128] See I. Barbadoro, *Storia del sindacalismo*, vol. I, pp. 119-148.

leagues in one area than unions and agitation would appear in another area. In this fashion, the authorities were unable to achieve any decisive or permanent victories, while the idea of mass action was carried on, inspiring laborers elsewhere to organize or to reconstitute their unions. Indeed, the power of example appears to have played a crucial role in the growth and persistence of the leagues. News or rumor of strikes in one province often provided the spark that ignited agitation in other areas as in 1897 when a work stoppage in the province of Cremona set off a chain reaction of strikes that spread rapidly to Mantua, Polesine, and the entire region of Emilia.[129]

The leagues also benefited enormously from their mutually supportive relationship with the Italian Socialist party (PSI). Founded in 1892, the PSI gave the rural labor movement an important new political voice both in the provinces and in Rome. Through its electoral propaganda and newspapers, the party helped sustain the agricultural workers in defeat and during the frequent periods of persecution, while its continuous organizational presence in the countryside reduced their isolation and gave them a sense of unity and participation in a movement that extended well beyond the confines of their old municipal or provincial worlds. In the Chamber of Deputies, Socialist leaders like Andrea Costa, Leonida Bissolati, and Gregorio Agnini advanced the previously neglected interests of the laborers, defended the goals and objectives of the leagues, and denounced the excesses of the police and the blind resistance of the landowners. By drawing national attention to local labor struggles, their impassioned speeches and writings began to influence public opinion and counteract official versions of events and the one-sided accounts of the moderate press.[130] In exchange for these services, the PSI gained substantial benefits; as one foreign observer noted in the 1890s, most of the Socialist deputies in Italy were "elected only by the agricultural laborers [and] they represent prevalently agricultural provinces." Indeed, in the wake

[129] *Ibid.*, p. 130.
[130] *Ibid.*, pp. 66-67.

of the electoral reforms of the previous decade that had lowered educational requirements for voters, the party found one of its first and strongest bases of mass support in the plains of the Po Valley. Its alliance with the leagues in this area not only provided a disproportionately large share of the small but growing number of Socialist deputies in parliament, but also enabled the PSI to capture many municipal administrations in rural communes such as Molinella where in the past agrarian notables had ruled supreme.[131]

The persistent, if halting, advance of the socialist labor movement in Bologna and other provinces of the northern plains took place against a background of mounting social and political unrest throughout the Italian peninsula in the last years of the century. The lingering effects of economic recession, rising food prices, and the growing political consciousness of the population all combined to fuel popular discontent and trigger recurrent demonstrations, strikes, and violent protests in virtually every major city. Between 1896 and 1900, the total number of strikes in the country nearly doubled; during the same period authorities confronted a swarm of bread riots and local rebellions. Widespread turbulence and exasperation reached a peak in 1898. In January of that year, angry mobs of protestors attacked grain dealers and administrators in a number of isolated uprisings in the south and center. By April, unrest had spread to the north as pitched battles erupted between rioters and police in the provinces of Ravenna, Piacenza, and Parma. These disturbances culminated in May when violent demonstrations in Milan led to the erection of barricades and three days of bloody fighting between demonstrators and troops that left over eighty dead and 450 wounded.[132]

Regardless of whether it was an agricultural strike in Bologna, a food riot in Bari, or a protest demonstration in Milan, Italy's

[131] W. Sombart, "Italienische Briefe," in *Sozialpolitisches Centralblatt*, 3, 1894, cited in *ibid.*, p. 71.

[132] For strike statistics, see Maurice F. Neufeld, *Italy: School for Awakening Countries* (Ithaca, 1961), p. 547; on the events of 1898, see Umberto Levra, *Il colpo di stato della borghesia. La crisi di fine secolo in Italia* (Milan, 1975).

moderate political class was inclined to see the revolutionary designs of the socialists in the social unrest and at least initially appeared disposed to sacrifice individual liberties in order to defend its uncontested leadership. Already in January 1897, one of the foremost moderate leaders, Baron Sidney Sonnino proposed a "return to the Constitution" of 1848 to disarm "the permanent armies of the extremist parties" by stripping the Chamber of Deputies of its control over the ministries and by strengthening the executive power of the king.[133] In the midst of the turmoil of the following year, landowners in the Agrarian Society argued that "the defense of property and the social order" required severe restrictions on the right of association, since the "rural masses" were "ignorant of their duties before the law and the society."[134] While the successive governments of Antonio di Rudinì and General Luigi Pelloux did not implement Sonnino's proposal, they took extreme measures against the unrest. After the events of May 1898, di Rudinì extended martial law from Milan to Naples, set up special military tribunals to punish the rioters, banned more than a hundred newspapers, and dissolved labor organizations. In the sweeping repression that followed, 828 so-called "political offenders," including most of the prominent Socialist leaders as well as numerous Republican and Radical politicians, were arrested and imprisoned.[135] The fall of the di Rudinì ministry in June 1898 did not lead to any enduring relaxation of his authoritarian policies. On the contrary, his successor General Pelloux introduced sweeping legislation for the defense of public order early the following year. When the strenuous opposition of the *estrema sinistra*, a leftist coalition of the Socialist, Republican, and Radical parties, prevented its passage in the Chamber of Deputies, Pelloux prorogued parliament and promulgated by royal decree his comprehensive coercion

[133] Sidney Sonnino, "Torniamo allo Statuto," *Nuova Antologia*, January 1, 1897; reprinted in Benjamin Brown, ed., *Sidney Sonnino: Scritti e discorsi extraparlamentari 1870-1902* (Bari, 1972), pp. 575-597.

[134] G. Grabinski, *Lo sciopero e la questione sociale*, pp. 5-7; G. Urtoller, "I movimenti agrari," pp. 225-226.

[135] M. Neufeld, *Italy*, p. 222.

bill that established penal colonies for banished political prisoners, placed severe restrictions on public meetings, and empowered the courts to dissolve all organizations threatening "to subvert the social order and the Constitution."[136]

By the summer of 1899, however, the unity and cohesiveness of the ruling moderates had begun to break down visibly. Protesting Pelloux's antiparliamentary methods, a group of some fifty moderate deputies, headed by Giolitti and Giuseppe Zanardelli, broke ranks with the government and joined the opposition in May.[137] Although the dissident moderates constituted a small minority in parliament, their influence was considerably greater than their numbers, since their ideas attracted a growing consensus outside the Chamber of Deputies in the press, university circles, chambers of commerce, and in the business world.[138]

The political disunity of the moderates reflected not only conflicts over constitutional and civil libertarian issues, but also new divisions within Italy's propertied classes over questions of foreign policy, trade, and tariffs. After nearly a decade of depression and stagnation, in 1896 the country entered a period of rapid industrial and commercial expansion. In the highly favorable international economic climate that prevailed in the last years of the century, influential cotton, chemical, and electrical interests from Liguria, Lombardy, and Piedmont began to argue for a reduction in tariffs and a return to free trade policies in order to take fuller advantage

136 *Ibid.* See also U. Levra, *Il colpo di stato*, pp. 223-310.

137 In a speech a few months later, Giolitti justified his break from the moderate majority, charging that "the path of reaction would be fatal to our institutions precisely because it puts them at the service of a small minority and alienates the most vital and irresistible forces of modern society." To avoid this danger, he advocated a more conciliatory strategy to diffuse the militancy of the extreme left by enlisting its support for a broadly based governing coalition. Such a strategy, Giolitti argued, represented an "eminently conservative undertaking" since it promised to give the Italian state a secure base "not in the interests of restricted privileged classes," but in the "affection of the immense majority of the country." See Giovanni Giolitti, *Discorsi extraparlamentari* (Turin, 1953), p. 220 as cited in Franco De Felice, "L'età giolittiana," *Studi Storici*, 1969, no. 1, pp. 142-143.

138 See Christopher Seton-Watson, *Italy from Liberalism to Fascism* (London, 1967), p. 194.

of rising foreign demand. Their support for a major revision of Italy's trade agreements, cuts in taxes and government spending, and an end to overseas military adventures brought them inexorably into conflict with agrarian protectionist interests as well as with the steel, armaments, and shipbuilding sectors who favored expansionist policies abroad and depended on massive state subsidies. These contracts came into public view in the spring of 1899 when Pelloux advanced a program tailored to the interests of the protectionist bloc. In March he attempted unsuccessfully to use the threat of armed intervention to gain an Italian sphere of influence in China and proposed, at the same time, substantial increases in military spending. In the face of strong opposition to his China policy and his budget from the extreme left, Catholics, and the followers of Giolitti and Zanardelli, the prime minister resigned in May, only to form immediately a new ultraconservative government that excluded all representatives of the "constitutional left," precipitating a formal split within the moderate camp.[139]

With both parliament and the country as a whole increasingly polarized into two hostile camps, the prime minister moved to break the stalemate by dissolving the Chamber of Deputies and calling new elections in June 1900. The results of the voting clearly revealed the inefficacy of repressive legislation as well as the isolation of Pelloux and his agrarian, monarchical, and military allies. While the government managed to maintain a majority in the Chamber, it gained a narrow plurality of the popular vote and actually won only a minority of the seats in the north. More importantly, the chief target of Pelloux's repressive legislation and electoral campaign, the parties of the extreme left, raised their strength from sixty-seven to ninety-five seats. In few provinces did the Socialist party achieve a greater success than in Bologna where it captured two out of eight seats.[140] Disheartened by the outcome, the prime minister resigned from office and withdrew

[139] U. Levra, *Il colpo di stato*, pp. 311-320; G. Procacci, "Appunti in tema di crisi dello stato liberale e di origini del fascismo," *Studi Storici*, 1965, no. 2, pp. 221-237; G. Carocci, *Giolitti*, p. 25.

[140] M. Neufeld, *Italy*, p. 225; for voting in Bologna, see *RdC*, June 16-17, 1900.

from political life at the end of June 1900. Although King Umberto chose another conservative, Giuseppe Saracco, to form a caretaker government, the fall of the Pelloux cabinet effectively marked the end of "political reaction" and set the stage for Giovanni Giolitti's return to power, this time with a bold new program of political and social reforms. As the dramatic developments of 1901 soon demonstrated, Giolitti's innovative policies would significantly alter the established systems of interest representation and social bargaining on the provincial level.

II. POLITICAL LIBERALIZATION AND AGRARIAN REACTION, 1901-1909

By the spring of 1901, the Italian peninsula had already entered a period of unparalleled industrial growth and social progress. With the chemical, metallurgical, and engineering sectors leading the way, manufacturing production more than doubled, the annual rate of growth reached record highs, and capital investments in plant and equipment rose by 114 percent. As the older textile firms completed their conquest of the domestic market and enlarged their export activities, modern steel, hydroelectric, and automotive industries were born. Indeed, in a highly favorable international economic climate, the state, capable entrepreneurs, and new commercial banks helped stimulate the greatest relative economic advance of any major European nation in the years from 1896 to 1908.[1]

The same period also witnessed major changes in Italian society. Industrialization and falling death rates led to an increase in population that was accompanied by a steady movement from the countryside to the towns and cities. After decades of economic stagnation and misery, large numbers of Italians began to experience a real improvement in their standard of living. Significantly,

[1] On the industrial expansion of this period, see Alexander Gerschenkron, *Economic Backwardness in Historical Perspective* (Cambridge, Mass., 1962); Rosario Romeo, *Breve storia della grande industria in Italia* (Bologna, 1963).

both *per capita* income and consumption of wheat rose sharply, while infectious diseases and illiteracy declined in the first decade of the century.[2]

The government formed in February 1901 under the leadership of Giuseppe Zanardelli clearly reflected these developments. From its inception, the new cabinet marked a decisive shift away from the authoritarian governments of the late 1890s by actively pursuing and gaining the support of the parties of the extreme left. Presenting his cabinet to the Chamber of Deputies on March 7, 1901, Zanardelli stressed its liberal stamp, affirming his commitment to the "principles of liberty" and his determination to apply "in letter and spirit the individual and collective guarantees sanctioned by the constitution."[3]

The new approach to the problem of labor militancy advanced by Giovanni Giolitti, Zanardelli's minister of interior, best expressed the innovative character of the government. Even prior to assuming office, Giolitti rejected the longstanding view of the moderate right that all workers' associations were subversive. Interviewed in early February, he claimed that the unions could be "a very noble intermediary between capital and labor"; if they had displayed a certain hostility toward the established order in the past, it was because "they felt themselves systematically persecuted."[4] During the spring of 1901, Giolitti expanded on these ideas in a series of parliamentary addresses. Portraying the labor movement as "an inevitable movement that no force will succeed in arresting," he argued that repression was counterproductive, since it encouraged the "masses to consider the government as their enemy" and thereby served to radicalize what were essentially peaceful organizations of economic amelioration. To halt such a process of polarization, the government had to limit its role in labor-management disputes to ensuring that "the worker is sat-

[2] For social progress in this period, see Maurice Neufeld, *Italy: School for Awakening Countries* (Ithaca, 1961), pp. 289-297.

[3] From speech of Zanardelli to Chamber of Deputies, quoted in S. F. Romano, *L'Italia del novecento*, Vol. I, *L'età giolittiana* (Rome, 1968) p. 107.

[4] *RdC*, February 16-17, 1901.

isfied with fair wages and the employer pays him his due." In this fashion, workers would acquire a more positive image of the Italian state as "an impartial authority that will do all it can to give them justice" as well as a "force that will keep them within the bounds of legality."[5]

Giolitti's advocacy of government neutrality in labor disputes represented just one aspect of his master plan to broaden the base of consensus for Italy's monarchy and ruling moderate oligarchy by domesticating the parties of the extreme left and by gradually assimilating the organized working class and peasantry of the north into the established political system. In order to achieve these objectives, he proposed not only to tolerate peaceful strikes, but also to recognize the legitimacy of the trade unions, to provide state aid to the labor cooperatives, and to respect the civil rights of the Socialist party. As conceived by Giolitti, such concessions would reduce mass discontent, isolate violent extremists, and strengthen the position of reformist elements within the PSI who could then be induced to participate as junior partners in an enlarged governing coalition under his leadership. At the same time, his plan entailed a new opening toward the various Catholic associations whose influence and potential voting strength he intended to use as a political counterweight to the extreme left.[6] The viability of this complex system of shifting political compromises, alliances, and trade-offs depended in turn on both labor's and capital's sharing in the rewards of economic growth. For with economic prosperity, employers could increase their profits and still meet the basic demands of the workers who would thus be encouraged to operate within the existing legal order.[7]

Giolitti did not have to wait long for the opportunity to test his

[5] *AP Camera dei Deputati*, Leg. XXI, 1st Session, Vol. VI, Discussioni, 2nd Tornata, June 21, 1901, p. 5498; *AP Senato*, Leg. XXI, 1st Session, Vol. II, Discussioni, April 31, 1901, pp. 1353-1355.

[6] On Giolitti's general strategy, see Giampiero Carocci, *Giolitti e l'età giolittiana* (Turin, 1971), pp. 50-51; Emilio Gentile, ed., *L'Italia giolittiana* (Bari, 1977), pp. 13-15; Richard Webster, *Industrial Imperialism in Italy* (Berkeley, 1975), p. 23.

[7] *Ibid.*

conciliatory labor policies in the countryside. Encouraged by the political promises of the new government and determined to secure their share of the wealth generated by economic expansion, Italian agricultural workers rose up in an unprecedented wave of strikes in the spring and summer of 1901. The previous peak of labor agitation, which had come in 1897 with twelve strikes involving 24,145 laborers, paled in comparison with 1901 when nearly a quarter of a million rural workers mostly from the Po Valley took part in over six hundred strikes in support of their demands for higher wages and shorter work hours.[8]

The peasant leagues were especially active in the province of Bologna where governmental statisticians reported twenty-two strikes with 17,378 participants between April and August.[9] Following a well-established pattern, the Bolognese strikes were spearheaded by salaried workers and day laborers in the wet crop areas of the low plains while sharecroppers remained for the most part uninvolved. Laborers struck first in the communes of Bentivoglio and Minerbio in early April after agrarian employers refused to negotiate the new wage scales and work schedules with league representatives. From these communes, the strike fever spread quickly to the rest of the plains and involved both rice workers and other field hands in what the local press described at the end of the month as "a general movement directed toward establishing uniform contracts for each of the various localities and crops."[10] Apart from their size, the strikes were distinguished by the ex-

[8] More than 90 percent of the agricultural strikes in Italy that year took place in the Po Valley. The vastness of the rural strike movement is reflected in the fact that only 197,000 industrial workers went on strike that year. See G. Procacci, *La lotta di classe in Italia agli inizi del secolo XX* (Rome, 1970), pp. 77-79; Società degli Agricoltori Italiani, *I recenti scioperi agrari in Italia e i loro effetti economici* (Rome, 1902), p. 13.

[9] G. Procacci, *La lotta di classe*, pp. 77-79. In numbers of agricultural strikers, Bologna was third in the country in 1901 behind Ferrara and Milan.

[10] *RdC*, April 18-19 and 22-23, 1901. The largest single strike took place in Molinella and involved over three thousand laborers who demanded formal recognition of their organization by the landowners. See ASB, C6 F2, Police report to Prefect, April 29, 1901.

ceptional militancy of the laborers. In his report on the situation in the plains late in April, the prefect Caravaggio claimed that large bands of strikers were roving about the countryside "armed with their tools," intimidating all those who "wanted to go to work."[11]

In the face of this extraordinary outburst of labor agitation, Giolitti remained calm and steadfastly maintained his commitment to governmental neutrality. To the calls of agrarian deputies for renewed use of soldier harvesters, he responded that such a measure would be not only "illegal and politically unwise," but would also reinforce the reluctance of the employers to "concede those wages that are just and equal."[12] Troops were brought into the province of Bologna to maintain order and mass demonstrations were temporarily banned in April, but in contrast to previous years, the prefect did not close the league offices, disband the Socialist municipal administrations, or imprison strike leaders. More importantly, for the first time a minister of interior actually criticized the intransigence of agrarian employers and pressured them to accept a compromise settlement with the laborers. In May, for instance, Caravaggio received orders from Giolitti to demand "greater fairness" from the landowners and leaseholders and to warn them that the government would "never use armed force" on behalf of "illegitimate interests." The same month Giolitti intervened directly in the Bolognese disputes, charging that wages in the plains were "inferior to those elsewhere" and that consequently the recalcitrant landowners were "in the wrong."[13] The significance of this shift in government policy was not lost on the reformist leaders of the PSI like Filippo Turati who praised Giolitti for not "at-

[11] ASB, C6 F2, Prefectorial Decree, April 24, 1901.

[12] *AP Senato*, Leg. xxi, 1st Session, Vol. ii, Discussioni, April 31, 1901, pp. 1366-1367. Giolitti reaffirmed this position to the prefect of Bologna in May. See ASB, C6 F2, May 20, 1901.

[13] For use of troops and ban on demonstrations, see prefectoral decree cited in note 11. On Giolitti's intervention in the Bolognese situation, see ASB, C6 F2, telegrams to Prefect of May 19 and 20, 1901. Prefectoral reports show that little more than one hundred persons were arrested during the strikes; virtually all arrests were for specific violations of the right to work. See in particular, ASB, C6 F2, Prefect to Giolitti, June 2, 1901.

tempting, as others before him, to suffocate [the leagues] in the cradle."[14]

In the new political climate of 1901, rural strikes were accompanied by an expansion of the socialist labor movement in the countryside that far surpassed the achievements of comparable organizations in other European countries. By late November when the strike wave had receded, over eight hundred leagues with 152,122 members had come into existence, concentrated for the most part in the plains of the Po Valley. That month league representatives from all over Italy gathered for the first national congress of agricultural laborers in the city of Bologna where they agreed to coordinate their activities and press for the socialization of the land. The congress culminated in the founding of the National Federation of Agricultural Laborers (the Federterra). The Federterra soon had a larger membership than any industrial or commercial union in the country, accounting for half of all workers organized in labor federations by the end of the following year.[15]

Despite their impressive strength in certain communes of the low plains, the Bolognese leagues lagged behind their comrades in neighboring provinces in the development of a provincial federation. Above all, the wide range of farming systems, crops, and forms of land tenure in Bologna hampered the efforts of local labor leaders to formulate a common program and organizational structure, since any provincial federation had to satisfy the needs and interests of both the large sharecropping population and the landless day laborers of the plains. The first attempt to unite all the peasant leagues in a single organization came in June 1901 when the Bolognese Chamber of Labor, the local umbrella organization of unions and cooperatives, announced plans for a "federation of agricultural laborers." But this project made little headway and at

[14] Filippo Turati, *Discorsi parlamentari*, vol. I, p. 181 quoted in Idomenao Barbadoro, *Storia del sindacalismo italiano dalla nascita al fascismo*, Vol. I, *La Federterra* (Florence, 1973), p. 120.

[15] On the congress, see *RdC*, November 22-23, 1901. For the comparative membership of the Federterra in relation to other federations, see M. Neufeld, *Italy*, p. 329.

the time of the national congress the rural labor movement in Bologna was still localized and fragmented. Only after the founding of the national Federterra was the first provincial congress of leagues convened. Meeting in January 1902, the heads of thirty-seven leagues founded the Provincial Federation of Agricultural Laborers (the Bolognese Federterra) that proposed not only to advance the wage and work demands of the day laborers, but also to agitate for the reform of local sharecropping contracts.[16] With this compromise program, the new organization made rapid progress; by October the Bolognese Federterra represented sixty leagues with over fourteen thousand members, making it the third largest provincial federation in the country after those of Mantua and Ferrara.[17] At the same time, representatives of seven labor cooperatives in the low plains set up a parallel federation to coordinate their activities and obtain "important public works from the government."[18]

The founding of the Bolognese Federterra coincided with a new burst of political activity in the province by the Socialist party that had immediately benefited from the growing size and discipline of the leagues. Indeed, 1902 saw the party strengthen its control over the municipal administrations in Molinella and Imola and begin to challenge the position of agrarian moderates in those communes of the plains where agricultural workers constituted the bulk of the local population. Relatively free from government interference, the PSI was able to use its labor and cooperative alliances to build powerful electoral coalitions in order to oppose the hastily assembled groups of moderate supporters. Commenting on the electoral activity of the Socialists in the commune of Baricella, for example, one police official warned that "their predominant numbers [and]

[16] See *La Squilla,* June 8, 1901, for the provincial federation project of the Chamber of Labor. On the provincial congress and the statute of the new federation, see *RdC,* January 18-19, 1901 and *La Squilla,* February 22, 1902.

[17] *RdC,* October 20-21, 1902. The Federation of Mantua had a membership of 23,104; that of Ferrara, 20,565. See G. Procacci, *Lotta di classe,* p. 88.

[18] *RdC,* January 20-21, 1902; ASB, C7 F1, Police Chief to Prefect, February 10, 1902.

the inexhaustible propaganda that animates them give them a strong possibility of victory."[19] Party efforts met with particular success in those rural areas where the league leaders were also Socialist candidates. The commune of Molinella, where Giuseppe Massarenti was the mayor, head of the leagues, and president of the cooperative, best exemplified this situation. Here, police officials complained, the vast majority of the laborers "follow blindly the counsels, indeed the orders, of the Socialist leaders and drag along the hesitant."[20]

As these developments suggest, political liberalization in Rome had helped bring about a dramatic shift in the balance of power at the provincial level. With the leagues firmly established in the countryside, the Bolognese daily, *Il Resto del Carlino* stressed how "the arbitrary action of the landowners can no longer determine the level of the laborer's pay, his future, and his participation in the fruits of civilized life; misery and death no longer set what the minimum wage level will be . . . but rather the workers themselves."[21] At the same time, the new freedom granted the left in the province allowed the Socialist party to develop its distinctive forms of organization and electoral mobilization and become an increasingly important political force, to which the propertied classes had to respond and adapt or else face the gradual loss of those prizes and distinctions of public life that had been their exclusive preserve.

1. *The First Response: Political Reaction and Agrarian Disarray*

For a generation of landowners and leaseholders accustomed to the partisan support of police, prefects, and prime ministers, Giolitti's neutrality came as a brutal shock, which caught

[19] ASB, C4 F1, Police Report to Prefect, May 10, 1902. On the special relationship between the PSI and the leagues, see Napoleone Colajanni, "Il movimento agrario in Italia," *Rivista d'Italia*, 1902, p. 733.

[20] ASB, C6 F2, Police Report to Prefect, February 18, 1902.

[21] *RdC*, July 4-5, 1901.

them unawares and left them woefully unprepared for the explosion of strikes that engulfed the Italian countryside in 1901. Isolated and unorganized, rural employers had little choice but to capitulate to the laborers' demands; they seemed powerless to halt the spread of the socialist leagues.[22] If the editorials of the agrarian press and the speeches of moderate deputies from the Po Valley are any indication, the initial reaction of the propertied classes to these developments was a blend of panic, outrage, and most of all untempered hostility toward a government that had betrayed their interests and opened the floodgates to anarchy and chaos for the sake of facile popularity.

The apocalyptic mood of the landowners in the spring of 1901 was clearly evident in the speeches of agrarian representatives in the Senate. Addressing his colleagues in April, Senator Arrivabene, a large landowner from the province of Mantua, portrayed the strikes as part of a growing subversive movement bent on reducing "the landowners, leaseholders, and peasants to misery in order to prepare for social revolution," a view also held by Senator Vitelleschi who warned that the socialists, left unchecked, would soon destroy "the state and . . . the social order."[23] These fears were shared by many of their constituents who claimed that all security of property and person had vanished in strike-torn areas where, as one Bolognese landowner expressed it, "one sees upright citizens, expert farmers, the pride of the province, threatened [and] compelled to shut themselves up in their homes."[24]

Agrarian interests, however, reserved their strongest invective for the new government and for Giolitti in particular. In attaching blame for the labor unrest, *Il Giornale dell'Emilia*, the leading moderate daily in Bologna, asserted that "the most guilty of all,

[22] In 1901 only 19.1 percent of the strikes ended in an unfavorable outcome for the laborers. See Sergio Zaninelli, *Le lotte nelle campagne dalla grande crisi agricola al primo dopoguerra 1880-1921* (Milan, 1971), p. 185.

[23] For Arrivabene's speech, see *AP Senato*, Leg. XXI, Vol. II, April 29, 1901, p. 1336; for that of Vitelleschi, *ibid.*, April 30, 1901, pp. 1356-1357.

[24] A. Feletti, *Gli scioperi a fronte del governo e dei possidenti* (Bologna, 1902), p. 14.

the most responsible, the one against whom all landowners and right-thinking people must unite, is not to be sought here in the rice fields . . . but in Rome at the seat of the government."[25] During the spring of 1901, the paper published a steady stream of attacks on the minister of interior, accusing him of "passivity" in the face of "impudent and unpunished violations of the right to work," encouraging the laborers to strike, and "cheerfully ruining the nation's agriculture." Giolitti's defense of his labor policies before the Chamber of Deputies in June did little to reduce the hostility of *Il Giornale,* which responded that no purpose "would be served by analyzing the speech of the minister of interior," since there was "not a word that is not an offense against truth, good sense, and the sentiments of the vast majority of Italians."[26]

At the same time, Bologna's moderate deputies rallied behind Sidney Sonnino who led the campaign in the Chamber of Deputies to bring down the Zanardelli ministry. Articulating the fears and resentments of the landowners, Sonnino told the Chamber in mid-June that the government's opening to the extreme left and its tolerance of strikes had served only to "dangerously accelerate the development of a mass movement under the socialist banner." For Sonnino, the upsurge of strikes and labor agitation in the spring provided more than ample proof that Giolitti's policy of "passive indifference" was seriously endangering the "entire edifice of liberty, civilization, and unity which our elders erected with so much courage and sacrifice after centuries of darkness and shame."[27] Sonnino and other spokesmen of the constitutional right used the supposed threat of revolution in the countryside to justify their demands for an immediate halt to Giolitti's experiment and the replacement of Zanardelli's cabinet by a strong government, resting on a healthy and responsible "constitutional majority" in parliament, which did not have to win "the support of extremist elements and groups as a condition for its survival." Such a government

[25] *Giornale dell'Emilia,* May 26, 1901. Hereafter cited as *GdE.*

[26] *Ibid.,* April 22, 23, 26; May 10, 13, 1901.

[27] *AP Camera,* Leg. XXI, Vol. VI, June 19, 1901, pp. 5390-5392.

could be "concerned more with the future of the country than with its own immediate popularity" and thus would be able to avoid "revolutions or precipitous evolutions" by preventing "collective strikes that use coercion and violence" and by dealing energetically with "agitators and instigators."[28]

Despite its vehemence and alarmist rhetoric, the campaign of the agrarian moderates in Rome did not achieve its primary objective. While many moderate deputies may have shared some of Sonnino's concerns, few were prepared to accept his authoritarian alternative that amounted to little more than a return to the bankrupt policies of repression and reaction of the late 1890s. Moreover, most moderates feared that the fall of the Zanardelli cabinet would result in the closing of parliament and early elections, a prospect that they wished to avoid at all costs in 1901. These considerations, together with the innate ministerialism of the southern deputies and the support of the extreme left, assured the government the necessary votes in the Chamber to withstand the challenge from Sonnino's supporters and to persevere in its liberal labor policies.[29]

Left to their own devices after the failure of the political reaction in Rome, local agrarian interests in the Po Valley took steps on their own to recapture the initiative in the countryside. With little hope of forcing a change in the government's approach to labor disputes, landowners and leaseholders began to organize themselves in order to prevent any repetition of their humiliating capitulation to the laborers in the spring of 1901. Already in mid-July, *Il Resto del Carlino* reported that "leagues of landowners—in opposition to the labor leagues of resistance—are spreading throughout most of Italy." Although the paper exaggerated the extent of the phenomenon, it is certain that associations of rural employers did arise in at least seven major provinces of Emilia and Lombardy during the summer and fall of 1901.[30] Following the

[28] *Ibid.*, p. 5389.

[29] G. Carocci, *Giolitti*, pp. 82-83.

[30] *RdC*, July 18-19, 1901. During this period organizations were set up in Vercelli, Mantua, Milan, Pavia, Rovigo, Parma, Ferrara, and Ravenna. See Confederazione

example of their adversaries, representatives of the new agrarian associations met in Ferrara in February 1902 to discuss the best methods to "oppose force against force, army against army" in what they characterized as the "harsh struggle that is being fought between capital and labor." A second gathering in the spring approved a statute for an Interprovincial Federation of Agrarian Associations that proposed to combat strikes and defend the rights of property by combining the resources of the various local organizations and coordinating their activities.[31]

During the spring of 1901, the idea of an agrarian association also had its proponents in the province of Bologna. As early as April, Agostino Ramponi, a prominent member of the Agrarian Society, predicted that "the organization of laborers will lead inevitably to the organization of landowners." The same month, Giovanni Enrico Sturani, the leading spokesman of the commercial farmers in the plains, insisted that, because of the growth of the leagues, the "organization of resistance by capitalists and landowners" had become an urgent necessity.[32] Yet in contrast to neighboring provinces, in Bologna agrarian leaders encountered serious obstacles in their efforts to organize rural employers.

Their organizational difficulties stemmed from the fact that, while virtually all local landowners and leaseholders opposed Giolitti's labor policies, there was little agreement among them on the most appropriate methods for dealing with the strikes and the demands of the leagues. This lack of consensus was already apparent during the strikes of 1901. Meetings of landowners and leaseholders to discuss strategies gave rise to bitter disputes and disagreements. As police officials reported in early May, one such meeting in the low plains had to be terminated prematurely after

---

Nazionale Agraria, *L'organizzazione agraria in Italia. Sviluppo, ordinamento, azione* (Bologna, 1911), p. 5.

[31] See *Bollettino della Società degli Agricoltori Italiani*, 1901, no. 3-4, p. 178; *RdC*, February 3-4, April 28-29, 1902. While the project for a regional federation was not implemented at this time, the various provincial organizations did continue to function.

[32] *GdE*, April 27, 30, 1901.

"tumultuous . . . exchanges of insults."[33] From the outset, the large commercial farmers took a hard line on the demands of the leagues. In mid-March, for example, the rice growers of Molinella informed the police that they intended not to accept the new contracts and to resist the leagues "even where this means refusing to cultivate the rice fields."[34] When strikes broke out in April, these intransigent growers refused, as in previous years, to meet with labor representatives or to accept the mediation of government officials. Nor did they limit their responses to passive resistance; late that month, Massarenti charged that striking workers had been "threatened with eviction from their homes and exclusion from future employment" unless they returned to work.[35] In communes where this hard line prevailed, the strikes dragged on for well over a month, sparking violent clashes between laborers and strikebreakers that led to police intervention.[36] But often the intransigent tactics of the rice growers were opposed by older absentee landlords like Count Francesco Massei, who saw "nothing wrong, nothing humiliating in the fact that landowners negotiate with workers' delegates by means of their own representatives."[37] Where these conciliatory voices prevailed, the strikes ended quickly with the laborers gaining significant improvements in wages and working conditions. In the commune of Minerbio, for instance, a committee of landowners did not delay in signing agreements with the leagues for both dry and wet crops so that the strike lasted little over a week. Similarly, the strike in San Pietro in Casale was relatively brief because of a compromise settlement reached by the two negotiating teams that, according to the local press, had given "proof of their mutual esteem and a well-intentioned spirit of conciliation."[38]

33 ASB, C6 F2, Police Report, May 4, 1901.

34 ASB, C6 F2, Police Report to Prefect, March 19, 1901.

35 *RdC*, April 23-24, 1901.

36 See ASB, C6 F2, Prefect to Giolitti, June 12, 1901.

37 *RdC*, April 27-28, 1901.

38 *Ibid.*, April 29-30, 1901. By May 1, growers in Baricella and Malalbergo had followed the same path of least resistance.

Such divergent responses to the strikes reflected not only the unpreparedness of the landowners and leaseholders, but also more profound territorial, economic, and ideological divisions within the provincial elite. The wide variety of farming systems in the province contributed to the fragmentation of agrarian interests. Landowners who relied on sharecroppers to farm their estates were largely unaffected by the strikes; in the districts where the sharecropping system predominated the unrest had been minor and the contracts had remained virtually unaltered.[39] Since the leagues had made little headway in organizing the sharecroppers and tenant farmers in 1901, these landlords tended to remain complacent and relatively indifferent to the supposed revolutionary menace in the countryside. Describing their attitude, one policeman wrote how their "entrenchment behind the still valid line of defense of the *mezzadria*" led them to consider the strikes and leagues "as facts that do not concern them directly."[40] The big commercial farmers of the low plains, and especially the rice growers, faced a very different situation. Both the structure of their farms and the specific labor requirements of rice cultivation made these growers dependent to a much greater extent on an ample supply of hired hands and consequently brought them directly into conflict with the leagues. Unlike their colleagues in more tranquil areas of the province, they could not afford to be complacent, since the strikes meant unharvested crops and the potential loss of an entire year's investments.

In the absence of energetic government intervention, the strikes of 1901 also sharpened economic conflicts of interest between the absentee landowners and the large leaseholders. Many of the biggest landowners in the province leased their lands in the plains on the basis of contracts which stipulated that "neither for damages caused by hail, nor for flooding, *nor for strikes* . . . would the lessee have the right to any decrease of the total sum owed."[41]

[39] Società degli Agricoltori Italiani, *I recenti scioperi*, p. 13. On the activities of the sharecroppers in Bologna, see S. Zaninelli, *Le lotte nelle campagne*, p. 202.
[40] ASB, C6 F2, Police Report, no date, 1901.
[41] *Bollettino Federale Agrario*, June 15, 1909.

Thus guaranteed a fairly secure income from their properties, the absentee landowners could view the strikes dispassionately and advocate policies of compromise and concessions to the laborers without sacrificing their own interests. The large commercial leaseholders enjoyed no such protection; strikes and work stoppages at critical stages of the harvest season immediately threatened their economic positions and predisposed them toward more extreme reactions. Moreover, the leaseholders had a far more pronounced interest in resisting tenaciously any increase in wages than the absentee landowners, since their profit margins were directly affected by labor costs. As Giolitti himself observed, the leaseholder "always believes he makes a profit when he succeeds in lowering the wage scale by a few cents."[42] Less scrupulous leaseholders found an additional incentive for intransigent opposition to labor demands in the lucrative benefits that prolonged strikes provided them; according to various police reports, some of the major leaseholders in the low plains drew "exaggerated profits" from long and violent strikes by furnishing lodging to the soldiers and straw and stables for their horses.[43] Even when the strikes had ended, their effects continued to be a source of tension between landowners and leaseholders. As a result of rising labor costs, for instance, the leaseholders intensified their pressure on the landowners to reduce rents and to provide compensation for capital investments and land improvements, concessions that many landowners were reluctant to grant.[44]

Agrarian disunity in 1901, however, was not only the product of economic conflicts between landlords and leaseholders, but also of contrasting perceptions of the propertied classes' role and responsibilities in the province. Apart from any material considerations, the preference of landed patricians like Count Cavazza, Count Nerio Malvezzi, and Enrico Pini for a conciliatory approach to labor unrest reflected their particular position in Bolognese so-

[42] *AP Senato*, Leg. xxi, Vol. ii, April 30, 1901, p. 1351.

[43] ASB, C6 F2, Police Report, July 13, 1907.

[44] See S. Zaninelli, *Le lotte nelle campagne*, p. 233, n. 6.

ciety. As the perennial arbiters of local political and cultural life, they preferred to see themselves as members of a disinterested ruling elite that stood above the vulgar struggles between capital and labor and concerned itself with the needs of all the people in the province. Consequently, they tended to view the strikes and leagues as symptoms of a more general crisis in the countryside that could be overcome only by restoring harmonious relations between proprietors and peasants. Not surprisingly, in their public utterances, they looked back to a happier, more tranquil time when the landlord assumed responsibility for the welfare of his dependents and was repaid by their deference and respect.

Most of the new commercial farmers recognized none of the old guard's broader social and political concerns. As active entrepreneurs rather than landed notables, they were more concerned with problems of production and markets than with status or political influence. While the absentee landowners might see agriculture as a way of life or the cornerstone of a rural community over which they exercised influence, the commercial farmers saw it exclusively as a business in which laborers represented a factor of production and not dependents whose well-being was their responsibility. From their more narrow perspective, unions and collective bargaining constituted little more than unacceptable infringements on their managerial prerogatives and profits that had to be opposed by any and all means.

These contrasting perceptions clearly shaped the debates that took place in agrarian circles during the winter 1901-1902 over proposals for a provincial association of agricultural employers. When the first discussions got under way in the Agrarian Society at the beginning of December, one group of landowners, for the most part older aristocrats, attacked the very concept of an agrarian association, arguing that it would serve only to aggravate "class conflict" in the countryside. Count Francesco Massei, the chief spokesman for this view, reminded the landowners that they had not just "firm rights to safeguard," but also "duties . . . to . . . reform the agricultural contracts." Attributing the labor unrest to the corrosive effects of commercial agriculture, he called upon his colleagues to sacrifice some of their profits for the sake of social peace in the countryside by transforming their agricultural workers into more stable small leaseholders, since in his opinion the "attachment of the laborers to the land" represented the "only way of separating them from the leagues."[45] Outside of a small circle of old-fashioned landowners, Count Massei's ideas attracted scant support. Many landowners shared his nostalgia for the traditional rural order, but most saw little possibility of and had even less interest in returning to what amounted to less efficient and lucrative forms of cultivation and land tenure. Moreover, most of the influential agrarian spokesmen did not share Count Massei's reservations concerning the value of an employers' association. Yet even among the proponents of agrarian organization, there was a pronounced lack of consensus about the form and goals of the proposed association.

The embattled commercial farmers of the low plains wanted a militant and disciplined association of employers that would defend their immediate economic interests against "strikes, impositions, and disorders" and would resist tenaciously "the unjustified moral and material violence" of the leagues. Their conception of organization rested upon a vision of the countryside as a battle zone where two opposing armies would have to fight an unconditional war with total victory as the ultimate goal. Citing the formal commitment of the leagues to the overthrow of the propertied classes, they rejected any compromise with organized labor as economically unacceptable and politically unwise, attributing essentially coercive functions to their proposed association. As conceived by its sponsors, this association aimed to break strikes, eliminate the leagues, and reassert agrarian supremacy over the agricultural labor market by "fighting with equal weapons . . . opposing organization to organization, resistance to resistance."[46]

[45] *Annali della Società Agraria Provinciale di Bologna*, Vol. XLII, December 1, 1901, pp. 302-303; *RdC*, February 17-18, 1902.

[46] Marchese Giuseppe Tanari, "Studi per una proposta di Statuto per una as-

Proposals for such a bellicose association, which paralleled the structure and functions of the leagues, alarmed some of the most prominent landed notables in the province who argued that it would only increase conflict and further polarize social relations in the countryside. Enrico Pini, one of the leading spokesmen of the agrarian old guard, reacted in no uncertain terms to the proposals:

> I would like first of all to express openly my conviction . . . about the inanity of capitalist organizations, counterposed to labor organizations, when they are created for the sole purpose of resistance. Such a project does not represent a means of defense, but . . . a danger of conflict which would retard rather than promote the settlement it seeks to achieve. A capitalist organization limited to being a bulwark against labor organizations would constitute solely and uniquely a coalition of interests, weak and uncertain before the more sturdy coalition of labor.

In line with the wider political and social concerns of the moderate notables, Pini advocated instead a more broadly based agrarian program that would neutralize the appeal of the leagues by encouraging cooperation and "harmonious moderation between capital and labor." Specifically, he envisioned an association that included all classes engaged in agricultural activity, an organization that not only defended landowning interests, but also sought to "elevate and reinforce every healthy concept of labor."[47] Already in the summer of 1901, a similar proposal had been advanced in the pages of *Il Giornale dell'Emilia* for an "agrarian brotherhood" that brought together "the poorest laborer" with the "wealthiest

---

sociazione mutua fra proprietari," *Annali della Società Agraria Provinciale di Bologna*, Vol. XLII, December 11, 1901, pp. 37-38. For a similar proposal advanced by other prominent commercial agrarian interests, see "Di una società mutua fra i proprietari," *Bollettino Mensile del Consorzio Agrario Bolognese*, December 31, 1901.

[47] Enrico Pini, "Quale deve essere il programma della proprietà agraria in Italia," *Annali della Società Agraria Provinciale di Bologna*, Vol. XLII, May 11, 1902, pp. 223-224.

agricultural entrepreneur" in order to facilitate "a direct understanding between capital and labor."[48]

While spokesmen for the commercial farmers of the plains attacked the cooperative model of organization as naive and impractical, it clearly appealed to other sectors of the provincial elite.[49] Wealthy absentee landowners such as Count Cavazza and Count Bianconcini saw it as a new means of preserving and institutionalizing their traditional, but informal, influence over the peasant classes. Other landowners like Count Giuseppe Grabinski, who took their cues from church teachings, were drawn to a program that seemed to reflect Catholic corporative ideals. Indeed, as early as 1891, delegates to the ninth Italian Catholic Congress had specifically endorsed the idea of rural unions that united both peasants and landowners in a single organization.[50] The cooperative model was also well suited to those areas of the province where the sharecropping system prevailed and landlords had more direct and continuous contact with the people who cultivated their fields. For less lofty reasons, landowners outside of the plains, who had not felt the pressure of the leagues, looked favorably upon an association that projected vague, longterm solutions and required few immediate sacrifices of time, wealth, and independence.

In the debates over these contrasting proposals, neither the older notables nor the new leaseholders were able to develop a consistent and coherent program that could overcome internal differences within the elite, so that no provincial association of landowners and leaseholders emerged in Bologna in the winter of 1901-1902. This lack of success, however, reflected not only a clash of interests and aspirations, but also the fact that as yet there was no impelling necessity to organize and overcome internal divisions. As agrarian employers began to recognize in the fall of 1901, the wave of

[48] *GdE*, May 6, 1901.

[49] For the initial debates on the various proposals, see *Annali della Società Agraria Provinciale di Bologna*, Vol. XLII, Minutes of Meeting of December 11, 1901, p. 299.

[50] Giovanni Spadolini, *L'opposizione cattolica da Porta Pia al 1898* (Florence, 1961), p. 267.

victorious strikes testified less to the irresistible strength of the leagues than to the surprise and unpreparedness of the propertied classes. By the spring of the following year, even hard pressed commercial farmers in the plains had discovered that they had a variety of instruments at their disposal, other than formal organization, to combat labor militancy and counteract the socialist leagues.

2. *Agrarian Economic Reaction and Labor Response: 1902-1904*

The dramatic events of 1901 ushered in a new era of social struggle in the Bolognese countryside characterized by stunning victories and sudden reversals. In the first decade of the century, the development of this struggle, with its quick transitions from triumph to desperation, was shaped by a number of factors that together gave all power relations in the province a distinctively fluid and evanescent quality. For both protagonists, the line between victory and humiliating capitulation was clearly drawn each year, since conflicts were concentrated for the most part in a few crucial weeks of the harvest season. The gains made one year either by organized labor or by agrarian interests always remained vulnerable and could easily be lost the next year in renewed struggles under continually changing economic and political conditions. While the overabundance of laborers and chronic underemployment constantly threatened the unity and morale of the leagues, agrarian employers had to contend with their own divergent interests and divisive feuds. Agrarian unity, quickly forged during strikes and contractual disputes, vanished just as quickly with the passage of the common danger. In the seesaw struggle between the leagues and the agrarians, the ambivalent relations that sharecroppers maintained with both landowners and day laborers functioned to buttress or isolate one or the other of the two opposing forces. If at one moment contractual disputes with landlords drove sharecroppers into the arms of the leagues, the next moment wage or hiring demands of the laborers led them to make common cause with agrarian employers. In addition, the form and direction of government intervention in local strikes and electoral contests, which varied in accordance with shifting parliamentary priorities in Rome, could tilt the balance of power on the provincial level. Finally, the rapid if uneven progress throughout the Italian economy in these years generated a new dynamism and instability that could not but affect all political and social relations in the province.

In 1902 and 1903, the particular mix of these various factors favored commercial farmers in Bologna and elsewhere in the Po Valley. Beginning in the winter of 1901, the Italian peninsula suffered the effects of a brief deflationary recession that was compounded in the agricultural sector by poor harvests. Indeed, the harvest of 1902 was the worst in nearly a decade, wheat production falling from 55 million to 41 million quintals that year. The region of Emilia registered one of the sharpest drops in wheat yields; in Bologna an extended drought during the summer months also damaged the sugar beet and hemp crops.[51] While the bad harvests certainly reduced agrarian profits, they also strengthened the position of commercial farmers in their dealings with organized labor. The high demand for labor and the resultant strong bargaining position of the leagues during the previous year's large harvest declined sharply in 1902. As the demand for hired hands slackened, the concern of agricultural laborers changed from questions of wages and work hours to the more basic problem of finding any work at all, a situation that the leagues were as yet ill-equipped to meet. At the same time, the economic recession led the government to reconsider its tolerant labor policies. Under mounting pressure from business and agrarian interests who attributed the slump to the strikes, which they claimed had paralyzed industrial and agricultural investments, Giolitti began to take a tougher line on labor agitation in 1902. After February, the tendency of prefects and police to intervene against striking workers became increas-

[51] G. Carocci, *Giolitti*, p. 68; G. Procacci, *La lotta di classe*, p. 301. For wheat production in Emilia, see *Bollettino della Società degli Agricoltori Italiani*, 1902, no. 17-19, p. 773; on the drought in Bologna, see *ibid.*, 1902, no. 16, p. 687.

ingly evident as the government moved to revive economic activity by preventing a repetition of the previous year's disruptive work stoppages.[52]

Bolognese commercial farmers quickly took advantage of these new economic and political conditions in the spring of 1902 to cancel earlier concessions to the leagues and to recapture the initiative in the countryside. Their counteroffensive, which unfolded simultaneously in other provinces of the Po Valley, involved first of all the rigid refusal to recognize the leagues or negotiate with their representatives and, in the event of renewed strikes, intransigent resistance. Such antistrike policies were bolstered in turn by a number of measures to minimize the dependence of agrarian employers on organized labor: greater reliance on sharecroppers and salaried dependents, expanded use of agricultural machines, curtailment of labor-intensive crops, and reduction of all unessential farm work that previously provided jobs in the winter months. In this fashion, the growers' response to the economic slump dovetailed with their campaign to destroy the socialist leagues. As *Il Resto del Carlino* charged in April 1902, agrarian employers were now seeking to reassert their unfettered control of the rural labor market by returning to "the system of scattered negotiations with isolated groups of laborers, unassisted by outsiders, unorganized, and deprived of leadership and protection from exploitation."[53]

Although local commercial farmers lacked the cohesion and unity that an association would have provided them, they did manage to achieve a certain degree of solidarity in 1902 through informal coordination of their antiunion policies. In Molinella, for instance, an investigative report of the Humanitarian Society concluded that even though the growers did not have their own organization, they were "united in supporting each other in resistance and owed their . . . victories over the laborers to this solidarity of theirs, which is not officially indicated in the records of an association, but op-

[52] G. Carocci, *Giolitti*, p. 67; on the rapprochement between Giolitti and the Constitutional Right in 1903, see Girolamo Sotgiu, *L'Italia di Giolitti. Testi e documenti* (Cagliari, 1972), p. 181.

[53] *RdC*, April 2-3, 1902.

erates automatically."[54] On the basis of such informal collaboration, Molinellese rice growers boycotted meetings called by league representatives and moderate landowners in the spring of 1902, negotiating exclusively with individual laborers, while in the neighboring communes of Budrio and Medicina the big leaseholders imposed "without discussion" new contracts that, according to league officials, tended "to decrease the pay scales and increase the hours of work."[55] The effectiveness of these policies became dramatically apparent in March when the leagues called strikes in various communes of the lower plains. In sharp contrast to the previous year, the strikes in Bologna, much like similar initiatives in Ferrara, Mantua, Rovigo, and Ravenna, ended in resounding defeats for the laborers.[56]

Agrarian employers owed much of their new success in resisting labor demands and breaking strikes to measures they had taken to cut labor costs after the strikes of 1901. In its survey in the winter of 1901-1902 on the effects of labor militancy in agriculture, the Society of Italian Agriculturalists, a national professional and technical organization, placed special emphasis on the tendency of growers in the Bolognese plains to reduce their cultivation of rice and to substitute it with laborsaving crops. In Molinella alone, over four hundred hectares were converted from rice to dry crop cultivation in 1901; in the spring of the following year, police officials reported that the large leaseholders in Medicina had begun to plant Spanish grass in many fields where rice had been grown, primarily as a response to "the continual strikes of the laborers and women rice workers." Significantly, total rice production in the province fell

[54] Ufficio del Lavoro della Società Umanitaria, *La disoccupazione nel basso emiliano* (Milan, 1904), p. 110. The Humanitarian Society was a Milanese radical cooperative which carried out a fairly extensive investigation of labor conditions in the lower plains of Emilia in 1903. Its findings were then published in the above-cited volume.

[55] ASB, C6 F2, Police Reports, March 21 and 22, 1902; *ibid.*, Provincial Federterra to Prefect, March 28, 1902; *RdC*, March 27-28, 1902.

[56] For information on the outcome of the strikes in 1902, see S. Zaninelli, *Le lotte nelle campagne*, pp. 184-186; I. Barbadoro, *Storia del sindicalismo*, Vol. I, p. 167.

more than 50 percent between 1901 and 1905.[57] Commercial farmers further reduced their demand for labor by halting or curtailing their land reclamation and farm improvement projects in the winter of 1901-1902. Immediate economic difficulties caused by the recession could explain this trend only in part. Some of the biggest leaseholders such as Annibale Certani, Alfredo Benni, and Roberto Magli made no secret of their intention to use winter employment to tame the laborers, informing the prefecture that they would provide jobs only if they received firm guarantees against "impositions of wage scales or demands by representatives of the leagues."[58]

The threat of strikes and the need to undermine the position of the leagues also encouraged commercial farmers in the lower plains to mechanize. The local Agrarian Committee claimed that "machines were introduced principally to avert strikes," a claim that both landowners and labor leaders in the plains confirmed.[59] Already during the summer of 1901, a group of local banks headed by the Cassa di Risparmio and the Banca Popolare came together with some of the "most noted and influential agriculturalists" in the province to found the Bolognese Agrarian Consortium. Following the example of similar institutions in other areas of the Po Valley, the consortium began to promote and facilitate the purchase of farm machines, chemical fertilizers, and insecticides by offering growers reduced prices and advantageous credit arrangements. The new consortium met with an enthusiastic reception in the strike-torn communes of the plains where its sales more than quadrupled

[57] ASB, C6 F2, Police Report, April 2, 1902; Società Umanitaria, *La disoccupazione*, p. 115; *Bollettino Federale Agrario*, December 15, 1908.

[58] See ASB, C6 F2, Special Commissioner to Prefect, November 27, 1902; on the reduction of winter work, see *ibid.*, Police Report, August 20, 1901; Società degli Agricoltori Italiani, *I recenti scioperi*, p. 58.

[59] Società degli Agricoltori Italiani, *I recenti scioperi*, pp. 58-61. The agrarian committees were among the first institutions created by the liberal state to encourage technical modernization in the Italian countryside. See Paola Corti, "Fortuna e decadenza dei Comizi Agrari," *Quaderni Storici*, XII, no. 36 (1977), pp. 738-758.

between 1901 and 1903.[60] In explaining this sudden success, the director of the Italian Federation of Agrarian Consortia (the Federconsorzi), stressed the decisive role of organized labor, declaring that "two years of strikes have been more valuable than twenty years of technical propaganda . . . for the spread of agricultural machines."[61]

Bad harvests, the general recession, and the economic policies of the commercial farmers all combined to swell abnormally the ranks of the rural unemployed in 1902 and 1903. With jobs scarce, agrarian employers were better able to exploit the perennial economic insecurity of the laborers as well as the divisions within the peasant classes. Wherever possible, landowners increased their use of sharecroppers, whose interest in the harvest made them less inclined to go out on strike.[62] In the lower plains, where the sharecropping system had all but disappeared, the big leaseholders moved to enlarge their staff of *salariati*, or full-time salaried workers. As early as June 1901, police reported from Molinella that the leaseholders were taking steps "to assure themselves an ever greater supply of . . . laborers under contract to specific employers."[63] A few months later, Ignazio Benelli, the largest agrarian employer in Medicina, signed a contract with the 122 laborers who lived on his estate, "guaranteeing them steady employment for the year 1902 and in compensation obligating them to work" regardless of strikes or work stoppages. Antonio Bonora, the biggest leaseholder in the province, went even further, setting up a cooperative for the salaried workers on his estate precisely to avoid "the enrollment of the laborers into the leagues."[64]

[60] Sales of the Agrarian Consortium rose from 44,095 lire in 1902 to 215,659 in 1904. See *Bollettino Mensile del Consorzio Agrario Bolognese*, April 1912, p. 25 for statistics.

[61] Società degli Agricoltori, *I recenti scioperi*, p. 16.

[62] On the increased use of sharecroppers, see ASB, C6 F2, Police Report, November 25, 1901; *RdC*, July 2-3, 1902.

[63] ASB, C6 F2, June 24, 1901. On the advantages of the contract workers, see Società Umanitaria, *La disoccupazione*, p. 77.

[64] For the activities of Benelli, see ASB, C6 F2, Police Report, August 9, 1901; on Bonora, see Luigi Zerbini, *Illustrazione delle principali aziende agrarie del Bolognese* (Bologna, 1913), p. 17.

During the harvest season, however, salaried workers and sharecroppers did not constitute an adequate supply of labor, particularly in the event of strikes by the leagues. In Molinella, for instance, the 72 contract workers and the 819 nonunion laborers could not compensate for the potential loss of the 1,761 day laborers enrolled in the socialist leagues.[65] To remedy this problem, commercial farmers began to collaborate with sympathetic local church officials in the promotion of Catholic "professional unions" in Molinella and the border areas of Ferrara, which combined bitter attacks on the Socialists with mild economic demands. Guided by the criteria of "justice and Christian charity," the professional unions took advantage of religious appeals and preferential treatment by employers to attract laborers away from the leagues. Already in August 1901, Molinellese leaseholders openly favored the laborers from these unions who, according to police sources, became "the most sought after because they are more docile and pliable."[66] By 1903 the professional union of Molinella counted over four hundred members whose ranks were enlarged in the harvest season by another eight hundred Catholic laborers imported from Ferrara. Collaboration between commercial farmers and the professional unions became so strong that by 1904 the latter had a virtual monopoly of agricultural employment in certain areas of Molinella.[67]

In the Po Valley as a whole, the agrarian economic reaction of 1902 had a devastating impact on the nascent agricultural labor movement. From the rice fields of Vercelli and the vast land reclamation projects of Mantua to the large capitalist farms of Ferrara, Rovigo, and Ravenna, agricultural laborers suffered a nearly unbroken string of setbacks. After the triumphs of 1901, both the

[65] Società Umanitaria, *La disoccupazione*, p. 98.

[66] ASB, C6 F2, Police Report, August 15, 1901. As the Humanitarian Society reported, imported Catholic workers represented "the best weapon which the landowners have to combat the leagues and resist the demands of the organized laborers." See Società Umanitaria, *La disoccupazione*, p. 112. For the professional unions in Ferrara, see Paul Corner, *Fascism in Ferrara 1915-1925* (London, 1975), p. 10.

[67] Società Umanitaria, *La disoccupazione*, p. 112; *RdC*, May 12-13, 1904.

number of agricultural strikes and the percentage of victorious strikes fell drastically in 1902 and 1903.[68] More importantly, the unsuccessful strikes and the desperate competition of the laborers for jobs led not only to the loss of earlier gains, but also to the complete collapse of the leagues in a number of provinces. Indeed, between 1902 and 1904, ten of the twenty-two provincial federations disappeared altogether, while membership in the national Federterra shrank from a high of almost 228,000 laborers to a mere 45,000 in the course of 1903.[69] In the province of Bologna, the reduced demand for hired hands in the countryside tempered the militancy of organized labor so that in 1903 only six strikes, involving 4,720 laborers, took place. At the same time, the initial expansion of the leagues came to an abrupt halt. Between December 1902 and December 1903, no new leagues were founded and the total membership in the Bolognese Federterra contracted slightly.[70]

Nonetheless, the Bolognese Federterra withstood the defeats of 1902, competition from the professional unions, and systematic blacklisting by employers far better than the larger and initially more aggressive federations of Ferrara and Mantua. In the fall of that year, the provincial secretary, Argentina Altobelli proudly affirmed that the broken strikes had constituted an economic but not a moral defeat for the leagues, since in their aftermath the laborers had "closed ranks and remained loyal to their organizations."[71] The Bolognese leagues owed their remarkable resilience in part to the victory of Socialist slates in several municipal elections during the summer of 1902 that helped sustain the morale of the organized laborers. More importantly, the distinctive pro-

[68] See note 56.

[69] I. Barbadoro, *Storia del sindacalismo*, vol. I, p. 167.

[70] On membership, see *La Squilla*, January 30, 1904; for information on strikes, see *Statistica scioperi, 1901-1905*, p. 144, cited in Silvio Fronzoni, "Dalle consociazioni" (Tesi di Laurea, University of Bologna, 1973), p. 303, table 3. According to the Humanitarian Society, 52 percent of the laborers in Molinella and 47 percent of those in San Giovanni in Persiceto were unemployed in 1903. See *La disoccupazione*, p. xxxi, table 7. *Il Resto del Carlino*, May 13-14, 1903 reported that Giolitti intervened, ordering the prefect "to induce the landowners and agents to give work to the unemployed."

[71] *La Squilla*, October 24, 1902.

gram of the leagues in Bologna enabled them to involve their members in a variety of other initiatives when the strikes failed to produce positive results. Thus, while the largest and most powerful provincial federations of 1901 had concentrated exclusively on the day laborers and had relied primarily on strikes to advance the cause of their rank and file, the Bolognese Federterra involved its membership in campaigns to organize sharecroppers and salaried workers, to promote reform of the *mezzadria* contracts, to develop labor cooperatives, and to assume collective farm leases.[72]

At least in the plains, the mounting discontent of the sharecroppers provided a fertile terrain for such campaigns. As the prefect warned his superiors early in 1902, the existing *mezzadria* contracts had become "too onerous" for many peasants who were expected to fulfill a number of traditional obligations that included "tribute (eggs, chickens, cheeses), transportation, and loading services."[73] The efforts of local landowners to cut labor costs and destroy the leagues only accentuated the pressures on the peasants by shifting the burden of rising wages onto the shoulders of the sharecroppers who were often compelled to work farms that were too large for their family labor force.[74] Taking advantage of this discontent, labor organizers began to circulate in the countryside, extolling the virtues of collective action and promoting model contracts that responded to the most pressing needs of the sharecropping families. Where persuasion proved insufficient, the leagues buttressed their appeals with selective coercion. Indeed, one of the leaders of the Bolognese Federterra freely admitted that the "guerilla warfare of the boycott" played no small part in convincing recalcitrant sharecroppers of the advantages of unionization.[75]

At the same time, the selective boycott also marked a significant

[72] G. Procacci, *La lotta di classe*, pp. 307-309.

[73] ASB, C6 F2, Prefect to Minister of Interior, February 2, 1902.

[74] In Baricella, for example, sharecroppers called for new contracts in 1902, claiming that they could not support the burden of increased labor costs. See *RdC*, March 19-20, 1902. The Humanitarian Society reported that the landowners had intensified "incredibly the exploitation of the sharecropper, who is compelled to assume . . . extensions of land superior to the forces of his family." See *La disoccupazione*, p. 117.

[75] See G. Procacci, *La lotta di classe*, p. 308n.

tactical innovation on the part of the Bolognese leagues in their relations with agrarian employers. After the setbacks of 1902, union strategists concluded that the large territorial strikes worked chiefly to the advantage of the more militant leaseholders who had been able to unite the bulk of employers against the common threat of a strike. Selective boycotts avoided this result by enabling the leagues to exploit divisions within agrarian ranks and to employ their own financial and human resources in a more efficient manner. The flexibility offered by the new tactic allowed the leagues to come to terms with moderate landowners and to concentrate maximum pressure on the more inflexible and intransigent leaseholders. Perhaps the strongest testimonial to the effectiveness of the selective boycotts came from agrarian spokesmen like Giovanni Enrico Sturani, who claimed that they posed far graver dangers to commercial farming interests than the mass strikes, since they divided the employers into two categories, "the privileged and the persecuted," and thereby "accentuated natural economic inequalities, encouraged self-interest, and favored defections" among the employers.[76]

The full impact of the Bolognese Federterra's organizational initiatives and tactical innovations became dramatically evident in the spring and summer of 1904 when the province once again became a major center of agricultural labor agitation. During this period, nearly fourteen thousand day laborers and salaried workers took part in nineteen strikes, accounting for approximately 40 percent of all the strikers in Emilia, which in turn had the largest regional total in the country that year. In June the leagues also made use of selective boycotts for the first time in order to disrupt the informal collaboration of the big Molinellese leaseholders.[77] Moreover, after the lull of 1903, union organizing picked up considerably with the resurgence of labor militancy in the countryside. In the course of the year, forty new leagues were founded; by the

[76] *Bollettino Federale Agrario*, November 1, 1908.

[77] For strike statistics, see *Statistica scioperi, 1901-1905*, p. 144, cited in S. Fronzoni, "Dalle consociazioni," p. 303, table 3; on the use of the boycotts, see *RdC*, June 15-16, 1904.

beginning of the following year, the Bolognese Federterra controlled a network of 103 leagues with a combined enrollment of over twenty-three thousand laborers.[78] The rapid expansion of the socialist labor movement came partially at the expense of the Catholic professional unions which entered into crisis in 1904 as a result of pressures from the leagues and internal conflicts between clerical conservatives and Christian democrats.[79] The Bolognese Federterra's greatest organizational breakthrough, however, came in the late spring of 1904 when the first unions of sharecroppers began to appear in the lower plains. By November, socialist organizers had set up twenty-five peasant unions with more than two thousand members. That month Bologna hosted the first provincial congress of sharecropper unions in Italy that approved a new model contract which, in the words of *Il Resto del Carlino*, transformed the *mezzadria* from an "old patriarchal society of agricultural production" into a form of "industrial contract with a capitalist member and one or more labor members."[80]

Such accomplishments significantly reinforced the position of the Bolognese federation's reformist leadership and ensured the continuity of its programs precisely at a time when more militant syndicalist elements were unseating reformist elements in many other provinces and capturing control of the Socialist party on the national level. The economic recession and employers' reaction that had proven so damaging to the rural labor movement in 1903 also favored a shift in the balance of power within the PSI. At the national party congress in April 1904, a coalition of so-called "revolutionaries" and syndicalists under the leadership of Enrico Ferri triumphed. Their victory signaled an open rupture between the PSI and the government and led quickly to an escalation of violent confrontations that culminated in a massive and tumultuous gen-

[78] *La Squilla*, February 18, 1905.

[79] On the difficulties of the professional unions, see Alessandro Roveri, *Dal sindacalismo rivoluzionario al fascismo. Capitalismo agrario e socialismo nel Ferrarese, 1870-1920* (Florence, 1972), pp. 176-177.

[80] *RdC*, May 5-6, December 6-7, 1904.

eral strike in the fall of that year.[81] For his part, Giolitti allowed the strike to run its course and then called new parliamentary elections in November. Exploiting the political backlash against the strike, the prime minister gave the government's campaign a pronounced antisocialist thrust and ordered his prefects to make sure that "monarchical electors intervene in large numbers."[82] The outcome of the elections more than fulfilled his expectations, marking a serious setback for the Socialists and their Radical allies who lost some fifteen seats in the Chamber of Deputies. As Giolitti subsequently observed, the elections had the "special benefit of serving as a lesson to the Socialists and revolutionaries by letting them see that the Italian people did not intend to permit any side to exceed certain limits."[83]

In the province of Bologna, however, the elections produced results for the left that sharply contrasted with the fortunes of the PSI elsewhere in the country, results that the local press attributed to "the intensive work of propaganda by the unified socialist organizations" of laborers and sharecroppers. Despite the active support of the prefecture, agrarian candidates emerged victorious in only two of the eight electoral colleges, while the entire zone of the plains fell to the Socialists. Particularly noteworthy in this respect was the defeat of Marchese Giuseppe Tanari, one of the most prominent leaders of the Bolognese moderates, in the college of Castelmaggiore, since according to *Il Resto del Carlino* it represented "the passage of a college into the hands of the Socialists that has been until now the traditional stronghold of the moderates."[84] The PSI owed much of its success here to the Bolognese

[81] G. Procacci, *La lotta di classe*, p. 362; pp. 382-416.

[82] ACS, B26, F71/4, telegram Giolitti to Prefects of Bologna and thirty-two other provinces, November 5, 1904, cited in G. Carocci, ed., *Dalle carte di Giovanni Giolitti*, Vol. II, *Dieci anni al potere, 1901-1909* (Milan, 1962), p. 365. Giolitti subsequently wrote that during the campaign he had stressed the "question of the responsibility of the parties and men . . . who . . . provoked . . . the general strike." See Giovanni Giolitti, *Memorie della mia vita* (Milan, 1922), p. 177.

[83] G. Giolitti, *Memorie*, pp. 177-178. On the outcome of the elections see G. Carocci, *Giolitti*, p. 88; M. Neufeld, *Italy*, p. 233.

[84] *RdC*, November 7-8, 1904.

Federterra, which had clearly emerged as the largest, most efficient, and politically influential provincial federation in the country. Indeed, by the fall of 1904, the local Federterra's militancy, able leadership, and varied programs had not only made Bologna the center of the entire agricultural labor movement in Italy, but also had provided the foundations for what Giuliano Procacci has described as "a profound movement of regeneration from below that invested the entire society . . . and created a new civilization."[85]

The awesome resurgence of the leagues in 1904, both in the countryside and at the ballot box, provoked considerable alarm within Bologna's propertied classes, dramatically underscoring their own disorganization as well as the inefficacy of their antiunion policies and political strategies. In his evaluation of the situation in the province, Giovanni Enrico Sturani stressed how "the labor movement proceeded in closed ranks to the battlefields, [while] the landowners and leaseholders, far from uniting in a common action of defense and legitimate resistance, remained in the most complete disarray." Blacklisting and selective hiring practices had proven to be unproductive for agrarian employers, since they entailed an exclusive reliance on contract workers and strikebreakers that led inexorably to "the gradual abandonment of the crop cultivations" and consequently to "an enormous sum of economic, social, and political damages."[86] At the same time, the apparent success of the Federterra in organizing the sharecroppers had shaken the confidence of the older landlords in the *mezzadria* as a bulwark of tradition and stability in the countryside. For the first time, agrarian interests faced the prospect of a united peasant front, in which the unions of sharecroppers greatly strengthened the leagues of day laborers, since as Sturani recognized, "with the threat of abandoning the livestock, they possessed the most formidable weapon of coercion against the employers."[87] Moreover, as the elections

[85] G. Procacci, *La lotta di classe*, p. 309.

[86] G. E. Sturani, *Le Consociazioni agrarie della Provincia di Bologna. Organizzazione e programma* (Bologna, 1905), pp. 5-7. This pamphlet was originally a speech read by Sturani to the Agrarian Society on May 7, 1905.

[87] *Ibid.*, p. 15.

of 1904 had demonstrated, the new peasant unions also constituted a serious challenge to the political power of moderate notables like Marchese Tanari who had always relied on their personal prestige and the deference of the peasant cultivators to control their respective rural districts.

Agrarian interests did not delay in reacting to these unfavorable political and economic circumstances. Above all, the unions of sharecroppers acted as a catalyst on the fragmented and factionalized propertied classes, instilling in them a much clearer sense of their shared interests. Already in the spring of 1904, absentee landlords and commercial leaseholders started to put aside their differences and collaborate in the development of a more systematic and longterm strategy to deal with the problems of labor militancy and electoral mobilization. Under pressure from an aggressive and disciplined labor movement, Bologna's agrarian elite now began to make the difficult transition from the old world of local notables and informal agreements to a new system of institutional arrangements in which interest-group organizations and collective action would prevail.

3. *Agrarian Organization and the Strategy of Class Cooperation*

On New Year's Day 1904, *Il Giornale di Bologna*, the local moderate daily, issued a ringing call to action. Agrarian employers had to realize, the paper declared, that never had the necessity for "serious and well-organized associations been so urgent as now when the working masses are so inclined to translate their organizational power into violence."[88] More than an isolated appeal, the editorial reflected a dynamic new activism that began to inform the Bolognese propertied classes in the spring of that year. In the press, promotional leaflets, and municipal gatherings, agrarian leaders repeated the same command: "Organize yourselves;

[88] *Il Giornale di Bologna*, January 1, 1904. Hereafter cited as *GdB*.

now is the time to leave individualism behind in the fight against the labor organizations!"[89]

If such appeals were familiar, the response they received in 1904 was truly novel. Indeed, renewed labor agitation and the emergence of the sharecroppers' unions combined to trigger a sudden and unprecedented burst of agrarian organizational activity. Already in mid-June, some two hundred fifty landowners and leaseholders from the district of Minerbio founded "a vast association for agricultural improvement and the resolution of labor disputes." Less than three weeks later, another assembly of landowners and commercial farmers announced the creation of an organization for the "defense of the general interests of agriculture" in the district of Budrio. During the fall, similar associations appeared in the communes of Granarolo and Castel San Pietro that, according to the local press, included "all the landowners, from the largest . . . to the smallest."[90] This organizational trend spread from the low plains to more tranquil areas in the spring of 1905, so that by June of that year Enrico Pini could boast how the "province of Bologna is now covered in every commune by agrarian associations of landowners and leaseholders."[91]

The chief architect of the Bolognese associations was Giovanni Enrico Sturani, a man peculiarly well-suited to the tasks of uniting the various factions of the provincial elite and mobilizing them in a common program of action. Born into an aristocratic family of Ancona, Sturani graduated from the University of Bologna in 1891 with a degree in jurisprudence. Thereafter he pursued a dual career as an attorney and journalist, writing for such prestigious journals and papers as *Il Giornale degli Economisti* and *Il Corriere della Sera*. His family background gave him easy access to the exclusive

[89] *Ibid.*, July 13, 1904. For other examples of agrarian promotional activities, see ASB, C6 F2, Police Report, May 20, 1904 and the leaflet distributed by the promotional committee of the Agrarian Association of the First and Fourth Districts of Bologna, May 1905.

[90] *GdB*, June 20, July 9, 1904; *RdC*, August 8-9, 1904.

[91] *RdC*, June 4-5, 1905. For additional accounts of organizational activity, see *ibid.*, January 15-16, March 24-25, 1905.

social circles of the old guard, and already in the 1890s he had established himself as an influential figure in the Agrarian Society. But unlike many of his titled colleagues, Sturani identified with the interests and aspirations of the new commercial farmers as his pivotal articles on the strikes in Molinella in the late 1890s clearly demonstrated. An outspoken proponent of a militant organization of agrarian resistance in 1901, he nonetheless recognized the ideological and economic heterogeneity of the provincial elite and consequently the need for associations that appealed to the old absentee landlords as well as the big leaseholders.[92]

Both the structure and program of the new associations represented a compromise between the immediate economic interests of the commercial farmers in the low plains and the larger political and social concerns of the moderate notables. Blending features of earlier proposals by Tanari and Pini, Sturani attributed two central functions to the organizations: "the immediate defense of [agrarian] interests against strikes and boycotts" and collaboration with "the other classes for the defense of the general interests of agriculture."[93] The statutes of all the associations guaranteed their members direct assistance and measures of collective protection in the event of strikes and boycotts. The agrarian association in Budrio, for instance, proposed "to counter the united action of the leagues against liberty and property with the equally united action of the organized agrarians" and to serve as a bulwark against "impositions, crimes, and violations committed by the leagues."[94] At the same time, Sturani hastened to assure absentee landlords that the organizations would not limit their activities to antiunion resistance. As he told a meeting of the Agrarian Society in the spring of 1905, exclusive reliance on lockouts and other strike-breaking measures had brought only pyrrhic victories, since they

[92] For information on Sturani, see *RdC*, July 3, 1912.

[93] G. E. Sturani, *Le consociazioni agrarie*, p. 8.

[94] ASB, C6 F2, 1904, "Statuto della Consociazione per la difesa degli interessi generali agrari nel Mandamento di Budrio," Article 2, III, 1. For similar clauses, see *ibid.*, "Statuto della Consociazione fra proprietari e conduttori di fondi di Minerbio," Article 2g.

tended to intensify social conflicts in the countryside. The employers' organizations had to go beyond "pure resistance" and provide "benefits to all agricultural classes."[95]

Appealing directly to the values and pretensions of Bologna's agrarian old guard, Sturani proclaimed "class cooperation" as the guiding principle of the associations. In line with this principle, the associations were designed to link landowners, leaseholders, sharecroppers, and laborers in a single hierarchical agricultural "sector," in which the various categories could resolve their differences and "share in a peaceful, ordered enterprise united by a common purpose."[96] Because of the different problems of the dry and wet crop areas, the lower plains and the foothills, Sturani favored a decentralized network of municipal or district associations rather than one provincial organization, so that each association could adapt its policies to specific local conditions. Likewise, many of the associations included separate sections for landowners and leaseholders, since as Sturani observed, the two groups had "essentially different interests that, when not regulated and contained within a system of cooperation, could become fiercely contrasting."[97] The most innovative feature of the Bolognese associations, however, were their auxiliary organizations for sharecroppers. Conceived by Sturani as a concrete response to the Federterra's peasant unions, the auxiliaries were to provide institutional channels for "continual contact and increased familiarity" between landlords and sharecroppers, encouraging "that mutual trust which is the moral foundation of the *mezzadria*."[98] To eliminate the primary source of tension between landlords and sharecroppers, peasant representatives from the auxiliaries were empowered to negotiate all features of their contracts and related agreements with agrarian spokesmen. Moreover, like the organized landowners and leaseholders, sharecroppers in the auxiliaries received the association's support and protection from the coercion and violence of

[95] G. E. Sturani, *Le consociazioni agrarie*, pp. 7-8.
[96] *Ibid.*, pp. 10-13.
[97] *Ibid.*, p. 14.
[98] *Ibid.*, p. 18.

the leagues. The auxiliaries in turn obligated their members to furnish their labor "for the defense of other peasants who are hit by boycotts or other hostile acts" and forbade them from employing "laborers who have . . . refused to work for the landowners and leaseholders."[99] In this fashion, the peasant auxiliaries served the interests of both the agrarian old guard and the commercial farmers by mediating conflicts between sharecroppers and landlords and by sharpening divisions within the agricultural labor force.

Despite the claims of agrarian leaders about the "political neutrality" of the auxiliaries, moderate notables could hardly ignore the possibilities they offered at election time. Already in the summer of 1904, *Il Giornale di Bologna* had underlined the political importance of the sharecroppers, insisting that "a tight network of agrarian associations" had to "regain the allegiance of the peasants whom the subversives are attempting to enlist in their campaign against the landowners."[100] In a province where the moderate party consisted of small clubs that revolved around a few notables, the auxiliaries had the potential for fulfilling many of the same functions as a mass party, since they provided an organized framework for communication, propaganda, and electoral mobilization.

At the same time, the new associations also sponsored the creation of "labor offices" in their respective communes or districts to curb the influence of the leagues and to systematize hiring practices in the interest of agrarian employers. According to the statutes of the associations, the labor offices had as their central task to "ensure the rational distribution of labor" by compiling rosters of agricultural laborers and collecting the employment requests of the landowners and leaseholders.[101] Laborers enrolled in the offices received preference in all field work as well as guarantees of protection from persecution by the leagues. In exchange, the

[99] *Ibid.*, p. 17; ASB, C7 F1, 1906, "Consociazione agraria di San Giorgio di Piano. Regolamento per l'Aggregazione dei Coloni," Article 4.

[100] *GdB*, June 3, 1904.

[101] ASB, C7 F1, 1906, "Consociazione agraria di Budrio. Regolamento per l'Ufficio del Lavoro," Article 2a-c.

offices obligated their laborers to accept work on the farms of any member of the associations and forbade them from belonging to any other "organization of resistance" or from participating in "labor disturbances of whatever nature."[102] Eventually, Sturani saw the labor offices evolving into cooperatives that contracted for public works projects and assumed collective leases of land under the direction of the associations. In contrast to the socialist organizations, they would be "truly cooperative" undertakings, since they did not attack "the capitalists and their enterprises, [but] collaborate with them."[103]

Armed with their innovative new program and phalanx of organizations, agrarian interests moved to recapture the initiative from the Bolognese Federterra in the spring of 1905. In response to demands from the socialist peasant unions for the implementation of their reformed *mezzadria* contract, the associations advanced a two-pronged strategy that combined coercion with concessions. Against the more militant sharecroppers, the landowners used clauses in the old contracts that allowed them to evict those peasants they deemed "too impatient for innovations." In the commune of Crespellano, for example, over five hundred sharecroppers had been evicted from their farms by the end of October, according to the local press, "for reasons of political repression." The fate of these men served as a warning to sharecroppers in other areas of the plains that economic ruin awaited those peasants who insisted too strenuously on the application of the Federterra's contract.[104] Simultaneously, the agrarian associations took steps to eliminate the most glaring sources of peasant discontent. Working closely with the associations, the Agrarian Committee of Bologna presented its own reform of the *mezzadria* contract in January 1905. In the words of its sponsors, this contract promised to "reinvigorate the *mezzadria* with a spirit of solidarity and understand-

[102] *Ibid.*, Articles 3, 5, and 9.

[103] G. E. Sturani, *Le consociazioni agrarie*, pp. 21-23.

[104] *RdC*, February 4-5, October 25-26, 1905. In addition, see *ibid.*, January 9-10, 1908 for a brief history of attempts by agrarians and Socialists to organize the Bolognese sharecroppers.

ing," while allowing for "the introduction of new methods of production."[105] Beginning in February, agrarian leaders organized a series of meetings with sharecroppers to promote the contract, which, Sturani claimed, met with "the favor of the peasants." To strengthen the resolve of those sharecroppers who accepted the contract and joined the auxiliaries, the associations provided protection from socialist boycotts, supplying them with threshing machines, drivers, and other personnel to help complete the harvest on their farms.[106]

This blend of repression, concessions, and protection proved to be remarkably effective in shifting the balance of power back in the favor of the landowners. Frightened by the prospect of losing their farms and lured by the pledges of the associations to implement immediately the contract of the Agrarian Committee, sharecroppers hastened to enroll in the auxiliaries. Indeed, various sources reported that in a number of communes in the plains both the rank and file and the leaders of the socialist peasant unions had transferred their allegiance to the auxiliaries in the course of 1905.[107] By February of the following year, the socialist weekly *La Squilla* conceded that none of the twenty-five peasant unions, which had shown so much promise in 1904, remained in existence. That month the Bolognese Federterra voted to abandon altogether its project for separate unions of sharecroppers.[108]

During the spring of 1905, the agrarian associations also began to impose new labor contracts and systems of cultivation in the rice areas of the low plains in order to curb strikes and boycotts by the leagues of day laborers and to provide commercial farmers with greater security for their investments. In mid-April, the as-

[105] *Ibid.*, January 26-27, 1905; ASB, C6 F2, Police Chief to Prefect, February 21, 1905. Agrarian spokesmen claimed to have encountered a favorable response from the sharecroppers. See G. E. Sturani, *Le Consociazioni agrarie*, p. 16.

[106] *RdC*, May 5-6, 1904; G. E. Sturani, *Le consociazioni agrarie*, p. 18.

[107] On the success of the peasant auxiliaries, see Consociazione fra proprietari ed affittuari del Mandamento di San Giorgio di Piano, *Relazione economico-morale del consiglio di amministrazione* (Bologna, 1906), pp. 7-8; *Bollettino Federale Agrario*, August 1-15, 1908; *RdC*, January 9-10, 1908.

[108] *La Squilla*, February 5 and 10, 1906.

sociation in the district of Minerbio announced its intention no longer to employ day laborers in the rice fields and to rely instead on the *mezzadria,* claiming that this system would "diminish the landowners' risks [and] give the laborers a more equal status by making them associates in the agricultural production." Sturani justified the change as a necessary response to the problem that "all farmers and especially the rice growers fear most . . . the lack of a dependable and loyal labor force."[109] Not surprisingly, the plans of the association provoked angry protests from labor leaders who charged that the use of the *mezzadria* would "nourish the egotism of the few," swell the ranks of the unemployed, and create conflicts between the sharecroppers and the mass of rice workers.[110] Initially, the organized growers ignored these protests and refused to consider any negotiated compromise with the leagues. When approached by the prefect, officials of the association affirmed their determination to leave the fields uncultivated or to plant other crops "rather than risk the loss of enormous investments that rice cultivation requires . . . because of the exorbitant demands of the leagues."[111]

Under the influence of Sturani, the association adopted a more flexible posture at the end of April. To avoid a costly abandonment of the rice fields, Sturani formulated a new set of contractual guidelines. Agrarian employers could now negotiate collective agreements with the leagues, provided that they included three crucial clauses: "the integral and complete observance of the wage-hour schedule of the association, the preferential hiring of laborers enrolled in the labor office, [and] the payment of a deposit of 30 percent of the workers' wages as a guarantee against strikes, to be returned at the end of the harvest."[112] By making it considerably more difficult for the laborers to go out on strike, these clauses served to protect the growers from disturbances at critical moments

[109] *RdC,* April 15-16, 1905. For Sturani's explanation, see *GdB,* March 16, 1905.

[110] On the Federterra's reaction to the new contracts, see *RdC,* April 23-24 and May 12-13, 1905.

[111] ASB, C6 F2, Prefect to Minister of Interior, April 14, 1905.

[112] *Ibid.,* C7 F1, "Norme per la conduzione della risaie," November 15, 1905.

of the harvest and to reduce the leagues to little more than labor contractors who supplied the farmers with the requested field hands. Despite such obvious disadvantages, the leagues finally accepted the terms dictated by the association. In the face of a compact agrarian front, they signed an agreement in May 1905, in which they not only dropped their demands for a system of rotating turns in the fields and commissions to oversee the work, but also accepted virtually without change the contract and strike deposit demanded by the employers.[113] Moreover, the victory of the growers in Minerbio encouraged other associations elsewhere in the plains to apply similar guidelines in the spring and summer of the following year.[114]

Significantly, the collapse of the socialist peasant unions and the setbacks suffered by the leagues coincided with the political resurgence of the parties of order in 1905. Already in February, a clerical-moderate slate, headed by Marchese Giuseppe Tanari, defeated the coalition of Socialists and Radicals who had controlled the municipal government in the city of Bologna since 1902. Far from being an isolated event, the election in the capital city reflected a new conservative trend in the province that became dramatically apparent in the summer of 1905 when moderate candidates captured eleven of the fifteen municipalities where elections were held. Encouraged by these results, the prefect reported to Giolitti in September that "this year there has been a noticeable change in the political parties; the star of the leftist parties is rapidly declining . . . [and] they are losing the support of many who . . . refuse to sacrifice their allegiance to the patriotic institutions."[115]

The agrarian associations played a vital behind-the-scenes role

[113] *RdC*, May 9-10, 12-13, 1905.

[114] See previously cited annual report of the Association of San Giorgio di Piano; ASB, C6 F2, Police Report from San Lazzaro di Savenna, May 2, 1906; *ibid.*, C6 F2, Mayor of Crespellano to Prefect, May 7, 1906.

[115] ASB, C5 F1, Prefect to Giolitti, September 21, 1905. For additional information on the municipal elections, see *ibid.*, "Prefettura di Bologna: Prospetto indicante i risultati delle elezioni amministrative avvenute nei comuni della Provincia di Bologna nel 1905"; *RdC*, February 1, July 3-4, 7-8, 17-18, 24-25, 1905.

in the preparation of these electoral successes. *Il Resto del Carlino* noted that in many of the communes of the plains "the municipal administrations held by the Socialists or popular coalitions fell into the hands of conservatives as a result of the dismantling of the peasant unions."[116] Since many agrarian leaders like Sturani, Tanari, and De Morsier were also prominent political figures, collaboration between the associations and the moderate clubs developed almost automatically. Assemblies called by the associations provided an invaluable forum for moderate candidates, who were often officials of the same associations, to address and influence sharecroppers and laborers. In this setting, the organizational loyalties of the peasants could be translated into electoral support for agrarian candidates.[117] The social makeup of the moderate administrations seemed to confirm the effectiveness of the associations as instruments of political mobilization. In the commune of Malalbergo, for instance, the newly elected mayor and five of the six aldermen were either large landowners and leaseholders; similarly, twelve of the twenty moderates elected in Minerbio were influential agrarian leaders such as Count Francesco Cavazza, Count Francesco Isolani, and Frank De Morsier, president of the association of Budrio.[118]

Victories on the municipal level in 1905 inspired a more formidable conservative coalition the following year when a special election was called to fill the parliamentary seat in the electoral college of Budrio vacated by the Socialist deputy Leonida Bissolati. Early in the spring of 1906, agrarian notables worked out a campaign strategy that entailed an unprecedented degree of collaboration between the employers' associations, moderate clubs, and clerical groups. As conceived by its sponsors, the strategy had two main objectives: to unite politically the propertied classes and to tap the voting strength of the Catholic peasants. The designated candidate of the coalition, Carlo Ballerini, clearly embodied this

[116] *RdC*, January 9-10, 1908.
[117] *Ibid.*, July 7-8, 1905; *La Fiaccola*, July 6, 1907.
[118] *RdC*, July 7-8, 1905.

merger of moderate and clerical interests. A leading clerical spokesman and future editor of the Catholic daily, *L'Avvenire d'Italia*, Ballerini was at the same time prominent in local banking circles and served as a director of the agrarian association in San Giorgio di Piano. Linked by economic interests and political beliefs to the large landowners and leaseholders, he also appealed to the more devout sharecroppers through his organizational and religious affiliations.[119] In addition, Ballerini's campaign received substantial assistance from the prefect, Dall'Olio, who had enthusiastically supported the employer's associations and maintained close ties with important agrarian leaders like Sturani. Dall'Olio's partisan efforts on behalf of Ballerini aroused bitter protests from the Socialists in Budrio, who charged that the "prefecture of Bologna" had been transformed into an electoral agency of the clerical-moderates, "impudently facilitating corruption [and] employing troops . . . for the purpose of intimidation."[120]

The results of the voting on April 1, 1906 represented a stunning triumph for the Bolognese propertied classes and their program of class cooperation. In an electoral college where two years earlier the left had won handily, Ballerini defeated his Socialist adversary. Moreover, his victory encouraged moderates and clericals in the summer of 1906 to unite and carry Marchese Tanari to victory in the college of Castelmaggiore, the site of his devastating defeat in 1904.[121] Thus, by the fall of 1906, it appeared that the provincial elite had not only broken the Federterra's sharecroppers' unions and curbed the militancy of the leagues, but that it had also developed an effective counterweight to the Socialist party at the ballot box. By using the network of economic associations to mobilize a mass constituency, the moderates had defeated Socialist

[119] For the various activities of Ballerini, see Nazario Sauro Onofri, *I giornali bolognesi nel ventennio fascista* (Bologna, 1972), p. 63.

[120] On Dall'Oglio, agrarians, and the electoral campaign, see ASB, C7 F1, Prefect to Ministry of Agriculture, Industry, and Commerce, May 9, 1905; *ibid.*, C5 F2, Police Report, March 28, 1906; *ibid.*, C5 F2, Circolo socialista di Budrio to Gruppo Socialista, April 6, 1906.

[121] *RdC*, April 2-3, June 2-3 and 7-8, 1906.

candidates without creating a centralized party apparatus or fundamentally altering their informal style of deference politics. Small cliques of wealthy electors continued to determine the selection of candidates and political programs, but now their decisions were buttressed by ostensibly "nonpartisan" associations that offered channels for the regimentation and mobilization of a much broader electorate.

4. *The Limits of Class Cooperation and the Search for a New Equilibrium in the Countryside*

The agrarian architects of class cooperation had little time to enjoy their success. Despite the impressive victories of Ballerini and Tanari in 1906, the political revival of the Bolognese parties of order rested upon an extremely fragile consensus. Indeed, from its inception, Sturani's strategy had required a wide range of disparate interests to compromise voluntarily on issues of contracts, wages, and hiring practices and to collaborate in a common program of political action. The events of 1904 and 1905 had shown that as long as the threat of an aggressive socialist labor movement remained strong, landowners, commercial farmers, and sharecroppers were prepared to submerge their differences and join together in the agrarian associations. But ironically the very achievements of the associations in 1906 removed precisely those conditions that ensured cooperation and internal cohesion. With the apparent passing of the socialist menace, each group began once again to pursue its own narrow interests, often at the expense of other groups within the associations. In the absence of a strong authority capable of enforcing internal discipline, old conflicts between absentee landowners and leaseholders, large and small proprietors, and landlords and sharecroppers reemerged, plunging the associations into disarray.

The first signs of internal discord appeared as early as the summer of 1906 within the powerful agrarian association of Budrio, largely as a consequence of the big leaseholders' intransigence in

Molinella. In May the local leagues went out on strike in support of their demands for higher wages. Initially, the entire membership of the association adopted a hard line, insisting on the application of existing wage rates and refusing "to come to any negotiations under the pressure of a strike."[122] Such unity, however, concealed important differences of opinion within the association. While many absentee landowners viewed intransigence as a temporary tactic to modify the demands of the laborers, the rice growers saw intransigence as part of a larger campaign to break, once and for all, the power of the leagues in Molinella. These clashing objectives became evident in June when the leaseholders blocked efforts by Count Piero Bianconcini, the moderate president of the association, to open negotiations with labor representatives. Under pressure from militant elements, an assembly of agrarian employers adopted a resolution stating that, although Bianconcini had promised his "personal" involvement in negotiations, he had "in no way committed the association, either for the present or the future." At the same time, the rice growers began to prepare on their own for a decisive confrontation with the leagues by setting up an emergency fund to cover strike losses and by importing large numbers of child workers, contract laborers, and other strikebreakers from the province of Ferrara.[123] The conflict between Bianconcini and the militant growers came to a head in the fall after he guaranteed the full participation of his association in renewed negotiations with the leagues. In an open breach with their president, the major leaseholders refused to take part in the meetings or to recognize any agreements made by Bianconcini, who angrily resigned his office and withdrew from the association in December. Other prominent absentee landlords soon followed Bianconcini's example; in March 1907, local authorities reported how a number of

[122] ASB, C6 F2, President of the Consociazione agraria di Budrio to Prefect, May 16, 1906.

[123] *RdC*, June 11-12, 1906. Two weeks earlier, the membership also voted to deposit 20,000 lire as a reserve fund for growers damaged by the strike. See *ibid.*, May 27, 1906. On the importation of strike breakers, see ASB, C6 F2, "Elenco dei minorenni adibiti ai lavori della risaia," July 15, 1906.

influential agrarian notables like Count Francesco Cavazza were "equally disheartened for the same reasons" and had resigned their posts in the association.[124]

The sudden exodus of these notables reflected not only specific policy differences, but also a growing awareness on the part of the absentee landlords that the agrarian associations had become instruments for the advancement of the leaseholders' special interests. According to the prefect, the intransigent policies of the association in Budrio had enabled the leaseholders "to exploit the landowners with low rental rates and leave them with the burden of the strikes by shifting on to their shoulders the expenses of the military forces needed to maintain public order." By his resolute resistance to the leagues, Alfredo Benni, for one, was able to extract a 50 percent reduction in the rental rate from the owner of the estate he leased in Budrio.[125] Similarly, the obligation imposed by the associations on their members to employ workers enrolled in the labor offices made it virtually impossible for landowners to lease their lands to less affluent entrepreneurs "whose scarce resources prevented their foregoing organized labor or bearing up under the boycotts" and, in this fashion, created a monopoly on agricultural leases that "depressed the price of leases and completely favored the major capitalist agrarians."[126] All these circumstances led the prefect to conclude in the spring of 1907 that the agrarian associations only aggravated the situation, in which "the aristocracy and the great landowners of yesteryear become impoverished and their places taken by the leaseholders."[127]

Giolitti appears to have shared many of the concerns of the Bolognese moderates. While the prime minister had initially encouraged the growth of the employer associations as essential components of a new system of collective bargaining and as useful

[124] *La Squilla*, December 15, 1906; ASB, C6 F2, Prefect to Ministry of Interior, March 16, 1907.

[125] ASB, C6 F2, Prefect to Ministry of Interior, March 16, 1907; *ibid.*, Prefect to Ministry of Interior, July 5, 1908.

[126] ASB, C6 F2, Police Report, April 23, 1907.

[127] *Ibid.*, Prefect to Ministry of Interior, March 16, 1907.

counterweights to the Socialist party, he was not prepared to support policies that only increased social conflict in the countryside. Already in the summer of 1906, he voiced his displeasure with the intransigence of the leaseholders in Molinella, ordering his prefect Dall'Olio to "make the agrarians understand that the government cannot aid them in unjust actions" and warning him: "I do not intend to provoke conflicts in order to reinforce the excessive demands of the agrarians; if any conflicts occur, I will hold you personally responsible."[128] When the militant growers ignored warnings from the prefecture as well as the counsels of their deputy Carlo Ballerini and continued to block negotiations, Giolitti took more drastic action. In October he transferred Dall'Olio from Bologna and replaced him with Giuseppe Dallari, a prefect far less sympathetic to the cause of the organized agrarians.[129]

The agrarian associations also had to contend with the mounting discontent of their small proprietors and sharecroppers during the winter of 1906-1907. The big commercial farmers' militant resistance to the leagues placed particularly heavy burdens on the meager resources of the small growers. As Sturani subsequently admitted, the intransigent policies of the associations had not entailed "an equal degree of sacrifice for everyone." While the wealthier growers could sacrifice an entire crop as a "definitive act of resistance," the family farmers could not since the loss of a harvest meant "the threat of complete ruin."[130] In a letter to *La Fiaccola*, the local Christian democratic weekly, one farmer eloquently summarized the plight of the small proprietors who belong to the associations: "What should we do? . . . We cannot unite with the large agrarians because they want violence, and provoke . . . strikes, boycotts, and repression. Men like Benelli, Benni, and Garagnani can afford the loss of entire harvests and can leave their stables

[128] *Ibid.*, Giolitti to Prefect, June 6, 1906.

[129] See *ibid.*, C6 F2, March 16, 1907 for the new prefect's critical appraisal of the big leaseholders.

[130] G. E. Sturani, *La Mutua-Scioperi. Sue basi economiche e suo ordinamento* (Bologna, 1909), p. 9.

abandoned for months, but not us for we live solely from the fruits of the soil."[131]

The increasing discontent of the sharecroppers in the peasant auxiliaries, however, constituted the most serious threat to the strategy of class cooperation. Despite the lavish promises made by the landlords and the associations in 1905, sharecroppers had gained little in the way of contractual reforms, especially after the collapse of the socialist unions. As one landlord admitted in the summer of 1907, "the majority of landowners reacted with annoyance to any requests for improvements; they did not want to deal at all with the peasants and had little regard for their individual requests."[132] The rising chorus of protests from the auxiliaries in the spring of 1907 finally led a few agrarian leaders like Marchese Tanari and Giovanni Marchetti of San Giorgio di Piano to encourage their colleagues to adopt more conciliatory policies toward their sharecroppers. They encountered only sullen indifference, and in mid-August a frustrated Tanari resigned from his association, while Marchetti lamented publicly that most landowners continued to "avoid any sacrifice . . . entrenching themselves behind an old peasant contract that no longer conforms to the exigencies of modern agriculture."[133]

Such internal dissension prevented the agrarian associations from developing any unified response to renewed pressure from the socialist leagues in 1907. In December 1906, the Bolognese Federterra repudiated the strike deposits and announced its intention not to negotiate with the associations "until they abandon their plan for sending strikebreaking squads throughout the province."[134] Sturani attempted to mobilize agrarian employers in defense of the deposits and labor offices, but he found little support among the absentee landlords. Typical of their attitude was that of Count Rene Talon whose agent informed police officials that he

[131] *La Fiaccola*, February 1, 1908.

[132] *Ibid.*, July 13, 1907. For a similar judgment, see *RdC*, January 9-10, 1908.

[133] *RdC*, August 16-17, 1907. On the mounting discontent within the peasant auxiliaries, see *La Fiaccola*, March 9, 16, May 25, 1907.

[134] *RdC*, December 9-10, 1906.

did not intend "to defer his interests in order to satisfy those who persist in their efforts to annihilate the leagues" and consequently planned "to have all the work in the rice fields performed by the leagues."[135] By the end of July, the prefect reported that Count Talon and more than a hundred other landowners, including Count Cavazza, Count Bianconcini, and Count Agostino Salina, had signed agreements with the leagues in Molinella, leaving the large leaseholders like Alfredo Benni and Roberto Magli "almost alone in their refusal to accept . . . the proposals of the labor organizations."[136] The following month the association suffered an even more devastating blow when most of their peasant auxiliaries collapsed in the wake of mass resignations by the sharecroppers.[137]

Much as in 1904, the Bolognese Federterra emerged in 1907 as the chief beneficiary of agrarian disunity and peasant discontent. With the Molinellese leagues leading the way, the Federterra saw the number of laborers enrolled in its organizations rise from 23,000 to 34,227 in the course of the year. Under the able leadership of Giuseppe Massarenti, the leagues in Molinella eliminated the strike deposits, imposed their own employment offices, and acquired an unprecedented new role in the technical operations of the farms. Landowners who accepted the demands of the laborers received guarantees of efficient work under the surveillance of league committees entrusted with taking "the necessary measures against those who do not perform the tasks according to the highest standards of agriculture."[138] At the same time, the Federterra launched a new organizational campaign among the sharecroppers in March 1907 in order to capitalize on the unrest inside the peasant auxiliaries. The campaign met with rapid success during the summer and fall, especially in the plains, and by November the Fe-

[135] ASB, C6 F2, Prefect to Ministry of Interior, July 22, 1907. On the efforts of Sturani to mobilize the agrarians, see *RdC*, December 13-14, 1906.

[136] ASB, C6 F2, Prefect to Ministry of Interior, July 22, 1907.

[137] On the collapse of the peasant auxiliaries, see *La Fiaccola*, November 9, 1907; *Bollettino Federale Agrario*, August 1-15, 1908.

[138] *La Squilla*, July 6, 1907. For the growth in membership, see Luigi Arbizzani, *Squardi sull'ultimo secolo. Bologna e la sua provincia, 1859-1961* (Bologna, 1961), p. 102.

derterra claimed to control thirty-nine peasant unions, representing over forty-four hundred sharecropping families in the province.[139] Significantly, these developments mirrored a more general resurgence of the rural labor movement throughout the Po Valley that year. Reconstituted in 1906 in Bologna, the National Federterra nearly doubled its membership in the following two years, ushering in a period of expansion that continued to the First World War.[140]

However, in contrast to 1904, the year 1907 also witnessed the emergence of a third force in the countryside: the Peasant Brotherhoods. While in the neighboring provinces of Romagna the Republican party had sponsored independent unions, the Bolognese brotherhoods appear to have been largely the work of Christian democratic groups associated with the Catholic weekly, *La Fiaccola*. As early as April 1907, *La Fiaccola* began to promote "the formation of neutral organizations of sharecroppers" that functioned independently of both the agrarian associations and the Federterra.[141] After the collapse of the peasant auxiliaries in the fall, the brotherhoods gained a sizeable following in those rural areas of the foothills where the *mezzadria* predominated and the socialists were relatively weak. Organizational efforts on the municipal level culminated in December with the founding of the Provincial Federation of Brotherhoods, which proposed to unite "the entire class of peasants in the province for the sole purpose of defending their collective interests." By the end of March 1908, the federation of brotherhoods boasted twenty-seven local organizations, with a membership of some several thousand sharecroppers, concentrated for the most part in the district of Imola.[142]

In a province like Bologna, where the division between the prop-

[139] On the campaign of the Federterra to organize the sharecroppers and its achievements, see *La Fiaccola*, March 16, 1907; *RdC*, August 23-24, 1907 and January 9-10, 1908; *La Squilla*, November 30, 1907; ASB, C6 F2, "Situazione delle organizzazioni delle classi medie (piccoli proprietari e coloni) della Provincia di Bologna," 1919.

[140] See I. Barbadoro, *Storia del sindicalismo*, vol. I, pp. 179-180.

[141] *La Fiaccola*, April 6, 1907. For the role of the Republican party in the brotherhoods of Romagna, see S. Zaninelli, *Le lotte nelle campagne*, pp. 366-420.

[142] *La Fiaccola*, March 28, 1908.

ertied classes and the laborers was so pronounced, the new organizations soon found it virtually impossible to maintain an independent and nonpartisan position. Despite their claims to political neutrality, competition for the "hearts and minds" of the sharecroppers immediately brought the brotherhoods into conflict with the socialist peasant unions. Above all, the stated intention of the brotherhoods to advance the exclusive interests of the sharecroppers even at the expense of the organized laborers aroused the untempered hostility of the Bolognese Federterra. Determined to forge their own alliance of sharecroppers and day laborers, socialist leaders looked upon the independent unions as divisive agents and tools of the landowners in the countryside. Thus, when the brotherhoods defended the *scambio di lavoro*, the reciprocal exchange of labor among sharecroppers to reduce demand for hired hands, the Federterra retaliated by organizing an indiscriminate boycott against all independent sharecroppers in the spring and summer of 1908.[143]

The increasingly bitter rivalry between the brotherhoods and the Federterra, and the resultant cleavages within the agricultural labor force, worked primarily to the advantage of agrarian interests who had begun to regroup in the fall of 1907. Once again the presence of socialist unions of sharecroppers provided the decisive catalyst for agrarian organization. Already in August, a group of local landowners founded the Agrarian Society of Imola to prepare for the renegotiation of the *mezzadria* contracts, an example that landowners and commercial farmers in a number of other communes soon followed.[144] In order to pool their resources and coordinate their policies, seven associations went one step further in November, founding the Intermunicipal Federation of Landowners and Leaseholders, which with its two thousand members consti-

[143] ASB, C6 F2, Police Report, June 13, 1908.

[144] On the founding of the Agrarian Society of Imola, see *La Fiaccola*, August 24, 1907. For the reorganization elsewhere in the province, see *Giornale dell'Emilia* (formerly *GdB*) October 26-27, 1907; *RdC*, November 17-18, 1907; MAIC, Labor Office, *Statistica delle organizzazioni padronali*, Vol. I, *Le Agrarie* (Rome, 1912), p. 80.

tuted the largest provincial agrarian organization in the country.[145] Similar considerations also led Bolognese agrarian leaders to establish closer ties with their colleagues in other provinces. In October 1907, they met in the city of Parma with representatives from throughout the Po Valley to launch the Interprovincial Agrarian Federation (Interprovinciale). Designed as an institutional counterweight to the national Federterra, the Interprovinciale proposed to "integrate the resistance of the single associations with the united resistance of the federated associations . . . in conflicts over grave questions of principle and general interest."[146] With a total membership of over six thousand landowners and leaseholders from the richest agricultural areas, the federation quickly became the most powerful and influential agricultural lobby in Italy. In homage to the key role played by the Bolognese group, agrarian representatives elected Count Francesco Cavazza as president of the Interprovinciale in December 1907.[147]

On the provincial level, the revived agrarian associations lost no time in exploiting the friction between the peasant brotherhoods and the Federterra. In the communes of Imola, Dozza, Casteldelico, Fontana Elice, Mondano, and Tossignano, the two leaders of the Agrarian Society of Imola, Antonio Bufferli and Giacobbe Manzoni, openly sponsored and then assumed direct control of the brotherhoods. Elsewhere the associations played a less visible role in the organization of the brotherhoods, giving special preference to "independent" sharecroppers even when, in the words of Raffaele Stagni of the association of Castelfranco, "their contracts are economically more onerous."[148] Both early proponents of the brotherhoods and prefectoral officials recognized the significance

[145] See *Statuto della Federazione intercomunale delle associazioni fra proprietari e conduttori di fondi della Provincia di Bologna* (Bologna, 1907). On membership, see *Bollettino dell'Associazione Agraria Parmense*, VI, no. 10-13, November 9, 1907.

[146] For the complete text of the statute, see *ibid.*

[147] Confederazione Nazionale Agraria, *L'organizzazione agraria in Italia. Sviluppo, ordinamento, azione* (Bologna, 1911), p. 12; *RdC*, December 17-18, 1907.

[148] On the role of agrarian interests in the brotherhoods, see *La Fiaccola*, March 7, 1908; *RdC*, May 12, 1908.

of these initiatives. In January 1908, *La Fiaccola* warned that the landowners of Imola were employing "the old tactic of divide and conquer" by encouraging the sharecroppers and small tenant farmers "to form an organization of their own in opposition to the chamber of labor." According to the Christian democratic weekly, the employers favored the brotherhoods only because they wanted "to divide the peasants, break their organizations, and fragment their resistance in order to dominate them and treat them as they please."[149] This view found confirmation in the retrospective report of the prefecture that attributed the landowners' sympathy for the brotherhoods to their plans for using them as "instruments of labor during the periods of struggle against the day laborers."[150]

Whatever might have been the original intentions of the brotherhoods, the pressure of circumstances drove them into the arms of the landowners in the spring of 1908. By April, the local press was reporting that the independent sharecroppers had effectively allied with the agrarian associations, if only to find protection from the Federterra's boycotts. For its part, the intermunicipal federation refused to negotiate with the socialist peasant unions, preferring instead to sign a separate *mezzadria* contract with the leaders of the brotherhoods, who reciprocated by releasing a communiqué that openly proclaimed the "antisocialist stamp" of their organizations.[151] Boycotts and sympathy strikes by the leagues continued through the summer, but they did little to slow the growth of the independent unions, and already in mid-August the house organ of the Interprovinciale was claiming that the agrarian associations had succeeded in creating a situation highly favorable to the landlords, in which "the class of peasants is divided into two camps, the one organized in the leagues belonging to the Chamber of Labor, the other in the brotherhoods."[152] By the fall of 1908, the

[149] *La Fiaccola*, January 18, 1908.

[150] ASB, C6 F2, "Situazione . . . classi medie" cited in note 139.

[151] On the policies of the agrarian associations, see *RdC*, March 14, May 19 and 24, 1908; *Bollettino Federale Agrario*, August 1-15, 1908. For the anti-socialist orientation of the brotherhoods, see *RdC*, April 23, 1908.

[152] *Bollettino Federale Agrario*, August 1-15, 1908.

landlords' tenacious resistance and competition from the independent unions finally forced the socialists to back down and accept a settlement on terms largely dictated by the agrarian associations. The new contract reconfirmed the position of the landowners as the sole directors of the farms as well as the responsibility of the sharecroppers for the maintenance of the tools, half the expenses of the livestock, and all the labor costs.[153]

At least on the surface, the struggles over the *mezzadria* seemed to mark the end of an era of bitter and often violent social conflict in the Bolognese countryside. In 1909 no strikes were reported in the province for the first time in more than a decade.[154] The absence of strikes led the prefect Dallari to write his superiors in the fall that "conditions have improved noticeably in recent years; in fact, I can say that the political parties have shifted the masses away from violent tyranny to discussions between league representatives and agrarians that establish agreements which have replaced the impositions and open conflicts." Dallari foresaw the dawn of a new era of social peace, since in his words, "the unrest and strikes are gradually losing intensity to the point of disappearing altogether."[155] A similar optimism pervaded the speeches of agrarian notables in the winter of 1909-1910. In his address to the Second National Agrarian Congress in December, Count Francesco Cavazza insisted that the propertied classes had finally come to terms with Giolitti's labor policies and the socialist leagues. Repudiating the intransigence that had characterized agrarian policies earlier in the decade, the president of the Interprovinciale declared that employers no longer had to "assume an *a priori* stance of blind resistance" to the demands of the laborers. On the contrary, collective bargaining between representatives of labor and management promised to settle all disputes without damage to persons or property. Indeed, the situation in Bologna during 1909 convinced him that the agrarian associations had finally achieved a dynamic "equi-

[153] For the terms of the contract, see ASB, C6 F2, 1908 cited in S. Fronzoni, "Dalle consociazioni agrarie," p. 209.

[154] MAIC, *Statistica scioperi, 1908-1909* (Rome, 1910), p. 101, p. 363.

[155] ASB, C6 F2, Prefect to Ministry of Interior, October 15, 1909.

librium between capital and labor." Older notables like Count Cavazza recognized that such an equilibrium involved the loss of unmediated agrarian domination of the labor market, but they saw more than adequate compensation in the new organizational arrangements, since in exchange for minor economic concessions, landowners and commercial farmers could look forward to a future of stable and productive relations with their agricultural workers.[156] The operations of the Intermunicipal Federation of Landowners and Leaseholders in 1909 appeared to justify both Cavazza's analysis and his optimism. With the sharp drop in strikes, the federation reduced its activity to the stipulation of wages and contracts, and for the most part remained "inactive in the periods between contractual negotiations."[157] Only the continued intransigence of a small group of large commercial farmers seemed to mar the general "normalization" of labor relations in the Bolognese countryside.

[156] For the text of Count Cavazza's speech, see *RdC*, November 29, 1909.
[157] See *Le Agrarie*, cited above, p. 77.

III. THE NEW AGRARIAN BOURGEOISIE AND THE STRATEGY OF MILITANT RESISTANCE, 1908-1911

Not all factions of the Bolognese agrarian elite shared Count Francesco Cavazza's acceptance of the new status quo or his optimistic appraisal of labor relations in the province. Despite the general trend toward collective bargaining and negotiated settlements in the countryside, a number of large commercial farmers in the low plains remained steadfastly opposed to any compromise with organized labor. During the winter of 1907-1908, for instance, a royal commissioner wrote from Molinella that some of the biggest leaseholders continued to be "no less tenacious in their opposition to every aspiration of the day laborers," engaging in what he described as an "organized war" against the leagues in order to "starve the mass of socialist laborers."[1] Similarly, labor leaders in Medicina complained the following year that they were still encountering the open hostility of the most important leaseholders in their commune, while even in the relative calm of 1909, the prefect could not ignore the vocal protests and provocative actions of certain big commercial farmers in the plains.[2]

[1] ASB, C6 F2, Royal Commissioner to Prefect, November 29, 1907. See also *ibid.*, telegram, G. Massarenti to *Avanti*, November 5, 1907.

[2] ASB, C6 F2, Comitato d'Agitazione to Prefect, June 12, 1908; *ibid.*, C6 F2, Prefect to Ministry of Interior, October 11, 1909.

Many of these recalcitrant farmers drew their inspiration from the personal vendetta of Alfredo Benni, one of the largest leaseholders in the province, against the leagues in the years between 1907 and 1910. In June 1907, organized laborers began to boycott Benni's vast estate in Budrio because, according to the police, he had been "always hostile to every attempt initiated by the leagues to set up negotiations and establish agreements."[3] Far from seeking to avoid the boycott, Benni actually provoked it in order to challenge the authority of the Bolognese Federterra. As the prefect observed in the summer of 1908, Benni was "a proud and authoritarian man . . . obsessed by the idea that he can dominate the situation with his firm behavior and give other landowners in the region an example of how they can overcome the labor organizations."[4] To lessen the impact of the boycott, he hired a full-time work force of five hundred contract workers whose loyalty he ensured through high wages; during the harvest season, non-union laborers from Ferrara were brought in to supplement the resident workers.[5] More importantly, Benni responded in kind to the intimidation and coercion of the leagues. A month after the boycott began, police reported that armed squads were accompanying the Ferrarese workers and standing guard over the fields of Benni's estate. The thirty-nine year old entrepreneur made no secret of his private security forces and the role they played. In a letter to the prefect, he and his business associates asserted that they were involved in a "civil war" with organized labor and consequently felt fully justified in providing "an energetic defense of our incontestable rights and in protecting our loyal workers."[6]

Contrary to the claims of the Bolognese prefect, who dismissed them as a small and isolated group in the province, Benni and like-minded commercial farmers constituted the vanguard of a new

[3] ASB, C6 F2, Police Report to Prefect, June 25, 1907.

[4] ASB, C6 F2, Prefect to Ministry of Interior, June 20 and 26, 1908.

[5] See ASB, C6 F2, Prefect to Ministry of Interior, June 20, 1908. According to the prefect, Benni paid his workers wages that were 50 percent higher than those requested by the leagues.

[6] ASB, C6 F2, Police Report to Prefect, July 6, 1907.

movement of agrarian insurgency in the Po Valley that was directed not only against the socialist labor movement, but also against the interest representation of the landed patricians and the political mediation of the old parties of order. This movement had its roots in the major expansion of industrial capitalism into the northern Italian countryside during the first decade of the century. After 1896 exceptional advances took place in the agriculture of the Po Valley that both reflected and stimulated the increasing involvement of commercial farmers with banking interests and the industrial supplying and processing sectors. Locally, rising levels of production and the growing interpenetration of agrarian and industrial groups chiefly benefited the large, market-oriented leaseholders who were able to increase their wealth and power at the expense of the smaller producers and less enterprising absentee landowners. At the same time, these developments also gave rise to new needs, pressures, and problems, spurring commercial farmers to seek an alternative to the inadequate, traditional channels of interest representation and influence on the provincial level and in Rome. Greater vulnerability to market fluctuations combined with the pressing need for an effective organizational counterweight to industrial wealth and organized labor to forge among commercial farmers a new interest-group and class consciousness that transcended the old provincial confines. Spearheaded by aggressive young entrepreneurs like Alfredo Benni, the movement of agrarian insurgency thus was an expression of the changing balance of power within the provincial elites as well as a response to the mounting rigors of economic competition and political lobbying.

In many respects, the accelerated industrialization of agriculture and the related interpenetration of economic interests in the northern plains closely paralleled earlier developments in other European countries. The latter half of the nineteenth century saw the growing subordination of agriculture to the industrial world's demands for foodstuffs and raw materials, as well as to the imperatives of technological innovations in the fields of communications and transportation. By the 1880s overseas competition led to an agricultural depression that converted European farmers to protectionist "iron and rye" alliances with industry, and forced them to cut costs while increasing the productivity of their lands. As a result, commercial farmers turned to mechanization, introduced chemical fertilizers, and started to produce for the expanding food-processing sector. In the decades before World War I, labor and tariff controversies also encouraged agrarian interests in many areas of Europe to consolidate their economic power by organizing modern pressure groups, affiliated with political parties.[7]

Deep structural problems in the Italian economy and polity, however, gave relations between industrialists and commercial farmers in the Po Valley a distinctive blend of instability and aggressiveness. A narrow domestic market, the excessive territorial concentration of industry, and an extreme dependence on favorable world economic conditions made Italian entrepreneurs highly susceptible to international recessions and sharpened conflicts between the two sectors. At a time when most European and American farmers faced a mounting shortage of hired hands because of the insatiable demand of the new industries and urban occupations for labor, agrarian interests in the northern Italian plains confronted a radically different situation. Delayed and uneven growth in the industrial sector slowed the absorption of surplus workers from agriculture, accentuating the "artificial over-population" in the countryside that intensified labor discontent and militancy.[8] While economic weakness increased the vulnerability of commercial farmers

[7] On the general economic trends, see E. J. Hobsbawm, *The Age of Capitalism 1848-1875* (London, 1975), pp. 173-192 and Carlton J. H. Hayes, *A Generation of Materialism 1871-1900* (New York, 1941), pp. 98-102. Karl Kautsky, *La questione agraria* (Milan, 1971), pp. 292-328 provides an analysis of the industrialization of agriculture. For the formation of pressure groups, linked to political parties, see Charles Maier, *Recasting Bourgeois Europe* (Princeton, 1975), p. 11.

[8] For a concise summary of the problems in the Italian economy, see Luciano Cafagna, "Italy 1830-1914" in Carlo Cipolla, ed., *The Fontana Economic History of Europe*, Vol. IV, Pt. 1 (London, 1973), pp. 279-328. On the concept of artificial overpopulation, see Emilio Sereni, *Il capitalismo nelle campagne* (Turin, 1968), pp. 345-369.

to pressures from both organized labor and industrial groups, a parliamentary system that lacked clearly defined, cohesive, and ideologically consistent parties made it extremely difficult for growers to advance their interests at the political level. Indeed, the absence of a modern bourgeois party and the continued dominance of a few parliamentary managers tended to alienate northern agrarian interests from the ruling moderate political class and drew them toward authoritarian solutions to the problems of production, labor relations, and political representation in the last years of the decade.

1. *Commercial Farmers and the Industrialization of Agriculture in the Po Valley*

In the first decade and a half of this century, the rapid growth of new industries sparked a general reawakening of the Italian economy that greatly encouraged expansion in the agricultural sector. The rising standard of living, the growth of cities, and improved transportation all stimulated demand for farm products. During the period, agricultural prices rose by 50 percent, interest rates fell, and the burdens of debt and taxation declined.[9] Production of wheat, Italy's most important crop, rose by more than 35 percent while dramatic progress was made in the cultivation of specialized crops.[10] The chief protagonists of the agricultural expansion were the large commercial farms of the Po Valley. With only 13 percent of the nation's farm land, they accounted for nearly a third of the agricultural production by 1910. In contrast to much of the rest of the peninsula, where wheat yields remained low or relatively stationary, growers in the provinces of Emilia substan-

[9] Christopher Seton-Watson, *Italy from Liberalism to Fascism* (London, 1967), p. 288; Giuseppe Orlando "Progressi e difficoltà dell'agricoltura" in Giorgio Fua, ed., *Lo sviluppo economico in Italia*, Vol. III (Milan, 1969), p. 22.

[10] For statistics on growing wheat production and rising productivity, see Giorgio Porisini, "Produzione e produttività del frumento in Italia durante l'età giolittiana," *Quaderni Storici*, V, no. 14 (May-August 1970), pp. 510-511. For sugar beet production, see Luigi Perdisa, *La bietola da zucchero nella economia italiana* (Rome, 1938), p. 16.

tially increased their output per hectare. By the outbreak of World War I, wheat productivity and farm incomes in the leading provinces of the north stood well above the national average.[11] Similarly, the Po Valley monopolized the development of highly profitable industrial crops. The region of Emilia accounted for over half the hemp and a quarter of the tomatoes grown in the entire country in 1911. The same year Emilia and the neighboring provinces of the Veneto provided over 80 percent of Italy's production of sugar beets. Dominating the market meant considerable financial gains for growers in these regions; the average profits per quintal of hemp and sugar beets in 1911-12 were respectively four and ten times that of wheat.[12]

In the province of Bologna, as elsewhere in the northern plains, the rewards of growth were not evenly distributed among the various classes in the countryside. With their richer lands, commercial orientation, and superior resources, the large farmers of the plains reaped the lion's share of the new wealth. Responding to favorable market conditions, Ignazio Benelli, the biggest farmer in the commune of Medicina, increased his wheat production six fold, expanded his annual rice harvest from fifteen hundred to twelve thousand quintals, and cashed in on the highly lucrative cultivation of the sugar beet plant between 1894 and 1909. Nor were Benelli's achievements unique. By 1910 large leaseholders like Benni, Antonio Bonora, Ettore Cacciaguerra, and Augusto Lenzi were obtaining exceptionally high wheat yields, averaging over twenty quintals per hectare or twice the national average.

[11] While the national average stood at 10.5 quintals per hectare, the major wheat-growing provinces of the north—Rovigo, Ferrara, Cremona, Milan, Padua, and Bologna—averaged over 17.5 quintals in the last years before the war. For the regional variations in wheat productivity, see G. Porisini, "Produzione e produttività," pp. 516-518. On the overall dominance of northern agriculture, see G. Valenti, "L'Italia agricola dal 1861 al 1911" in *Cinquanta anni di storia italiana* (Milan, 1911), p. 91. For farm incomes, see G. Orlando, "Progressi e difficoltà," p. 28.

[12] E. Sereni, "Note per una storia del paesaggio agrario emiliano" in R. Zangheri, ed., *Le Campagne emiliane nell'epoca moderna* (Milan, 1957), pp. 44-45; MAIC, *Annuario statistico italiano, 1911* (Rome, 1912), pp. 102-103; Giovanni Proni, *La canapicoltura italiana nell'economia corporativa* (Rome, 1938), p. 41.

That year a select group of leaseholders and commercial growers managed ten of the twelve largest and most productive farms in the plains.[13] Conversely, many of the old absentee landowners saw their economic position decline, since rental incomes did not keep pace with rising agricultural productivity and prices, a situation that led the Bolognese prefect in 1907 to contrast the gradual "impoverishment" of the aristocratic landlords with the new fortunes of the leaseholders.[14] The success of the commercial farms also appears to have encouraged the increasing concentration of land holdings in the province, chiefly at the expense of the smaller proprietors; between 1901 and 1911, their numbers fell significantly.[15] Likewise, the new opportunities and necessities of production for the market highlighted the advantages of direct management over the *mezzadria* system, leading many local farmers to reduce further their use of sharecroppers. In the first decade of the century, the number of sharecroppers in Bologna dropped from 66,185 to 60,333, while the population of day laborers rose from 47,024 to 52,263.[16]

During the same period, some of the more prominent commercial farmers began to diversify their economic activities outside the agricultural sector. Vittorio Venturi, one of the most successful leaseholders in the province, became an important exporter, opening up markets for Bolognese rice in Austria, Hungary, Yugoslavia, and Greece.[17] Other growers moved into the agricultural processing and supplying sectors. In 1903, for example, Antonio Bonora founded and became president of the Bonora Sugar Refinery in Ferrara. Seven years later, he branched out into the field of chemicals by

[13] Luigi Zerbini, *Illustrazione delle principali aziende agrarie del Bolognese* (Bologna, 1913), pp. 6-69.

[14] See ASB, C6 F2, Prefect to Ministry of Interior, March 16, 1907.

[15] Between 1901 and 1911, this category shrunk from 10,352 to 6,509. See MAIC, *Censimento della popolazione del Regno d'Italia 1901* (Rome, 1902), p. 217; Franco Cavazza, *Le agitazioni agrarie in Provincia di Bologna dal 1910 al 1920* (Bologna, 1940), p. 40.

[16] *Ibid.* Unfortunately, these figures must be treated with caution, since the criteria for each category changed from one census to the next.

[17] Agostino Bignardi, *Costruttori di terra* (Bologna, 1958), p. 39.

setting up a factory to produce organic nitrate fertilizers in his native commune of Galliera; the following year, his brother and business associate, Cesare Bonora became a director of one of the major local banks, the Monte di Pietà.[18] The Bonora brothers' activities were relatively modest in comparison to those of Ignazio Benelli. By 1914 Benelli presided over the Bolognese Electricity Company and the Emiliana Romagnola Bank, as well as serving on the boards of directors of the Canonica Grain Mills and the Bolognese Company for the Industry of Fertilizers and Chemical Products. In a similar fashion, other leaseholders such as Benni, Augusto Peli, and Augusto Lenzi moved into influential positions in the Bolognese Agrarian Consortium and the Cassa di Risparmio, the most important bank in the province, in the years before the war.[19]

Both the economic diversification of the commercial farmers and the rising productivity of agriculture in Bologna testified to a more general process of agrarian-industrial interpenetration in the Po Valley after 1900. This process found its earliest and most important institutional expression in the agrarian consortia that began to appear in Emilia during the late 1880s. Organized as commercial intermediaries by groups of enterprising landowners and leaseholders, the consortia offered growers a range of benefits on a cooperative basis. By establishing direct contacts with manufacturers and making bulk purchases, the consortia could provide their members with industrial supplies and equipment at reduced prices. Moreover, their technical experts could check the quality of supplies to protect growers from fraud and could give them valuable counsel on the types of machines and fertilizers best suited to local

[18] For the activities of the Bonora brothers, see *ibid.*, p. 13; *L'Agricoltura Bolognese*, October 15, 1921; *RdC*, October 12, 1922; Credito Italiano, *Società Italiane per azioni 1914* (Rome, 1915), p. 1025; Mario Maragi, *I cinque cento anni del Monte di Pietà* (Bologna, 1972), p. 354.

[19] On Benni's activities, see *RdC*, October 1, 1908; Credito Italiano, *Società Italiane 1914*, p. 999; *ibid.*, 1920, vol. I, p. 109, vol. III, p. 1101. For the other leaseholders, see *RdC*, April 2, 1913; *Annali della Società Agraria Provinciale di Bologna*, vol. LXIII, 1913, p. 84.

conditions.[20] After 1892 the activities of these local consortia were buttressed by a national organization, the Italian Federation of Agrarian Consortia or Federconsorzi, which assumed as its main functions the promotion of new consortia and the acquisition of chemical fertilizers. Gradually, the Federconsorzi broadened its activities to include the purchase of machines and feed, the leasing of machinery and tools, the collective sale of members' produce, and the encouragement of more rational methods of cultivation.[21]

The formation of the consortia on the provincial level marked the convergence of agrarian and banking interests. In order to assure farmers the credit required to enlarge their purchases of industrial supplies, the consortia needed to establish a privileged relationship with the rural banks. In a region like Emilia, these banks, which were dominated by agrarian interests, recognized how "their own prosperity [was] intimately tied to the progress of agriculture."[22] Often the rural banks directly took part in the creation of the consortia. Cooperation between the banks and the consortia proved beneficial to both parties. The growers in the consortia were quick to avail themselves of the advantageous credit terms and greatly increased their purchase of fertilizers and machines. For the banks, involvement in the consortia led to a tremendous and profitable expansion of their activities in the countryside.[23]

[20] Federconsorzi, *Federconsorzi ed i consorzi agrari. Note informative* (Rome, 1947), pp. 5, 12; Federconsorzi, *Federconsorzi. Sessant'anni di vita al servizio dell'agricoltura italiana 1892-1952* (Rome, 1952), p. 46; C. Pareschi, "La cooperazione agraria in Emilia," *L'Italia Agricola*, April 1928, p. 186; *Bollettino Mensile del Consorzio Agrario Bolognese*, no. 11, 1902, pp. 253-254.

[21] *Federconsorzi. Note informative*, p. 6; *Giornale di Agricoltura*, July 10, 1977, p. 9.

[22] *Bollettino Mensile del Consorzio Agrario Bolognese*, II, no. 11, 1902, p. 257. In the province of Bologna, the director of the Banca Popolare, Vincenzo Sani, was one of the most important local landowners; the commercial farmer, Augusto Peli, served on the boards of directors of both the Consortium and the Cassa di Risparmio. On the activities of Sani, see *L'Agricoltura Bolognese*, v, no. 3 (March 1911), pp. 55-58; for Peli, see Cassa di Risparmio, *La Cassa di Risparmio in Bologna nei suoi primi cento anni* (Bologna, 1937), pp. 163, 269.

[23] On the mutual benefits of cooperation between the rural banks and the con-

Despite their goal of buying industrial products at lower prices, the consortia also provided advantages to designated manufacturing interests. The expanded demand for industrial goods, the simplification of commercial operations, and the enhanced market stability offered by the Federconsorzi all served to attract the interest of industrial suppliers. During the first decade of the century, when the chemical and machine industries had not yet attained a high degree of concentration, collaboration with the Federconsorzi appeared as the best alternative to ruinous competition among producers. Some industrial leaders recognized that the consortia potentially represented a "defense against the risks of competition" and envisioned a new market system in which prices and conditions could be discussed and accorded "between . . . two general federations."[24] In addition, the Federconsorzi served as a research and publicity department for chemical and machine manufacturers. Beginning in the late 1890s, the organization published and distributed a stream of pamphlets, promoting and illustrating the rational use of nitrate and phosphate fertilizers, and agricultural machines; the provincial consortia reinforced this service on the local level in their monthly bulletins. At the same time, the technical office of the Federconsorzi carried out extensive research on the construction and modification of plows, reapers, and tractors that it placed at the disposal of manufacturers.[25]

---

sortia, see Antonio Bizzozero, *Diciotto anni di cooperazione agraria 1893-1910. Consorzio Agrario Cooperativo Parmense* (Parma, 1911), p. XIX and statistical tables; *Bollettino Mensile del Consorzio Agrario Bolognese*, December 1916; Cassa di Risparmio, *La Cassa di Risparmio*, pp. 381-403; G. Porisini, "Aspetti e problemi dell'agricoltura ravennate dal 1883 al 1922" in *Nullo Baldini nella storia della cooperazione* (Milan, 1966), pp. 271-272. In the province of Bologna, a group of banks, headed by the Cassa di Risparmio and the Banca Popolare, joined with "the most noted and influential farmers" to found the Bolognese Agrarian Consortium in 1901. In addition, the Cassa di Risparmio arranged special credit terms, enabling the growers to buy seed, fertilizers, and machines prior to the growing season and then pay for them after the sale of their crops. See *Bollettino Mensile del Consorzio Agrario Bolognese*, III, no. 3 (1903), pp. 51-53.

[24] See letter of chemical manufacturer to president of the Federconsorzi, cited in Angelo Ventura, "La Federconsorzi dall'età liberale al fascismo" in *Quaderni Storici*, XII, no. 36 (December 1977), p. 691.

[25] On the promotional and research activities of the Federconsorzi, see Giuseppe Ravasini, "L'attività culturale della Federazione Italiana dei Consorzi Agrari" *L'I-*

Chemical fertilizers were the first products to be extensively marketed through the consortia, since they were in high demand among growers and did not require substantial capital investments. For the Italian chemical industry, with its shortage of experienced scientists and technicians, the market for fertilizers was a natural area of expansion prior to World War I.[26] As a result, contact between the consortia and manufacturers developed rapidly after 1900. For the purchases of phosphates, which were largely produced in northern Italy, the Federconsorzi gave its provincial affiliates a model contract that they used to establish specific agreements with individual firms. Beginning in 1903, the Federconsorzi also assumed responsibility for purchases of imported fertilizers through the creation of special import companies that arranged agreements with foreign producers for supplies that the organization eventually distributed to the various consortia. In quantitative terms, such arrangements appeared to provide definite benefits to both commercial farmers and chemical firms.[27]

The marketing of agricultural machines also gave rise to collaboration between the consortia and manufacturing groups, but commercial operations in this area did not attain the same levels as those for fertilizers because of the small size of the Italian industry and the limited capital of the consortia. These circumstances, however, favored a far more pronounced convergence of interest be-

---

talia Agricola, March 1932, pp. 225-233; Federconsorzi, *Federconsorzi. Sessant' anni*, p. 55.

[26] For a general discussion of the Italian chemical industry before 1914, see L. Cafagna, "Italy, 1830-1914," pp. 316-317.

[27] Between 1895 and 1910, total sales of phosphates by the Federconsorzi rose from 36,621 quintals per year to nearly 900,000. By 1910 the Federation could claim to control 40 to 50 percent of the national market for chemical fertilizers and even higher percentages in the northern plains. During the same period, the Italian chemical industry had its greatest area of expansion in the production of fertilizers for agriculture. Output of fertilizers jumped six fold in the fourteen years after 1895. In 1905 the industry also began to extend its activity beyond phosphates to the production of nitrogeneous fertilizers and by 1913 provided one-third of the country's consumption of this product. Significantly, growing production was accompanied by the technological innovation and mechanization of the industry. See A. Ventura, "La Federconsorzi," pp. 696-697 and p. 735; Giovanni Morselli, *Le industrie chimiche italiane* (Milan, 1911), pp. 33-34; R. Romeo, *Breve storia della grande industria in Italia* (Bologna, 1963), p. 67.

tween the two groups. While the high costs of imported machines pushed the consortia to encourage the growth of a domestic industry, manufacturers needed the consortia to help develop a market and to refine and specialize their equipment. Although imports of farm machines rose steadily after 1897, the real surge in demand did not come until after the agricultural strikes of 1901. To meet part of the new demand, the provincial consortia established direct contacts with local firms for the acquisition of relatively unsophisticated machinery. In a region like Emilia, where industry had traditionally been tied to the agricultural sector, collaboration between the consortia and industrialists encountered few obstacles. The leading manufacturers of Bologna, for instance, were integrated into the provincial elite so that the consortium merely provided an institutional channel for arrangements between them and the big commercial farmers, who steadily increased their purchases of machines in the first decade of the century.[28] Similar agreements in other neighboring provinces stimulated the development of a small- and middle-sized agricultural machine industry; by the war seven firms in Bologna and nineteen in the region of Emilia specialized in the manufacture of ploughs, motors, pumps, and harvesting machines.[29]

A second and politically more important area of agrarian-industrial integration involved growers and processors of specialized crops such as hemp, tomatoes, and sugar beets. Hemp was one of the first industrial crops in the Po Delta. As early as the sixteenth century, the plains in Bologna, Ferrara, Modena, Ravenna, and Forlì had been a major center of hemp cultivation. During the

[28] Frank De Morsier, for example, owned the second largest machine firm in Bologna and was a prominent figure in both local liberal political circles and provincial agrarian organizations. As a result, he was able to establish close ties with the Bolognese Consortium, which awarded his firm a direct commission for the construction of certain specialized farm machines as early as 1904. See *Bollettino Mensile del Consorzio Agrario Bolognese*, 1904, supp. 2, p. 53. For statistics on sales, see *ibid.*, XI (1911), no. 2, pp. 7-16.

[29] See ACS, Ministero delle Armi e Munizioni, B2, F20, "Elenco delle ditte del Veneto ed Emilia specializzate nella fabbricazione di macchine agricole," March 12, 1917.

nineteenth century, production rose steadily until the 1880s, when competition from other textiles provoked a slump in the hemp market. Growers reduced the cultivation to the best suited lands so that quality and productivity rose, and by the opening years of the twentieth century they had achieved a new level of stability and prosperity.[30] An Italian hemp-processing industry to absorb domestic production developed only gradually, however. The first processing factories were founded in the 1840s in Emilia, but as late as 1876 growers exported 75 percent of their harvest. The dominance of the English, French, and German textile industries discouraged Italian initiatives in the sector throughout the second half of the century. Only with the economic boom after 1896 did the Italian hemp industry begin to expand. In the north a small number of entrepreneurs founded the first large companies, sparking a general modernization in the sector.[31]

A far more dynamic development took place in the cultivation and processing of tomatoes and sugar beets in the first decade of the century. Increased foreign demand, combined with certain technological innovations, triggered the rapid growth of an industry for the production of tomato concentrate and the spread of tomato cultivation in Emilia. In the province of Parma, where this new industry was centered, the first modern factories were built in 1902. Within a decade the number of factories grew from three to forty-four; exportation of tomato preserves increased from 48,000 quintals to over 400,000. The tremendous demand created by the processing industry and the high profits it assured led growers to extend their cultivation of tomatoes, which rapidly became the most important crop in the high plain of Parma.[32]

30 For the history of hemp cultivation, see Roberto Roversi, *Canapa ed autarchia* (Rome, 1939), pp. 11-13; Giovanni Proni, *La canapicoltura italiana*, p. 40; Vittorio Peglion, *Piante industriali. Produzione, commercio, regime doganale* (Rome, 1917), p. 29.

31 The leading firms were the Linificio e Canapificio Nazionale, the Manifatture Italiane Riunite, and the Ditta Ing. Clateo Castelini. See Ernesto Sessa, *Della canapa e del lino in Italia* (Milan, 1930), pp. 53-54; G. Proni, *La canapicoltura italiana*, pp. 54-55.

32 Attilio Todeschini, *Il pomodoro in Emilia. Importanza economica della col-*

Advances in tomato processing paled in comparison to the tremendous growth of the sugar-refining industry. Before 1880 the industry was virtually nonexistent in Italy, while a mere 250 hectares in the entire country were under cultivation with sugar beets. Refiners received their first great stimulus from the government in the midst of the agricultural depression in the form of indirect subsidies and a tariff, which assured them control of the internal market.[33] Exploiting these favorable conditions, a few entrepreneurs began to experiment with beet cultivation in the Po Delta. The crop soon found a favorable reception among the large commercial farmers. In provinces such as Ferrara, where the Bank of Turin and major land reclamation companies had invested vast sums of capital, sugar beets offered the fullest return. In other provinces, growers were drawn to the cultivation of the crop by the fall in hemp and wheat prices in the 1890s.[34] The success of the initial experiments sparked a remarkable burst of activity in the sector at the turn of the century. In just two years from 1898 to 1900, twenty-eight refineries were founded in the Po Delta, annual sugar production rose from 59,000 to nearly 600,000 quintals, and acreage devoted to the cultivation of sugar beets increased tenfold.[35] After the international Brussels Agreement of 1902, which gave Italian refiners a monopoly of the domestic market, industrial and agricultural production grew at a steady but less dramatic pace until shortly before the First World War. By 1913-1914 seventeen plants in Emilia and thirty-nine in the country as a whole produced

tivazione (Rome, 1938), pp. 3-34; P. Giulio Gennari, *Le provincie di Parma, Reggio Emilia, e Modena nella struttura generale della loro economia agraria e nei rapporti fra datori di lavoro e lavoratori* (Parma, 1921), p. 2; Gaetano Briganti, "Le colture intensive specializzate" in *L'Italia agricola e il suo avvenire* (Rome, 1919), pp. 190-191.

33 Luigi Perdisa, *La bietola da zucchero*, pp. 10-13; C. J. Robertson, "The Italian Beet-Sugar Industry," *Economic Geography*, XIV (January 1938), p. 12.

34 Alessandro Roveri, *Dal sindacalismo rivoluzionario al fascismo. Capitalismo agrario e socialismo nel Ferrara, 1870-1920* (Florence, 1972), p. 139; C. J. Robertson, "The Italian Beet-Sugar Industry," pp. 7-9.

35 L. Perdisa, *La bietola da zucchero*, pp. 14-16; L. Zerbini, "Le bietole da zucchero," *L'Italia Agricola*, April 1927, p. 208; A. Roveri, *Dal sindacalismo*, pp. 139-140; "Bieticoltura ravennate," *L'Italia Agricola*, December 1927, p. 788.

nearly 3 million quintals of sugar per year while the area under the crop was over 200,000 acres.[36]

Despite the overall growth of production and commercial activity, relations between commercial farmers and industrial suppliers and processors were far from smooth and untroubled. On the contrary, problems of overproduction, price instability, and financial speculation provoked recurrent tensions and conflicts between the two interests. Already in 1900, overproduction in the chemical sector unleashed a fierce competition that drove fertilizer prices down to, and sometimes below, costs. In response to this disastrous situation, virtually all manufacturers joined together in 1901 to form a marketing cartel, which regulated production and set prices according to the average costs of production. As a result of these agreements, fertilizer prices rose to an acceptable level, but the attempts of certain firms to undercut the Federconsorzi by offering more advantageous terms to independent growers provoked no small discontent in the consortia.[37] Similar difficulties strained relations between sugar beet growers and refiners. From its founding, the refining sector was dominated by a few large companies who quickly extended their influence over the smaller firms in the first decade of the century.[38] Alarmed by the disorderly and speculative expansion of the industry, the major firms formed their own cartel in 1904, the Sugar Refiners' Union, to regulate production, distribute supplies equally among the factories, and standardize contractual relations with the growers.[39] The concentrated might of the sugar cartel in the local markets undermined the bargaining power of the agrarians and forced them to begin organizing. As early as 1900, sugar beet growers held a national congress in order to establish uniform criteria in their dealings

[36] V. Peglion, *Piante industriali*, p. 92; L. Perdisa, *La bietola da zucchero*, p. 16.

[37] A. Bizzozero, *Diciotto anni*, p. 117, pp. 135-137.

[38] For the major corporations of the sugar-refining industry, see Credito Italiano, *Società Italiane 1914*, pp. 1012-1030. On the expansion of the Società Eridania, in particular, see A. Roveri, *Dal sindacalismo*, p. 140.

[39] L. Perdisa, *La bietola da zucchero*, pp. 251-252.

with the refiners and to prepare the ground for eventual organizations of their own.[40] As a relatively small and highly capitalized group, the sugar beet growers found it relatively easy to join together in marketing organizations. After the creation of the Unione Zuccheri, the first growers' syndicates soon arose in the provinces of Rovigo, Adria, Ferrara, and Bologna to control the cultivation of the crop and to represent the farmers in negotiations with the trust and independent firms.[41]

These tensions and strains marked only a prelude to the far more serious conflicts that arose in the last years of the decade. The financial crisis and economic recession of 1907-08 profoundly altered relations between commercial agriculture and industry. They accelerated the processes of concentration and cartelization in the supplying and refining sectors and pushed manufacturers to transfer the burdens of credit stringency and overproduction on to the less organized and more competitive agrarians. It was in response to these developments, and the renewed militancy of organized labor, that commercial farming interests in the Po Valley began to free themselves from the tutelage in the old landed patricians and formulate distinctive new programs and organization strategies in the years after 1907.

2. *Economic Crisis, Labor Militancy, and the Ideology of Bourgeois Renewal*

Italy's golden era of industrial expansion, prosperity, and stability came to an abrupt halt in 1907. In the second half of that year, a worldwide depression and financial crisis hit the fragile Italian economy with devastating force. The effects of credit stringency, which spread from the United States to Europe, hurt in

[40] See "Atti del primo Congresso nazionale dei bieticultori" reprinted in *Rassegna Economica del Polesine*, November 1951, pp. 43-44.

[41] For the information of the growers' syndicates, see L. Perdisa, *La bietola da zucchero*, pp. 252-253; V. Peglion, *Le nostre piante industriali* (Bologna, no date), p. 101; Julo Fornacciari, "La Federazione nazionale bieticultori," *L'Italia Agricola*, March 1932, pp. 235-236; *Bollettino Mensile del Consorzio Agrario Bolognese*, v, no. 10-11 (1905), p. 202.

particular the mixed credit banks in Italy that had committed most of their deposits in loans to industry and in stock ventures. One of the largest credit banks, the Società Bancaria Italiana, nearly collapsed and the remaining financial institutions reacted with strong measures to restrict credit.[42] Industrial recession accompanied the financial crisis. The deflationary policies of the banks, along with excess production and rising prices for raw materials, proved especially damaging for the automobile, cotton, steel, and ship-building sectors. Nor was the slump of 1907-1908 simply a temporary phenomenon. Although the Italian economy began to recover in 1909, investments, industrial profits, and employment in the last six years of the prewar period remained below the levels they had reached before 1907.[43]

Reduced demand and high interest rates forced significant structural changes in those industrial sectors with close ties to commercial agriculture. Overproduction and price instability in the chemical industry, for instance, led to growing concentration in the sector and by 1913 two firms controlled two-thirds of the domestic production of phosphate fertilizers. Such concentration greatly facilitated the revival of a marketing cartel that already controlled nine-tenths of all domestic fertilizer production in 1911.[44] Similar trends were evident in the industrial processing and refining sectors. After a period of rising prices and expansion in the first years of the century, hemp manufacturers encountered serious marketing problems in 1907-1908 as a consequence of the American financial crisis and declining demand in England.[45] The lively competition that had previously characterized the industry gave

[42] See Franco Bonelli, *La crisi del 1907. Una tappa dello sviluppo industriale in Italia* (Turin, 1971), pp. 8-11.

[43] Adolfo Pepe, *Lotta di classe e crisi industriale in Italia. La svolta del 1913* (Milan, 1978), pp. 10-19; Alexander Gerschenkron, *Il problema storico dell'arretratezza economica* (Turin, 1965), pp. 74-77.

[44] The two major chemical firms were the Unione Italiana Concimi and the Società Colla e Concimi. The first of these had emerged by 1911 as the largest supplier in the Po Valley with its twenty-six factories (five in Emilia alone). For developments in the chemical industry, see G. Morselli, *Industrie chimiche*, pp. 33, 125.

[45] For the causes of the recession, see *Bollettino Federale Agrario*, October 15, 1908.

way to general agreements among the major northern firms that culminated in the formation of a cartel for the purchasing of raw hemp and the marketing of their finished products in 1913. One company, the Linificio e Canapificio Nazionale, emerged as the dominant force within the cartel and in the following five years gradually absorbed the other big firms to become the largest Italian textile corporation.[46] In the sugar industry, the economic slump accelerated earlier tendencies toward concentration. Interlocking directorates testified to the increasingly oligopolistic structure of the sector; in 1914 a select group of industrialists and financiers either managed or sat on the boards of the twelve biggest sugar-refining companies in the country.[47] Thus, in the years after 1908, growers confronted a considerably more compact and powerful bloc of industrial suppliers and buyers with the capacity to dictate the terms of exchange with the fragmented and less organized agricultural sector.

Those commercial farming interests who were heavily involved with these industries were also hard hit by the slump. The Bolognese Agrarian Consortium, for example, had to halt its ambitious program of expansion in 1908, its board of directors reported, because of the plight of "industries closely linked with our business operations." The same year, textile processors and sugar refiners drastically reduced their purchases of hemp and sugar beets, with disastrous consequences for the growers.[48] Not surprisingly, such difficulties gave rise to new tensions and bitter conflicts between agrarians and industrialists. The leaders of the Federconsorzi openly criticized the major chemical companies, charging that consumers of fertilizers were having to pay for the excessively high dividends

[46] On the growing concentration in the sector, see E. Sessa, *Della canapa*, pp. 54-55; ACS, Ministero delle Armi e Munizioni, B189, Verbali del Comitato regionale della Mobilizazione industriale, Bologna, September 15 and 22, 1917.

[47] See Credito Italiano, *Società Italiane 1914*, pp. 1012-1030.

[48] On the financial difficulties of the Bolognese Consortium, see the annual report of the board of directors in *Bollettino Mensile del Consorzio Agrario Bolognese*, x, no. 1 (1910), pp. 6-7. For the problems of the hemp and sugar beet growers, see *Bollettino Federale Agrario*, October 15, 1908.

they paid to their stockholders. After the sugar refiners abruptly cancelled their contracts with the beet growers in 1908, agrarian spokesmen denounced their "excessively industrial spirit" and accused them of attempting to unload their losses on the farmers.[49]

Precisely at a time when the commercial farmers of Emilia felt squeezed by their industrial suppliers and clients, they had to contend with renewed pressures from an aggressive rural trade union movement. The most immediate dangers confronted growers in the provinces of Ferrara and Parma where revolutionary syndicalists had gained control of the local labor organizations in 1907. The syndicalists did not delay implementing their program of direct action and physical violence. In the spring and summer of that year, Michele Bianchi orchestrated a massive general strike of day laborers and salaried workers in Ferrara, in which the Catholic unions and large numbers of sharecroppers took part. During the same period, Alceste De Ambris, the syndicalist leader in Parma, called a strike of all laborers and stable hands that resulted in the abandonment of some sixty thousand head of cattle and the quick capitulation of the landowners.[50] In those provinces like Bologna where reformist elements remained in command of the leagues, commercial farmers faced a less dramatic, but perhaps equally alarming challenge. Responding to the chronic unemployment in the Po Valley that had negated many of the gains won on issues of wages and work hours, the national Federterra adopted a strategy designed to gain control of hiring in the countryside. In accordance with its guidelines, the local leagues demanded their own employment offices to ensure equal distribution of the available work and to regulate the migrational currents of the day laborers. Despite their seemingly innocuous functions, the offices potentially

[49] See *Bollettino Federale Agrario*, December 1 and 15, 1908. For the discontent of the consortia, see A. Bizzozero, *Diciotto anni*, pp. 117, 135-137.

[50] On the strike in Ferrara, see A. Roveri, *Dal sindacalismo*, pp. 189-208; for the strikes in Parma, see Biagio Riguzzi, *Sindacalismo e riformismo nel Parmense* (Bari, 1931) and Thomas R. Sykes, "Revolutionary Syndicalism in the Italian Labor Movement: The Agrarian Strikes of 1907-08 in the Province of Parma" *International Review of Social History*, XXI, pt. 2 (1976), pp. 189-191.

gave the leagues the means for unprecedented intervention in areas of farm management previously the exclusive domain of the employers.[51]

Pressure from industry and labor violence not only sharpened the awareness of commercial farmers in the region of their shared interests, but also instilled in them a new militancy that younger agrarian leaders began to articulate in the fall of 1907. In the wake of the bitter syndicalist strikes that year, Giovanni Enrico Sturani, the Bolognese organizer, and Lino Carrara, the president of the Agrarian Association of Parma, emerged as the most outspoken critics of moderate class cooperation and the traditional methods of agrarian interest representation. Already in August, Sturani voiced his dissatisfaction with the old strategy, claiming that the moderate landowners who "have not hesitated during strikes to come to terms with the leagues, to cede their lands to laborers with collective contracts, and to agree to continual improvements" were following the "direct path toward socialism amid the applause and praise of those who are gradually supplanting them." Sturani conceded that these policies brought temporary peace in the countryside, but warned that in the long run they benefited exclusively a socialist movement that was proceeding to the slow but relentless "expropriation of industry and private property."[52] In a similar vein, Carrara told a regional agrarian congress in November 1907 that the program of class cooperation no longer corresponded to the harsh realities of the northern plains. Despite all their "fine institutions and good intentions," Carrara argued that the moderate agrarian leaders had not achieved their primary objective: to convince the leagues "to renounce the doctrine of class conflict."[53]

[51] See Idomeneo Barbadoro, *Storia del sindacalismo italiano dalla nascita al fascismo*, Vol. I, *La Federterra* (Florence, 1973), pp. 210-211 as well as E. Dugoni and N. Mazzoni, "Gli uffici di collocamento. La loro utilità, norme, moduli, istruzioni per l'impianto e funzionamento degli uffici" in R. Zangheri, ed., *Lotte agrarie in Italia*, pp. 219-227.

[52] *Il Giornale dell'Emilia*, August 24-25, 1907.

[53] See *Bollettino dell'Associazione Agraria Parmense*, VI, no. 10-13, November 9, 1907.

Sturani and Carrara did not limit their criticisms to specific policies and programs of the agrarian associations. Indeed, they broadened their attack to include the entire structure of clubs and provincial notables that had perennially served as the political mediators of landed interests in the Po Valley. In their view, such informal and impoverished arrangements were hopeless anachronisms in an era of mass politics and organized pressure groups. As Sturani expressed it, they offered programs "so vague and generic that they no longer signify anything, only a history by now gloriously exhausted [and] not a program for future conquests."[54] Dissatisfied agrarian spokesmen cited developments in other sectors of the economy to underscore the need for commercial farmers to look beyond the politics of prestige: "Look about us: all the classes are organizing . . . for commercial, industrial, and professional ends, always with the single objective of conquering a just position for themselves in the social balance of economic interests. The entire world is being transformed before our very eyes and is assuming this special direction. . . . The agrarians must recognize the full importance and multiple benefits of class action."[55] In a society increasingly dominated by compact and well-organized interests, Sturani insisted that the growers had to unite on their own, independently from the old notables, if they hoped to protect "the legitimate interests of capital and business enterprise in all legislation, in all the political activity of the government."[56]

Both the rhetoric and proposals of these militant spokesmen reflected a new corporative and authoritarian vision of labor relations, production, and agrarian interest representation.[57] Dis-

[54] See article by G. E. Sturani in *RdC*, May 26, 1910.

[55] *Bollettino Federale Agrario*, July 31, 1909. See also *Bollettino Mensile del Consorzio Agrario Bolognese*, VI, no. 1 (1906), pp. 5-6.

[56] *RdC*, May 26, 1910.

[57] The use of the term "corporative" in this context is not intended to link the militant agrarians' program with the Fascist system of corporations in the 1920s and 1930s. Rather the term is used here in a more generic sense used by Charles Maier to describe a vision of institutional arrangements involving "the displacement of power from elected representatives or a career bureaucracy to the major organized

taining the old ideal of the paternalistic and gentlemanly landowner, Lino Carrara celebrated instead the figure of the innovative and efficient commercial farmer who, in his words, represented "the most vital, most energetic, most active bourgeoisie" that had "created the wealth by drawing higher levels of production from the land" and consequently had earned the right to command.[58] Carrara and Sturani attributed the upsurge of labor militancy and the growing power of the Socialists less to any intrinsic economic weakness of the agrarians than to their passivity and their habit of "giving in for love of peace" to the demands of the leagues. As a result, they saw the pressing need for new forms of organization that galvanized commercial farmers by stimulating their "class consciousness, good faith, [and] confidence in our cause." Contrary to the moderate leaders who favored organizations that included all the rural classes, Carrara and Sturani called for a more exclusive, disciplined, and bellicose association composed of a "small nucleus of men who are prepared for any contingency."[59] Such an association, they argued, which placed "the defense of the class before the interests of the individuals," offered the best means of reasserting managerial authority in the countryside and of advancing the position of commercial farmers in the national economy as a whole.[60]

From its inception, the militants' program aimed to restrict drastically, if not eliminate altogether, the role of organized labor in social and economic bargaining. Significantly, they denied the possibility of domesticating the leagues through a policy of concessions, rejecting Giolitti's distinction between the legitimate interest-group agitation of the reformist unions and the subversive class

forces of European society and economy." See C. Maier, *Recasting Bourgeois Europe*, p. 9. Moreover, agrarian opponents of Carrara used the term to characterize his program. See, for example, *Bollettino Federale Agrario*, November 15, 1908.

[58] *RdC*, June 7, 1910.

[59] *Ibid.*; G. E. Sturani, *La Mutua-Scioperi. Sue basi economiche e suo ordinamento* (Bologna, 1909), pp. 33-34; CNA, *Atti del II Congresso Agrario, Bologna*, (Bologna, 1911), p. 111.

[60] G. E. Sturani, *La Mutua-Scioperi*, p. 34.

attacks of the revolutionary syndicalists. Despite the apparent moderation and gradualism of the reformist leagues in Bologna, Sturani charged that they had produced the same results as their syndicalist comrades in Parma or Ferrara, since in most cases their agreements and contracts were "extorted in violation of all fundamental rights and involve arbitrary impositions that deprive independent laborers of work." Regardless of whether it was "reformist guerilla warfare" or violent syndicalist general strikes, growers had little choice but to resist the leagues or else accept "the gradual elimination of the leaseholders, the small proprietors, [and] ultimately the elimination of all property rights" in the countryside.[61]

In line with this monolithic conception of organized labor, Carrara and Sturani proposed policies designed to combat all initiatives of the leagues and to enforce the absolute obedience of the laborers to the dictates of the growers. In order to create the cohesive and tightly disciplined employers' associations required for such policies, Carrara advocated the use of *cambiali in bianco*, or promissory notes, signed by all members of the association for the value of their crops. According to Carrara, the promissory notes represented "the guarantee of all for one and one for all," since they served to ensure the loyalty of the individual growers to their colleagues and the policies of their organizations.[62] As an additional measure for promoting solidarity within the agrarian associations, Sturani advanced the idea of a new insurance company, the Strike Insurance Fund, that indemnified all members of the Interprovinciale for losses they suffered in "unjust agricultural strikes, boycotts . . . and other disturbances." Sturani conceived of the fund less as a form of protection than as an offensive weapon allowing the agrarian associations to expand their use of lockouts in order to enlarge the area of unemployment and compel the leagues to exhaust more quickly their limited resources. While in the past the leagues had largely determined the time and place of

[61] *Bollettino Federale Agrario*, November 1, 1908; *Giornale dell'Emilia*, August 24-25, 1907.

[62] CNA, *Atti del II Congresso*, p. 117.

strikes and boycotts, Sturani claimed that the Strike Insurance Fund would enable the employers to initiate hostilities, selecting "the opportune moment to open the conflict before their adversaries have consolidated their forces of resistance."[63]

Apart from these financial initiatives, the young agrarian leaders also envisioned special combat units for use once conflicts with the leagues had erupted. Carrara, in particular, favored the formation of mobile squads of nonunion workers or "free laborers" that could be rapidly dispatched into troubled areas to complete the most essential farm work and thereby lessen the impact of strikes and boycotts. To protect the permanent squads of strikebreakers from the inevitable wrath of the leagues, Carrara advocated an armed "interprovincial corps of volunteers" that guarded fields and energetically opposed any efforts by striking laborers to halt the work. The outspoken agrarian leader from Parma made no secret of what he hoped to achieve through such measures: "Hit by boycotts, we will respond with the lockout; we will answer violence with violence. The working class may be strong, but the employer class is equally strong."[64]

While Sturani and Carrara devoted most of their attention to the issue of labor control in the countryside, they did not neglect the perhaps equally important problems of production and marketing that faced commercial farmers in the last years of the decade. Much as in their approach to labor relations, the two agrarian leaders looked to disciplined organizations of producers as the best means of regulating agricultural production, rationalizing marketing operations, and counteracting the concentrated might of industrial processors and refiners. Already in 1902, Sturani emerged as a strong proponent of specialized commodity organizations that he characterized as the growers' only defense against "the risks of competition" and the damages resulting from "natural or artificial

[63] G. E. Sturani, *La Mutua-Scioperi*, pp. 6, 23, 34, 39-40.

[64] *Bollettino dell'Associazione Agraria Parmense*, VII, no. 1, January 2, 1908; CNA, *Atti del II Congresso*, p. 108.

monopolies" which distorted the normal operations of the market.[65] Sturani's views were echoed in the following years by commercial farming interests in the Bolognese Agrarian Consortium who enthusiastically publicized the activities of the agricultural cooperatives in Germany as examples of the benefits that local farmers could gain "from a well-conceived cooperation in the various branches of agricultural industry."[66]

With the financial crisis and economic recession of 1907-08, these ideas provided the basis for a systematic campaign to develop growers' syndicates in the Po Valley. In the pages of the Interprovinciale's bulletin and the newsletters of the agrarian consortia, exponents of commodity organization advanced plans for self-regulating syndicates of hemp and sugar beet growers, run by the leading farmers, to control the market, limit production, stabilize agricultural prices, and act as strong bargaining agents in contractual negotiations with industrial processors. Uniting all producers of a particular commodity at the provincial level, these cartels would collect information on local and foreign market conditions, locate new outlets, negotiate collective sales of their members' crops, establish storage facilities for surpluses, and arrange credit assistance.[67] Promoters claimed that the syndicates would not only assure growers remunerative prices and protection from "the excessively industrial spirit" of the processors and refiners, but would also facilitate economic integration of the two sectors. Thus, for example, they saw ample opportunities for collaboration between the syndicates of sugar beet growers and the Sugar Refiners' Union in the containment of labor costs, the maintenance

[65] See Sturani's article in *Bollettino Mensile del Consorzio Agrario Bolognese*, II, no. 11 (1902), p. 230.

[66] For the views of the consortium's leaders, see *ibid.*, VII, no. 8-10 (1907), pp. 100-102.

[67] On the hemp syndicates, see "I produttori di canapa si muovono," *Bollettino Mensile del Consorzio Agrario Bolognese*, VII, no. 8-10 (1907), pp. 98-102; and *Bollettino Federale Agrario*, October 15, 1908. For the sugar beet growers, see note 41 in this chapter.

of tariffs, and in the coordination of production, marketing, and credit.[68]

The pronounced emphasis on class solidarity and corporative organization that informed the young agrarian militants' labor policies and marketing proposals also shaped their approach to political action. Under the direction of patricians like Count Francesco Cavazza, the Interprovinciale and the local agrarian associations had tended to restrict themselves to economic matters and to rely on provincial notables and the established parties of order for their political representation. Carrara and Sturani rejected this separation of politics and economics, arguing that the rise of a national party of labor and the growing commercialization of agriculture, which had created new configurations of interest that transcended the old provincial borders, had made such arrangements inadequate and outdated. In their view, the loose network of municipal and provincial political clubs that comprised the Liberal party could not provide the type of organized representation and coherent national programs that commercial farming interests required, since they constituted little more than "occasional regroupings of particular interests" tied to the "parliamentary ambitions of certain individuals."[69] The effectiveness of the Socialist party in advancing the interests of organized labor further underscored the insufficiencies of the old parties of order. As Sturani observed, the socialist trade unions had their own "deputies who carry on an activity completely coordinated with their interests," while commercial farmers had no "authoritative representatives in the Chamber who can interpret their ideas and interests."[70]

To remedy this situation, Carrara and Sturani advocated the transformation of the Interprovinciale into an independent political force, directly involved in electoral and parliamentary struggles. In his speeches to agrarian groups throughout Emilia, Carrara repeated the same message: "Since we represent a great national

[68] See *Bollettino Federale Agrario*, January 15, March 15, and September 1, 1909.

[69] *Ibid.*, October 1, 1909.

[70] *Ibid.*, May 1, 1910.

energy, we must have the right to make our voice heard in the halls of parliament, and we will be able to do this only when we become a truly vital electoral force, when we no longer rely on ministerial alliances or any force other than ourselves."[71] Agrarians, therefore, had a clear "political mission . . . to alter profoundly the existing situation with the forces of our own organization."[72] As a first step, the militants called for the creation of a farm bloc or parliamentary "Agrarian Group" composed of deputies and senators from agricultural provinces who obediently followed the directives and advanced the objectives of the Interprovinciale and its affiliated associations in Rome. United by shared class, professional, and regional interests that shielded it from the lures of transformism, the Agrarian Group would make its support of any government contingent on the responsiveness of ministers and other officials to the program of the Interprovinciale. Eventually, the Agrarian Group would give way to a new Agrarian party, "completely independent from the so-called political parties," that would provide the agricultural sector with its own "authoritative representatives in the Chamber."[73]

With its rhetoric of bourgeois renewal and its advocacy of intransigent resistance, commodity cartels, and agrarian political autonomy, the program advanced by the militant young Emilian leaders represented not only an open repudiation of Giolitti's strategy of social compromise, but also a direct challenge to the leadership, methods, and ideals of the provincial notables who still guided the Interprovinciale and many of the local associations. Not surprisingly, Carrara, Sturani, and their supporters encountered strong opposition from prominent moderate leaders like Count Francesco Cavazza and old fashioned liberals such as Marchese Giuseppe Tanari. Indeed, the last years of the decade witnessed an intense power struggle within the Interprovinciale and at the provincial level as proponents of bourgeois renewal moved to wrestle

[71] CNA, *Atti del II Congresso*, p. 122.
[72] *Bollettino Federale Agrario*, January 15-February 1, 1910.
[73] *Ibid.*, September 30, 1908; *ibid.*, May 1, 1910.

organizational control from the defenders of class cooperation and deference politics.

3. *Agrarian Insurgency Within the Interprovinciale*

The first great test of the agrarian militants' new strategy came in the spring of 1908 in Lino Carrara's native province of Parma where revolutionary syndicalist elements had given all labor conflicts a distinctively political and violent character. After the local agrarian association suffered a humiliating defeat at the hands of the leagues the previous summer, Carrara took steps in the winter of 1907-1908 to forge a compact and disciplined antiunion front of all agricultural, industrial, and commercial employers in the province. He received unexpected assistance in his campaign from the syndicalist leader, Alceste De Ambris, who announced in November 1907 that the laborers would once again "desert the fields, stables, and offices, [and] bring all social life to a halt" the following spring.[74] In preparation for what appeared to be a decisive confrontation with the syndicalists, Carrara had the growers sign promissory notes, recruited squads of "free laborers," and organized a corps of "volunteers" to defend at all costs the right to work. Significantly, he made sure that his volunteers were well-armed; in the commune of Noceto alone, the association distributed some two hundred seventy licenses to carry weapons.[75] To protect the capital of its members, the association also set up a special mutual fund against strike damages and made arrangements for transporting livestock to nearby provinces and for purchasing farm machinery to replace the striking laborers during the harvest. By January 1908, Carrara confidently proclaimed the readiness of his association to repel any challenge or attack from the syndicalists.[76]

When the syndicalists called a boycott of landowners in the

[74] *L'Idea*, November 2, 1907, as cited in B. Riguzzi, *Sindacalismo e riformismo*, p. 120.

[75] B. Riguzzi, *Sindacalismo e riformismo*, p. 120.

[76] See note 64.

communes of Noceto and Colorno in February, Carrara made good his claim, ordering a lockout of all organized laborers in those areas. As the local boycotts escalated into a general strike involving every category of agricultural labor in the late spring, he proceeded to extend the lockout to the entire province. Aided by other employer organizations in the region, the Agrarian Association of Parma evicted striking peasants from their farms, transported unattended livestock out of the province, and recruited nonunion labor from every part of Italy.[77] At the same time, Carrara retaliated against threats and collective violence by the leagues by dispatching his own squads of club-wielding toughs to intimidate and rough up striking laborers. While such tactics helped to make the Parma strike the most violent rural labor conflict in the prewar period, they did achieve their immediate objectives. By mid-July, De Ambris had fled the province, most of the wheat had been threshed, and the strike had collapsed. More importantly, Carrara succeeded in forcing the contract workers to resign from the syndicalist chamber of labor and enroll in the "free" unions of the agrarian association.[78]

The repercussions of Carrara's victory extended well beyond the borders of his province. With the methods and organization of the Agrarian Association of Parma as their models, militants began in the fall of 1908 to agitate for a drastic reorientation of the Interprovinciale's program and structure. Already in the first issue of *Il Bollettino Federale Agrario*, house organ of the Interprovinciale, they harshly attacked Giolitti and moderate proponents of class cooperation for their isolation from "the real life of the country." In particular, they denounced the idea of governmental neutrality in labor disputes as "the grossest partisanship," since the authorities always wound up sacrificing "the right to produce, the right to work, which requires intervention to remove those obstacles to free and legitimate activity." The militants called upon the organized commercial farmers to take matters into their own hands

[77] B. Riguzzi, *Sindacalismo e riformismo*, pp. 125-132.
[78] *Ibid.*, pp. 128-129.

and compel a change in the government's policies. Instead of passively accepting the dictates of Giolitti and the leagues, the agrarian associations had to follow the example of Parma by organizing their own squads of volunteers, so that in moments of conflict they could confront the authorities with a clear choice: "Either you intervene or we will defend the liberty of our workers."[79]

The militants' criticisms and proposals aroused an immediate reaction from moderate spokesmen who stressed the uniqueness of the Parma situation and warned that Carrara's corporative program would only exacerbate labor strife and increase the isolation of agrarians at the provincial level and in Rome. The moderates reaffirmed their view that the agrarian associations should not represent narrow class interests, but rather "the general interests of the society," providing leadership and direction to all elements involved in agricultural production.[80] In an attempt to placate the militants, the leaders of the Interprovinciale advanced a program in November 1908 that incorporated features of both the "orthodox liberal" and "corporative" program. Summarizing the main tenets of the program, *Il Bollettino Federale Agrario* reported: "A more ample formula has prevailed that can include and conciliate the two tendencies by bringing them together on one common goal, the defense of property. The defense of property implies a program of resistance against the direct action of the syndicalists and the erosion of the reformists. . . . Where economic conflict—class conflict—emerges, the corporative strategy will be employed. In other places where class conflict is concealed in a battle of ideas and principles, pure orthodox liberalism will rule supreme."[81] Simultaneously, the Interprovinciale proposed to lobby in Rome on behalf of issues, around which both absentee landlords and commercial farmers could unite, such as grain protectionism, favorable agricultural trade agreements, local tax reforms, and stronger right-to-work laws.[82]

[79] *Bollettino Federale Agrario*, August 1-15, 1908.

[80] *Ibid.*, November 15, 1908.

[81] *Ibid.*

[82] For an outline of the issues upon which the Interprovinciale proposed to lobby, see *ibid.*, October 15, 1908.

This program, however, did not eliminate the clash of vested interests and divergent conceptions of agrarian organization within the Interprovinciale. Already during the winter of 1908-1909, moderates and militants came into conflict over the issue of government intervention in agricultural labor disputes. Count Francesco Cavazza presented a resolution to the council of the Interprovinciale in December that called upon the government to establish a system of compulsory arbitration for all controversies between capital and labor. Carrara vehemently opposed the resolution on the grounds that too often agrarians had had to accept unfavorable contracts because of the "partisan pressure from those who represent the government." After a heated debate, the council defeated Count Cavazza's proposal and instead approved Carrara's substitute resolution that "the agrarians, as individuals and as a *class*, have to draw upon their own moral and political resources to obtain and eventually *impose* the real observance of contracts."[83] As the language and tone of the victorious resolution suggest, the vote marked a major setback for Giolitti and the moderates' plan to institutionalize labor-management relations in the countryside.

The most serious clashes between moderates and militants, however, involved the question of the Interprovinciale's political role and its relations with the existing parties of order. From the outset, Carrara's proposal to politicize the agrarian associations through the creation of a parliamentary agrarian group alarmed the landed notables who controlled the local liberal political clubs. Voicing their concern, Marchese Giuseppe Tanari cautioned that any parliamentary groups, which represented exclusively "the defense of special interests," were dangerous because they pushed the country "away from a healthy liberalism."[84] Despite Tanari's warnings, the militants prevailed in the spring of 1909 when the Interprovinciale founded an Agrarian Central Committee composed of deputies and senators who embraced its program. Although agrarian leaders insisted that the new body did not constitute a "true par-

[83] *Ibid.*, December 1, 1908.

[84] *Ibid.*, September 15, 1908; for Carrara's response, see *ibid.*, September 30, 1908.

liamentary group," it clearly fulfilled the main aim of the militants by serving as a "union of all those politicians who have committed themselves to the fundamental principles of agrarian action."[85]

Significantly, the creation of the Agrarian Central Committee coincided with new parliamentary elections in 1909. At the urging of the militants, the Interprovinciale announced its intention in February to take part actively in the electoral campaign on the basis of a program of "social conservatism [and] the defense of private property."[86] For the first time, the agrarian associations officially endorsed only those candidates who formally accepted the political program of the Interprovinciale. Mario Missiroli, a young agrarian propagandist from Bologna, defined the objective of the policy in early March, writing that the organized agrarians now preferred "to have a few parliamentary friends who are truly sincere and reliable, and who are prepared to sustain the great battles in the Chamber," rather than "those innumerable vague supporters on whom the agrarians have learned from experience that they cannot rely."[87] Moreover, the Interprovinciale did not hesitate to circumvent the old liberal clubs and sponsor its own candidates. In Bologna, for instance, Carlo Cremonini, who ran in the electoral college of San Giovanni in Persiceto, freely admitted that his candidacy had been designated by the local agrarian associations.[88]

The attempt of the Interprovinciale to impose its program on the parties of order encountered some resistance from certain established politicians like Marchese Tanari. As a candidate in one of Bologna's urban colleges, Tanari agreed to accept the agrarian program solely on the condition that it did not signify "the aspiration to create future agrarian parliamentary groups" which he considered "harmful to the principles of liberty and justice."[89] But

[85] CNA, *L'organizzazione agraria in Italia. Sviluppo, ordinamento, azione* (Bologna, 1911), pp. 82-83.

[86] *Ibid.*, p. 79.

[87] *Giornale d'Italia*, March 5, 1909.

[88] *Bollettino Federale Agrario*, March 1, 1909.

[89] *Ibid.*

these reservations did not prevent the agrarian associations and the liberal clubs from reaching an agreement. At the beginning of March, the Interprovinciale publicly endorsed an electoral slate in the Po Valley that included four Bolognese candidates: Tanari, Cremonini, Enrico Pini, and Filippo Bosdari.[90]

In its first major plunge into electoral politics, the Interprovinciale achieved some notable successes in Ferrara, Parma, Rovigo, and Milan where its candidates won eleven of the thirteen races they contested. The province of Bologna stood out as the glaring exception. Here, Socialist candidates dominated the rural areas, capturing four of the five electoral colleges in the countryside, while the only two agrarian victories, those of Pini and Tanari, came in the capital city.[91] Predictably, the militants blamed these setbacks on the parties of order. Evaluating the outcome in Bologna, *Il Bollettino Federale Agrario* concluded that the old liberal and monarchist clubs had not lived up to their mandate because of their impoverished campaign organization and "hurried and convulsive activity . . . after years of inertia and silence."[92] In this fashion, Carrara and his supporters used both the victories and the defeats to justify their demand for greater political activism and independence.

Encouraged by the results of the elections, the militants aggressively promoted their program at the Second National Agrarian Congress in Bologna at the end of November 1909. In his address to the delegates, Sturani reiterated the view that the organized agrarians had to "struggle in the political arena in order to have [their] ideas triumph" and consequently should support only those politicians "who recognize our aspirations and give assurance of promoting them."[93] At the same time, the militants accompanied their calls for political mobilization with resolutions in favor of sugar protection and the general adoption of those measures that

[90] *Ibid.*

[91] For the electoral defeats of the agrarians in Bologna, see *RdC*, March 5, 1909. On their victories elsewhere, see *Bollettino Federale Agrario*, March 15, 1909.

[92] *Bollettino Federale Agrario*, April 1, 1909.

[93] CNA, *Atti del II Congresso*, pp. 140-141.

had proven so effective in Parma: promissory notes, permanent strikebreaking squads, corps of "volunteers," and the Strike Insurance Fund.[94]

Virtually all these proposals met with strong opposition from the defenders of class cooperation. Ignazio Zampieri, a moderate agrarian delegate from Imola, attacked Carrara's resolution in support of high sugar tariffs, charging that such tariffs benefited exclusively the big refiners.[95] On the plan for mobile squads of strikebreakers, moderates warned that they increased the prospect of violent clashes with the leagues which could result in "tragic consequences." They favored instead measures to organize the mass of agricultural workers into unions "without political flags" that negotiated peacefully with employers on issues of wages and work hours.[96] Moderates, however, reserved their strongest criticisms for Sturani and Carrara's political proposals. Citing the political heterogeneity of the agrarians, Count Francesco Cavazza cautioned that any attempt to transform the Interprovinciale into an independent political force would endanger the organizational unity essential for the protection of specifically agricultural interests. Against his militant adversaries, Count Cavazza counseled the congress that the agrarian associations should concern themselves only with economic issues: "We must be united in the defense of our common interests and aspirations, but in the political arena . . . you must make your own decisions according to your diverse ideals."[97]

The congress concluded without either faction achieving a clearcut victory. In deference to Count Cavazza and the moderates, the delegates avoided any official stand on Carrara's antistrike measures. But on the controversial questions of sugar tariffs and agrarian political action, the militants prevailed. Despite the opposition of Count Cavazza, the congress approved Carrara's sugar tariff resolution and Sturani's proposal that the agrarian associations

[94] *Ibid.*, pp. 109, 117, 138-139.
[95] *Ibid.*, p. 155.
[96] *Ibid.*, p. 138.
[97] *Ibid.*, p. 149.

"intervene directly in every area of public life and especially in municipal and parliamentary elections."[98]

Already three months before the congress, the militants had acquired a powerful new instrument in their campaign "to conquer a broad consensus in public opinion" at the national level, when the Interprovinciale and a consortium of prominent agrarians and sugar refiners purchased controlling shares in *Il Resto del Carlino*. Early in September, the Interprovinciale made public its role in the change of ownership and announced that the Bolognese daily would now assume "an attitude of objectivity, truth, and justice in the various controversies that involve our organization."[99] With the purchase, the Interprovinciale not only acquired the most influential and prestigious paper in the region, but also established its independence from *Il Giornale dell'Emilia*, longtime organ of the local moderate establishment. Under the direction of Sturani, Carrara, and Mario Missiroli, *Il Resto del Carlino* rapidly emerged as the most authoritative defender of commercial farming interests and critic of the government in the Po Valley, much to the dismay of Giolitti.[100]

Throughout 1910, the militants used the Bolognese daily as a platform to promote the creation of a national agricultural lobby and an agrarian party. The first of these proposals, which also had the support of moderate spokesmen, became a reality in June with the founding of the National Agrarian Confederation (CNA). Significantly, Carrara chose the first meeting of the CNA to launch his plan for a party that, in his words, would make the agrarians "the victors of tomorrow who will impose their victory . . . [by] re-establishing . . . a government that will be a secure and solid bulwark against all pressures and disturbances."[101] A week later,

[98] *Ibid.*, p. 216.

[99] *Bollettino Federale Agrario*, September 1, 1909.

[100] See Nazario Sauro Onofri, *I giornali bolognesi nel ventennio fascista* (Bologna, 1972), p. 91; Maria Malatesta, *Il Resto del Carlino* (Turin, 1978), pp. 190-192.

[101] *RdC*, June 7, 1910. With its headquarters in Bologna, the CNA began operations on July 10, 1910 under the presidency of Count Francesco Cavazza.

Carrara repeated the same message to a meeting of commercial farmers in Ferrara, affirming that the agrarian organizations should aspire to be "a party of bourgeois regeneration."[102]

To a large extent, the increased influence of Carrara and the militants within the Interprovinciale reflected their strength at the grass-roots level. As early as 1908, Luigi Facta, undersecretary of state for internal affairs, voiced his concern over the growing militancy of the provincial agrarian associations. In a speech to the Chamber of Deputies that year, he charged that the associations had fallen under the sway of "those leaseholders . . . who because of their attitudes, position, and activities are the most combative." In particular, the undersecretary stressed how the profit-maximizing tendencies of the big commercial leaseholders had created a situation "in which conflicts between labor and capital are becoming increasingly intense and tenacious."[103] While Facta addressed his remarks chiefly to developments in Parma, by 1909 the insurgent trends he had noted were apparent not only in provinces where the syndicalists predominated, but also in that stronghold of the reformist leagues, Bologna.

4. *Agrarian Insurgency Within the Province of Bologna*

In 1907 and 1908, the Intermunicipal Federation of Landowners and Leaseholders represented the most important organizational bulwark of moderate class cooperation in the Po Valley. Founded in response to the growth of socialist sharecroppers' unions, the federation had built up a loose coalition of local employer associations and forged an alliance with the independent peasant brotherhoods against the Federterra and the Socialist party. Collaboration between the two organizations had not only strengthened the landowners in their negotiations with the Socialist unions, but had also seemingly laid the foundations for a renewed con-

[102] *Bollettino Federale Agrario*, June 15, 1910.

[103] *AP, Camera dei Deputati*, Leg. XXII, 1st Session, Discussioni, March 16, 1908, p. 20383.

servative electoral coalition in the province. In April 1908, the Provincial Federation of Brotherhoods had made known that it was "disposed to combat Socialist candidates and to support the liberals."[104] Provincial authorities had also noted the political potential of the alliance. The subprefect of Imola, for instance, reported in June that "the recently constituted agrarian association and the peasant brotherhoods have united the landowners and sharecroppers in strong groups which, if well-guided, represent a considerable electoral force."[105]

However, even as the subprefect made his optimistic prediction, strains were beginning to appear in the alliance, largely over issues of reciprocal duties and responsibilities. As in the past, these strains resulted primarily from unwillingness of agrarian leaders to accept an autonomous role for their peasant allies and their inability to discipline their own rank and file. Already in May the federation of brotherhoods angered agrarian leaders by refusing to join them in support of the Agrarian Association of Parma.[106] Later the same year, the brotherhoods forbade their sharecroppers from helping the landowners to break a strike in Anzola dell'Emilia, on the grounds that they were organized "to defend their own category, their own families, and not the interests of the [agrarians]."[107] For their part, the agrarian associations proved to be equally unreliable allies. Despite promises made by the Imolese association, large numbers of independent sharecroppers informed a prefectoral commissioner in the summer of 1908 that "they have been utterly abandoned by the landowners [and] intend to enroll in the Chamber of Labor."[108] Similarly, the head of the agrarian association in San Giovanni in Persiceto denied any aid to the local brotherhoods because, in his words, they were "still too few and imperfectly

[104] *La Fiaccola*, April 18, 1908.

[105] ASB, C5 F2, Subprefect of Imola to Prefect, June 23, 1908.

[106] The federation ordered all its members "not to give support either as volunteer laborers or as recipients of livestock from the province of Parma." See *La Fiaccola*, May 16, 1908.

[107] ASB, C6 F2, 2, "Situazione delle organizzazioni delle classi medie (piccoli proprietari e coloni) della Provincia di Bologna" Prefect to Ministry of Interior, no date, 1919.

[108] *Ibid.*, C6 F2, Prefectoral Commissioner to Prefect, June 18, 1908.

organized to be of any real utility."[109] These incidents provoked charges of disloyalty and betrayal by both the brotherhoods and the organized agrarians. In August, *La Fiaccola,* principal organ of the brotherhoods, reported on the growing discontent among the independent sharecroppers that it blamed on "the unwillingness of many landowners to assist them."[110] Prominent agrarian spokesmen reciprocated in December, accusing the brotherhoods of having forsaken their original "Christian democratic" credo for "revolutionary anarchist" ideas.[111]

Mutual recriminations led to an open rupture in the alliance early the following year. In February 1909, the federation of brotherhoods expelled the two agrarian representatives from its ranks and shortly thereafter resolved that leadership be entrusted to a council "composed exclusively of peasants and no one else."[112] Proponents of class cooperation suffered a far more serious setback in March when the independent peasant unions refused to collaborate with the agrarian associations in their electoral campaign. In a hurried effort to reconstruct the alliance with the brotherhoods, the Interprovinciale and the agrarian federation of Bologna had proposed in mid-February to support a peasant candidate, Augusto Federici, in the electoral college of Castelmaggiore in exchange for the brotherhoods' endorsement of their candidate, Carlo Cremonini, in San Giovanni in Persiceto. Peasant leaders, however, rejected the offer and instead used the campaign to criticize Cremonini and the policies of the agrarian associations. With such unexpected assistance from the brotherhoods, the Socialists captured both electoral colleges.[113]

The disintegration of the peasant-agrarian coalition, the electoral debacle, and the elevation of Raffaele Stagni to the presidency of

[109] *La Fiaccola,* August 1, 1908.

[110] *Ibid.,* August 28, 1908.

[111] *La Tribuna Agraria,* December 19, 1908.

[112] *La Fiaccola,* April 17, 1909.

[113] *Ibid.,* March 6, 1909. In mid-February, the *Bollettino Federale Agrario* called upon its readers to give Federici "all our sympathy and . . . our most warm and loyal support."

the Bolognese agrarian federation set the stage for the emergence of a small but vocal group of militants in the fall of 1909. Stagni, a land reclamation engineer with close ties to commercial farming interests, Sturani, and Augusto Pellicioni were the key figures in the group, which sounded the alarm against the reformist leagues, attacked the strategy of class cooperation, and agitated for a drastic reorientation of the Bolognese associations along lines laid down by Lino Carrara. Not surprisingly, Stagni found his principal base of support, as the prefect reported in October, among the big capitalist leaseholders of the lower plains.[114]

In sharp contrast to moderate spokesmen like Count Francesco Cavazza, Stagni saw the absence of strikes in the summer of 1909 not as a sign of a new social compromise in the province, but rather as "the capitulation and wartime imprisonment of our soldiers who fall one by one." According to Stagni, the local propertied classes had paid a high price for the quiet life: "We must recognize that this peace in our province is the result of an uninterrupted series of individual surrenders . . . either on wages or more often on those contractual clauses that tend to strengthen the monopoly of the leagues."[115] Echoing the views of Sturani, Stagni portrayed the initiatives of the socialist cooperatives and employment offices a far graver menace than the more dramatic general strikes of the revolutionary syndicalists. Despite their apparent moderation and gradualism, the reformist leagues were quietly but steadily eroding basic property rights and entrepreneurial prerogatives in the Bolognese countryside. Indeed, he warned that the Bolognese Federterra, if left unchecked, would soon become "the real employer who establishes the locality, form, schedule, and wages of work."[116]

Stagni and the militants attributed the relentless advance of the

[114] ASB, C6 F2, Prefect to Ministry of Interior, October 15, 1909. Specifically, the prefect mentioned the names of Benni, Roberto Magli, Antonio Bonora, Giuseppe Bolognesi, and Filippo Dal Rio. For Stagni's activities as a reclamation engineer, see ASB, Carte di amministrazione del Ducato di Galliera, "Progetti di Bonifica 1909," Titolo 1.

[115] *Bollettino Federale Agrario*, September 15, 1909.

[116] *Ibid.*, April 15, May 15, 1909.

local socialist labor movement, both at the ballot box and the negotiating table, to the weak structure and program of the existing agrarian organizations. In his address to the Second National Agrarian Congress in November 1909, Stagni painted a grim picture of the agrarian federation's operations: "The Federation would appear to be strong if one looks at the number of members and the acreage they represent. However . . . the organization exists in name only. Everyone attends to his own business without regard for the interests of others or more general class interests. There is no spirit of solidarity and resistance so that proprietors must continually give in to the demands of the manual laborers."[117] The Bolognese agrarian leader blamed this situation in part on the loose-knit federal system of organization that prevented unified action on the provincial level and reduced the central leadership to little more than a "consultative body without any real authority." Since the federation required the approval of all the associations before taking action, it invariably intervened "too late . . . when the question has already been resolved in favor of those who have acted with greater speed."[118] The strategy of class cooperation, militants charged, accentuated these organizational difficulties by encouraging compromises and concessions and by obscuring the harsh reality that the agrarians were engaged in what Pelliccioni described as "a class war which . . . will be resolved only through the energetic action of the landowners."[119]

The Bolognese militants' proposed remedies to these problems were clearly inspired by the ideas and achievements of Lino Carrara. As early as November 1908, Sturani had advised the agrarian associations "in those areas afflicted by the reformist program of erosion" to follow the example of Parma "where the agrarian association decided to eliminate once and for all that system which was reducing it to impotence."[120] Upon taking office in 1909, Stagni began to carry out this advice, promoting a series of organizational

[117] CNA, *Atti del II Congresso*, p. 90.

[118] *Bollettino Federale Agrario*, November 15-December 1, 1909.

[119] *Ibid.*, December 1, 1908.

[120] *Ibid.*, November 1, 1908.

changes and innovations, which he claimed would provide agrarian interests with "the weapons necessary for fighting the war" against the leagues and their political allies. Thus, he advocated the introduction of high membership fees and promissory notes to weed out the weak and uncommitted and enhance discipline and unity within the associations.[121] To meet the new challenge posed by the socialist employment offices, he called upon the agrarian associations to set up their own hiring halls. As conceived by Stagni, such halls would enable growers to organize squads of "free laborers," reassert control over employment procedures, and restore wage scales to a level "consistent with the merit and effective output of each worker."[122] Finally, Stagni insisted that the successful implementation of these measures required a new and highly centralized organizational structure that concentrated all authority in the hands of a provincial ruling council and integrated the local associations into a single unit capable of mobilizing "the mass action of the agrarians against the mass action of the laborers."[123]

Much as at the regional level, the militants' program did not go unopposed by moderate propertied elements in the province. Doctrinaire liberals protested that Stagni's proposals constituted a serious menace to the personal freedom of the landowners, since they aspired to "suppress the individual cultivator in order to replace him with the agrarian association." In their view, the associations should not be "an end in themselves or a permanent and crystalized expression of social reality, but simply an instrument for overcoming the critical period of socialism and proletarian organization."[124] At the same time, moderate spokesmen warned that the militants' program would unnecessarily rekindle labor conflicts in a province where they had been gradually losing intensity. Many moderates shared the view of the Imolese agrarian, Ignazio Zampieri, who criticized the militants' propensity for "all-out war" with the leagues over issues that were too insignificant

[121] *Bollettino Federale Agrario*, July 9, 1909.
[122] *Ibid.*, July 15, 1909.
[123] *Ibid.*, September 15, 1911.
[124] *RdC*, August 21, 1910; *Bollettino Federale Agrario*, September 15, 1911.

to warrant such extremism when a satisfactory settlement could be reached through "mutual concessions."[125]

New conquests by the leagues in 1910 appeared, however, to contradict the moderates' optimism and confirm both the militants' analysis and their prescriptions. In the summer of that year, the Bolognese Federterra finally gained recognition of its employment offices in certain areas of the lower plains. The agrarian association of Baricella, for example, accepted a contract requiring rural employers to hire only laborers from the leagues for all field work, while the contract signed by growers in Medicina gave the local leagues virtually complete control over the distribution of jobs.[126] The same year also saw the Federterra extend its influence outside the farms by supporting the unionization of workers engaged in the transportation of agricultural products within the province. Such initiatives alarmed not only the big commercial farmers, but also older landed patricians like Marchese Tanari who characterized them as dangerous steps in the direction of a "new slavery that will kill every liberty and install a new tyranny."[127] In this setting of mounting agrarian alarm and discontent, Stagni and his militant supporters shifted from words to deeds in the fall of 1910.

5. *The Organizational Triumph of the "New Bourgeoisie"*

In September 1910, the Bolognese prefecture began to receive police reports on a series of local meetings in the plains, called by militant agrarians to urge the landowners and leaseholders "to resist in earnest and to . . . leave promissory notes as a guarantee of their allegiance." Significantly, police officials cautioned that the meetings were only the first symptoms of what they saw as a general reawakening of the propertied classes: "The

[125] I. Zampieri, *Note sull'agitazione agraria imolese nel 1910* (Bologna, 1910), p. 6.

[126] MAIC, Ufficio del Lavoro, *Statistica delle organizzazioni padronali*, Vol. I, *Le Agrarie* (Rome, 1912) p. 77.

[127] *RdC*, August 8, 1910.

agrarians, and with them all the capitalists who are menaced by the exorbitant demands of the Federation of Transport Workers, have felt the need to unite their previously dispersed and discordant forces in order to resist more efficaciously."[128] This view found confirmation in November when Raffaele Stagni resigned from the Intermunicipal Federation of Landowners and Leaseholders and launched a new employer organization, the Bolognese Agrarian Association (AAB).

From its inception, the AAB reflected the ideas, aspirations, and interests of the province's militant commercial farmers. As Stagni told "the elite of Bolognese landowners and farmers" at the founding meeting, his association had three main objectives. In collaboration with the Bolognese Agrarian Consortium and the various commodity organizations, it aimed to promote the modernization of agricultural industry in the province "by assisting the farmers in understanding and implementing all those improvements, modifications, and transformations that together allow for the greatest profits."[129] At the same time, the AAB aspired to be an aggressive lobbying agency that "imposed itself on dissident farmers, public opinion, and . . . the authorities." Finally and most importantly, the AAB proposed to eliminate "outside interference in the management of the farms" and to reconquer those prerogatives and privileges that rural employers had relinquished to the leagues during the previous decade in the areas of wages, work schedules, and hiring.[130]

In pursuit of these objectives, Stagni patterned the structure and programs of the new association after those of Lino Carrara's Agrarian Association of Parma. Unlike the old intermunicipal federation, the AAB adopted a highly centralized structure in which all authority rested in a provincial ruling council whose decisions were uniformly implemented by its branch offices on the local level. To strengthen internal discipline and ensure that the association con-

[128] ASB, C6 F2, Police Report to Prefect, September 13, 1910.
[129] *Bollettino Federale Agrario*, November 15-December 1, 1910.
[130] *Ibid.*

stituted "a band of organized agrarians who are animated by a true spirit of solidarity," Stagni required promissory notes and high membership fees.[131] The AAB commanded, in addition, various specialized auxiliary organizations. In the spring of 1911, for instance, it sponsored the Azienda Agricola Industriale, a new company that purchased farm machines operated by nonunion personnel, which it placed at the disposal of the growers. Following the example of Carrara, the AAB also organized permanent squads of strikebreakers as well as a corps of volunteers, composed primarily of young farmers and the sons of men in the association. Spokesmen for the association portrayed the volunteers as idealistic young men who protected the right to work, while they claimed that the "free laborers" were poor unfortunates who had enrolled to find work and escape the league's persecution. The Bolognese Federterra presented a sharply contrasting image: in a petition to Giolitti, it charged that the squads represented "an armed body of . . . 'free criminals' scrapped together from the refuse of the leagues or discovered . . . in the slums of the city."[132]

The first issue of *L'Agraria Bolognese*, the association's organ, clearly indicated the pugnacious policies the AAB intended to pursue: "For far too long we have passively allowed the [socialist] movement to expand at our expense. . . . We are rebelling in defense of our dignity and our right to exist. We will . . . defy the attacks of our adversaries . . . affirming that, if they have brute strength, we have an intelligent strength that derives from the lofty function that agriculture fulfills in modern society. . . . We do not depend on anyone; we are strong men."[133] In accordance with this new hard line, the AAB displayed an unprecedented

[131] *Ibid.* The effectiveness of these innovations did not go unnoticed by prefectoral officials who stressed that "within the Associazione Agraria an iron discipline is enforced and only the central council . . . in Bologna has the authority." See ASB, C6 F2, Subprefect to Ministry of Interior, May 16, 1913.

[132] *L'Agraria Bolognese*, July 9, 1911; Franco Cavazza, *Le agitazioni agrarie*, p. 91. For the Federterra's views on the free laborers, see ASB, C6 F2, petition to Giolitti, September 1911, p. 18.

[133] *L'Agraria Bolognese*, January 15, 1911.

intransigence in its initial dealings with organized labor. When a dispute arose between the growers and the leagues of Budrio and San Pietro in Casale during the summer of 1911, the association refused to negotiate, rejected prefectoral arbitration, and dispatched its squads of strikebreakers and volunteers to complete the harvest. Commenting on the actions of the AAB, police officials charged that it had prevented a peaceful resolution to the dispute, "exacerbated tensions [and] created an even more serious situation."[134] Similarly, the association called a general lockout in September to break a boycott against one of its members in the commune of Baricella.[135]

The local economic situation in 1911 greatly enhanced the appeal of such belligerent rhetoric and policies. In its annual report, the Bolognese Agrarian Consortium concluded that "the year 1911 does not leave very happy memories from the agricultural standpoint." As a result of bad weather, both the hemp and rice harvests had been well below normal, so that the slight rise in prices was not sufficient to compensate growers for their reduced production.[136] With their profits down, agrarian interests became all the more vulnerable to pressures from organized labor. Demands from the leagues, which had been granted with relative ease in the past, began to encounter the bitter hostility of Bolognese landowners and farmers, hostility that the new association was quick to articulate and mobilize. Indeed, as one prefectoral official reported, "many landowners and leaseholders who previously did not belong to an agrarian association now have enrolled, determined to resist to the bitter end."[137] By the end of 1911, the AAB had over twenty branch offices in the province and had replaced the old agrarian

[134] ASB, C6 F2, Police Report to Prefect, July 4, 1911. For additional information on the activities of the AAB in these communes, see *RdC*, July 4, 8, 1911; and the Federterra's petition to Giolitti, pp. 23-24, pp. 35-37.

[135] *RdC*, October 8, 1911.

[136] *Bollettino Mensile del Consorzio Agrario Bolognese*, April 1912, annual report to general assembly, February 18, 1912.

[137] ASB, C6 F2, Subprefect of Imola to Prefect, February 20, 1912.

federation of Bologna as the organizational representative of the major agrarian employers.

Not surprisingly, the younger commercial farmers of the plains constituted the backbone of the AAB. Both the prefecture and Socialist spokesmen insisted that the great majority of the association's most active members as well as the heads of its branch offices came from the ranks of the big leaseholders.[138] Noticeably absent from key positions in the association were older landed notables such as Count Cavazza and Count Piero Bianconcini; aggressive professional organizers like Alberto Donini had taken their place. Described by the prefect as "one of the firmest advocates of the new, dangerously reactionary policies," Donini took over as secretary of the AAB in January 1911 after having previously served in a similar capacity with the Agrarian Association of Carpi. In sharp contrast to his moderate predecessors, Donini displayed little interest in having employers peacefully coexist with the leagues. On the contrary, he championed the ideas of Carrara, advocating an agrarian association that would give, in his words, "a vigorous trumpet blast to reawaken the class consciousness of the bourgeoisie [and] reinvigorate its exhausted fibers with the hot blood of idealism and ardent youth [*giovenezza*]."[139]

The emergence of a militant agrarian association in the province of Bologna mirrored more general trends at the national level in 1911. In the spring of that year, a decisive confrontation between moderates and militants took place when agricultural leaders and political representatives from all over Italy met in Bologna for the Third National Agrarian Congress. As president of the National Agrarian Confederation, Count Francesco Cavazza gave the opening speech to the delegates, in which he reaffirmed the moderates' position that the agrarian associations should avoid direct political

[138] See ASB, C6 F2, Federterra to Giolitti; *Ibid.*, Prefect to Ministry of Interior, no date, 1914; in addition see Maria Adelaide Salvaco, "Riflessi parlamentari delle lotte agrarie emiliane" in R. Zangheri, ed., *Le campagne emiliane nell'epoca moderna* (Milan, 1957), p. 224.

[139] *Bollettino Federale Agrario*, November 15-December 1, 1910; for the prefect's judgment of Donini, see ASB, C6 F2, June 21, 1912.

activity or the narrow defense of class interests, and instead should work with the responsible elements of organized labor for the creation of a mutually beneficial "social and economic equilibrium" in the Italian countryside. Tacitly endorsing Giolitti's labor policies, he chastised the militants for their intemperance and insisted that "by now . . . there should not be anyone who refuses to recognize the right of the laborers to unionize and to seek the improvement of their conditions."[140]

Lino Carrara and the militants, however, more accurately captured the angry and resentful mood of the congress. In his address, the agrarian leader from Parma made a sweeping indictment of the moderates and Giolitti whom he blamed for "the chronic lack of authority . . . that has rendered difficult, if not impossible, any peaceful advance of agricultural industry." Dismissing the old parties of order as anachronisms that had lost all sense of direction "in the fog of vague and abstract aspirations," Carrara repeated his call for commercial farmers to act decisively in defense of their class and sectoral interests by constituting an agrarian party that united "a strong contingent of the productive bourgeoisie."[141] With the enthusiastic support of Raffaele Stagni, Alberto Donini, and agrarian leaders from Ferrara and Ravenna, Carrara's views prevailed. At the end of the congress, the delegates approved overwhelmingly Carrara's resolution affirming "the necessity of intensifying a strong and uniform agrarian political consciousness within the associations [and] requiring all agrarian representatives to follow the directives of the CNA in the conquest of public power."[142] In recognition of this defeat for the moderates, Count Cavazza resigned his office after the congress, while Carrara and other prominent militant leaders moved into influential positions in the Interprovinciale and the national federation.[143]

The congress of 1911 marked not only a major victory for the agrarian militants, but also a crucial turning point in the evolution

[140] *Bollettino Federale Agrario,* May 1, 1911.

[141] *Ibid.*

[142] *Ibid.*

[143] *RdC,* August 4, 1911.

of agricultural interest-group politics in the prewar era. During the course of the year, spokesmen for aggressive commercial farming interests in the Po Valley had largely supplanted the old guard of landed notables at the helm of both the regional and provincial organizations. Under the direction of men like Carrara, Stagni, and Donini, the agrarian associations now dropped all pretense of collaboration and compromise, adopting instead a strategy of direct confrontation with organized labor and governmental authorities. Thus, at a time when economic elites in other European countries were beginning to develop the new institutional arrangements that would create a conservative consensus in the 1920s, northern Italian commercial farmers embarked on a path leading to intensified social conflict and political polarization in the last years before World War I.[144]

[144] See C. Maier, *Recasting Bourgeois Europe*, pp. 9-11.

IV. THE POLITICS OF CONFRONTATION, 1912-1914

If the organizational triumph of agrarian militants in 1911 seemed to foreshadow an era of renewed reaction in the Italian countryside, political developments in Rome the same year suggested a quite different trend. Indeed events in the first half of 1911 appeared to mark a major advance for mass-party democracy and organized labor. In March Giolitti formed his fourth prewar government. Overlooking the foremost political figures of the constitutional right, the Piedmontese statesman turned to the moderate left for the personnel to staff his cabinet. Despite the refusal of the Socialist Bissolati to accept a ministerial post, the composition of the new government reflected a clear shift to the left. Three radicals joined the cabinet while only the Marchese Antonio di San Giuliano, the minister of foreign affairs, represented the right.[1]

The same month Giolitti also launched the most far-reaching and ambitious reform program of his long political career. The program he presented to the Chamber of Deputies contained two central proposals that were certain to win support on the left: universal manhood suffrage and the nationalization of the life

[1] Christopher Seton-Watson, *Italy from Liberalism to Fascism* (London, 1967), p. 281; Giampiero Carocci, *Giolitti e l'età giolittiana* (Turin, 1971), pp. 134-135.

insurance industry. Giolitti subsequently justified his electoral reform, claiming that the "notable progress in the economic, intellectual, and moral conditions of the masses" had earned them "the right to a more direct participation in the country's political life."[2] The suffrage bill the government sent to the Chamber in June 1911 extended the vote to all literate men over twenty-one and to illiterates who had completed their military service or who had reached the age of thirty. Under its provisions, the electorate was to be enlarged from 3.5 million to 8.6 million, with at least 5 million of the new voters being illiterate.[3] Similarly, Giolitti portrayed his state insurance monopoly as a device to protect the mass of his countrymen from "the numerous cases of failure of insurance companies that were unable to carry out their obligations after having taken the premiums." To make the project even more attractive to the left, the prime minister also promised to use the profits from the proposed National Insurance Institute to supplement the existing workers' old age and sickness pensions.[4]

Immediate political calculations as well as ideological commitments underlay the reform package. For Giolitti characteristically balanced his concessions to the left with a third project that was bound to appeal strongly to the right. At the same time that he was leaning in public to the left during the summer of 1911, the prime minister secretly planned for military intervention in Libya. Various factors apparently influenced Giolitti's decision to involve Italy in a new overseas adventure: the desire to stimulate a flagging domestic economy, pressures from the Bank of Rome, the diplomatic situation following the French occupation of Morocco.[5] In any event, after hasty military preparations, Italy declared war on Turkey and occupied Tripoli at the end of September.

Taken together, the reforms and the war were calculated to

[2] Giovanni Giolitti, *Memoirs of My Life* (London, 1923), p. 220.

[3] *Compendio delle statistiche elettorali italiane dal 1848 al 1934* (Rome, 1947), vol. I, pp. 68-69 as cited in C. Seton-Watson, *Italy from Liberalism*, p. 220.

[4] G. Giolitti, *Memoirs*, p. 224; Nino Valeri, *Giovanni Giolitti* (Turin, 1971), p. 206.

[5] See G. Carocci, *Giolitti*, pp. 138-145.

consolidate Giolitti's political position and neutralize his enemies both within the Socialist party and on the right. Although the government officially attributed the war to diplomatic exigencies, contemporary observers also saw it as a means of weakening conservative opposition to electoral reform and the state insurance monopoly; Giolitti himself later conceded that foreign intervention helped create a situation in which "conflicts of interests and opinions at home tended to diminish greatly."[6] In the same fashion, the domestic reforms were to reduce Socialist hostility to the war and thereby ensure the broadest possible base of popular support for the government's imperial adventure.[7]

Initially, Giolitti's gamble appeared to pay off. The war not only divided the parties of the left, who mounted ineffectual resistance to it, but also disarmed his conservative opponents, assuring the smooth passage of his reform bills in 1912.[8] The prime minister's political calculations, however, ultimately depended upon renewed economic prosperity and the continued moderation of the major political forces in the country. Neither of these conditions developed in the years after 1911. The Libyan War alienated most of Giolitti's reformist Socialist friends and strengthened the position of extremist elements who captured control of the PSI in 1912. Under the leadership of men like Benito Mussolini, Costantino Lazzari, and Giacinto Menotti Serrati, the Socialists adopted a program that stressed class struggle, republicanism, and open hostility to all bourgeois governments. As the war dragged on forcing a curtailment of Giolitti's social welfare program, the radicalization of the PSI was accompanied by the resurgence of revolutionary syndicalism.[9]

Extremism on the left had its counterpart in the growing militancy of Italy's productive bourgeoisie. Above all, a severe economic recession in 1913 greatly intensified the intransigence of both industrial and agrarian employers. Much as in 1907-1908,

[6] G. Giolitti, *Memoirs*, pp. 249-250.
[7] G. Carocci, *Giolitti*, pp. 134-135.
[8] C. Seton-Watson, *Italy from Liberalism*, pp. 381-382.
[9] *Ibid.*, pp. 384-387.

an international downturn, characterized by tight money and scant investment capital, hit the already sluggish Italian economy with particular force. Excessive inventories, slackening demand, and falling prices and profits in key industrial sectors led to cutbacks in production that swelled the ranks of the unemployed and eroded the bargaining position of the trade unions.[10] Under the pressure of economic difficulties, agrarian and industrial interests achieved an unprecedented unity of outlook and purpose that enabled them to launch a major counteroffensive against organized labor. Through their employer fronts and lockouts, they attempted to cancel earlier concessions, break the power of the unions, and reassert unchallenged authority over the labor market.[11]

The new arrogance and class spirit of management after 1911 not only inflamed labor strife, but also seriously restricted the mediating role played by the government in the previous decade. Efforts by Giolitti to arbitrate conflicts between labor and capital met with mounting resistance from the employers' associations. Such resistance found expression on the political level in the estrangement of powerful industrial and agrarian groups from the liberal parliamentary oligarchy and in their increasing enthusiasm for the authoritarian, technocratic, and protectionist program of the Italian Nationalist Association. In this context, developments in the province of Bologna provided a microcosm of the more general process of political polarization and class conflict that had begun to destroy the parliamentary moderation and social compromises of the Giolittian system as the prewar era drew to a close.

1. *Agrarian Militancy in the Province of Bologna*

The intransigence displayed by the Bolognese Agrarian Association (AAB) in its dealings with the leagues during the summer of 1911 was only the prelude to a far more systematic campaign against the provincial Federterra the following year. Be-

[10] See Adolfo Pepe, *Lotta di classe e crisi industriale in Italia. La svolta del 1913* (Milan, 1978), pp. 23-32.

[11] *Ibid.*, pp. 8-9.

ginning in the spring of 1912, the AAB intentionally provoked a series of confrontations with the laborers in order to cancel prior agreements and reassert entrepreneurial prerogatives lost during the previous decade. Under the leadership of Stagni and Donini, the association transformed even the most minor disputes into battles of principle involving recognition of the leagues, collective bargaining rights, and control of the labor market.

The issue of socialist employment offices provided the first major test of the AAB's new offensive strategy. In late March the prefect called a meeting of agrarian and labor representatives to establish guidelines for the negotiation of agricultural labor contracts in the province. Before the meeting, the Federterra announced its intention to seek recognition of its employment offices throughout the lower plains. Labor leaders justified the request, arguing that wage agreements would be "utterly useless" if the employers were "then free to hire whomever they pleased."[12] Stagni and Donini rejected the proposal out of hand as an unacceptable infringement on managerial freedom and a threat to efficient production. Indeed, they refused to grant even a "simple preference" to laborers enrolled in the leagues on the grounds that it would constitute "a privilege that is irreconcilable with the principles of liberty that the AAB is pledged to defend." To the argument of the Federterra that its offices had already been recognized in earlier local contracts, the agrarian leaders replied that those agreements no longer had any legitimacy, since they "had been made by the old federation [while] the new association is taking a completely different direction."[13] Significantly, the prefect placed the blame squarely on the shoulders of Stagni and Donini for the failure of the meeting to produce an agreement. "Under the cover of defending principles," he wrote his superiors, the AAB was displaying "an intransigence that reveals the desire, and perhaps the need, for conflict."[14]

The AAB's policies in the ensuing months appeared to confirm

[12] ASB, C6 F2, Prefect to Ministry of Interior, March 12, 1912. For additional information, see also *RdC*, March 19, 1912, which contains the resolution of the general council of the Federterra.

[13] ASB, C6 F2, Prefect to Ministry of Interior, March 24, 1912.

[14] *Ibid.*

the prefect's charges. Even after the leagues in Sala Bolognese dropped their demand for an employment office, the association ordered its branch there to reject any agreement because the approach of the laborers in its view had "the character of an imposition." Similarly, the AAB's branch in the commune of Bologna refused to negotiate with labor representatives, charging that the leagues used methods "harmful to the free life of agriculture."[15] These practices were not simply the result of local circumstances. By June the prefect warned of mounting labor unrest throughout the plains which he attributed to the "resolutely reactionary posture of the agrarian association." The chief obstacles to social peace in the countryside now came from the employers who, in his words, were "provoking conflicts by any means to prevent the customarily friendly negotiations between capital and labor which they view as signs of weakness and compromise that, however small, constitute limitations on the absolute right of the landowner to impose work conditions and wages."[16]

A number of such incidents during the spring and summer of 1912 set the stage for a more protracted and bitter confrontation between the AAB and the Federterra at the beginning of September. After agrarian leaders in the commune of Granarolo refused to consider a request for preferential hiring, the leagues began to boycott some of the bigger local growers. With the full support of the provincial leadership, the head of the AAB's branch in Granarolo, Luigi Calori, imported squads of strikebreakers and farm machines from the Azienda Agricola Industriale to counteract the boycotts. At the same time, Calori informed prefectoral officials that any negotiations with the leagues were impossible as long as "the hostility and pressure against the liberty of the employers" persisted.[17] Far from seeking a peaceful resolution, the AAB broad-

[15] ASB, C6 F2, Police Reports to Prefect, March 27, May 13, 1912. For other statements by agrarian leaders on the issue of the employment offices, see *L'Agraria Bolognese*, June 22, 1912 and *RdC*, September 7, 1912.

[16] ASB, C6 F2, Prefect to Ministry of Interior, June 21, 1912.

[17] ASB, C6 F2, letter, Luigi Calori to Prefect, September 7, 1912. For the policies of the AAB, see "La questione di Granarolo" leaflet of the AAB, October 5, 1912;

ened the scope of the conflict in mid-November by calling a lockout on all the farms in Granarolo. While the boycotts continued through the winter of 1912-1913, the tenacious refusal of the agrarians to negotiate and the economic pressures created by their lockout gradually weakened the resistance of the laborers. Finally in March 1913, the leagues dropped their initial demands and voted to end the boycotts against members of the AAB.[18] Victory in Granarolo led agrarian militants to employ their strategy elsewhere. Ignoring all calls to come to the bargaining table, the AAB used its squads of "free laborers" and harvesting equipment to break strikes in five other areas of the plains during the spring and summer of 1913.[19]

A similar intransigence also informed the AAB's policies toward the socialist sharecropper unions as the Zerbini-Pondrelli affair clearly illustrates. In the fall of 1911, a large landowner from Molinella, Giacomo Zerbini, refused to implement reforms stipulated in the *mezzadria* contract of the previous year and began legal proceedings to evict one of his sharecroppers, Germano Pondrelli. Since Pondrelli was the secretary of the local peasant union, Giuseppe Massarenti and other labor leaders interpreted the proposed eviction as a union-busting measure and immediately ordered a total boycott of Zerbini's estate.[20] By October, the AAB had entered the fray, dispatching its squads of volunteers to work

---

ASB, C6 F2, Subprefect to Prefect, September 10, 1912 and Police Chief to Prefect, September 2, 1912.

[18] ASB, C6 F2, Police Chief to Prefect, March 2, 1913. On the lockout, see ASB, C6 F2, Police Chief to Prefect, November 18, 1912.

[19] ASB, C6 F2, Police Report to Prefect, January 17, 1913; Police Chief to Prefect, March 4, 1913; *RdC*, June 15, July 9, and August 17, 1913. The areas involved were Castel San Pietro, Budrio, Argelato, Altedo, and Minerbio

[20] ASB, C6 F2, Police Report to Prefect, August 22, 1911. For an account of Zerbini's rather unsavory background, see *ibid.*, Police Report to Prefect, April 23, 1912. In the 1880s, Zerbini and a friend formed a contracting company which brought him a small fortune in government-financed public works projects. But in 1892 the faulty construction of one of their jobs led to the arrest of the two men on charges of fraud. Zerbini escaped prosecution only after his partner committed suicide and had been generously burdened with full responsibility for the affair.

on Zerbini's property. Not surprisingly, *L'Agraria Bolognese* portrayed the dispute in terms of general principles that could not be compromised under any circumstances. As a result, Stagni and Donini demanded unqualified acceptance of Zerbini's position and sabotaged every initiative by the police, prefect, and moderate landowners in the winter of 1911-12 to arrange a negotiated settlement.[21] Even after Zerbini and his sharecroppers indicated a willingness to accept a compromise, the AAB continued to obstruct negotiations and prolong the dispute. During meetings called by the prefect in the summer of 1912, the association's representative refused to participate in any settlement and threatened to seize Zerbini's promissory note if he capitulated. When the landowner did sign a contract with the Molinellese leagues in June, the AAB expelled him on charges of indiscipline.[22]

These aggressive and intransigent policies of the AAB reflected a general upsurge in agrarian militancy throughout Emilia in the last years before the war. As an investigation by the Ministry of Agriculture, Industry, and Commerce in 1912 concluded, most of the agrarian organizations in the region had embraced the program and methods of the Bologna and Parma associations in order to challenge more effectively the leagues.[23] Much as in Bologna, these more disciplined and combative organizations achieved some notable successes. In Ferrara, for example, the provincial agrarian association enrolled in the Strike Insurance Fund, organized squads

[21] For the position of the AAB in the dispute, see "La Vertenza Zerbini" leaflet in ASB, C6 F2, 1912. On the use of strikebreakers and agrarian volunteers, see *RdC*, November 15, 1911 and ASB, C6 F2, Police Report to Prefect, November 15, 1911. Accounts of the AAB's obstructionist tactics can be found in ASB, C6 F2, Police Chief to Prefect, November 25, 1911; *ibid.*, Massarenti's telegram to *Avanti!*, January 1, 1912; *RdC*, November 11 and 19, 1911. For a more detailed account of the dispute, see Francesco Saverio Solari, "Lotte agrarie a Molinella: 1905-1915" *Storia Contemporanea*, IX, no. 5-6 (December 1978), pp. 859-861.

[22] ASB, C6 F2, Prefect to Ministry of Interior, June 6 and 8, 1912; Franco Cavazza, *Le agitazioni agrarie in Provincia di Bologna dal 1910 al 1920* (Bologna, 1940), p. 198.

[23] MAIC, *Le organizzazioni padronali: le agrarie* (Rome, 1912), vol. I, pp. 16-17.

of nonunion laborers and volunteers, and used a lockout to break a general strike called by the revolutionary syndicalists in 1913.[24]

2. *The Agrarian-Industrial Offensive Against Organized Labor*

In the last five years before the war, resistance to organized labor also provided the basis for unprecedented collaboration between agrarian and industrial groups. Faced with sluggish markets and falling profits, both commercial farmers and manufacturers began to discover a common interest in reducing labor costs and in opposing the political and social demands of the socialist trade unions.[25] As early as 1909, the sugar beet growers syndicates and the Sugar Refiners' Union had demonstrated the potential benefits of systematic collaboration. Despite recurring conflicts over marketing arrangements, growers and refiners found ample opportunity for cooperation in resisting organized labor. The pressing need for collaboration against the unions became evident in the winter of 1908-1909 when agricultural laborers and refinery workers in Bologna coordinated a series of strikes and boycotts on the beet farms and in the refineries. With their reciprocal interests damaged by a common enemy, agrarian and industrial groups forgot their recent differences and began to prepare a unified strategy of defense. Their preparation culminated in a joint agreement in the spring of 1909, which agrarian leaders characterized as "the first strand of what will become a tighter network of economic relations between agricultural and industrial producers."[26] The agrarian federation of Bologna, the growers syndicate, and the refiners union committed themselves to work together for a "victorious resist-

[24] See Alessandro Roveri, *Dal sindacalismo rivoluzionario al fascismo. Capitalismo agrario e socialismo nel Ferrara, 1870–1920* (Florence, 1972), pp. 271-280.

[25] See Anthony Cardoza, "Agrarians and Industrialists: The Evolution of an Alliance in the Po Delta, 1896-1914" in John Davis, ed., *Gramsci and Italy's Passive Revolution* (London, 1979), pp. 191-194.

[26] *Bollettino Federale Agrario*, March 15, 1909.

ance'' against the unions and to create a mutual insurance fund against strike damages. The pooling of resources and the coordination of antistrike initiatives proved highly effective; by the fall of 1909 the coalition had broken the strikes and boycotts. More importantly, the alliance in Bologna set an example for other provinces where agrarian and industrial interests were beset by labor unrest.[27]

The leadership of the two major interest-group organizations, the Interprovinciale and the Industrial League of Turin, were also early advocates of intersectoral collaboration to combat labor agitation and advance common political and economic policies in Rome. Gino Olivetti and Luigi Bonnefon Craponne of the industrial league were well aware of the benefits that had resulted from agrarian-industrial cooperation in Germany, and they saw the natural convergence of interests with agrarian groups of the Po Valley, who also faced a powerful and aggressive labor movement.[28] For its part, less than a year after its founding, the Interprovinciale called for the unification of ''the entire employer class in the various branches of economic activity'' into a single bloc in order to protect their general interests.[29]

With the founding of the Italian Industrial Confederaion (CII) and the National Agrarian Confederation (CNA) in 1910, active cooperation began to develop, both in Rome and on the provincial level. During the summer of that year, the CII came to the aid of the Interprovinciale in a protracted dispute with the leagues of Ravenna over ownership and control of the threshing machines. In a letter of protest to the Italian Senate, the secretary of the industrial confederation strongly defended the stand of the agrarian employers and denounced the league demands as threats to the entire industrial class, since their general implementation would lead to the ''total subversion of the established order in our com-

[27] *Ibid.*, September 1, 1909.

[28] Guido Baglioni, *L'ideologia della borghesia industriale nell' Italia liberale* (Turin, 1974), pp. 542-544.

[29] *Bollettino Federale Agrario*, September 15, 1908.

panies."[30] Such support did not go unnoticed by agrarian spokesmen. After its victory in the dispute, the official organ of the Interprovinciale rejoiced that in the agrarians' "great battle in defense of industrial liberty" they could now count on the "strong phalanx of the Italian industrial bourgeoisie."[31]

The same year the two employer organizations began to intervene jointly in the corridors of power in Rome. At first, agrarian and industrial representatives focused their lobbying activity on the reform of the High Council of Labor. Founded in 1902, the council provided a seat for the discussion of social and labor legislation; its opinions on important economic questions were influential and it reflected the impulse for social reforms. Lobbyists of the two confederations, claiming to express "the complete agreement between the employer classes, industrial and agrarian," promoted a sweeping restructuring of the council in 1910 that would ensure an effective role for the "real capitalist Italy" and curtail the excessive influence of the socialist labor organizations.[32] They demanded that the confederations, rather than the minister of agriculture, industry, and commerce, select the employer representatives on the council. These representatives, being "particularly competent and free from any parliamentary concerns," could prepare the legislation that best responded to the "real needs of the population." To combat the influence of the socialists, the lobbyists insisted on the inclusion of representatives from the Catholic, republican, and liberal unions on the council. The advantages to agrarians and industrialists were evident. Not only did these changes promise to give them a direct role in the formulation of social policy, but they would also reinforce divisions within the trade union movement.[33] After 1910 cooperation developed within the Chamber of Deputies as well. Parliamentary supporters of the

[30] CII, "La questione delle macchine" cited in Silvio Fronzoni, "Dalle consociazioni agrarie" (Tesi di Laurea, University of Bologna, 1973), pp. 244-245.

[31] *Bollettino Federale Agrario*, April 1, 1911.

[32] CII and CNA, *Per la riforma del Consiglio Superiore del Lavoro* (Turin, 1910), pp. 1-2.

[33] *Ibid.*, pp. 2-15; G. Baglioni, *Borghesia industriale*, pp. 540-541.

two confederations—organized respectively in the Agrarian Central Committee and the Industrial Parliamentary Group—collaborated closely to resolve potential conflicts of interest and to build a common front on issues of social legislation, labor policies, trade agreements, and tariffs.[34]

Outside of Rome, the national confederations pursued a number of joint initiatives. In April 1911, Olivetti of the CII participated in the third National Agrarian Congress in Bologna to demonstrate, in his words, "the solidarity that unites all those who, in different areas of activity, contribute to the production and development of national wealth at a time when every principle of liberty and justice is threatened with subversion."[35] In the fall of the same year, the CII and the CNA sponsored the first International Congress of Industrial and Agricultural Organizations in Turin. Although the congress did not approve Olivetti's proposal for an "Employer International," it did pave the way for more systematic collaboration the next year, when the two confederations cofounded a monthly journal, *L'Italia Industriale ed Agraria,* to elaborate and promote a unified policy on issues of mutual concern.[36]

Agrarian-industrial cooperation on the provincial level in 1912 and 1913 assumed the form of a united employer front against the unions, both syndicalist and reformist socialist. In the province of Bologna, such cooperation found its clearest expression in the alliance between the AAB and the Federation of Building Contractors (Edile). Founded in early 1912, the Edile, under the aggressive leadership of Ettore Lambertini, quickly adopted the strategy and methods of the AAB, leading the prefect to write later that year how both organizations were taking the same position of "tenacious and intransigent" resistance to the unions in order to "destroy . . . the current labor agreements."[37] Already in the spring

[34] CNA, *L'organizzazione agraria in Italia. Sviluppo, ordinamento, azione* (Bologna, 1911), pp. 82-83; G. Baglioni, *Borghesia industriale,* p. 544; Valerio Castronovo, *Storia d'Italia,* Vol. I, Bk. I (Turin, 1975), p. 199.

[35] *Bollettino Federale Agrario,* April 1, 1911.

[36] See sources cited in note 34.

[37] ASB, C6 F2, "Movimento economico, politico, e sociale della provincia," Prefect to Ministry of Interior, September 22, 1912.

and summer of 1912, the organized agrarians actively supported the Edile in a series of struggles with the construction unions. In mid-April for instance, when the contractors decided to lock out striking bricklayers in various communes, the AAB instructed its members "not to employ bricklayers who refuse to work for the federated contractors." Stagni proclaimed that this support was "inspired by the principle that agricultural and industrial property owners have common aims and defense needs."[38]

Early the following year, the Edile refused to renew its existing contract with the construction unions and demanded recognition of the contractors' right to fire workers without notice and hire nonunion labor.[39] When the bricklayers' and transport workers' unions rejected these demands and ordered a boycott of nonunion workers, the two employer organizations joined forces. Beginning in mid-February, the secretaries of the Edile and the AAB accompanied squads of armed "volunteers for the freedom of labor" who brought in strikebreakers and protected the boycotted laborers. Within a week the boycott collapsed and the unions voted to return to work.[40] While this incident marked only the opening phase in a long struggle that continued until the late summer, it revealed the determination and solidarity of the employers. Significantly, the final agreement signed in August constituted a victory for the Edile.[41]

Developments in Bologna exemplified the general counteroffensive launched by agrarian and industrial employers throughout the Po Valley in 1913. In sharp contrast to the ideologically and factionally divided trade unions, the employers' associations displayed an exceptional unity and militancy. As the economist Riccardo Bachi reported, "employer unionism" had shown renewed vitality, engaging in "great struggles . . . in order to triumph on issues of principle, without defections, with a method and spirit analogous

[38] *RdC*, April 20, 1912. For an account of the lockout, see ASB, C6 F2, Mayor of Imola to Prefect, April 15, 1912.

[39] A. Pepe, *Lotta di classe*, pp. 110-111.

[40] *RdC*, February 3, 11, and 14, 1913.

[41] A. Pepe, *Lotta di classe*, pp. 112-114.

to those of the labor organizations."[42] Imposing a rigid discipline on individual employers and utilizing lockouts and strikebreakers, the associations handed organized labor a string of defeats from Turin to Reggio Emilia. As a result, employers were able to transfer many of the burdens of the recession on to the unions and workers.[43] More importantly, the counteroffensive demonstrated that powerful industrial groups now shared the militant agrarians' hostility to even moderate reformist unions as well as their determination to restrict drastically the role of organized labor in social and economic bargaining.

3. *The Agrarian-Industrial Bloc and Giolittian Liberalism*

The new militancy of agrarian and industrial associations in their dealings with organized labor profoundly altered relations between the northern economic elites and Giolitti. From the outset, the Piedmontese statesman's attempt to broaden support for the liberal state by assimilating the working class into Italian politics had depended upon the willingness of employers to bargain in good faith with the unions and to make at least some concessions to the workers. Although for the most part industrialists had gone along with Giolitti's program during the prosperous first years of the century, recurrent recessions and relative stagnation after 1908 led gradually to a change in their attitudes. Faced with stiffer foreign competition and reduced profits, entrepreneurs became increasingly hostile to the prime minister's social policies, his tolerance of strikes, and his treatment of labor's demands as legitimate interest-group grievances.

Even in the best of times, agrarian support for Giolitti had been only lukewarm. With the rise to prominence of young militant leaders like Lino Carrara, this fragile support gave way to a new

[42] Riccardo Bachi, *L'Italia economica nell'anno 1913* (Turin, 1913), pp. 249-250.

[43] *Ibid.*, p. 178; Giampero Carocci, *Storia d'Italia dall'Unità ad oggi* (Milan, 1975), pp. 206-207.

and more strident opposition, intensified by the apparent unresponsiveness of the government to agrarian lobbying on issues of municipal tax reform, selection of farm machines, and agricultural strikes.[44] By the second decade of the century, the government's policies in labor-management disputes began to draw similar criticisms from industrial associations. Much like their agrarian colleagues, industrial spokesmen charged that Giolitti's policies unjustly favored organized labor at the expense of the productive needs and rights of entrepreneurs. Under his tutelage, they claimed, the right to strike had become an obligation: "Almost daily we must report acts of violence by strikers . . . while the authorities look on impassively"—a situation which they saw as a menace to individual freedom and the nation's productive base.[45] Agrarian and industrial interest groups were equally united in their opposition to Giolitti's social programs that, in their view, imposed "major sacrifices without corresponding benefits because their underlying principles ignore the most fundamental realities."[46]

In 1911 the employer associations' criticisms of Giolitti extended to his proposals for universal suffrage and a state insurance monopoly. Although the local liberal clubs officially supported electoral reform, Giuseppe Bacchelli, the deputy closest to the AAB and a former secretary of the Strike Insurance Fund, publicly attacked it, charging that the "triumph of the illiterates did not seem to him the triumph of progress and civilization."[47] In the case of the insurance monopoly, economic as well as political considerations dictated the opposition of leading commercial farming interests, since prominent agrarian deputies like Marchese Giuseppe

[44] On the mounting opposition of the agrarians, see Maria Malatesta, *Il Resto del Carlino* (Turin, 1978), pp. 255-259.

[45] CII, *Conflitti del laboro e legisluzione sociale*, p. 7 cited in G. Baglioni, *Borghesia industriale*, p. 537.

[46] See the joint communiqué issued by the two confederations at the first International Congress of Industrial and Agricultural Organizations, reprinted in *Bollettino Federale Agrario*, September 15, 1911.

[47] *RdC*, October 30, 1911. When the suffrage bill came to a vote in the Chamber of Deputies, Bacchelli was one of the five deputies who opposed it; see *Ibid*, May 12, 1912.

Tanari, Enrico Pini, and Pietro Niccolini of Ferrara also sat on the boards of a number of big life insurance companies.[48] The opposition campaign in Bologna was led by Giuseppe Franchi, a member of the AAB's ruling council and a local representative of four major insurance companies. In various meetings held in the winter of 1911-12, Franchi stressed the technical deficiencies of the monopoly plan, but usually concluded on a political note by declaring that the government had not demonstrated the plan's urgency at a time when "Italy needs the unanimous support of all the vital forces of the Nation to bring its African enterprise to a successful conclusion."[49]

The attempt to portray the insurance monopoly as a hindrance to the war effort is especially significant, for it reflected the way in which agrarian spokesmen sought to use military priorities and inflamed nationalism to sabotage Giolitti's domestic political strategy. While the prime minister hoped to minimize leftist opposition to military intervention, the employer associations exploited the initial public enthusiasm for the war in order to mobilize a domestic crusade against the Socialist party and its unions. Not surprisingly, the agrarian press dwelled on the subversive threat that the Socialists ostensibly posed to the nation at arms.[50] The identification of patriotism with antisocialism was also a central theme of the prowar rallies organized by the employer associations. Before one

[48] On the role of agrarian notables in the insurance industry, see ACS, B17, F39, July 7, 1911, "Informazioni relative al disegno di legge per il monopolio delle assicurazioni sulla vita" reprinted in Claudio Pavone, ed., *Quarant'anni di politica italiana* (Milan, 1962), Vol. III, pp. 47-48.

[49] Giuseppe Franchi, "Il monopolio di Stato delle assicurazioni sulla vita," *Annali della Società Agraria Provinciale di Bologna*, Vol. LII, February 11, 1912, p. 24. For his part, Giolitti later wrote that "these conservative organs fought the insurance monopoly not so much for itself as to be able to strike in this manner at the government which had placed in the forefront of its program the question of electoral reform with a suffrage that was almost universal." See G. Giolitti, *Memoirs*, p. 230.

[50] In this vein, Mario Missiroli wrote that since "Italian socialism is against the war in Tripoli, against the undertaking which has unified the national consciousness," it was therefore "against the patria." See *RdC*, February 21, 1912. For the views of the AAB on the war, see *L'Agraria Bolognese*, October 21, 1911.

such "patriotic demonstration" in Bologna, the AAB distributed leaflets throughout the province, in which it urged all loyal citizens to participate in a "solemn display of *Italianità*" as a protest against "those who want to offend and degrade our legitimate national pride in this magnificent show of heroism which is enhancing the prestige of our Italy in the eyes of the entire civilized world."[51] In addition, agrarian spokesmen used Italy's enlarged imperial responsibilities to pressure the government into curtailing its social programs at home. As *Il Resto del Carlino* expressed it, the financial burdens of the new colony required the government to stop subsidizing "public works of no utility, monopolistic cooperatives, [and] the sordid indolence of a reformist proletariat which in the past has tasted the . . . fruits of ministerialism."[52]

With the employers' offensive against organized labor in 1912 and 1913, criticism of specific policies escalated into a direct confrontation with government authorities, both in the countryside and in industrial centers. Relations between the prefecture and commercial farming interests in the province of Bologna steadily deteriorated after the founding of the AAB. The potential for conflict was already evident in one of the first issues of *L'Agraria Bolognese*, where Stagni and Donini proclaimed their determination to challenge "whoever attacks our rights, whether they are socialists, municipal governments, or the *State*."[53] Tensions between the AAB and local authorities finally erupted into an open clash in the summer of 1912 when Donini accused the prefect Dallari of intentionally ignoring the criminal character of the leagues' activities in order not "to compromise a political program that for many years has been characterized by concessions and surrenders."[54] Angered by these charges, Dallari informed Giolitti that he could no longer maintain "cordial relations" with agrarian leaders who "offend representatives of the government."[55] Evidently,

[51] *RdC*, March 29, 1912.
[52] *Ibid.*, February 21, 1912.
[53] *L'Agraria Bolognese*, February 1, 1911.
[54] See "La vertenza Zerbini," AAB leaflet, in ASB, C6 F2, 1912.
[55] ASB, C6 F2, Prefect to Ministry of Interior, June 21, 1912.

he also made this point clear to the AAB, for the following day Donini stormed out of a meeting in the prefecture, declaring: "I will not allow myself to be imposed upon by prefects or even by Giolitti." In his report of the incident, Dallari emphasized Donini's deliberately offensive attitude, which he interpreted as part of a strategy "to provoke a rupture that the Bolognese Agrarian Association considers useful to its policy of reaction and hostility to the directives of the government."[56]

By the summer of 1913, this strategy of confrontation had spread to important industrial centers of the north. The most serious clash occurred in Turin at the end of May after militant elements gained control of the industrial league and called a lockout in all steel and automobile plants to break union resistance to a general wage revision. Alarmed by the industrialists' intransigence, Giolitti took stern measures to curtail what he considered their "excesses." Under orders from Rome, the prefect of Turin forced the president of the industrial league to resign his office and threatened to deny police protection to the factories and to withhold government contracts from firms involved in the lockout. While Giolitti succeeded in ending the lockout, he did so at the price of further alienating an embittered and hostile industrial lobby.[57]

The increasingly antagonistic relations between the prime minister and the employer associations were symptomatic of more than personality conflicts or disagreements on specific policies. Indeed, they reflected the deeper dissatisfaction of powerful sectors of agriculture and industry with the entire liberal political class and the Italian parliamentary system as a whole. In their propaganda, the associations stressed the enormous gulf between the "legal" country and the productive classes, and strongly criticized

[56] ASB, C6 F2, Prefect to Ministry of Interior, June 23, 1912.

[57] See Mario Abrate, *La lotta sindacale nella industrializzazione in Italia, 1906-1926* (Turin, 1966), p. 101; G. Baglioni, *Borghesia industriale*, p. 547; Valerio Castronovo, *Giovanni Agnelli* (Turin, 1971), pp. 41-46. For a sample of the industrialists' views on Giolitti, see Bonnefon Craponne's article in *L'Italia Industriale ed Agraria*, III, no. 2 (1913).

the methods of political recruitment of the old parties of order. The Industrial League of Turin, for instance, denounced in 1911 the "wide and deep separation between the people who produce and pay, and the fraction that governs, drawn for the most part from among the provincial lawyers, professors, and state functionaries."[58] Both agrarian and industrial spokesmen frequently lamented that production was being sacrificed because of the political personnel's economic incompetence and because of the excessive influence of parliamentary factions. The Agrarian Central Committee and the Industrial Parliamentary Group were designed precisely to bypass the old political groupings and to insert "the productive elements of the nation" into the political arena.[59]

Discontent was most evident in their relentless attacks on parliamentary transformism and ministerial coalitions, based on personal ambitions and shallow electoral concerns. Agrarian spokesmen, in particular, blamed the practices of transformist rule, with its constantly shifting coalitions and its lack of ideological consistency, for what they perceived as the dangerous weakness and indecisiveness of government officials at the provincial level. As the leaders of the AAB affirmed in 1911:

> The prefects and all the authorities, as organs of transmission between the government and the citizens, suffer the tragic consequences of these continual parliamentary acrobatics. . . . This is reflected in their uncertain and contradictory behavior which encourages the masses to have contempt for our basic institutions and to ignore the rights of others. . . . Obsessed by the fear of contradicting the current political trends, the authorities do not evaluate situations . . . according to the standards of the general welfare, but instead adapt themselves to the dictates of immediate opportunism.[60]

[58] *Bollettino della Lega industriale di Torino*, v, June 6, 1911 cited in G. Baglioni, *Borghesia industriale*, p. 536n.

[59] See sources in note 34.

[60] *L'Agraria Bolognese*, August 11, 1912.

Significantly, Stagni and Donini openly looked to an antidemocratic solution of these problems, advocating a strong government that would defend bourgeois power and influence, and impose its will "without concern for its parliamentary fortunes."[61]

While much of this rhetoric had been the stock and trade of militant agrarian propaganda since 1908, it was coupled in the last years before the war with a new willingness to explore political alternatives to the liberal parliamentary oligarchy. Above all, the growing antiparliamentarianism of industrial and agrarian interests drew them toward the authoritarian proposals for economic development and labor discipline of the Italian Nationalist Association.[62] A clear affinity of ideas and language had already existed between young agrarian leaders like Lino Carrara and the early nationalist intellectuals, Giuseppe Prezzolini and Giovanni Papini. Despite important differences, both shared a strong antipathy to the socialist movement, Giolittian reformism, and the old liberal leadership with its "platitudes of '48 and '59." Moreover, both rejected the politics of compromise and concessions, favoring instead a "bourgeois resurgence" spearheaded by a dynamic and combative new economic elite.[63] After the recession of 1908, there was also a convergence of ideas between entrepreneurial groups and leading Nationalist economists such as Enrico Barone. With his proposals for producers' syndicates to supplant cut-throat competition, rationalize production, and resist labor demands, Barone found a highly receptive audience among prominent industrial and

[61] *Ibid.*

[62] For information on Italian nationalism and the Nationalist Association in particular, see Franco Gaeta, *Nazionalismo italiano* (Naples, 1965), and Alexander De Grand, *The Italian Nationalist Association and the Rise of Fascism in Italy* (Lincoln, Nebr., 1978).

[63] See Giovanni Papini, "A Nationalist Programme," in A. Lyttelton, ed., *Italian Fascisms from Pareto to Gentile* (New York, 1975), p. 100. For the similarity of ideas between early Nationalist intellectuals and the agrarian militants see *ibid.*; F. Gaeta, *Nazionalismo italiano*, p. 77, p. 184n.; Nicola Tranfaglia, *Dallo stato liberale al regime fascista* (Milan, 1973), pp. 100-101; the speeches of Lino Carrara in CNA, *Atti del II Congresso Agrario, Bologna* (Bologna, 1911), and in *RdC*, April 25, 1909 and June 7, 1910.

agrarian groups who were actively forming cartels, marketing syndicates, lobbying groups, and leagues of resistance.[64]

Il Resto del Carlino represented the first important institutional link between the nationalists and commercial farming interests of the Po Valley. Even prior to the official founding of the association, the agrarian-owned daily was providing the nationalists with an influential forum to espouse their ideas. Beginning in the summer of 1910, the paper opened its pages to Enrico Corradini and other leading figures of the nascent movement.[65] During the same period, Mario Missiroli, the foremost agrarian publicist and cultural editor of the Bolognese daily, published a series of articles in which he sought to adapt key nationalist ideas to the concrete political and economic goals of the organized farmers. Along the same lines, Missiroli greeted the first Nationalist Congress in December 1910 with obvious approval, seeing in it the potential for a strong new movement of those forces "who place the interests of an entire industry before the narrow and contingent interests of the leagues, the success of an entire harvest before the victory of a strike."[66]

Enthusiasm for the Nationalist Association became steadily more evident in employer circles after 1912. When Nationalist leaders came to speak in Bologna, for instance, the agrarian press gave special attention to their speeches and extolled the virtues of their organization.[67] In the spring of 1914, the CNA strongly endorsed the Nationalists' economic program which, it asserted, "truly seems a copy of the program for which . . . the Italian agrarian associations have fought for many years."[68] The same year Gino Olivetti of the Italian Confederation of Industry envisioned an alliance between the Nationalists and the "producer classes" for the expansion

[64] On Barone, see Richard Webster, *Industrial Imperialism in Italy, 1908-1915* (Berkeley, 1975), p. 373.

[65] See for instance, E. Corradini, "Il nazionalismo," *RdC*, July 9, 1910 and "La politica della vittoria," *ibid.*, August 3, 1910.

[66] M. Missiroli, "Il congresso nazionalista," *RdC*, December 2, 1910. For a more detailed evaluation of Missiroli's role, see M. Malatesta, *Il Resto del Carlino*, pp. 264-272.

[67] See for instance, *RdC*, March 13, 1913.

[68] *L'Italia Industriale ed Agraria*, April-May 1914.

of Italian markets abroad and the containment of the socialist movement, while the major industrial associations began a strident campaign for economic nationalism or the so-called "national product."[69]

Despite differences on certain policies, influential figures from the agrarian and industrial world became directly involved in the Nationalist Association after its founding. In Bologna two officials of the AAB and a couple of large landowners were part of the committee that launched the provincial Nationalist Group in 1911; in the following years, the ruling council of the AAB frequently participated in the meetings of the group.[70] In 1913 Dante Ferraris, president of the Industrial League of Turin and vice-president of FIAT, joined with some of the most important sugar refiners and arms manufacturers to finance the Nationalist daily, *L'Idea Nazionale.* Ferraris also became an active member of the Nationalist Group of Turin and by the summer of 1914 served as the chief interlocutor between the Nationalists and major industrial consortia.[71]

This convergence of northern economic interest groups with the Nationalist Association signaled a crucial shift in political behavior and objectives on the part of the most aggressive sectors of the agrarian-industrial bloc. As Valerio Castronovo has noted, on the eve of the First World War, the Nationalist Association was rapidly emerging as the new "party of opinion" of the productive bourgeoisie, with an ideology and program that clearly marked it as a forerunner of the Fascist totalitarian state of the 1920s and 1930s.[72]

[69] Gino Olivetti, "I nazionalisti e la borghesia lavoratrice" in *Ibid;* M. Abrate, *La lotta sindacale*, p. 55.

[70] See *RdC*, May 29, 1911 for the founding of the Bolognese Nationalist Group. Among the founders were Augusto Pellicioni and Sebastiano Sani, officials of the AAB, as well as the landowners Marchese Camillo Malvezzi Campeggi and Count Guido Alessandretti. On the participation of the AAB's ruling council in the group's activities, see *ibid.*, December 18, 1911.

[71] See Valerio Castronovo, *La stampa italiana dall'Unità al fascismo* (Bari, 1973), pp. 210-211 and *Giovanni Agnelli*, pp. 54-55.

[72] V. Castronovo, "Il potere economico e fascismo," Guido Quazza, ed., *Fascismo e società italiana* (Turin, 1973), pp. 53-55.

4. The Rewards of Confrontation: Rebellion and Reaction in 1914

The last years before the war saw not only a new militancy on the part of the economic elites, but also a growing radicalization of the labor movement. The combination of economic recession and the employers' offensive in 1912-1913 had a devastating impact on the employment, wage, and living conditions of Italian workers, both in the countryside and in the cities. As the economist Riccardo Bachi noted, "The general situation of the labor market has noticeably worsened in 1913, even in relation to the recent depressed years." Despite the most massive emigration flow in Italian history that year, the government still paid out four times as much in unemployment benefits as it had in 1909. Particularly hard hit were workers in the building, sugar, cotton, and hemp industries where work hours were steadily reduced and many factories temporarily closed.[73] As a result of problems in these sectors and government cutbacks in public works projects, the perennial phenomenon of agricultural unemployment reached alarming new heights, above all in Emilia and Romagna. In January 1914, the Federterra reported that more than half the day laborers in the provinces of Ferrara, Bologna, Ravenna, and Forlì were without work.[74] Even those workers who found employment suffered a decline in their standard of living. While wages either remained stationary or actually fell, food prices and rents continued an upward spiral that had begun in 1911, leading to a sharp drop in the consumption of wheat, oils, and sugar.[75]

Massive unemployment and the refusal of employers to accept collective bargaining enhanced the position of extremist elements within the labor movement. In the face of an intransigent employers front, the moderate reformist unions were unable to protect

[73] R. Bachi, *L'Italia economica nel 1913*, p. 177; Maurice Neufeld, *Italy: School for Awakening Countries* (Ithaca, 1961), p. 354; A. Pepe, *Lotta di classe*, pp. 33-36.

[74] R. Bachi, *Italia economica nel 1913*, p. 178.

[75] A. Pepe, *Lotta di classe*, p. 38.

their rank and file or defend the gains of previous years. Frustration with the apparent inefficacy of the reformists' gradual and legalistic tactics made workers in many areas more receptive to the appeals and methods of revolutionary syndicalism, which underwent a strong revival in 1913. Under the leadership of syndicalist firebrands like Errico Malatesta and Filippo Corridoni, a record number of nearly half a million workers took part in over nine hundred strikes that year. Apart from their sheer numbers, an exceptional bitterness and violence distinguished the strikes, especially in Milan and the Ferrarese countryside.[76]

While the strikes of 1913 ended for the most part in total defeat for the workers, they did succeed in sharpening divisions within the labor movement and in inflaming popular discontent. At the same time that the General Confederation of Labor (CGL) and reformist Socialists deplored the syndicalists' general strikes, the so-called revolutionary wing of the PSI enthusiastically supported them as part of "the psychological preparation of the proletariat for the use of violence."[77] The divisive struggle between the CGL and the Italian Syndical Union had serious repercussions on the provincial level. Even in the reformist citadel of Bologna, ideological and factional strife led to the creation of two opposing chambers of labor; the one syndicalist, representing mostly urban industrial workers, the other reformist with its primary base of support in the rural peasant leagues.[78]

Political developments in Rome during the spring of 1914 did little to reduce polarization or ease social tensions in the country. On the contrary, the resignation of Giolitti's government in March and its replacement by a new cabinet under the leadership of Antonio Salandra appeared to mark a major victory for proponents

[76] For strike statistics, see MAIC, *Annuario statistico italiano 1919-1921* (Rome, 1922), p. 512. On the syndicalist strikes in Ferrara and Milan, see C. Seton-Watson, *Italy from Liberalism*, pp. 386-387.

[77] C. Seton-Watson, *Italy from Liberalism*, p. 387.

[78] Brunello Vigezzi, *L'Italia di fronte alla prima guerra mondiale*, Vol. I, *L'Italia neutrale* (Milan, 1966), p. 959.

of bourgeois renewal and antisocialist reaction.[79] An old ally of Sonnino and a leading parliamentary foe of Giolitti's state insurance monopoly, the southern lawyer and notable had spelled out his own political alternative to the Piedmontese statesman's "healthy democracy" as early as 1912. Significantly, Salandra repudiated his predecessor's compromises with the left as an "unjustified negation of the fundamental principles of liberalism and the frank acceptance of the postulates of socialism." Instead he envisioned a reinvigorated and doctrinaire Liberal party that would strengthen "the authority of the state" and allow the bourgeoisie to reassert its political dominance as a "national party." Thus, he opposed any collaboration with or concessions to the parliamentary left and favored a government coalition of the constitutional right, conservative Catholics, and the nationalists.[80] In line with these aims, the cabinet he formed in 1914 contained no strict Giolittians or Radicals, drawing most of its personnel from the conservative camp. Governmental change in Rome also had its repercussion on the provincial level. As part of a general administrative reorganization, Salandra transferred Dallari, Giolitti's prefect in Bologna and a longtime adversary of agrarian militants, and replaced him with Domenico Quaranta, a staunch supporter of his "national policy."[81]

To a great extent, reactions to the new government mirrored the larger social divisions on the peninsula. The agrarian and industrial associations greeted its advent with obvious approval. Praising Salandra's program as the "masterful course to follow," their organ, *L'Italia Industriale ed Agraria,* portrayed his government as the "first stone of a new edifice of moral and political reconstruction."[82] The extreme left, on the other hand, met the Salandra cabinet with renewed protests and turbulent demonstrations, while

[79] See G. Carocci, *Giolitti e l'età giolittiana,* pp. 158-161.

[80] Antonio Salandra, *La politica nazionale e il partito liberale* (Milan, 1912), pp. xv-xxx.

[81] C. Seton-Watson, *Italy from Liberalism,* p. 392.

[82] Frank De Morsier, "Il ministero Salandra ed una politica nazionale," *Italia Industriale ed Agraria,* April-May 1914.

even reformist labor leaders warned that the government's opposition to the "moderate requests of the workers" was leading the country into "dangerous times."[83] A number of incidents in May seemed to confirm their warnings. From the dairy farms of Pavia to the state tobacco factories of Lucca, Modena, Venice, Florence, and Palermo, and the sulphur mines of Sicily, the Italian peninsula became the scene of serious disturbances and strikes.[84]

This spirit of popular rebellion reached its peak the following month. A violent clash between leftist demonstrators and police during an antimilitarist rally in Ancona on June 7 provided the spark for what soon became known as "Red Week." With the support of the CGL and the Socialist party, a general strike called in the Adriatic port city quickly spread to the entire country. Both chambers of labor and the Federterra in Bologna joined the strike on June 9, effectively halting all activity in the province for three days. With the railwaymen's union taking part in the strike, government communications and troop movements broke down as a wave of insurrections spread over the regions of Romagna and the Marches.[85] In the key cities of Rome, Milan, Turin, and Florence, however, the police succeeded in containing the unrest, and by June 10, the CGL ordered its affiliates to return to work. Two days later a defeated and discredited railwaymen's union also ended its strike. Without leadership or plans, the various local insurrections gradually collapsed, so that by June 14, the government had regained control of the situation.[86]

Salandra and the right in general emerged as the chief beneficiaries of Red Week. For in its aftermath, a strong and outspoken portion of Italy's propertied classes rallied to the new prime min-

[83] *Il Metallurgico*, May 1, 1914 cited in R. Webster, *Industrial Imperialism*, p. 169.

[84] R. Webster, "From Insurrection to Interventionism: The Italian Crisis of 1914," *Italian Quarterly*, v, no. 20 (Winter 1961-Spring 1962), pp. 37-38.

[85] For the most detailed account of Red Week, see Luigi Lotti, *La settimana rossa* (Florence, 1965). On developments in the province of Bologna during the week, see N. Sauro Onofri, *La grande guerra nella città rossa. Socialismo e reazione a Bologna* (Bologna, 1966), p. 53.

[86] R. Webster, "From Insurrection," p. 41.

ister and his vision of the state as a bulwark of the bourgeois elite. While radicals and reformists withdrew their support after Red Week, a bloc of conservatives, nationalists, and Catholics increased their support of Salandra's government, thereby accentuating its right-wing cast.[87] Moreover, conservatives were able to exploit the political backlash to the disorders in the administrative elections of June, which saw the victories of clerical-moderate coalitions in Turin and Genoa, and of a Catholic-Nationalist slate in Rome.[88]

The reaction to Red Week assumed more ominous forms in some of the major urban centers where rightist violence often exceeded that of the left. The mood of the propertied classes in Bologna was dramatically captured by one local businessman in a letter to the prefect after order had been restored:

> That which has just taken place was . . . a dress rehearsal for the revolution that will take place, I fear . . . when the troops are out on maneuvers and the bourgeoisie is at the seaside. If the government orders the troops to shoot in the air instead of on the anarchic mob, the revolution will certainly triumph. . . . The authorities for years now have shown themselves to be weak because of the "laissez-faire" attitude of the Honorable Giolitti. . . . Now Giolitti has introduced universal suffrage in a way that has put the country in the hands of the mob. . . . I fear that there will be massacres . . . and then the victory of the anarchic mob, if the government does not know how to confront energetically the first disturbances, shooting on the demonstrators. This would be an example of civilized severity and courage in the defense of the civilized classes.[89]

In a sense, the events of early June were a dress rehearsal, but for counterrevolution rather than revolution. Already during Red Week, a number of prominent notables displayed a new willingness to take the law into their own hands by joining with Nationalists to

[87] See *ibid.*, pp. 43-45.

[88] C. Seton-Watson, *Italy from Liberalism*, p. 395.

[89] ASB, C6 F2, letter, Montanari to Prefect, June 24, 1914. For a similar reaction, see letter of local merchant in *ibid.*, June 9, 1914.

sponsor squads of "volunteers for the defense of order." After the labor federations had gone out on strike, the Bolognese Nationalist Group organized counterdemonstrations of students and merchants, who were incited by men of Marchese Giuseppe Tanari's stature to take strong action against the "red peril." In a situation that the prefect characterized as one of incipient "civil war," armed volunteers clashed with leftist demonstrators on June 10. The prefect claimed in a report to his superiors that only his pressures on the liberal clubs and the Nationalists prevented more serious confrontations.[90] Such extremism was not simply a visceral response to the perceived threat of revolution. More importantly, it expressed the accumulated frustration and resentment of a propertied elite that had been unable to halt by legal means the advance of well-organized reformist socialist movement, which had seriously undermined its old prestige and power by the summer of 1914.

5. *The Costs of Confrontation in Bologna, 1913-1914*

Despite the victories in the counteroffensive of 1912-1913 and the electoral gains in 1914, the employer associations did not represent a cohesive and hegemonic bloc on the eve of World War I. The unity of employers in the campaigns against organized labor and Giolitti temporarily masked, but did not resolve, important contrasts and conflicts of interest among the various elements that comprised the bloc. On the issues of taxation, credit, and terms of exchange, commercial farmers and manufacturers remained divided. Moreover, growing economic interpenetration led to new conflicts that often cut across traditional sectoral divisions between agriculture and industry. The protectionist interests of the sugar lobby, for instance, clashed with the export-oriented coalitions that linked hemp and rice growers to their respective processing sec-

[90] ASB, C6 F2, Prefect to Ministry of Interior, June 12, 1914. On the nationalist counterdemonstrations, see N. Sauro Onofri, *La grande guerra*, p. 53; L. Lotti, *La settimana rossa*, pp. 235-236. The available sources provide little information on the social make-up of the Nationalist squads.

tors.[91] An additional weakness derived from the lack of political unity within the bloc. Certain prominent agrarian and industrial leaders continued to support Giolitti and his methods of political mediation in the last years before the war. Nor was there any effective consensus among the forces hostile to the Piedmontese statesman. Although many influential financial, industrial, and agrarian interests rallied to the Nationalist Association, others remained loyal to the constitutional right headed by Salandra and Sonnino.[92]

The more aggressive and militant factions of the productive bourgeoisie, in particular, faced a serious political dilemma. While rejecting the tutelage of the old parties of order, they were unable to find a viable replacement for them. As economic lobbies representing well-defined interests, the agrarian and industrial associations could scarcely assume the role of a new political elite capable of winning a broad base of support among the other classes in Italian society. Indeed, they encountered major difficulties in formulating a political program that went beyond the partisan defense of special interests and entrepreneurial prerogatives.[93] Far from cultivating a benevolent or populist image, militant agrarian and industrial leaders tended to exalt resistance and coercion, giving priority to immediate economic concerns at the expense of long-range needs for social consensus and political stability. Their narrow corporative vision of class relations left little room for the mass appeals essential to the creation of a conservative majority within an increasingly democratic parliamentary system.

All these problems and their disastrous political consequences were strikingly evident in the province of Bologna. Despite its rhetoric of class solidarity, the AAB remained a voluntary association, not a dictatorial oligarchy, and consequently it had to mediate between the desires of the different agrarian groups. Its

[91] See A. Cardoza, "Agrarians and Industrialists," p. 204.

[92] Among the industrial supporters of Giolitti was Giovanni Agnelli, founder of FIAT; see V. Castronovo, *Agnelli*, p. 56. For an example of support for Salandra, see Frank De Morsier's article previously cited in note 82.

[93] See A. Cardoza, "Agrarians and Industrialists," p. 204.

bellicose program and methods, however, served to accentuate divisions within the local propertied classes. From the outset, Stagni and Donini's strategy of confrontation alienated the moderate old guard of landed patricians who gave little support to their organization. Marchese Carlo Malvezzi, scion of one of the oldest families of the Bolognese aristocracy, summarized the moderates' reservations about the AAB in a letter to Mario Missiroli in the fall of 1913:

> It is clear that the AAB is . . . only an organization of material defense and reaction, just reaction if you like, but simply reaction, and its most noted actions have always been reactionary. In my view, the employer associations have too readily adapted to class struggle and self-defense; they have forgotten that they represent the ruling classes [and] that the difficult duty of he who rules and must educate is to be patient. . . . They have not realized that the idea "ruling class" is in some respects analogous to the idea "pater familias" and that it would not be a beneficial norm of fatherly education to make excessive use of thrashings.[94]

For their part, the leaders of the AAB made no attempt to placate the moderates. On the contrary, *L'Agraria Bolognese* printed a steady stream of abuse against independent landowners, whom it stigmatized as agrarian "scabs" and the benefactors of socialism. When Count Piero Bianconcini, for example, chose not to join the association and instead signed a longterm contract with the leagues of Molinella, Donini distributed a leaflet that attacked him with an unusual viciousness, leading the prefect to protest the AAB's presumed attempt "to control the free will of a landowner who, not being enrolled in it, should not be the object of polemics only for having stipulated those contracts."[95]

The absence of prominent absentee landowners limited the effectiveness of the AAB in more than one way. Apart from their personal prestige, the moderate notables held influential positions

[94] ASB, C5 F1, letter, Marchese Carlo Malvezzi to Mario Missiroli, September 17, 1913.

[95] ASB, C6 F2, Prefect to Ministry of Interior, June 4, 1912.

in the Cassa di Risparmio and the other local banks that controlled agricultural credit in the province. The dominance of these older financial institutions made it difficult, if not impossible, for the AAB to follow the path of Parma's agrarian association, which had set up its own cooperative bank and agricultural exchange in the first decade of the century.[96] Similarly, the AAB was able to exercise little direct or systematic influence over agricultural supplying operations, which remained firmly in the hands of the independent Bolognese Agrarian Consortium and its national organization, the Federconsorzi. Efforts to promote commodity organizations also met with limited success. With the exception of the sugar beet growers syndicate, organizers encountered enormous obstacles in trying to unite the large number of highly varied farm units involved.[97] In the absence of a strong network of supporting financial and economic institutions, the AAB thus lacked perhaps the most powerful instruments for organizing, controlling, and mobilizing the mass of small- and middle-sized farmers in the province.[98]

The deliberately elitist policies of the AAB and its almost exclusive concern for resistance exacerbated these organizational shortcomings. By requiring high membership fees and promissory notes, Stagni and Donini excluded the smaller peasant proprietors and tenant farmers. Although the AAB included in its ranks the biggest commercial leaseholders, it actually represented only a minority of the landowners and farmers.[99] Moreover, the dominant position of the leaseholders within the association limited its ca-

96 For the initiatives of Parma's association, see *Bollettino dell'Associazione Agraria Parmense*, October 17, 1908; November 28, 1908; August 14, 1908; October 2, 1908. On the credit situation in Bologna, see M. Malatesta, *Il Resto del Carlino*, pp. 245-246.

97 On the problems of the hemp syndicates in particular, see *Bollettino Federale Agrario*, January 1, 1910; Vittorio Peglion, *Piante industriali. Produzione, commercio, regime doganale* (Rome, 1917), p. 53.

98 The example of the powerful Agrarian League in Germany clearly illustrates the importance of such instruments; see David Abraham, "Intra-Class Conflict and the Formation of Ruling Class Consensus in Late Weimar Germany" (Ph.D. Dissertation, University of Chicago, 1977), p. 75.

99 On the membership of the AAB, see MAIC, *Statistica delle organizzazioni padronali*, Vol. I, *Le agrarie* (Rome, 1912), p. 1.

pacity to mobilize and manipulate the support of that pivotal intermediate class of sharecroppers. As the prefect observed in 1914, the leaseholders' "special interest in exploiting the land" led them to treat the sharecroppers with a "greater severity . . . that then characterizes the entire association."[100] In the summer of 1912, for instance, the attempt by sharecroppers in the peasant brotherhoods to use machines from their new cooperative met with the open hostility of the organized landowners, who threatened them with eviction unless they leased machines from the AAB's subsidiary, the Società Agricola Industriale.[101] While such policies provided immediate economic benefits to landlords, the prefect Quaranta pointed out their longterm political costs in 1914:

> These peasant forces should constitute the true reserves of the constitutional party, an especially precious quantity today when the extension of suffrage has made numerical strength the key to victory. It is essential, however, that the landowners put aside their narrowly egoistic attitude in order to consider the needs of the peasants with greater generosity. The latter cannot see in the landowner a boss whom one obeys without discussion; eventually the landowner must become either an enemy or a partner. This latter solution . . . requires a spirit of magnanimity from the landowners that in large part they have not displayed. . . . Often they do not respect the stipulated agreements and antagonize the peasants with threats of repression, so that during electoral campaigns they cannot turn to them for support. The ballot . . . becomes a weapon of the sharecropper, not to show his socialist convictions, . . . but to revenge himself against the landowner by opposing any candidate he supports.[102]

Quaranta no doubt based his analysis on what happened prior to the parliamentary elections of 1913, above all in the district of

[100] ASB, C7 F1, Prefect to Ministry of Interior, no date, 1914.

[101] ASB, C6 F2, 2, Subprefect to Prefect, July 20, 1912; *RdC*, August 14, 1912; ASB, C6 F2, 2, "Situazione delle organizzazioni delle classi medie (piccoli proprietari e coloni) della Provincia di Bologna," no date, 1919.

[102] ASB, C7 F1, Prefect to Ministry of Interior, no date, 1914.

Imola where the peasant brotherhoods had a large mass base and consequently represented a powerful electoral force. Despite their distrust and fear of the socialists, the independent peasants remained "diffident and discontented" with the parties of order, an attitude local authorities attributed to the AAB's policy of treating the brotherhoods "from moment to moment either as economic adversaries or as political allies." Stressing the intimate connection between politics and landlord-peasant relations, the subprefect reported on the eve of the balloting that in Imola "a true constitutional party no longer exists; its leaders . . . feel discouraged and incapable of developing any action."[103]

The situation in Imola reflected the general disarray and fragmentation of the Bolognese parties of order in 1913. As in previous years, the Liberal-Monarchist Federation theoretically provided unity and direction to the various political clubs and circles in the province. In their behind-the-scenes reports, however, governmental officials depicted a poorly organized cluster of clerical, moderate, and conservative factions, active only in the city of Bologna and divided by bitter political differences and personal rivalries. Already in the spring of 1913, the prefect warned of a growing split within the provincial political establishment between the followers of Enrico Pini, who were favorably disposed toward Giolitti and his programs, and the ultra-conservative supporters of Giuseppe Bacchelli, who remained "firm in their commitment to the old traditions." The prefect voiced particular concern over the attempt by the right wing of the federation to purge progressive elements from the local clubs and forge an anti-Giolittian slate headed by Bacchelli and Frank De Morsier, "the politicians most akin to the ideas and aims of the AAB."[104] His concern proved to be well founded, since this initiative only sharpened divisions within the constitutional camp. In the third electoral college of Bologna, the major political club transformed itself into the autonomous Liberal Union, rejected the federation's candidate, and instead en-

[103] *Ibid.*; ASB, C5 F1, Subprefect to Prefect, August 20, 1913.
[104] ASB, C5 F1, Prefect to Ministry of Interior, March 20, 1913.

dorsed Pini's protégé, Germano Mastellari. Likewise, supporters of Giolitti in the first electoral college openly opposed Bacchelli's candidacy on the grounds that he had always maintained "a hostile attitude toward the government, even voting against the extension of suffrage."[105] Catholic political forces were no less divided. While clerical conservatives allied with the Liberal-Monarchist Federation, Christian democratic elements threw their support to certain Socialist candidates in the plains.[106]

The intransigence of the AAB contributed significantly to the disarray and fragmentation of the non-socialist parties. After its campaign for an anti-Giolittian bloc encountered stiff opposition that forced the withdrawal of De Morsier's candidacy, the association refused to support publicly the other constitutional candidates, leading the prefect to lament the "political absenteeism" of the agrarians who, in his view, "should have constituted the backbone of the constitutional party in the countryside."[107] Left to their own devices, a number of commercial farmers made their own deals with less doctrinaire Socialist leaders. In Castelmaggiore some of the biggest leaseholders quietly backed Giacomo Bentini, the reformist Socialist candidate, in exchange for his assurances of "tranquility during the periods when labor contracts and wage schedules are stipulated."[108]

The apparent inability of the various feuding factions to settle their differences finally led Giolitti to intervene in the fall, if only to try and head off a Socialist landslide. To prevent a disastrous split of the non-socialist vote in the third college of Bologna, the prime minister ordered the prefect in September "to induce Mastellari to campaign in Budrio where he can win." The same month, the prefect received instructions to pressure Marchese Giuseppe Tanari to run in the college of Castelmaggiore, since according to

[105] *Il Secolo*, June 25, 1913; ASB, C5 F1, Prefect to Giolitti, September 15, 1913.

[106] See, for example, the letter of the priest of one village in Molinella in support of Giuseppe Massarenti's candidacy. ASB C5 F1, Prefect to Ministry of Interior, April 12, 1913.

[107] ASB, C7 F1, Prefect to Ministry of Interior, no date, 1914.

[108] ASB, C5 F1, Prefect to Giolitti, September 20, 1913.

Giolitti, he was "the only one who can defeat Bentini . . . [and] a victory in Castelmaggiore will raise the fortunes of the constitutional party in the entire province."[109] The prime minister's mediation met with no success; Tanari refused to run while Mastellari stubbornly maintained his candidacy in the third college. As the prefect concluded pessimistically in late September, "the Socialists are perhaps not the majority, but they represent a compact bloc; the constitutional forces instead appear as an amorphous mass."[110]

The election results in Bologna more than confirmed the authorities' pessimism. Commenting on the outcome, the prefect underscored the striking contrast between the Socialists, who had given "admirable proof of their discipline," and the constitutionalists with their innumerable "misunderstandings and petty jealousies."[111] Both in the countryside and in the cities, the left emerged from the elections as the chief beneficiary of the suffrage reform. Apart from the easy victory of the Giolittian incumbent, Luigi Rava, in the isolated mountain district of Vergato, just one constitutional candidate prevailed, and then only after a run-off election in November. The Socialists swept the remaining six colleges, attracting the lion's share of those voters who cast their ballots for the first time in 1913. Bologna had become, in the words of Raffaele Stagni, "the red province" of Italy not simply because her deputies were Socialists, but because "the spirit of the masses . . . is completely dominated by revolutionary ideals."[112]

In the absence of any strong party organization capable of imposing order, humiliating defeat led only to increased factional strife within the constitutional camp. Indeed, government officials

[109] *Ibid.*, Giolitti to Prefect, September 3 and 15, 1913.

[110] ASB, C5 F1, Prefect to Giolitti, September 20, 1913.

[111] ASB, C7 F1, Prefect to Ministry of Interior, no date, 1914.

[112] *RdC*, October 27; November 3, 1913. In the city of Bologna, the Socialists doubled their vote from 21,870 in 1909 to 42,441 in 1913. See N. Sauro Onofri, *La grande guerra*, pp. 17-18. For Stagni's pessimistic appraisal of the situation in Bologna, see "A che cosa è ridotta la proprietà terriera nella Provincia di Bologna," *Italia Industriale ed Agraria*, December 15, 1913.

claimed that the situation had actually worsened in the months after the parliamentary elections. In Medicina, for instance, the subprefect wrote in April 1914 that, despite growing discontent with the Socialist municipal administrations, he saw little hope of a change in personnel, since "the constitutional-agrarian party is divided between liberals and clerical-moderates." Prospects for a united front of the propertied classes in Budrio appeared equally remote, the prefect reported, because "the liberal currents are not responding to the urgings from the Catholics." Significantly, the prefect blamed much of the divisiveness on the loose-knit structure of the parties of order that encouraged "confusion and power struggles."[113]

With the municipal elections slightly more than a month away, the new government of Salandra stepped in, proposing the creation of "a commission of men, who enjoy the trust of the different groups as well as the masses, and who can take the initiative of forming a common electoral slate." Such a commission, the prefect argued, could assure "the most important economic groups, as well as all the other people, threatened by the Socialists . . . that a constitutional administration will protect their interests."[114] In response to overtures from the prefecture, three of Bologna's leading citizens—Marchese Tanari, Enrico Pini, and Alberto Dallolio—formed a committee in May with the aim of bringing together the various associations, clubs, and political circles in what they portrayed as a vast new anti-socialist crusade. Marchese Tanari reflected the tone of the committee's campaign in a speech on the eve of the city elections: "The Bolognese people must choose whether to be their own bosses, bosses in their homes and their businesses, or to live as slaves to that Socialist party that has degenerated . . . living today outside the law. . . . Everything depends on us; only we can prevent it . . . [and] save the reputation of our city."[115]

Much as in the previous year, however, factional rivalries, per-

[113] ASB, C5 F1, Subprefect to Prefect, April 8, 1914; ASB, C7 F1, Prefect to Ministry of Interior, no date, 1914.

[114] ASB, C5 F1, Prefect to Salandra, May 9, 1914.

[115] *RdC*, June 25, 1914.

sonal feuds, and private ambitions proved stronger than the fear of a Socialist victory. Neither the appeals of the committee nor the pressures of the prefecture produced an electoral slate acceptable to all groups of the proposed coalition. As a result, the Bolognese Electoral Association, the chief organization of the Catholic political forces in the city, withdrew and presented its own list of candidates.[116] To make matters worse, the committee was unable to eliminate, or even reduce, the "tensions, discord, confusion, conflicts, and divisions" that continued to characterize relations between the conservative Liberal-Monarchist Federation and the progressive Liberal Union in the weeks before the elections. The disunity of the parties of order, the prefect later reported, made the outcome of municipal contests a foregone conclusion, since it "led inevitably to the victory of the Socialist party."[117]

The full extent of the Socialist victory emerged with stunning clarity from a report of the prefect Quaranta on the local political situation after the municipal elections. Of the sixty-one communes in the province, only twenty-five remained in the hands of the parties of order, and of these a mere three were in the plains. The Socialists controlled twenty-seven communes, while the remaining nine were administered by Christian democratic elements "who generally express socialist tendencies because their supporters belong to the labor organizations of the Federterra." Moreover, the Socialists ruled over the two principal cities of the province, Bologna and Imola, as well as the other eleven municipalities with populations over eight thousand. Capturing thirty-one of the fifty seats, the left also dominated the Provincial Council and consequently all elective positions on the many local public agencies.[118]

More importantly, the parliamentary and municipal elections of 1913 and 1914 revealed the inability of either traditional deference politics or agrarian militancy to preserve the power and influence of the propertied classes. In the new era of mass politics ushered

[116] N. Sauro Onofri, *La grande guerra,* p. 48n, pp. 54-55.

[117] ASB, C7 F1, Prefect to Ministry of Interior, no date, 1914.

[118] ASB, C7 F1, "Relazione sulle condizioni politiche della provincia," Prefect to Ministry of Interior, no date, 1914.

in by Giolitti's reform of 1911, covert government intervention and improvised coalition-building by local notables were no match for the disciplined and well-organized electoral machines of the Socialist party. While militant spokesmen for commercial farming interests rightly criticized the outdated methods of the moderate old guard, their own strategy of confrontation hardly constituted a viable political alternative. On the contrary, the AAB's intransigent defense of narrow corporative interests not only sharpened divisions within the propertied classes, but also had alienated the mass of peasant proprietors and sharecroppers, whose support was essential for any conservative resurgence in an increasingly democratic polity. On the eve of World War I, Bologna's divided and isolated elite appeared powerless to halt the growth of what Mario Missiroli described as a socialist "state within the state with its own special laws and . . . executive organs."[119]

[119] *RdC*, July 18, 1913.

V. POLITICS AND SOCIETY IN WARTIME BOLOGNA

The Bolognese Socialists had little time to luxuriate in their victories or the propertied classes to lament their political setbacks after the municipal elections of 1914. Indeed, even as the balloting was taking place in late June, momentous events beyond Italy's borders began to overshadow provincial issues and conflicts. After the assassination of Archduke Franz Ferdinand on June 28 and the subsequent ultimatum, the Austro-Hungarian Empire declared war on Serbia on July 28; within a week this local conflict mushroomed into a general European war as Germany, Russia, France, and Great Britain rushed to the aid of their respective allies. The outbreak of hostilities in August caught the Italian government poised between the two opposing alliance systems. Formally tied to Germany and Austria-Hungary in the Triple Alliance, Italy had also continued to maintain friendly relations with Great Britain and had a nonaggression treaty with France as well as a sphere-of-influence agreement with Russia.[1]

A combination of foreign policy and domestic considerations led Salandra to declare officially his government's neutrality on August 2, 1914. In his diplomatic exchanges, the foreign minister San

[1] G. Chapman, "In Comparison: Italian Neutrality and Intervention, 1914-1915," epilogue to "Decision for War: The Domestic Political Context of French Diplomacy, 1911-1914" (Ph.D. dissertation, Princeton University, 1971), p. 274n.

Giuliano justified such a decision, citing the army's lack of preparedness and Austria-Hungary's refusal to provide firm guarantees for Italian territorial compensation.[2] The situation at home in the wake of Red Week also encouraged Salandra to avoid belligerency. In a message to the Italian ambassador in Vienna, San Giuliano voiced the government's concern that military intervention might provoke renewed domestic disorders that would disrupt any war effort and further undermine internal stability:

> In a democratic country such as Italy, it is not possible to conduct a war, and even less a large-scale and dangerous war, in opposition to the will and sentiment of the nation. With the exception of a very small minority, the nation immediately and unanimously pronounced itself to be against participating in a war that stems from Austrian arrogance. . . . In the event of war, we would have had to impose immense burdens on the state budget and the national economy, and would thereby have aggravated the widespread and perilous discontent that stems from our unsatisfactory financial and economic conditions. We would have exposed our existing institutions to serious dangers and would have set back by a half-century the increase in national wealth that is so vital to the preservation of the country from yet greater political and social cataclysms.[3]

Echoing these views in a report to the king, Salandra argued that internal stability represented a vital necessity for "a state whose lot it is to face the supreme test of full-scale war." Yet, the prime minister wrote, "the first few months of my government, which unfolded amid large and small strikes and open acts of revolt, revealed that in Italy's case this prerequisite was lacking."[4]

As San Giuliano's comments suggest, the decision for neutrality

[2] Christopher Seton-Watson, *Italy from Liberalism to Fascism* (London, 1967), p. 416.

[3] *Documenti diplomatici italiani*, 5th series, Vol. I, pp. 2-3, dispatch date 2 August 1914, cited in G. Chapman, "In Comparison: Italian Neutrality," p. 275.

[4] Antonio Salandra, *La neutralità italiana, 1914. Ricordi e pensieri* (Milan, 1928), p. 107, cited in *ibid.*, p. 276.

was well attuned to the general drift of public opinion on the peninsula in the summer of 1914. The Socialist party and the trade unions were militantly pacifist, while Radicals, Republicans, and democrats opposed intervention in what they saw as a dynastic, militaristic war of expansion. Despite their partiality to the Habsburgs, most Catholics also displayed little enthusiasm for war. Only a small group of Nationalists, conservatives, soldiers, and diplomats advocated belligerence in the first weeks of the war, either for reasons of national prestige or out of a sense of loyalty to the Triple Alliance.[5]

This broad national consensus, however, disintegrated in the fall of 1914. With the halt of the German advance in the west and the beginning of an Austrian retreat in the east in September, a movement in favor of Italian intervention on the side of the Entente began to gain momentum both within government circles and in the country at large. The ensuing national debate on the war had a traumatic impact on Italian politics, sharpening divisions within the ruling political class and shattering the initial unity of the left. While the official Socialist party remained firmly committed to absolute neutrality, the democratic left reversed its original position. As early as the end of August, prominent democratic leaders were advocating participation in a "war of liberation" against Germany, a position that soon brought them into an unnatural alliance not only with revolutionary interventionists like Mussolini, but also with Nationalists and conservatives who espoused a war for the "moral regeneration" of Italian society and the enhancement of the nation's great power status.[6]

The heterogeneous prowar coalition clearly illustrated how the question of intervention was inseparably linked to more profound political and social conflicts, and above all to the increasingly diffuse hostility toward Giolittian transformism. Despite their divergent

[5] C. Seton-Watson, *Italy from Liberalism*, p. 416.

[6] For the development of the democratic interventionists, see Renzo De Felice, *Mussolini il rivoluzionario, 1883-1920* (Turin, 1965), pp. 229-232. On the Nationalists, see Alexander De Grand, *The Italian Nationalist Association and the Rise of Fascism in Italy* (Lincoln, Nebr., 1978), pp. 60-71.

aims and aspirations, left-wing and conservative interventionists alike saw the war as a means of weakening the neutralist Giolitti and dismantling his system. Domestic political calculations were especially important for Salandra and Sonnino, who became foreign minister in September. Apart from the opportunities war offered for territorial expansion, the two looked to intervention as a way to escape the tutelage of Giolitti and his parliamentary majority, curb the influence of the extreme left, and restore "the prestige of the monarchy, the army, and conservative liberalism."[7]

For the besieged Bolognese elite, local more than national or international considerations dictated the appropriate stance on the issue of Italian participation in the war. In a province dominated by the Socialists, interventionism provided a unifying cause for the parties of order that allowed them to solidify ties with other antisocialist forces and to recapture the political initiative they had lost in the parliamentary and municipal elections. Beginning in the fall of 1914, Bologna's propertied classes skillfully exploited their new prowar coalition to challenge the earlier verdict of the ballot box and to bring about a change in the government's policies toward the socialist leagues.

1. *Interventionism and Political Reaction in Bologna*

In the first few months after the outbreak of war, the Bolognese elite displayed little unanimity of opinion on the question of intervention. Prominent spokesmen for the agrarian old guard such as Marchese Tanari begrudgingly accepted neutrality, but vehemently opposed Italian involvement in a war against her former partners in the Triple Alliance. Expressing the view of many traditional conservatives, Tanari wrote at the beginning of September: "I cannot comprehend how suddenly the substantial rea-

[7] See Adrian Lyttelton, *The Seizure of Power: Fascism in Italy, 1919-1929* (New York, 1973), p. 24; R. Webster, "From Insurrection to Intervention: The Italian Crisis of 1914" *Italian Quarterly*, v, no. 20 (Winter 1961-Spring 1962), p. 46.

sons that led Italy to become a member of the Triple Alliance . . . have now become obsolete, so that today we are supposed to desire the defeat of the two states with whom until recently, I repeat, we wished to remain united. . . . I appreciate that in the present moral, social, economic, and military situation of my country . . . one could certainly explain, if not justify, our neutrality. But this is a long way from stabbing Austria in the back or desiring the ruin of Germany.[8] Mario Missiroli was a considerably less ambiguous defender of neutrality. Already in mid-August he praised the government's decision as part of a "courageous and knowledgeable preparation for the defense of our interests, of our rights."[9] Conversely, militant agrarian leaders and younger factions with the parties of order emerged in the fall as outspoken proponents of Italian intervention on the side of the Entente. Addressing a meeting of the Liberal Union at the end of September on the theme, "national discipline against absolute neutrality," Lino Carrara called upon the "bourgeoisie . . . to seize the sword . . . for the defense of our Italy."[10] In a similar vein, the Young Liberal Association attacked neutrality early the following month as "only a blind renunciation of our interests."[11]

Despite their evident lack of agreement on the larger issue of Italian intervention in the war, virtually all factions of the elite concurred in the view that the new international situation could be used to obstruct any reform experiments by the Socialist municipalities and to curb labor militancy in the countryside. As early as July, Frank De Morsier, the local farm machine manufacturer and agrarian spokesman, argued that the growing war clouds over Europe made it imperative that "the great law of national solidarity prevail," a law that would have to be "imposed even on the un-

[8] Biblioteca Comunale di Bologna, MS Tanari, Cart. xxxix, no. 3, "Attegiamenti del Tanari all'inizio della guerra europea, 1914-16," letter, September 7, 1914.

[9] M. Missiroli, "Intemperanze" *RdC*, August 13, 1914. For a sampling of the diversity of views on the war issue, see Maria Malatesta, *Il Resto del Carlino* (Turin, 1978), pp. 299-300.

[10] *RdC*, October 1, 1914.

[11] ASB, C7 F1, Police Chief to Prefect, October 10, 1914.

willing."[12] The ruling council of the AAB was even more explicit on the subject. It affirmed in mid-August that the outbreak of war required an immediate end to strikes and labor agitation, since "internal conflicts and disturbances can only prejudice and weaken . . . the supreme interests of the Patria."[13]

Agrarian interests did not have to wait long for the opportunity to exploit the war crisis. In October a nine-month old dispute between the AAB and the leagues of Molinella erupted into violence. Prior to the violence, the association appeared to be on the brink of defeat. A number of big leaseholders had deserted its ranks and signed contracts with the leagues; the remaining holdouts faced disastrous crop losses as a result of the prolonged strikes and boycotts.[14] Finally the first week in October the AAB elected to dispatch its "free laborers" to Molinella in a desperate attempt to break the deadlock. Previously, provincial authorities had greeted such initiatives with open disfavor on the grounds that the association tended to use the squads, as the prefect Dallari complained, "not to complete the work, since they are insufficient, but to necessitate the presence of police and troops to intimidate its opponents."[15]

In the altered political situation of 1914, however, the AAB gambled that the new prefect Quaranta, who had attacked the leagues as "true and proper criminal organizations," would be more amenable to armed intervention on behalf of the employers.[16] Thus, on the morning of October 5, Donini and a squad of strikebreakers entered the commune. News of their impending arrival had spread among the local population the previous night, so that

[12] "Gli agrari e la guerra," *Italia Industriale ed Agraria*, July 1914.

[13] *RdC*, August 11, 1914.

[14] *Ibid.*, August 6, 1914. For the background and evolution of the dispute, which involved a drastic reform of the *mezzadria*, see Francesco Saverio Solari, "Lotte agrarie a Molinella: 1905-1915" *Storia Contemporanea*, IX, no. 5-6 (Dec. 1978), pp. 862-865.

[15] ASB, C6 F2, Prefect to Ministry of Interior, November 18, 1912.

[16] On the new prefect's views of the socialist organizations, see Natalia De Stefano, "Moti popolari in Emilia-Romagna e Toscana, 1915-1917," *Rivista Storica del Socialismo*, no. 32, 1967, p. 199.

an angry crowd of some two thousand men, women, and children was on hand to confront the agrarian scabs in the village of Guarda di Molinella. In the one-sided conflict that followed, four strikebreakers were killed, while Donini and three others were seriously injured.[17]

Before the bodies were cold, agrarian spokesmen were portraying the incident not just as a brutal crime, but as an act of treason against the entire nation. "While the nation is apprehensive about its future and beyond the Alps every country is putting aside divisions of party and class and rallying around its own flag," the Nationalist agrarian Giorgio Ghigi told the Bolognese municipal council, "we have the shame of witnessing the appalling slaughter in . . . Molinella."[18] For the AAB, considerations of national security dictated a strong government action to "eliminate as soon as possible a situation that for too many years has kept Molinella outside the limits of every human and civilized law."[19] The Nationalist and conservative press quickly transformed the local conflict into an event of national importance, the "massacre of Guarda," which they depicted as the end result of fifteen years of Giolittian permissiveness and "an entire system of *democratismo*."[20]

In the hysterical climate of public opinion fomented by the agrarians and their supporters, the Salandra government instituted a program of repression in Molinella without parallel since the 1890s. The day after the conflict, the prefect reported to his superiors that thirty-five individuals had been arrested, and that both the headquarters of the leagues and the homes of prominent labor leaders had been searched. In the succeeding weeks, 166 persons were jailed or had outstanding arrest warrants—including nearly all the league officials and Socialist administrators in the commune, whom the authorities charged with indirect responsibility for the

[17] ASB, C6 F2, Molinella, "Omicidi e violenze in Guarda di Molinella" Prefect to Ministry of Interior, October 6, 1914.

[18] *RdC*, October 9, 1914.

[19] ASB, C6 F2, Molinella, Resolution of the AAB, October 14, 1914.

[20] For the press reaction to the conflict, see Brunello Vigezzi, *L'Italia di fronte alla prima guerra mondiale*, Vol. I, *L'Italia neutrale* (Milan, 1966), pp. 962-966.

violence.[21] At the same time, the government went beyond simple police measures. Quaranta immediately removed Giuseppe Massarenti from his post of mayor and appointed a special royal commissioner to replace him; the noted labor leader escaped arrest only by fleeing to the Republic of San Marino. In response to pressures from the AAB and the landowners, the royal commissioner proceeded to cancel the previous municipal budget and introduced a new one that cut property taxes substantially and eliminated a host of social services and welfare measures.[22]

Not surprisingly, the AAB took advantage of the military occupation and the disarray in the Molinellese labor movement to break the strike and dismantle Massarenti's organizational empire. With the protection of troops and the unqualified support of the prefect, the association refused to reopen negotiations with the leagues and imported nonunion labor to complete the harvest. Big leaseholders like Giuseppe Bolognesi and Alfredo Benni capitalized on the new balance of power to disavow prior agreements with the leagues, claiming that they "were invalid because they had been extorted with violence."[23] To soften the resistance of the socialist sharecroppers, the AAB's emissaries pressured peasants to accept its contract "so as to avoid eviction." By the late spring of 1915, Count Francesco Cavazza, the sole constitutional deputy from the province, boasted that such pressures had largely achieved their objective. After "the reestablishment of law and order in Molinella," Count Cavazza wrote the Minister of Interior, "the overwhelming majority of the peasants . . . reached agreements with their respective employers [and] only a tiny group of the most irreducible subversives have not remained on their farms."[24]

[21] The government immediately dispatched 3,000 troops to occupy the municipality and surrounding countryside. See ASB, C6 F2, Prefect to Ministry of Interior, October 6, 1914; *ibid.*, Prefect to Ministry of Interior, no date, 1915.

[22] On Massarenti's flight, see Arturo Colombi, *Pagine di storia del movimento operaio* (Rome, 1951), p. 201. For the activities of the royal commissioner, see F. Saverio Solari, "Lotte agrarie a Molinella," pp. 869-870.

[23] F. Saverio Solari, "Lotte agrarie a Molinella," pp. 867-868; on the actions of Benni and Bolognesi, see ASB, C6 F2, Prefect to Ministry of Interior, July 12, 1919.

[24] ASB, C6 F2, Honorable Count Francesco Cavazza to Ministry of Interior, May

Agrarian interests launched a more ambitious organizational undertaking in November with the goal of permanently dividing and weakening the Molinellese labor movement. That month Count Cavazza and Marchese Carlo Malvezzi sponsored an "apolitical league of Molinella" which affirmed the principle that "the greatest distribution of work can come only from good relations with the employers."[25] A few days later, the AAB announced the founding of its own Cooperative Consumers Union of Molinella as an alternative to Massarenti's cooperative. These initiatives met with the enthusiastic approval of the prefect Quaranta who urged the creation of similar "neutral workers' organizations" elsewhere in the province to meet the needs of laborers and prevent the Socialists from "monopolizing the working masses for their own political aims."[26] Despite the prefect's backing and the persecution suffered by the socialist organizations, neither of the two new unions in Molinella acquired a mass following. At its peak the apolitical league had no more than two hundred to three hundred members, a paltry figure when compared to the three thousand laborers in the local red leagues. Nonetheless, for the time being, the AAB had succeeded in breaching the monolithic structure of the Molinellese leagues and in reintroducing a competitive labor market that worked decisively to the advantage of agricultural employers.[27]

Significantly, reaction in the countryside coincided with the growing militancy of the interventionist movement in the capital city. Beginning in mid-November after the congress of the provincial socialist federation affirmed its commitment to "defend energetically the position of neutrality," *Il Resto del Carlino* initiated a press campaign that virulently attacked the city's leftist municipal government and glorified the interventionist forces.[28]

17, 1915; on the pressures put on the sharecroppers by the AAB, see *ibid.*, C6 F2, Police Report to Prefect, November 3, 1914.

[25] *RdC*, November 20, 1914.

[26] ASB, C7 F1, Prefect to Ministry of Interior, January 12, 1915. On the founding of the agrarian cooperative, see *RdC*, November 21, 1914.

[27] F. Saverio Solari, "Lotte agrarie a Molinella," p. 868.

[28] Valerio Castronovo, *La stampa italiana dall'Unità al fascismo* (Bari, 1973), p. 222; Nazario Sauro Onofri, *La grande guerra nella città rossa. Socialismo e reazione a Bologna* (Bologna, 1966), pp. 129-130.

The following month a small group of dissident Socialists left the party and joined with anarcho-syndicalists and republicans to form the Fascio d'Azione Rivoluzionaria in order to promote the prowar cause in the streets and piazzas of Bologna.[29] The actions of the revolutionary interventionists did not weaken the links between political reaction and interventionism, which became even more intimate in February 1915 when the parties of order founded the Anti-Socialist Association. According to its charter, the new association proposed "to struggle against socialism" and to provide a "vigilant and strong defense of the homeland and every legitimate national interest."[30] By the spring of 1915, the city of Bologna became the scene of increasingly turbulent prowar demonstrations by a heterogeneous coalition of Nationalists, revolutionary interventionists, the University Republican Association, and various patriotic organizations such as the "Trento Trieste" Association and the Irredentist Committee.[31]

Despite their activism and the support they received from the propertied classes, the Bolognese interventionists remained a minority movement even within the capital city. In late March, for instance the PSI easily triumphed in a special election called to fill the parliamentary seat vacated by Alberto Calda in the first urban college.[32] Yet the Socialists were unable to translate their electoral power into an aggressive movement against the war. The very character of the neutralist position, namely the preservation of the status quo, seemed to preclude any peace demonstrations comparable to those of the interventionists. As the prefect observed, "the subversive masses [were] indifferent, because they are neutralist." Quaranta attributed those counterdemonstrations that did

[29] See announcement of the Fascio in ASB, C7 F1, December 27, 1914. In addition, the revolutionary interventionists had two local papers, *La riscossa*, edited by Guido Bergami and Maria Rygier, and *L'appello dei giovani* by Luigi Andreini. See R. De Felice, *Mussolini, il rivoluzionario*, p. 297.

[30] On the founding of the Anti-Socialist Association, see ASB, C7 F1, Police Chief to Prefect, February 21, 1915.

[31] For the make-up of these demonstrations, see *RdC*, February 22, 1915, for example.

[32] V. Castronovo, *La stampa italiana dall'Unità*, p. 223.

take place less to the Socialists' neutralist fervor than to the fact that they were "irritated by the energy with which the interventionists were holding the piazza."[33] On the whole, economic difficulties rather than the war issue provided the chief source of labor unrest, as witnessed by the numerous demonstrations for "bread and work" that took place in twenty-five rural communes during the first three months of the year.[34]

The interventionist campaign in Bologna, much as in the other major cities of the north, culminated in the "radiant days of May." With the war issue coming to a head in Rome, on May 12 the local interventionist groups met to call a mass demonstration for the next day and to dispatch a telegram to Salandra, in which they demanded that "the government prepare the work of national vindication" and warned that they would "not tolerate any deviation from the designated path."[35] Accordingly, the evening of May 13 some one thousand interventionists paraded through the city, shouting "Viva la guerra, down with Giolitti, down with the traitors" and attacking groups of suspected neutralist sympathizers. News of Salandra's resignation further aroused the prowar camp and led to renewed demonstrations in the following days. Only the energetic action of the prefect and the relative inertia of the Socialists prevented any serious conflicts between the opposing forces.[36] For its part, the agrarian press encouraged the protests and gave them a sharp political focus by proclaiming how "the entire nation, from Milan, Turin, and Bologna to Rome, has clearly disavowed the insidious and underhanded actions of its [parliamentary] representatives and has raised its eyes on high . . . to the King."[37]

[33] See B. Vigezzi, "Le 'Radiose giornate' dell maggio 1915," *Nuova Rivista Storica*, January-March 1960, pp. 82-83.

[34] On these demonstrations, see ASB, C6 F2, Police Report, March 30, 1915. For the unemployment situation, see Arrigo Serpieri, *La guerra e le classi rurali italiane* (Bari, 1930), p. 79.

[35] *RdC*, May 13, 1915. Notable among the signers of the telegram was Lino Carrara.

[36] B. Vigezzi, "Le 'Radiose giornate' del maggio 1915," pp. 82-83.

[37] *RdC*, May 13, 1915.

Victor Emanuel's decision to reject Salandra's resignation on May 16 was interpreted by the war party as a victory. That evening Quaranta reported a "spontaneous demonstration of joy" by crowds of cheering interventionists who marched through the center of the city, "singing the praises of Italy, the king, [and] Salandra."[38] Such enthusiasm proved to be well-founded; on May 20 the government received full powers for war, and four days later Italy was officially at war on the side of the Triple Entente. As if to underscore the connection between war and political reaction in the province, the Bolognese interventionists celebrated the declaration by storming Palazzo d'Accursio, seat of the Socialist municipal government in the city.[39]

2. *Wartime Labor Relations in the Bolognese Countryside*

The first steps taken by the government in May 1915 appeared to confirm the hopes of Bologna's propertied classes that the war would require an authoritarian state which emasculated the local Socialist power structure and elevated prominent bourgeois politicians to commanding positions in the province. With the declaration of war came a series of emergency decrees that severely restricted the rights of the press and political associations. One decree specifically forbade all mass meetings in public places; another empowered the prefect to confiscate any publications that in his judgment "depress public spirit, shake its faith in the authority of the state, provoke unrest among the political parties, or prejudice the supreme national interests connected to the war and the domestic or international position of the state."[40] Moreover, the government declared the entire region of Emilia a war zone, allowing military authorities to impose additional limitations on normal political and administrative activities in Bologna. During

[38] B. Vigezzi, "Le 'Radiose giornate' del maggio 1915," p. 83.

[39] See V. Castronovo, *La stampa italiana dall'Unità*, p. 223.

[40] *Leggi e decreti. Il Regio Decreto, May 23, 1915*, Articles 2 and 3, quoted in N. De Stefano, "Moti popolari," pp. 192-193.

the summer of 1915, the Socialist municipalities saw their reform programs halted and much of their power removed to new war mobilization committees.[41]

Even before the official declaration of war, *Il Resto del Carlino* had asserted that "the Italian bourgeoisie must lead the people in this great challenge."[42] Accordingly, agrarian interests responded to the war with a burst of patriotic fervor and organizational initiatives. Old notables like Marchese Tanari and Marchese Carlo Alberto Pizzardi spearheaded the initial fund-raising drives in the province, to which employer organizations such as the Strike Insurance Fund contributed handsomely, while certain big commercial farmers not only made large donations, but also placed their villas at the disposal of the Italian army.[43] More importantly, agrarian leaders dominated the mobilization committees that emerged in the summer of 1915. The Bolognese Committee of Wartime Preparation, for instance, was founded less than a week after Italy had entered the war by Marchese Tanari, Enrico Pini, Donini, Stagni, and three of the leading leaseholders from the plains. In addition to his work on this committee, Pini also assumed the presidency of the new Committee of Agricultural Preparation in mid-July.[44]

Local landowners and commercial farmers soon discovered, however, that the imperatives of a total war did not necessarily coincide with their own political and economic interests. As in other belligerent countries, the need to mobilize all material and human resources in Italy forced the government to seek the active par-

[41] See Ignazio Masulli, "Il movimento operaio e contadino e le origini del partito comunista del Bolognese," *Studi Storici*, XIV, no. 1 (1973), p. 195; Romano Mattarelli, "Un momento del 'socialismo municipale': l'amministrazione Zanardi a Bologna nel periodo 1914-1918," *Rivista Storica Italiana*, LXXXI, no. 1 (1969), pp. 98-99.

[42] *RdC*, May 17, 1915.

[43] On these initiatives, see *ibid.*, June 16 and July 17, 1915.

[44] For the formation of the Committee on Wartime Preparation, see *ibid.*, May 29, 1915. The three leaseholders on the committee were Alfredo Benni, Roberto Cremonini, and Augusto Lenzi. On the agricultural committee, see *ibid.*, July 10, 1915.

ticipation of all social groups in the war effort.[45] To achieve the social cohesion dictated by military necessity, high ranking officials put pressure on the prefects to involve organized labor in the mobilization initiatives and to impose a new relationship between capital and labor in the countryside that entailed significant concessions to the socialist leagues. Such concessions were particularly important in a province like Bologna where the cooperation of a well-organized network of Socialist municipalities, unions, and cooperatives was essential to any effective mass mobilization.[46]

For its part, the leadership of the national Federterra did not delay in responding to the government's overtures. Despite the PSI's official position of "neither support nor sabotage," the Federterra ordered its provincial affiliates "to accept all those agreements that, being inspired by a spirit of fairness, correspond to the compelling necessities of the hour" and began in the summer of 1915 to advance its own proposal for the defense of agricultural production. As early as mid-July, it called upon the government to adopt emergency measures for the more rational cultivation of the land; shortly thereafter, it announced its intention to function as a "national employment office for the duration of the war."[47] In this fashion, the Federterra moved to turn an initially unfavorable situation to its advantage by assuring itself an institutional role in the war effort and by using military priorities to legitimize its solutions to the problems confronting Italian agriculture.

Moderate municipal Socialist leaders like Francesco Zanardi, mayor of Bologna, were equally enterprising and receptive to the government's appeals. After Italy's entrance into the war, Zanardi

[45] On wartime developments in Germany, for instance, see Gerald D. Feldman, *Army, Industry, and Labor in Germany, 1914-1918* (Princeton, 1966).

[46] See Francesco Piva, "Mobilitazione agraria e tendenze dell'associazionismo padronale durante la 'grande guerra'," *Quaderni Storici*, no. 38, September-December 1977, p. 814.

[47] See ASB, C6 F2, "Per il collocamento nazionale dei lavoratori della terra durante la guerra," letter of Federterra, no date, 1915; Antonio Papa, "Guerra e terra, 1915-1918," *Studi Storici*, x, 1969, no. 1, pp. 3-4.

immediately set up a program of assistance to the families of men drafted into the army. In July the minister of agriculture Cavasola urged Zanardi to take advantage of "the opportunity for a quick and efficacious intervention in the markets to regulate prices."[48] The mayor responded by creating the Independent Agency for Provisions to regulate commerce in the city and ensure the fair distribution of primary necessitites at controlled prices. This initiative, which led to increasingly close collaboration between the municipal council and the war mobilization committees, won Zanardi the praise of the central authorities as well as of his former critics at *Il Resto del Carlino*.[49]

In the countryside, Bolognese agrarian interests got their first indication that the war might be a mixed blessing in June, when the prefect pressured the AAB to accept a truce with the Federterra, so that "there will be no dissent or anything that disturbs the harmonious union of all the national forces during the period in which Italy confronts its historical destiny."[50] That month the two organizations signed an extraordinary contract for the entire province. According to its terms, an arbitrational commission—presided over by the prefect with representatives of labor and management—would settle all disputes over wages and work conditions. Far from restoring their dominance, the wartime government forced the organized agrarians to make unprecedented concessions to the leagues. For the first time, they had to recognize officially the provincial Federterra and make recourse to its employment offices for their day laborers. The leagues helped sweeten this bitter pill by guaranteeing labor peace and recognizing certain rights of non-union laborers for the duration of the war.[51]

The formal truce between the AAB and the Federterra continued throughout the war, with the original agreement of 1915 being

[48] *RdC*, July 18, 1915.

[49] See R. Mattarelli, "Un momento del 'socialismo municipale'," p. 101.

[50] *RdC*, June 10, 1915.

[51] Franco Cavazza, *Le agitazioni agrarie in Provincia di Bologna dal 1910 al 1920* (Bologna, 1940), p. 122.

renewed and revised in March 1916 and again in May 1917.[52] As a result, no major strike or labor dispute occurred between 1915 and 1918. Summarizing the situation in the Bolognese countryside during this period, the prefect proudly wrote in the summer of 1918: "Thanks to a series of agreements, in which I was constantly the intermediary or arbitrator, it has been possible to maintain a general tranquility that has permitted the efficacious operation of the farms and the peaceful development of those factors so essential to the national economy."[53] In fact, the situation in Bologna reflected the relative calm that prevailed throughout rural Italy in the war years. Between 1915 and 1918, government officials reported fewer than two hundred strikes, involving a mere seventy thousand laborers.[54]

The provincial agreements and the absence of major strikes did not mean, however, that all conflict had disappeared from the Bolognese countryside. On the contrary, the constricted labor market created by the war became a constant source of tensions and disputes. As commercial farmers frequently lamented, the military draft had reduced the previously abundant supply of labor, greatly enhancing the bargaining power of the Federterra. The controversies and polemics that reached the office of the prefecture after June 1915 invariably involved efforts by agrarian employers to minimize their dependence on the leagues by increasing their use of salaried workers and nonunion laborers imported from other provinces. Numerous prefectoral reports in 1915 and 1916 cited these practices as the main cause of discord.[55]

In response to protests from the Federterra and the inquiries of the prefect, the major leaseholders justified their actions on the grounds that the league offices lacked the manpower to meet their

[52] *RdC*, March 7, 1916; ASB, C6 F2, Prefect to Ministry of Interior, May 12, 1917.

[53] ASB, C7 F1, Prefect to Ministry of Interior, June 13, 1918.

[54] For strike statistics, see Maurice F. Neufeld, *Italy, School for Awakening Countries* (Ithaca, 1961), p. 547.

[55] See for instance, the record of agrarian contractual violations in 1915 in ASB, C6 F2, 1, 1916.

needs. Already in August 1915, for instance, Federico Dal Rio and Augusto Lenzi, two of the biggest growers in Medicina, informed police officials that the local employment office had failed to satisfy their requests for laborers and complained how the laborers whom they did receive were "either too old or too young to do the necessary work."[56] The AAB supported the claims of the leaseholders, warning in the spring of 1916 that "the manual labor in our province has been so insufficient that it is unclear whether the threshing will be completed." Stagni reiterated this view in a special report to the prefect, in which he charged that conditions in the labor market "threatened not only their private interests, but also necessarily the general interests of the nation."[57] The Federterra strongly contested the AAB's predictions of imminent catastrophe and accused commercial farmers of intentionally exaggerating the problem in order to disrupt the employment offices and escape paying the official wage scales. Thus in the commune of Medicina, where agrarian leaders reported the most serious labor shortages, the Federterra noted in the summer of 1916 how 15 percent of the work force was idle "and even greater unemployment is expected in the future."[58]

Despite the Federterra's optimistic appraisal of the labor market, the AAB began to pressure the government in 1917 to furnish its members with squads of soldiers and prisoners of war during the harvest season. When the government finally conceded to their demands in January 1918, commercial farmers immediately took advantage of the cheap prisoner labor to break off relations with the socialist employment offices and thereby circumvent the 25 percent wage increase stipulated in the previous year's contract. To mention only one among many examples, in the fall of 1918 the Federterra charged that not a single laborer "was requested from our office" by the six major agrarian employers in Medicina who instead completed the work exclusively with prisoners of war.

[56] ASB, C6 F2, 3, Vice-Chief of Police to Prefect, August 20, 1915.

[57] ASB, C6 F2, Raffaele Stagni to Prefect, March 29, 1916; *L'Agraria*, January-March, 1916.

[58] ASB, C6 F2, Federterra to Prefect, June 5, 1916.

These growers reaped handsome financial benefits from the use of the war prisoners since, as local police officials pointed out, they paid them wages substantially "less than those fixed for this work by the agreements."[59]

The AAB and the landowners displayed considerably less concern for labor shortages suffered by their peasant tenants following Italy's entrance into the war. Military conscription hit sharecropping families particularly hard. In June the mayor of Savigno painted a grim picture of their plight:

> As a result of the general mobilization, numerous families of peasant sharecroppers have lost their men, and the women cannot complete . . . the especially difficult field work in this period. This problem could be overcome with hired hands, but since the present contracts, signed in peacetime, require peasant families to pay the relative expenses for hired labor, such a remedy creates serious difficulties and leads to gross injustices: difficulties because the sharecroppers do not have at their disposition the means to pay the laborers . . . injustices because the greatest damages and sacrifices of the present crisis fall on the sharecroppers, while the landowners remain protected.[60]

After the leagues had won a 15 percent wage hike for the day laborers in mid-June, spokesmen for the sharecroppers began to demand that the government enact an emergency decree, requiring the landowners to pay the wages of day laborers hired to replace the peasant draftees.[61]

The Bolognese Committee for Wartime Preparation intervened in July with a compromise plan whereby the landowners would pay half the costs for additional labor hired by the sharecropping families. While both the socialist and independent peasant unions

[59] ASB, C6 F2, 1919, Police Report to Prefect, November 16, 1918. For the protests of the Federterra, see *ibid.*, C6 F2, Federterra to Prefect, July 27, and October 12, 1918.

[60] ASB, C6 F2, Mayor of Savigno to Prefect, June 4, 1915.

[61] *Ibid.*, C6 F2, Commissione colonica di San Giovanni in Persiceto to Prefect, June 18, 1915.

as well as a number of moderate landowners endorsed the plan, the AAB objected strenuously to its compulsory character. Stagni instead proposed a voluntary plan that merely invited the landowners to contribute to the labor costs of the sharecroppers on a case by case basis, taking into consideration specific economic conditions and the supposed rise in peasant incomes from the increase in agricultural prices. As the Federterra quickly pointed out, the AAB plan meant in effect that "the peasant will have to suffer all the damages created by the mobilization, while the landowners will limit themselves to taking advantage of the profits due to the rise in prices."[62] Neither the appeals of the prefecture nor the protests of peasant spokesmen had any apparent effect on the AAB. Stagni steadfastly refused to compromise on the issue, and in the summer of 1915 the landowners proceeded to take legal steps to evict those sharecroppers who had failed to fulfill their contractual obligations.[63]

Once again the wartime government's concern for the maintenance of social peace in the countryside took precedence over the short-term economic interests of the landowners. In the fall of 1915, Salandra announced a series of emergency decrees, extending all agricultural contracts for the duration of the war and requiring landlords to pay half the expenses of hired hands "in cases where the labor of the family members proves insufficient."[64] Even after the government's intervention, the question of labor expenses continued to be a source of conflict between sharecroppers and landlords, who sought to circumvent the decrees or hamper their enforcement. In late December 1915, for example, the police warned of serious unrest among the sharecroppers in various communes of the plains and foothills that they attributed to landowners who still "do not intend to contribute to the expenses for hired labor . . . required by peasant families that have lost men to the armed

[62] On the proposals and reactions to them, see *RdC*, July 4 and August 14, 1915.

[63] *Ibid.*, August 19, 1915 and ASB, C6 F2, 2, Federterra to Prefect, October 29, 1915.

[64] R. Bachi, *L'Italia economica nel 1915* (Turin, 1916), pp. 185-186.

services."[65] Other landowners found more devious ways to avoid their responsibilities. In the spring of 1917, a prefectoral commissioner accused certain agrarian employers in the lower plains of attempting to neutralize the government decrees by putting pressures "on their respective sharecroppers to avoid the employment of . . . day laborers."[66]

Economic considerations rather than political criteria appear to have dictated these practices, since the landowners applied them indiscriminately to sharecroppers in the independent and socialist unions. Thus, it was the peasant brotherhoods rather than the Federterra who protested to the prefect in 1917 that twenty-one landowners, including the seven richest commercial farmers, in the commune of Minerbio had violated the decrees in their dealings with the sharecroppers.[67] Likewise, both socialist and independent peasant leaders charged the big landowners with using their wealth and influence to control the arbitrational commissions and assure themselves favorable rulings. At least in the district of Budrio, these charges were confirmed by the government prosecutor who reported that the prefectoral representative on the commission had allowed the agrarian representative, Cesare Baroni, a free hand and had supported his "illegitimate pressures on the peasants to accept reimbursements smaller than what was owed them."[68]

Taken together these innumerable local protests and disputes form a picture of labor relations in the Bolognese countryside that fell somewhat short of the prefect's description of harmonious and productive collaboration between capital and labor. While government intervention and the restrictions imposed by military authorities precluded the vast strikes and violent confrontations that had characterized the province before 1915, the struggle between

[65] ASB, C6 F2, Police Report to Prefect, December 27, 1915.

[66] *Ibid.*, C6 F2, 1918, Prefectoral Commissioner to Prefect, April 10, 1917.

[67] *Ibid.*, C6 F2, 1918, Fratellanza Colonica to Prefect, no date, 1917. Among the landowners and commercial farmers mentioned were Count Filippo Cavazza, Roberto Cremonini, Count Gualtiero Isolani, Antonio Bonora, Fernando Bragaglia, Ignazio Benelli, and Alfredo Saltarelli.

[68] *Ibid.*, C6 F2, 1918, Procuratore del Re to Prefect, April 21, 1917.

agrarian employers and organized labor persisted in the form of continual minor skirmishes over the interpretation and implementation of wartime contracts and decrees. More importantly, this pattern of labor relations after 1915 ran directly counter to the original expectations of the propertied classes, for the war had not led to the dismantling of the socialist labor movement or to the reestablishment of agrarian supremacy in the countryside. On the contrary, as a result of the pressures of mobilization and the over-riding need for social cohesion on the homefront, the Federterra was able to acquire a new institutional legitimacy, increase its power and influence both with provincial authorities and in the ministerial world of Rome, and consolidate further its organizational control over the agricultural labor force in the Po Valley. By the armistice, agrarian interests confronted a considerably more formidable adversary in the socialist leagues.[69]

3. *Agricultural Production and Social Change in Wartime Bologna*

The absence of prolonged strikes and labor conflict in the period from 1915 to 1918 masked not only the persistence of class conflict, but also the profound social changes that took place in the countryside as a result of Italy's involvement in World War I. Indeed, special economic conditions, military conscription, and state intervention all combined to affect the structure of rural society, accelerating some major prewar social trends and reversing others. Thus, the war accelerated the advance of the big commercial leaseholders, who greatly strengthened their economic position at the expense of the old absentee landlords. At the same time, these circumstances sharpened divisions within the peasant classes. While the mass of day laborers and sharecroppers were hard hit by conscription and inflation, certain categories of small peasant propri-

[69] On the enduring strength of the Bolognese Federterra during the war years, see Luigi Arbizzani, "Lotte agrarie in provincia di Bologna nel primo dopoguerra," in *Le campagne emiliane nell'epoca moderna*, ed., R. Zangheri, (Milan, 1957), p. 298.

etors and sharecroppers, whose numbers had been shrinking in the decades prior to 1914, took advantage of wartime contractual and price conditions to amass substantial savings and acquire an extraordinary new economic vitality.

With Italy's entrance into the war, conditions within the agricultural sector improved dramatically. Harvests of wheat, rice, sugar beets, and hemp were all larger in 1915 than in the previous year. Moreover, increased production coincided with a sharp rise in prices for farm commodities. In the course of 1915 alone, wheat prices increased more than 30 percent, hemp prices nearly 20 percent.[70] Of course the war also created new problems for commercial farmers who faced growing shortages of chemical fertilizers, insecticides, and farm machines. Between 1913 and 1917, the supply of imported fertilizers and insecticides fell by almost two-thirds. Despite a tremendous rise in prices, the total value of imported farm machinery during the same period dropped from 18.5 million to 7.4 million lire. Military authorities compounded these problems by requisitioning some 2.5 million head of cattle in the course of the war.[71] Nonetheless, agricultural production, with the exception of the disastrous year 1917, remained only slightly below its prewar levels. In the province of Bologna, wheat harvests in the first two years of the war actually exceeded peacetime levels, while farm productivity in Bologna and the region of Emilia stayed close to what it had been in 1914.[72]

Even more than in peacetime, the benefits and burdens of agricultural production during the war were not shared equally by all the classes in the countryside. Arrigo Serpieri, leading agricultural expert of the period, claimed that the economic position of the day laborers in particular seriously deteriorated in the years from 1915 to 1918, a view shared by union representatives and the left in general. Since they were paid in monetary wages, the

[70] MAIC, *Annuario statistico italiano* 1917-1918, p. 160; A. Serpieri, *La guerra*, p. 38 and 100.

[71] A. Serpieri, *La guerra*, p. 49.

[72] *Ibid.*, p. 95; on conditions in Bologna and Emilia, see MAIC, *Annuario statistico italiano* 1917-1918, p. 167 and 172.

day laborers did not benefit from rising farm prices and were extremely vulnerable to the general increase in the cost of living, the index of which rose from 100 in 1914 to 264 by 1918.[73] The government did little to help these workers, providing them at best with meager family subsidies. In partial compensation, government officials could point to the improved employment opportunities for hired hands because of military conscription.[74] Moreover, in those provinces like Bologna where the leagues had already organized a large portion of the agricultural work force, the Federterra was able to win substantial wage hikes that amounted to a total increase of approximately 220 percent in the period from 1915 to the middle of 1919.[75] The precise relationship between the wage scales in the contracts and the real income of the laborers remains unclear, however. The enormous number of protests and complaints lodged by the Bolognese Federterra against agrarian employers for contractual violations and the use of nonunion labor suggests that often there was a sizeable gap between what the contracts stipulated and what the workers actually received. Likewise, the increased availability of work did not necessarily compensate for the decline in real wages, since agricultural employment remained seasonal and laborers still faced long periods of enforced idleness.[76]

At the same time though, the war created exceptional economic opportunities for ambitious peasant tenants and sharecroppers who had large families or who managed to avoid the draft. As a result of a series of government decrees, their prewar contracts were frozen, while the landlords were obligated to help defray their labor costs.[77] Paid a share of the harvest, those fortunate peasant cultivators who produced for the market directly benefited from the enormous rise in farm prices after 1914. Indeed, with a single

[73] A. Serpieri, *La guerra*, pp. 143-144.

[74] *Ibid.*, p. 139; Luigi Preti, *Le lotte agrarie nella valle padana* (Turin, 1955), p. 345.

[75] See R. Bachi, *L'Italia economica nel 1919* (Città di Castello, 1920), p. 420.

[76] For the protests of the Federterra, see ASB, C6 F2 for the years 1915-1918.

[77] See L. Preti, *Le lotte agrarie*, p. 345.

harvest, they earned sums that previously would have required years of hard work and sacrifices. By 1917, many of them had doubled and sometimes even tripled their prewar incomes. One study of a group of twenty Bolognese sharecroppers, for instance, reported that their net income rose nearly 500 percent between 1914 and 1918.[78] The annual reports of the rural banks further testified to the new-found prosperity of these peasant strata. Deposits in traditional peasant savings institutions, which had grown by only 5 percent in the three years prior to 1914, more than doubled during the war. Total deposits in the Cassa di Risparmio of Bologna jumped more than 70 percent already in the first two years of the war.[79] More importantly, by 1918 successful tenant farmers and sharecroppers had begun to use their earnings to purchase land, prefiguring what would be the most important social phenomenon in the countryside after the armistice: the emergence of a new class of small peasant proprietors.[80]

The large commercial leaseholders of the Po Valley plains reaped even greater financial benefits. A variety of circumstances conspired to enrich these big growers in the years after 1914. Unlike the sharecroppers, who provided their landlords with a portion of the harvest, the leaseholders paid their rents in cash. With rents frozen at prewar levels, they were thus in a position to earn huge profits from the sale of their crops as farm prices soared. According to Serpieri, the real income of the capitalist leaseholders in the Po Valley more than quintupled during the war.[81] The same leaseholders enjoyed a host of other advantages. For the most part,

[78] Giuseppe Tassinari, "Le recenti agitazioni agrarie nell'Italia Centrale e le condizioni economiche dei mezzadri" in *Atti della R. Accademia dei Georgofili*, Vol. XVII, 1920, quoted in Osvaldo Passerini, *Inchiesta sulla piccola proprietà coltivatrice formatasi nel dopoguerra*, Vol. VII, *Emilia e Le Marche* (Milan, 1932), p. 33n.

[79] On the growth in deposits, see A. Serpieri, *La guerra*, p. 118 and Cassa di Risparmio, *La Cassa di Risparmio in Bologna nei suoi primi cento anni* (Bologna, 1937), p. 397.

[80] See O. Passerini, *Inchiesta sulla piccola proprietà*; E. Sereni, *La questione agraria nella rinascita nazionale italiana* (Rome, 1946), p. 117. For its social and political consequences see Chapters VI and VII in this study.

[81] A. Serpieri, *La guerra*, p. 116.

they did not have to pay the rising property and war-profits taxes. The greater efficiency and size of their farms also assured them preferential treatment by military and government authorities. Favoritism was perhaps most evident in the distribution of exemptions from military service for persons engaged in agricultural activity. From Italy's entrance into the war until mid-1917, the large leaseholders enjoyed a virtual monopoly of these exemptions.[82] In a similar fashion, the leaseholders were the chief beneficiaries of the new wartime agencies founded to stimulate agricultural production. Following the example of England and France, the Italian government created the State Tractor Agency (Motoaratura di Stato) in 1917 to facilitate the importation of farm machines. The vast majority of the 6,580 tractors, which this agency imported during the last two years of the war, wound up in the hands of the commercial leaseholders of the Po Valley who had the land, capital, and technical expertise to utilize them.[83]

The leaseholders' enrichment came largely at the expense of the absentee landowners. Government decrees, tax policies, and price trends all worked decisively to the disadvantage of those landowners who had leased their lands prior to 1915. With rents frozen at the level of 1915, they received none of the financial benefits of rapidly climbing farm prices. While their rental income from the land remained stationary, they had to shoulder the burdens of increased property taxes and rising living costs. Thus absentee landowners in the Po Valley saw their real income fall by as much as a third during the war, leading to what Serpieri characterized as a massive "shift of wealth from the landowner to the leaseholder."[84] The altered balance of power within the propertied classes found expression not only in the redistribution of wealth, but also in the changing structure of landholding in the decade after the

[82] *Ibid.*, pp. 64, 100-102.

[83] Utenti Motori Agricoli, *Quarant'anni di motorizzazione agricola in Italia 1928-1967* (Rome, 1968), pp. XVII-XVIII; A. Cadeddu, S. Lepre, F. Socrate, "Ristagno e sviluppo nel settore agricolo italiano (1918-1939)" *Quaderni Storici*, no. 29-30, May-December 1975, pp. 503-504.

[84] A. Serpieri, *La guerra*, pp. 116-118.

war. More immediately, its effects could be seen in the leadership and policies of the agrarian interest-group organizations. Beginning in 1917, Bolognese commercial farming interests in particular took the lead in formulating and lobbying for a new, more comprehensive agricultural program that responded to both the challenges and opportunities created by the war.[85]

4. *Commercial Agriculture and the Wartime State: Agrarian Interest-Group Politics, 1917-1918*

Writing in the fall of 1917, Mario Missiroli issued an ominous warning to northern commercial farmers:

> The entire world is rising up: all things are about to undergo profound changes. We are witnessing the concentration of wealth in the hands of a small group . . . [and] the radical transformation of the ruling classes. . . . At the same time, we see the agrarians standing by the wayside, cowering, timid, afraid to move. . . . Perhaps they do not know that an African wind is blowing from Russia. . . . Don't these agrarians realize that there are men in Italy capable of becoming Lenins? . . . Haven't [they] become aware that a colossal union against landed property is being organized?[86]

At least in the province of Bologna, Missiroli's words did not fall on deaf ears. On the contrary, they reflected the already evident concern of Bolognese agrarian leaders over the organizational weakness and disarray of commercial farming interests, in the face of increasingly menacing challenges from organized labor and the powerful war industries. Such weakness and disarray had their origins in the situation created by Italian belligerency. After Italy's entrance into the war brought an end to strikes and serious labor

[85] On the changing structure of landholding in Bologna, see the conclusion of this study.

[86] See Missiroli's two articles in *L'Agraria*, November and December 1917.

agitation in the countryside, the National Agrarian Confederation lapsed into inactivity, while the action of the various provincial associations became fragmented in countless purely local initiatives. Although certain agrarian notables held prominent positions on the mobilization committees, commercial farmers as a group lacked any effective organization in the first two years of the war to defend their interests, either at the regional level or in Rome.[87]

By the fall of 1916, new and more drastic proposals by organized labor for sweeping land reform exposed the dangers of agrarian organizational absenteeism. The Federterra and the CGL used mounting food and production problems to justify a campaign against the absolute rights of private property and to demand that the government expropriate some 7 million hectares of uncultivated or inadequately cultivated land.[88] Enthusiasm on the left for land reform increased the following year as news of events in Russia reached the Italian peninsula. Inspired by the growing peasant revolution in the Russian countryside, one contemporary observer wrote in the spring of 1917: "We are in a period in which the idea of land to the peasants is triumphing in all of Europe. Will our country not feel the repercussions of this?"[89] The significance of these developments was not lost on old agrarian notables like Marchese Giuseppe Tanari. As early as April, Tanari called upon the propertied classes to formulate their own land reform proposals, warning that otherwise they would find themselves "in a permanent state of revolution."[90]

At the same time, commercial farmers confronted a powerful new military-industrial-bureaucratic complex that was advancing its own interests at the expense of the agricultural sector. Much

[87] On the organizational disarray of the agrarians, see F. Piva, "Mobilitazione agraria," pp. 809-813; A. Serpieri, *La guerra*, p. 238.

[88] See A. Papa, "Guerra e terra," pp. 9-11.

[89] *Ibid.*, p. 21.

[90] *RdC*, April 22, 1917. In this issue, Tanari presented his own proposal for land reform to develop "a strong and numerous class of cultivators and small landowners who work and live on the land." In addition, see Giuseppe Tanari, *Studi sulla questione agraria* (Bologna, 1918).

like in other belligerent states, the imperatives of war production forced the Italian government to become, in the words of Riccardo Bachi, "the center, the motor of the national economy, the only or chief client of the most varied industries, the despotic ruler of vast numbers of economic enterprises." Emergency decrees in the summer of 1915 brought into existence the Industrial Mobilization, an enormous bureaucracy empowered to designate official war industries, control labor relations, and regulate the distribution of resources, transportation, and the stipulation of contracts.[91] Government contracts and generous subsidies encouraged those companies deemed essential to the war effort to expand their production without regard for costs. To guarantee labor peace, the factories were placed under military law and became veritable armed camps surrounded by troops and controlled internally through a network of informers and spies. Under these circumstances, management was able to denounce any labor agitation as "defeatist" maneuvers harmful to national production and the domestic war effort.[92]

Wartime state intervention had a dramatic impact on the structure of Italian industry. Above all, the metallurgical, mechanical, and chemical sectors underwent a rapid process of expansion and concentration. By 1917, a few industrial giants such as Ansaldo, FIAT, Ilva, Breda, and Montecatini had gained a virtual monopoly of production for the war. In the period from 1915 to 1918, FIAT climbed from thirtieth to third place among Italian corporations, increased its capital five-fold, and enlarged its work force from four thousand to forty thousand. By the end of the war, the automotive firm accounted for 92 percent of the country's production of trucks and 80 percent of its airplane engines.[93]

[91] See R. Bachi, *L'Italia economica nell'anno 1918* (Città di Castello, 1919), pp. XIII-XVI.

[92] For the industrial mobilization and its effects on production and labor relations, see Luigi Einaudi, *La condotta economica e gli effetti sociali della guerra italiana* (Bari, 1933), p. 113; Roberto Vivarelli, *Il dopoguerra in Italia e l'avvento del fascismo* (Naples, 1967), p. 100; Alberto Caracciolo, "La crescita e la trasformazione della grande industria durante la prima guerra mondiale," in Giorgio Fuà, ed., *Lo sviluppo economico in Italia*, Vol. III (Milan, 1969), pp. 215-216.

[93] See V. Castronovo, *Giovanni Agnelli* (Turin, 1971), pp. 109-110. On the

The growth of the Industrial Mobilization also stimulated an extraordinary new fusion of private and public power by bringing industrial leaders into direct and continuous contact with the war ministries and the army general staff. Both on the central and regional committees set up to determine economic priorities and direct production, men of the stature of Giovanni Agnelli, Dante Ferraris, and the Perrone brothers worked closely with General Alfredo Dallolio, head of the Industrial Mobilization, and the various military commanders and government officials. For the first time, leading industrial entrepreneurs found themselves in charge of state agencies with virtually unlimited power over entire sectors of production in which their own firms were involved. Not surprisingly, such arrangements translated into exceptional profits for these strategically situated business groups.[94]

Bolognese agrarian spokesmen viewed the government's promotion of the war industries with a mix of resentment and envy. Alberto Donini voiced the feelings of many growers when he charged that the "gigantic edifice of the Industrial Mobilization" had put commercial farmers "in a position of unjust inferiority" by absorbing resources and equipment that "had been taken away from agriculture."[95] The paucity of state initiatives on behalf of the agricultural sector seemed to confirm this view. In the first two years of the war, the government required numerous sacrifices from farmers with few corresponding benefits. There had been no shortage of special decrees and ordinances, imposing price controls, requisitions, export restrictions, and crop substitutions. Government aid, on the other hand, had consisted of only three measures: exemptions from military service, licenses for soldier workers, and provincial agricultural commissions.[96] Even these few measures

growth in industrial concentration, see Renzo Pacci, "Le trasformazioni ed innovazioni nella struttura economica italiana," in *Il trauma dell'intervento, 1914-1919* (Florence, 1968), pp. 29-55.

[94] See A. Caracciolo, "La crescita e la trasformazione della grande industria," pp. 216-217.

[95] *Libertà Economica*, February 10, 1918.

[96] AAB, *Per la Mobilitazione Agricola. Memoriale presentato a S.E. Ministro*

did not function properly according to the AAB. While bureaucratic red tape and the hostility of the Socialist municipalities obstructed the distribution of exemptions and licenses, the commissions had not received any real "effective and conclusive power."[97]

Commercial farming spokesmen in Bologna, however, saw in the Industrial Mobilization not only a threat, but also a model for a comparable mobilization of their sector as well as for a new relationship between the state and agriculture. Indeed, the "excellent results" achieved by the semipublic agencies in the war industries had demonstrated to the leaders of the AAB how a strong interventionist state might serve commercial farmers equally well by promoting their economic interests, curbing the independent power of the socialist leagues, and by regimenting agricultural labor in the cause of greater national production. These objectives were clearly evident in the proposal for an "Agrarian Mobilization" which the AAB presented to the Ministry of Agriculture in January 1917. Citing the precedent of what had taken place in the war industries, the association called upon the government to transform the agricultural sector into "an immense state workshop in which all the forces engaged in production are rigidly disciplined for a single purpose."[98] Specifically, the proposal envisioned a network of committees with absolute authority over all the rural classes that could impose a "rational distribution" of labor and any other measures required "to assure food for the soldiers and the civilian population" and to eliminate existing distortions in the division of economic resources. The AAB made no secret of its plan's authoritarian character, insisting that "a superior intelligence and a strong authority are needed to deliberate and give orders. Everyone else is expected to obey."[99]

If the Industrial Mobilization provided agrarian leaders with an

---

dell'Agricoltura (Bologna, 1917), pp. 5-6. For an account of the burdens assumed by growers, see A. Serpieri, *La guerra*, p. 75.

97 AAB, *Per la Mobilitazione Agricola*, pp. 5-6.

98 *Ibid.*, p. 8.

99 *Ibid.*, pp. 10-14. In addition, see *RdC*, January 12, 1917 and *L'Agraria*, January-April 1917.

operational model, the "productivist" ideas of the Nationalist Association provided a doctrine that allowed them to identify the private interests of commercial farmers with the general interests of the nation in arms. With the publication of *La marcia dei produttori* in 1916, Enrico Corradini brought together earlier partial analyses into a general theory of productivism. According to the Nationalist leader, the war had shown how national survival ultimately depended upon large-scale economic organization directed by a strong and capable "productive bourgeoisie." National power and expansion made it imperative that both state and society be geared to achieve the over-riding goals of economic growth and enhanced productivity. Corradini denied, moreover, the necessity of class conflict and envisioned a new form of class collaboration: the solidarity of producers, from the biggest entrepreneur to the lowliest worker, all united against the parasites of parliament and the antinational forces of the left.[100]

Productivist arguments clearly permeated the AAB's proposal for an Agricultural Mobilization. Echoing the views of Corradini, the association affirmed that victory in World War I required not only a strong military, but also a "more efficacious economic organization that fully utilizes all energies and all activities." Under the guise of promoting national agricultural production and internal resistance, local agrarian leaders demanded that the government use its authority to impose solutions to a range of problems that plagued commercial farming interests in previous decades:

[100] A. De Grand, *The Italian Nationalist Association*, pp. 83-86. While the Nationalists tailored their ideas to fit the interests of their industrial benefactors, they did not neglect the commercial farmers of the Po Valley. *L'Idea Nazionale* supported all efforts to increase cooperation between agriculture and industry; Filippo Carli, the Nationalist economist and head of the Brescian Chamber of Commerce, urged commercial farmers to follow the example of the industrial cartels by developing an association of agrarian producers to regulate marketing activities and standardize agricultural production "as it is done in heavy industry." Nationalist ideas appeared to find a favorable reception in Bolognese agrarian circles. In the summer of 1917, for instance, *L'Agraria* published and enthusiastically endorsed the postwar economic program drawn up by Carli for the Association of Italian Joint Stock Companies. See Filippo Carli, *L'altra guerra* (Milan, 1916), pp. 287-297; F. Piva, "Mobilitazione agraria," p. 828.

the short-sighted individualism of many growers, the lack of economic coordination among the rural classes, and most especially the workers' "passive and blind obedience to organizations whose principles are often in complete contrast to the present national imperatives." While the AAB claimed to eschew class objectives in favor of expanded production and economic efficiency, its proposal stressed the strict regimentation of labor, which was expected to make substantial sacrifices by "prolonging work hours and renouncing every limitation on the free development of agricultural production."[101]

Significantly, Bolognese agrarian leaders viewed their proposed mobilization as something more than a temporary response to special wartime conditions. Indeed, they saw it as the cornerstone of a new social and economic order in the Italian countryside, in which the state intervened to rationalize production and discipline relations between capital and labor on a permanent basis. Donini, for instance, insisted that many mechanisms of the Agricultural Mobilization "could remain in the postwar period where they might be perfected and adapted to resolve the formidable and inescapable problems of the future."[102] With this goal in mind, they drastically altered the program of the AAB in the summer of 1917. The first indication of an impending change came in May with the resignation of Raffaele Stagni, the chief architect of the prewar strategy of confrontation, from the presidency of the association and his replacement by Count Filippo Cavazza, son of the prominent moderate Count Francesco Cavazza. Despite his parentage, Filippo Cavazza was not an old-fashioned absentee landlord or an agrarian moderate of the traditional stamp. On the contrary, he was an agricultural expert, with a degree in zoology and zootechnics from the University of Bologna, who had founded with the big capitalist leaseholder Roberto Cremonini a joint-stock company, the Società Cavazza-Cremonini, to farm commercially his father's estates in

[101] AAB, *Per la Mobilitazione Agricola*, pp. 3-9; ASB, C6 F2, Resolution of the AAB, April 5, 1917.
[102] *L'Agraria*, July 1917.

the plains prior to the war. His elevation to the head of the AAB thus signaled not a return to the prewar strategy of the moderates, but rather the adaption of commercial farming interests to the problems and opportunities created by the war.[103]

Evidence for this interpretation came two months later when Cavazza and Donini unveiled a new longterm program that espoused productivist ideals while largely ignoring the plight of the absentee landowners. Jettisoning the rhetoric of class conflict and confrontation, they emphasized the mission of the AAB to forge an alliance of all rural producers, both large and small, in order to "create and perfect an environment conducive to the intensified production of wealth and its more equal distribution."[104] In addition to measures for the industrialization of agriculture, the program included proposals to stimulate the growth of a class of small peasant proprietors. Two decades of strikes and bitter labor conflicts had demonstrated, in their view, that a large class of landless day laborers constituted the chief threat to efficient farming and productive collaboration in the countryside. Consequently, the two agrarian leaders called for measures to encourage "every form of contract that, by involving the laborer directly in production, gives him a secure livelihood and the possibility of savings."[105] In this fashion, the AAB now sought to pose as the voice not only of the big growers but of all the supposedly productive elements involved in agricultural activity.

Much like the proposal for the Agricultural Mobilization, the new program of the AAB envisioned a major role for the state in the prevention of strikes and other disturbances that endangered production and discouraged capital investments in agriculture. As

[103] On the changing of the guard at the helm of the AAB, see *Libertà Economica*, March 10, 1918, for Donini's report on the association in the period 1916-1917. For a brief biography of Filippo Cavazza, see *Panorama biografico degli italiani d'oggi* (Florence, 1956), Vol. I, p. 344. On his work on his father's estates, see L. Zerbini, *Illustrazione delle principali aziende agrarie del Bolognese* (Bologna, 1913).

[104] See *L'Agraria*, July 1917.

[105] *Ibid.*

Donini expressed it, the government had to guarantee "the progress of the sharecroppers, small tenant farmers, and small landowners" by ensuring that "the labor unions are kept within legal limits and their [political] goals are modified."[106] To this end, the program demanded the continuation of compulsory arbitration on a permanent basis and the official recognition of the leagues as legally responsible parties in all contracts and agreements. Noticeably absent from the program were measures to aid the agrarian old guard. Far from coming to the defense of the absentee landowners, Cavazza and Donini indicated their support for government intervention to facilitate the division of the large aristocratic estates and the requisitioning of land left uncultivated by "inept" landowners.[107]

Bolognese agrarian leaders, however, soon discovered that it was considerably easier to draw up programs than to dictate national agricultural policy from a provincial base. From the outset, the Federterra attacked their planned regimentation of labor, charging that it would encourage "private speculation rather than meet the real and effective needs of agriculture."[108] Moreover, the AAB's proposals lacked a broad base of support among Italy's rural propertied classes. For the most part, large landowners from southern and central Italy seemed to prefer the program of the new Association for the Defense of National Agriculture, which strongly opposed "excessive state interference" in the countryside. Even in the Po Valley, the AAB's program met with resistance from other agrarian associations like that of Parma, which continued to advocate a strategy of bourgeois solidarity and unmediated confrontation with the socialist leagues.[109]

In the absence of a solid national agrarian consensus or a strong lobby in Rome, the AAB was able to exert little influence on governmental authorities who rejected its proposal for massive

[106] *Ibid.*

[107] Dino Donati, "Aspetti dell'organizzazione agraria bolognese tra guerra e dopoguerra (1915-1919)," *Studi Storici*, XIV, no. 2 (1973), p. 407.

[108] See F. Piva, "Mobilitazione agraria," p. 820.

[109] *Ibid.*, p. 827.

state intervention in agriculture in the summer of 1917. Not until February 1918, nearly three years after the creation of the Industrial Mobilization, did the minister of agriculture receive sweeping emergency powers to promote agricultural production and control the distribution of labor and farm supplies. Coming in the last year of the war, the official Agrarian Mobilization did not exist long enough to allow the development of a stable system of state regulatory agencies that commercial farmers could utilize after the armistice. As Riccardo Bachi noted, "the complex mechanism of so many commissioners and so many committees did not function or else added to the confusion . . . by creating obstacles and slowing down the already difficult development of the means of production."[110] Lack of clout in Rome also had its repercussions at the provincial level. When Cavazza demanded the creation of a powerful regulatory commission in the spring of 1918 "for the superior interests of production," the Bolognese prefect dismissed his demand on the grounds that the AAB represented only a minority of the growers who "should not be placed by the government in a privileged position in relation to the others."[111]

Nevertheless, the paucity of concrete results should not obscure the significance of the proposals emanating from the AAB in the last two years of the war. For the plan of agricultural mobilization as well as the other projects outlined by Donini and Cavazza in the summer of 1917 reflected a dramatic change in the approach of Bolognese commercial farming interests to the key questions of class relations in the countryside and state intervention in the private sector. Under new leadership, the AAB had disavowed its prewar methods of intransigent resistance and begun instead to promote a broad alliance of all rural producers, through which it posed as the guardian of national production and the disinterested spokesman for an ostensibly homogeneous agricultural sector. Likewise, the old hostility to government meddling gave way to a pronounced enthusiasm for state action to integrate the leagues

[110] R. Bachi, *L'Italia economica nel 1918*, pp. 224-225.

[111] ASB, C6 F2, Prefect to Ministry of Interior, September 9, 1918.

into a rigid new system of social bargaining that precluded strikes and ensured productive expansion. Such ideas were not merely temporary responses to special wartime conditions; they constituted the main tenets of the program that Bolognese agrarian leaders would pursue in the postwar period, both at the provincial level and in Rome.

VI. AN ELITE BESIEGED: THE POSTWAR CRISIS IN BOLOGNA

After three and a half years of enormous material and human destruction, World War I came to an end in the late fall of 1918. On November 3, the Italian and Austrian military delegations signed an armistice at Villa Giusti near the city of Padua; the following day hostilities officially ceased. The sudden return to peace had immediate domestic repercussions in Italy, for in no other victorious country were the expectations of radical change in the postwar period so pronounced and widespread. In the spring of 1919, *Il Corriere della Sera* captured the climate of euphoria and utopian hopes that characterized Italian society in the first months of peace:

> The end of the war has removed that moral force which constrained every citizen to control himself, to wait with patience, to limit his own desires. Now that this bridle has broken, all aspirations have a free field and all desires have been unchained. Everyone seems to feel the need to live newly his life. It is no longer the old life, which today appears so serene and easy, but a new life that must be full, rich, more than before. Thus all classes are agitated; they all want something more than they have now, not simply increases in monetary wages or shorter

work hours, but all that . . . in order to enjoy a more intense and elevated life.[1]

In the wake of revolution in Germany and the Austro-Hungarian Empire, Italians from every walk of life came to see sweeping political and social change as an inevitable feature of the world emerging from the war. Demands for constitutional reform, land to the peasants, workers' control of the factories, and public regulation of industry now dominated all political discussions and debates. The rhetoric of radical change seemed to infect even old conservatives like Antonio Salandra, who declared in November 1918: "The war is a revolution, yes, a very great revolution. Let no one think that after the storm it will be possible to make a peaceful return to the old order. Let no one think that the old habits of leisurely life can be resumed."[2]

Above all, the war brought about a profound transformation in the habits and expectations of Italy's rural population. Intervention in May 1915 had wrenched the mass of peasants from their familiar village surroundings and thrown them into a war they experienced as a form of obscure punishment. They provided the bulk of the frontline troops; from their ranks came the great majority of casualties. Established habits of deference and subservience vanished in the crucible of the trenches. In their place came new aspirations that found expression in the slogans "land to the peasants," the "last war," and the "democratic and proletarian war," which increasingly circulated along the front lines as the war dragged on.[3] The government and the political parties encouraged these aspirations during the latter phases of the war in order to sustain morale in the trenches as well as on the homefront. While the parties drew up competing proposals for land reform, the government propaganda machine distributed a steady stream of leaflets that exhorted the troops to defend "the land on which you will

[1] *Corriere della Sera*, April 11, 1919, quoted in Roberto Vivarelli, *Il dopoguerra in Italia e l'avvento del fascismo* (Naples, 1967), p. 407.

[2] Gaetano Salvemini, *The Fascist Dictatorship in Italy* (New York, 1967), p. 4n.

[3] R. Vivarelli, *Il dopoguerra in Italia*, p. 27.

toil and from which you will draw for yourself all the products of your labor."[4] As a result, peasant soldiers returned home after the armistice, expecting immediate recognition of their sacrifices and immediate satisfaction of their demands for land.

The economic realities of postwar Italy, however, precluded even the partial satisfaction of popular expectations. The war had taken a heavy toll on the economy: the pattern of industry had been distorted, the land exhausted, the balance of trade disrupted, and the transportation system allowed to deteriorate seriously.[5] With the return of peace, the enormous war industries cut back on their production and laid off thousands of workers, precisely at a time when demobilized soldiers were flooding back into the labor market. Unemployment, which had virtually disappeared during the war, reached alarming proportions in the spring of 1919. Between the beginning of March and the end of April alone, the number of jobless persons rose more than 25 percent, with the provinces of the Po Valley leading the way.[6] Skyrocketing inflation compounded the plight of the unemployed workers and veterans. The termination of wartime allied supports and price controls had a disastrous impact on the Italian monetary system. When London and New York abolished controls in late March 1919, the value of the lira plummeted, sparking a rapid rise in prices. By June the general price index had quadrupled its prewar levels and showed no signs of leveling off.[7]

[4] F. M. Fiecchi, *La terra ai contadini quale fu promessa al fante*, quoted in *ibid.*, p. 26. For a general discussion of the land reform proposals advanced by the various political parties, see Antonio Papa, "Guerra e terra 1915-1918," *Studi Storici*, x, no. 1 (1969), pp. 14-37.

[5] See Christopher Seton-Watson, *Italy from Liberalism to Fascism* (London, 1967), p. 519.

[6] On these problems, see R. Bachi, *L'Italia economica 1918* (Turin, 1916), p. 392; Arrigo Serpieri, *La guerra e classi rurali italiane* (Bari, 1930), p. 165; Idomeneo Barbadoro, *Storia del sindacalismo italiano dalla nascita al fascismo*, Vol. I, *La Federterra* (Florence, 1973), p. 347; R. Tremelloni, "La disoccupazione in Italia nel dopoguerra" *Rassegna della Previdenza Sociale*, August 1923, pp. 2-27, cited in R. Vivarelli, *Il dopoguerra*, p. 406n.

[7] The average cost of 100 Swiss francs rose from 130 lire in the second half of

Already in the winter of 1918-19, local authorities began to warn that frustrated popular expectations might lead to serious disorders. In the province of Bologna, for instance, the prefect wrote in January:

> The return of the soldiers from the front is, as I predicted, an element of new concern. Returning to their families, they cannot find provisions or obtain work. They are not willing to accept these conditions, and their unemployment is added to that of the masses of workers who are gradually being released from the factories that previously produced our war materials. Now it is important to remember that . . . those men who are returning from the front were continually encouraged . . . by morale propaganda which made certain promises. Every sacrifice asked in periods of grave crisis was preceded by preparation of this sort. All this created in the soldiers a firm and secure conviction that today they see brutally destroyed.[8]

Such concern proved to be more than justified. High unemployment and inflation helped trigger not only an extraordinary resurgence of labor militancy in 1919, but also more chaotic and explosive forms of social protest. Beginning in June, the peninsula became the scene of a wave of "cost of living" riots that spread rapidly from the port city of La Spezia to other urban centers. Between the end of June and the middle of July, riots broke out in over twenty-six cities, including Bologna, Rome, Milan, Genoa, and Naples. Significantly, the most serious violence erupted at Imola in the province of Bologna, where five people were killed and three wounded in clashes with the police after mobs had sacked

---

1918 to 326.5 lire by the beginning of 1920. See G. Salvemini, *The Fascist Dictatorship*, p. 5.

[8] ASB, C7 F1, "Spirito e ordine pubblico nella Provincia di Bologna," Prefect to Ministry of Interior, January 5, 1919, quoted in R. Vivarelli, *Il dopoguerra*, pp. 400-401. Already in December of 1918, the military commander warned that in the province "the conditions have become more serious" because "here the unemployment is real." See ASB, C7 F1, "Spirito pubblico nel Bolognese," December 30, 1918.

and destroyed scores of stores and private homes.[9] Two months later, peasant veterans in the south began to act unilaterally on the government's wartime promises of land. In August groups of them seized uncultivated lands in the Roman campagna, setting an example that their comrades in Puglia and Sicily soon followed. By the end of the year, some 79,000 acres had been seized without prior consent of the owners, another 172,000 acres occupied after "friendly" agreements.[10]

The Nationalists and various paramilitary groups added to the confusion with their violent counterdemonstrations and their annexationist demands in the Adriatic. During the summer of 1919, collaboration between the Nationalists and military officials in the disputed cities of Trieste and Fiume gave rise to rumors of a possible coup d'etat. Right-wing agitation in the area culminated in September when the local garrison mutinied and under the command of Gabrielle D'Annunzio seized control of Fiume, in open defiance of the government.[11]

Italy's ruling political class was unprepared to cope with the breakdown of old loyalties and respect for law and order that confronted it in the first year of peace. Bitter divisions over the war, foreign policy, and domestic reform had dramatically accentuated the pre-existing fragmentation of the constitutional forces. As a result, the governments of Giuseppe Orlando and his successor Francesco Saverio Nitti lacked the solid base of political support needed to deal effectively with mass unrest and right-wing sedition, let alone to direct the difficult transition from war to peacetime production and to carry out a coherent program of social and political reform. Throughout the first nine months of 1919, po-

[9] On the riots in Imola, see ASB, C7 F1, Police Report to Prefect, July 27, 1919. For developments on the peninsula as a whole, see R. Vivarelli, *Il dopoguerra*, pp. 412-415.

[10] See G. Salvemini, *Fascist Dictatorship*, p. 29.

[11] On the activities of the Nationalists and D'Annunzio, see Alexander De Grand, *The Italian Nationalist Association and the Rise of Fascism in Italy* (Lincoln, Nebr., 1978), pp. 95-111; R. Vivarelli, *Il dopoguerra*, pp. 342-385; Charles Maier, *Recasting Bourgeois Europe* (Princeton, 1975), pp. 113-116.

litical leaders in Rome ricochetted from one emergency to another with improvised measures that alienated both the right and the left. At the same time, government instability undermined the authority of the state machine. In the absence of strong political leadership in Rome, the public administration gradually broke down into a myriad of separate power centers at the periphery that became increasingly susceptible to pressures from well-organized private interests.[12] It was under these inauspicious circumstances that Bolognese agrarian leaders attempted to refine and implement their wartime proposals.

1. *Toward an Alliance of Producers: The Agrarian Program of 1919*

As Filippo Cavazza and Alberto Donini had foreseen in 1917, the return of peace confronted commercial farming interests with a number of extremely serious problems and challenges. In the wake of war and revolution abroad, the socialist labor movement had assumed a level of organization and militancy that the employer associations could no longer contain with the methods used prior to 1914.[13] At the same time, growers faced a greatly enlarged and concentrated heavy industrial sector that threatened to subordinate and sacrifice the needs of agriculture during the

[12] See Adrian Lyttelton, *The Seizure of Power: Fascism in Italy, 1919-1929* (New York, 1973), pp. 40-41 for the relationship between governmental instability and the piecemeal disintegration of the liberal state.

[13] After the armistice, the leagues in many northern provinces began to elaborate schedules, fixing the number of laborers to be hired per hectare, agricultural operation, and season of the year. In Bologna the Federterra abruptly terminated its wartime truce with the AAB in November, refusing to participate in negotiations for a new general contract. Instead, the leagues announced an extensive program of demands that included significant wage increases, the eight-hour day, equalization of salary scales, and the extension of socialist hiring halls throughout the province. For developments in Bologna, see *La Squilla*, February 22, 1919; developments elsewhere are discussed in Luigi Preti, *Le lotte agrarie nella valle padana* (Turin, 1955), pp. 373-389.

difficult period of reconversion to peacetime production.[14] These challenges were closely linked in turn to the larger problems of electoral mobilization and interest representation requiring fresh and innovative initiatives by the propertied classes in the increasingly democratic polity emerging from the war.

Bolognese agrarian leaders responded to these problems in 1919 by developing their wartime proposals into a program, both at the provincial level and in Rome, that represented an uneasy marriage of economic self-interest and political necessity. Reflecting the influence of the Agrarian Mobilization and fashionable "productivist" ideas, their program advocated the industrialization of agriculture, a return to older forms of integration between capital and labor, and most importantly the creation of a broad coalition of agricultural producers that united commercial farmers, agrarian technicians, small peasant proprietors, and sharecroppers. Indeed, such a "productive alliance of capital, labor, and expertise" was the cornerstone of agrarian hopes for political renewal and economic expansion in the postwar era.[15]

Economic growth and increased productivity remained the dominant themes of the AAB after the armistice. According to Cavazza and other local organizers, all "agricultural producers," from the biggest landowners to the humblest field hands, had a patriotic duty to help make "the industry of the fields . . . produce as much and as well as possible."[16] Much like industrial spokesmen and the

[14] In the chemical fertilizer sector, for instance, the Montecatini group gradually absorbed the largest firms in the country in the years after 1917. A similar process took place in the hemp processing sector, where one firm, the Linificio e Canapificio Nazionale, emerged from the war as the biggest Italian textile company. The most immediate menace came from the steel producers whose protectionist demands threatened to obstruct the mechanization of agriculture. On the chemical sector, see Angelo Ventura, "La Federconsorzi dall'età liberale al fascismo," *Quaderni Storici*, no. 36, September-December 1977, p. 699; for the situation within the hemp processing industry, see Ernesto Sessa, *Della canapa e del lino in Italia* (Milan, 1930), pp. 54-55.

[15] See F. Piva, "Mobilitazione agraria e associazionismo padronale," *Quaderni Storici*, no. 36, September-December 1977, p. 823.

[16] *RdC*, March 2, 1919.

economists of the Nationalist Association, they portrayed the pursuit of economic growth as a superior national mission that transcended old ideological conflicts and narrow class interests. Yet while the AAB claimed to espouse nonpartisan technocratic values, the proposals it advanced to achieve growth—mechanization, marketing organization, farm export campaigns, and the regulation of agricultural processing industries—were tailored primarily to the interests of the large commercial farmers.[17]

In the course of 1919, agrarian leaders from Bologna and the Po Valley proposed a variety of institutional arrangements to modernize agricultural production. From the outset, they strongly advocated closer collaboration between the employers' associations and the agrarian consortia to encourage the increased use of chemical fertilizers, farm machines, and high-yield seed. To cut production and transportation costs and to reduce the growers' dependence on industrial giants like Montecatini, Cavazza also favored greater agrarian involvement in the production of chemical fertilizers through the factories owned by the Federconsorzi.[18] Along similar lines, agrarian leaders envisioned a new alliance between agricultural interests and the major firms of the mechanical industry to expand the domestic market for farm machines and to lobby against high steel tariffs that made Italian machinery more costly than that of its foreign competitors.[19]

These proposals to raise output and productivity were closely tied to plans to develop new markets for farm products. Agrarian

[17] For a more general discussion of productivist and technocratic ideas, and their ideological uses in the postwar period, see Roland Sarti, "Fascist Modernization in Italy: Traditional or Revolutionary?" *The American Historical Review*, LXXV, no. 2 (1970), pp. 1032-1035; C. Maier, "Between Taylorism and Technocracy: European Ideologies and the Vision of Industrial Productivity in the 1920's," *Journal of Contemporary History*, V, no. 2 (1970), pp. 27-61.

[18] See *RdC*, October 19, 1919 and *Libertà Economica*, January 13, 1920. On the Federconsorzi, see A. Ventura, "La Federconsorzi dall'età liberale al fascismo."

[19] On relations between agrarian and machine interests, see F. Piva, *Lotte contadine e origini del fascismo. Padova-Venezia: 1919-1922* (Venice, 1977), pp. 59-60. For information on local farm machinery companies, see ACS, Ministero delle Armi e Munizioni, B2, F20, "Elenco delle ditte del Veneto ed Emilia specializzate nella fabbricazione di macchine agricole," March 12, 1917.

spokesmen portrayed the two as interdependent, arguing that demand abroad would stimulate the adoption of more efficient methods of production, while the penetration of foreign markets would require the use of "those technical means that produce the highest yields with the lowest per capita costs."[20] By 1919, the Russian Civil War and the collapse of the German and Austrian empires appeared to open up unprecedented opportunities for Italian expansion into the European markets. Accordingly, agricultural technicians and commercial farming leaders called for the creation of central marketing organizations to locate areas of peak foreign demand, negotiate collective trade agreements, and coordinate export campaigns.[21]

Similar considerations led the AAB to urge the consolidation of the commodity associations on the national level in order to control and standardize the production of the major industrial crops and to assure a more stable and equal relationship between growers and their respective processors and refiners. The National Federation of Sugar Beet Growers provided them with a model. Founded in the spring of 1917, it had unified the various local sugar beet syndicates and managed to pressure the government into regulating its relations with the refiners during the 1918-19 season.[22] Cavazza, Donini, and Professor Vittorio Peglion from the University of Bologna proposed a parallel organization for hemp growers in 1919 that would represent them in negotiations with domestic buyers, aggressively pursue markets in Northern Europe,

[20] G. Valenti and G. Briganti, "Organizzazione del commercio dei prodotti agricoli e delle industrie all'interno e all'estero," in Federconsorzi, *L'Italia agricola e il suo avvenire* (Rome, 1920), p. 236; V. Peglion, *Piante industriali. Produzione, commercio, regime doganale* (Rome, 1917), pp. 68-69.

[21] G. Valenti and G. Briganti, "Organizzazione del commercio," pp. 223-248. For an early work by Valenti on the same subject, see *L'agricoltura e la politica commerciale italiana* (Rome, 1917).

[22] On the growth of the sugar beet syndicates, see L. Perdisa, *La bietola da zucchero nella economia italiana* (Rome, 1938), pp. 252-253; Julo Fornaciari, "La Federazione nazionale bieticultori," *L'Italia Agricola*, March 1932, pp. 235-236. The initial activities of the federation in the last year of the war are discussed in Riccardo Bachi, *L'Italia economica nel 1919* (Rome, 1920), pp. 271-272.

and lobby for favorable government policies in Rome. Peglion went so far as to envision an eventual national export campaign in which hemp growers would be integrated with the processing sector in a single giant marketing monopoly.[23]

Bolognese agrarian leaders justified these proposals on the grounds of productivity, efficiency, and expertise rather than the rights of property. In fact, Cavazza openly attacked absentee landowners, who neglected their property or treated it as an "absolute and unconditional possession," and demanded that they be replaced by men who recognized a "social responsibility . . . to make their land productive." Where the land had been abandoned or "irrationally" cultivated, he advocated "state intervention to assure a management capable of drawing from the land the highest levels of production."[24] Yet productivist rhetoric and criticism of the agrarian old guard did not alter the class character of the AAB's program. For the measures it advanced to modernize agricultural production also had the function of legitimizing the position of the propertied classes by exalting their managerial role at a time when organized labor and the left were mounting a major offensive against the established economic hierarchies in the countryside.[25] On a more concrete level, mechanization and other measures to increase crop yields necessarily favored the big growers who had the land, capital, technical knowledge, and market orientation to take the fullest advantage of them. Plans for marketing cartels, specialized commodity associations, and agricultural supply organizations had a similar class bias, since they were designed to organize and integrate the mass of small and medium proprietors into a new system of institutional arrangements dominated by the

[23] *RdC*, January 26, 1919; V. Peglion, *Piante industriali*, pp. 65, 70-71; G. Valenti and Briganti, "Organizzazione del commercio," pp. 230-231.

[24] See *RdC*, June 15, 1919. For a further discussion of tensions between absentee landowners and commercial leaseholders, see F. Piva, *Lotte contadine*, pp. 69-70.

[25] On the problems of legitimizing economic authority in the work place after the war, see C. Maier's article cited in note 17 as well as his larger study, *Recasting Bourgeois Europe*.

commercial farming interests who controlled the agrarian consortia and rural banks.[26]

On the crucial issue of labor-management relations, however, political imperatives took precedence over considerations of economic rationality in shaping the policies of the AAB. Developing ideas he and Donini had first expressed during the war, Cavazza called for a return to older forms of collaboration between agrarian employers and their work force that tended to transform the agricultural laborer from a simple wage earner to a "producer and partner" in the productive process.[27] In particular, he urged government legislation to help employers restructure their farm work in ways that would allow them to hire laborers on the basis of limited-sharecropping or *compartecipazione* contracts. Because of the tremendous range of crops and local conditions on the Italian peninsula, such contracts could take a variety of forms, but essentially they entailed the assignment of small plots or specific tasks to individual laborers for a fixed period of time, usually one year. Whatever their specific terms were, all the contracts had to rest on two principles: the "duty" of the landowner or leaseholder to direct the farm work and the "right" of the laborer to "share in the division of the products."[28]

In his speeches and writings, the president of the AAB stressed above all the psychological and social benefits of *compartecipazione* contracts for the laborers. By receiving a portion of the crops his labor had helped to produce, the worker would be "morally uplifted" and would acquire a material stake in the success of the harvest. Moreover, Cavazza saw the contracts as a means of encouraging

[26] See Chapter III, Section 1, for the control of rural banks and consortia by the big commercial farmers. A general analysis of the role of cooperatives in capitalist agriculture is provided by Karl Kautsky, *La questione agraria* (Milan, 1971), pp. 138-151.

[27] Filippo Cavazza, *La compartecipazione ai prodotti agricoli in rapporto all'elevazione economica dei lavoratori della terra e all'incremento della produzione* (Bologna, 1919), p. 14.

[28] *Ibid.*; *RdC*, March 2, 1919.

individual social mobility by providing "a practical school for the laborer, a school through which . . . he can rise to the true partnership of the *mezzadria* system, which in turn will offer the technical preparation for the development of small landowners." Ultimately he envisioned the rise of a new class of peasant proprietors tied to the big agrarians by shared values and interests.[29]

While Bolognese leaders claimed that individual contracts provided significant economic advantages to employers in the form of higher labor productivity and greater technical specialization, their primary benefits were political rather than economic in nature.[30] As Cavazza himself repeatedly insisted, *compartecipazione* would give the laborers a "broader and more serene vision of national economic and political problems" and thereby encourage a "natural tendency toward class collaboration [and] a balanced and peaceful social and political order." More precisely, the AAB's contractual proposals were designed to nourish aspirations of private advancement among the laborers, sharpen divisions with the agricultural work force, and favor the consolidation of a conservative bloc of rural classes—an "alliance of producers" hostile to the "absolutist and war-mongering" appeals of the socialist labor movement.[31]

Such a coalition of rural producers constituted the foundation of a larger project of agrarian political reorganization and renewal in 1919. The electoral debacles of 1913-14 had already exposed the inability of a loose network of local gentlemen's clubs to mount a unified campaign or mobilize widespread political support under conditions of near universal suffrage.[32] The war only exaggerated

[29] F. Cavazza, *La compartecipazione*, p. 29; *RdC*, June 15, 1919.

[30] F. Cavazza, *La compartecipazione*, pp. 26-28.

[31] *Ibid.*, pp. 30-33. Local socialist leaders charged that the limited sharecropping contracts were designed to "nourish egotistical sentiments and fratricidal competition among the laborers, extinguish the spirit of collective solidarity, disintegrate the organizations of resistance, and annul the function of the employment offices." See *La Squilla*, July 23, 1921.

[32] In the winter of 1916, Mario Missiroli wrote how "the vicissitudes of the past two years have sanctioned in a definitive manner the decline of the moderate party [which as] the typical expression of the old Italy, is finished." See M. Missiroli, *La repubblica degli accattoni* (Bologna, 1916), p. 11.

these problems by raising popular expectations and by weakening, if not destroying altogether, traditional habits of deference to authority. Certainly by 1917, both older agrarian notables and the younger leaders of the AAB recognized the pressing need for drastic changes in the structure and methods of the parties of order. "In the face of new moral, economic, social, and political conditions which the Great War has unleashed in Europe," Marchese Tanari wrote that year, "the old political parties . . . no longer have any reason for existing; they have completed their time and have to disappear."[33] Donini echoed this view, proclaiming in the summer of 1917 that the faction-ridden Liberal party was destined "to die in the great funeral pyre the war has prepared for old-fashioned notions."[34]

Bolognese agrarian spokesmen proposed to replace the prewar political clubs with a new and more modern party of order that brought "the bourgeoisie that works and produces in industry, agriculture, commerce, and the professions" together with the intermediate classes of sharecroppers and peasant proprietors in the countryside, as well as with student and veterans' groups in the city.[35] Productivist, anti-socialist, and patriotic appeals were to provide the ideological cement to unite and mobilize this heterogeneous coalition of interests and classes. The leaders of the AAB, in particular, stressed the close connection between economic growth and electoral strength, since in their view "greater production combined with an improved social order [were] the essential factors for political renewal." Much like agrarian moderates in the first years of the century, they looked to productive collaboration on the farms as the prerequisite for a political partnership between the propertied classes and certain sectors of the agricultural work force.[36]

On a more visceral level, the AAB and conservative political

[33] See Biblioteca Comunale di Bologna, MS Tanari, XL, no. 4, "Azione controbolscevica e altre questioni politiche."

[34] *L'Agraria*, July 1917.

[35] *Libertà Economica*, October 15, 1919.

[36] See Alberto Donini's article in *L'Agraria*, July 1917.

leaders portrayed the proposed party as the sole bulwark against revolution and the "tyrannical actions of the socialists" in order to transform into votes the fears and resentments not only of the wealthy classes, but also of peasant cultivators, small businessmen and tradespeople. Indeed, they argued that the dangerous advance of the left made it imperative that the "various fragments of the bourgeoisie reunite" if only out of a "spirit of self-preservation."[37] Their pronounced anti-socialist orientation did not prevent proponents of a unified party of order from claiming, at the same time, to stand above the vulgar concerns of class and faction, and to be representing "the superior interests of the Patria." As the self-proclaimed defenders of patriotic, national values, they aimed to attract the support of students and returning war veterans whose enthusiasm and energy would give the anti-socialist forces "new blood, new tendencies, new visions which the changing times require to confront securely and with deliberation the great problems of the society."[38]

Significantly, both the political and economic features of the postwar agrarian program involved an unprecedented degree of state intervention in the agricultural sector. Despite their periodic complaints about bureaucratic inefficiency, the leaders of the AAB in 1919 did not share the prewar militants' fears of government action. On the contrary, they attributed a prominent role to the state in depoliticizing labor conflicts and in assuring the efficient development of agricultural production. After the armistice, they reiterated their calls for the legal recognition of the socialist leagues and compulsory arbitration to guarantee contracts and prevent strikes that endangered "the general interests of the country."[39] To encourage class collaboration and help resolve the labor problem in the countryside, they also demanded that the government introduce new legislation to facilitate the spread of crop-sharing contracts. Likewise, their plans for the industrialization of agri-

[37] Biblioteca Comunale di Bologna, MS Tanari, XL, no. 4.

[38] *Ibid.*

[39] See *Libertà Economica,* November 23, 1918; *RdC,* March 2, 1919.

culture and the development of new markets required a government that would assure the necessary commercial treaties and a moderate tariff regime to contain industrial prices and protect wheat and sugar beet growers without sacrificing the interests of export-oriented groups of hemp and rice growers. Conversely, agrarian spokesmen insisted upon the immediate abrogation of those wartime decrees that in any way limited the expansion of agricultural production. Price controls, livestock requisitions, and crop restrictions all had to be abolished and replaced by new measures that defended farm prices, assured advantageous credit terms to growers, and provided subsidies for land reclamation.[40]

Cavazza and Donini were acutely aware that the responsiveness of the postwar governments to their programs would depend on the presence of a strong agrarian interest-group organization in Rome, capable of applying pressure both at the ministerial level and within the Chamber of Deputies. Consequently, in December 1918 the two leaders of the AAB sponsored a series of meetings, attended by prominent agrarian spokesmen from the Po Valley as well as representatives of the peasant brotherhoods, in which they proposed a new farmers' organization to replace the virtually defunct National Agrarian Confederation. These meetings led in February of the following year to the creation of a special committee, headed by Cavazza, to promote the launching of the National Agricultural Secretariat (SAN). As conceived by its Bolognese promotors, the SAN was to serve as the sole organizational representative for the entire agricultural sector, "a vast and unified association of farmers that will engage in constant and useful action in Rome in defense of the interests of production, not in order to impose the interests of one class on those of the others, but to coordinate all elements of agriculture . . . for the general welfare of the country."[41]

[40] In addition to the sources cited in notes 20 and 21, see F. Piva, *Lotte contadine*, pp. 66-69.

[41] See *Libertà Economica*, February 15, 1919; D. Donati, "Aspetti dell'organizzazione agraria bolognese tra guerra e dopoguerra (1915-1919)," *Studi*

With the backing of agrarian associations from Piedmont, Lombardy, Veneto, Romagna, and Tuscany, Cavazza presented his labor proposals and his plan for the SAN to the forty-ninth congress of the Society of Italian Agriculturalists later the same month. While spokesmen for southern landed interests voiced strong reservations about Cavazza's enthusiasm for extensive state intervention, the majority of delegates endorsed his call for a law on *compartecipazione* contracts, and were favorably disposed toward the idea of a new national organization. In March the SAN was officially constituted and opened its offices in Rome. Not surprisingly, the top leadership of the organization reflected the predominant influence of the Bolognese agrarians: Cavazza assumed the presidency, Donini became the director of the political office.

The SAN immediately became involved in tariff and tax issues in the capital that brought it into conflict with the General Confederation of Italian Industry (CGII). Founded in April 1919, the CGII rapidly developed into the most powerful economic pressure group in the country. Under the direction of spokesmen from the steel, chemical, machine, and sugar industries, it endorsed high protective tariffs, a position that clashed sharply with agrarian export ambitions and Cavazza's plans for a low-cost industrialization of agriculture.[42] After overcoming efforts to exclude it from the committees preparing the new tariff schedules, the SAN launched a propaganda campaign in the summer against what it denounced as the excessively protectionist demands of the steel manufacturers.[43] At the same time, Cavazza and Donini intervened on fiscal questions, lobbying for an equalization of the burdens imposed on agricultural and industrial profits, the abolition of certain taxes on land purchases and livestock, and the limitation of local property

---

Storici, XIV, no. 2 (1973), p. 417; Franco Cavazza, *Le agitazioni agrarie in Provincia di Bologna dal 1910 al 1920* (Bologna, 1940), p. 151.

[42] D. Donati, "Aspetti dell'organizzazione," pp. 419-420; F. Cavazza, *Le agitazioni agrarie*, pp. 151-152.

[43] See A. Serpieri, *La guerra e le classi rurali*, p. 332; R. Sarti, *Fascism and the Industrial Leadership in Italy, 1919-1940* (Berkeley, 1971), pp. 12-16; V. Castronovo, *Giovanni Agnelli* (Turin, 1971), pp. 130-132.

taxes. By the fall, the SAN had organized a group of parliamentary deputies and senators around a program for tariff moderation, tax reform, compulsory arbitration, and union regulation.[44]

During the spring of 1919, Bolognese agrarian leaders also began to implement their proposals for political renewal at the provincial level. In March they joined with leading industrial and commercial groups in the city of Bologna to found the Union of Economic Forces with the stated aim of compelling the parties of order to "recognize the real and preeminent importance of national economic problems." Despite disagreements on tax and tariff issues, local agrarian and industrial interests were united in their shared fear of the socialist labor movement. Indeed, promotors portrayed the union as an "economic party that unites entrepreneurs and employers of labor" against the "privileges and excesses of the bolsheviks and socialists [that] are menacing the farms, industries, and the land."[45] Significantly, the union gave decisive impetus to a major reorganization of the parties of order in Bologna. In the summer of 1919, the old gentlemen's clubs were consolidated into a single political organization, the Bolognese Liberal League, on the basis of a general program that affirmed the principles of liberty, class collaboration, support for veterans, and "faith in the young people."[46]

Agrarian leaders did not limit their political initiatives to the propertied classes. In addition they attempted to broaden the mass base of the parties of order by pursuing new alliances both in the countryside and in the provincial capital. Above all, in the countryside they sought to develop and strengthen organizational ties with the independent peasant brotherhoods, which claimed to rep-

[44] For the activities of the SAN, see its weekly publication *Il Giornale Agrario*

[45] *Libertà Economica*, March 30, 1919. Joining agrarian leaders on the board of the union were Alessandro Taburi, the textile manufacturer; Adolfo Calzoni, owner of the largest metal foundry in the province; Giuseppe Masotti, head of an important chemical fertilizer company; and Cristoforo Turri of the sugar refining industry. See D. Donati, "Aspetti dell'organizzazione," p. 421.

[46] See *La Cittadina*, 1919, p. 54, cited in D. Donati, "Aspetti dell'organizzazione," pp. 422-423.

resent several thousand families and constituted, according to the prefect, "the only nonsocialist mass force upon which significant political activity can be based."[47] Electoral considerations played a crucial part in the decision of agrarian interests to involve the brotherhoods in the formation of the SAN and the new Consortium of Hemp Growers, and to include their leaders in certain private economic ventures.[48]

The spring of 1919 also saw agrarian notables like Marchese Giuseppe Tanari begin to cultivate closer relations with other non-socialist parties and organizations in the city of Bologna. In April, for instance, Tanari became one of the sponsors of the Anti-Bolshevik League, a paramilitary organization that proposed "to resist energetically as citizens and soldiers any revolutionary movement that . . . menaces the fate of the Patria." Under the leadership of Giorgio Ghigi, an official of the AAB and head of the Bolognese Nationalist Group, the league drew some three hundred veterans and students to its founding meeting. But even with the covert financial assistance of the prefecture, it quickly lapsed into inactivity and by early May had an active membership of only seventy men.[49] Provincial authorities were considerably more optimistic about the possibilities of collaboration between the Bolognese Liberal League and the new veterans' organizations. As early as April, the police chief reported that the local branch of the National Association of Combatants included large numbers of men who were either already enrolled in the parties of order or were at least disposed to cooperate in "the struggle against bolshevism."[50] With

[47] ASB, C6 F2, Prefect to Ministry of Interior, January 7, 1919.

[48] The provincial secretary of the independent peasant brotherhoods, Massimo Federici became a director of the new agricultural development company, the Società Agricola Bolognese which had been founded by a group of commercial farmers in February 1919. See Credito Italiano, *Società Italiane per azioni 1920*, Vol. I-III (Rome, 1921), p. 2233. On the founding of the Consortium of Hemp Growers, see *RdC*, January 22 and 26, 1919.

[49] On the rise and decline of the Anti-Bolshevik League in Bologna, see *RdC*, April 19, 1919; ASB, C7 F1, Police Chief to Prefect, April 18, 1919; *ibid.*, Police Chief to Prefect, May 8, 1919. For information on government subsidies to the League, see ASB, C7 F1, Minister of Interior to Prefect, August 14, 1919.

[50] ASB, C7 F1, Prefect to Ministry of Interior, April 22, 1919.

these considerations in mind, the Liberal League opened negotiations in the fall of 1919 with veterans' spokesmen as well as with representatives of the Republican, Radical, and Reformist Socialist parties for the creation of a broad-based anti-socialist electoral bloc.

These political initiatives, together with the production and labor proposals advanced by Cavazza and Donini, closely paralleled developments in other European countries in the first year after the war. Indeed, the spring of 1919 saw not only the founding of the National Agricultural Secretariat in Italy, but also the reconstitution of the Junker-dominated Agrarian League in Germany and the creation of the French Confédération Nationale des Associations Agricoles by a group of prewar agrarian syndicalist leaders. Despite the significantly different political and economic problems confronting them, all three organizations aspired to assure the control of the big growers over the peasantry and to forge a united farm bloc capable of defending sectoral interests in their respective national arenas.[51] At the same time that the spokesmen of the AAB were espousing the gospel of bourgeois political solidarity, French landowners were rallying to the Bloc National, while German rural conservatives sought to regain their political influence through the new German National People's party. Thus, to a certain extent, the Bolognese agrarian program fits into a general European context, in which embattled agrarian elites experimented with new institutional arrangements to contain the left and defend their old positions of wealth, power, and prestige in the wake of war and revolution.[52]

In pursuit of these objectives, however, northern Italian agrarians were considerably less successful than their French and Ger-

[51] On the activities of French agrarians, see Gordon Wright, *Rural Revolution in France: The Peasantry in the Twentieth Century* (Stanford, 1964), pp. 35-36; Pierre Barral, *Les agrariens francais de Méline à Pisani* (Paris, 1968), pp. 206-207. For those of the German agrarians, see Alexander Gerschenkron, *Bread and Democracy in Germany* (Berkeley, 1943), pp. 105-106; Dieter Gessner, "Agrarian Protectionism in the Weimar Republic," *Journal of Contemporary History*, VII, no. 12 (1972), pp. 764-765; Alan Kovan, "The Resurgence of the Landbund and Its Organized Power" (Ph.D. dissertation, University of California, Berkeley, 1973).

[52] Apart from the sources cited above, see C. Maier, *Recasting Bourgeois Europe*, chap. 1.

man colleagues. The sense of crisis and vulnerability within the ruling elite of Italy was especially pronounced, as Charles S. Maier has written, because "its members could not regain security through mastery of parliament as in France or manipulation of the economic arena as in Germany."[53] In this respect, the situation in the province of Bologna clearly mirrored the larger difficulties facing Italian business leaders and political notables in 1919 and 1920. The tremendous surge of the socialist labor movement, which had one of its greatest centers of power in Bologna and the neighboring provinces of Emilia, paralyzed and demoralized the local propertied classes, severely hampering the efforts of agrarian leaders to organize an effective resistance to the leagues, let alone implement their ambitious economic and political plans. The advance of the left in Bologna and the Po Valley resulted not only from the rapid growth and militancy of organized labor, but also from the inability of the provincial elites to surmount their own internal divisions or mobilize mass support in defense of the status quo. The plight of the agrarians at the local level was accentuated by government instability and parliamentary paralysis in Rome, which undermined the authority of the state in the countryside precisely at a time when the leagues were challenging basic entrepreneurial privileges and prerogatives. For the Bolognese propertied classes, the parliamentary elections of November 1919 provided the first dramatic indication of their apparent weakness and vulnerability.

2. *The Politics of Agrarian Disarray: The Elections of 1919*

The political situation in Rome during the fall of 1919 gave Bolognese agrarians little time to organize a solid coalition of anti-Socialist parties and associations. In the wake of bitter clashes between the government and nationalist elements in the Chamber of Deputies over D'Annunzio's Fiume expedition, Nitti dissolved parliament in late September and forced early elections,

[53] *Ibid.*, p. 47.

the first under a system of proportional representation.[54] The timing of the electoral contest could not have been more unfortunate for the parties or order. The first six months of the year had witnessed not only the rapid expansion of the Socialist party, but also the emergence of a new Catholic party, the Popular party (PPI), which had a significant mass appeal in the countryside. To make matters worse, the parties of order entered the electoral campaign deeply divided over issues of war, domestic reform, foreign policy, and personalities at a time when proportional representation made party organization and bloc voting essential for political survival.[55]

The parties of order in Bologna confronted an especially formidable adversary in the Provincial Socialist Federation. Already the dominant political force in the province in 1914, the federation was the chief beneficiary of the popular frustrations and discontent in the months after the armistice. By the fall of 1919, it had grown enormously in membership largely as a result of support from a union movement representing some seventy thousand laborers in the countryside and another sixteen thousand in the provincial capital.[56] Apart from their numerical strength, the Socialists aroused the alarm of the prefect and police because of the increasingly radical posture they assumed as the balance of power within the federation shifted decisively to the left. In the first half of 1919, the reformist leaders, who had worked closely with the government and military authorities during the war, gradually lost control of

[54] See C. Seton-Watson, *Italy from Liberalism to Fascism*, p. 547. On the basis of the new electoral law of August 1919, Italy was divided into fifty-four constituencies, with five to twenty members each, to be elected on party lists. In addition, the vote was given to all men over twenty-one, and to those under twenty-one who had served in the armed forces.

[55] See C. Maier, *Recasting Bourgeois Europe*, pp. 123-124.

[56] Angela De Benedictis, "Note su classe operaia e socialismo a Bologna nel primo dopoguerra (1919-1920)," in Deputazione Emilia-Romagna per la storia della Resistenza, *Movimento operaio e fascismo nell'Emilia-Romagna 1919-1923* (Rome, 1973), p. 80; L. Arbizzani, "Lotte agrarie in provincia di Bologna nel primo dopoguerra," in R. Zangheri, ed., *Le campagne emiliane nell'epoca moderna* (Milan, 1957), pp. 298-299.

the party organization to a more intransigent maximalist faction, which won a resounding victory at the provincial party congress in September. With these extremist elements at the helm of the federation, the Socialists now advanced a program that violently denounced the war, repudiated any cooperation with "bourgeois" parties, and glorified the dictatorship of the proletariat.[57]

The impressive strength and militancy of the left contrasted sharply with the situation of the Bolognese parties of order. The initiatives of the Union of Economic Forces and the AAB produced few tangible results in the spring and summer, amid the strikes and riots that seemed to disorient and dishearten all the nonsocialist groups. Barely a month prior to the dissolution of parliament, political observers were reporting that the Socialists were the only active force in Bologna, while the Liberals, Nationalists, and Republicans did "absolutely nothing."[58] Indeed, despite the founding of the Bolognese Liberal League, the parties of order displayed little sign of life until the calling of new elections. On September 30, two days after the closing of the Chamber, the Union of Economic Forces published a manifesto, calling for an electoral alliance of the "legalitarian parties" and announcing its intention to participate in the campaign along with "all the forces of the producers."[59] In a province where the neutralist cause of 1914-15 had been associated with the PSI, agrarian notables set out to build their coalition on the basis of a platform that exalted interventionism, the war, and patriotism. Marchese Tanari clearly articulated these themes at the first campaign meeting of the Liberal League, invoking "the union of all those who, with the declaration of war, put the interests of the Nation before those of the individual parties," a union that would be "inspired by the higher interests of the Patria."[60]

[57] See A. De Benedictis, "Note su classe operaia," pp. 84-98.

[58] ACS, Mostra della Rivoluzione Fascista, B100, letter, Pedrini to Pasella, August 22, 1919.

[59] ASB, C7 F1, resolution of the union, quoted in the report of Police Chief to Prefect, September 30, 1919.

[60] See ASB, C7 F1, Police Chief to Prefect, October 13, 1919.

A combination of old conflicts and new challenges, however, seriously handicapped efforts to forge such a political coalition. In the countryside, calls for an alliance of rural producers aroused little enthusiasm among the unaffiliated peasant cultivators and sharecroppers. As the prefect noted, the peasant brotherhoods viewed agrarian overtures with understandable skepticism after more than a decade in which the AAB had steadfastly rejected the notion that "the peasants could be organized in an independent federation" and had sought chiefly to "exploit them politically and economically for its own profit."[61] Moreover, in 1919 the AAB was not in a position to offer very much to the independent peasants in exchange for their political support. With their postwar program still in an embryonic stage, the big growers were unable to mount any collective resistance to the newly militant leagues of the plains. By May the pressure of strikes and boycotts had forced employers to accept twenty-two local labor contracts that stipulated wage hikes of 18 to 20 percent.[62] As a result of its own weakness, the AAB could not provide the independent peasants with any real protection from the Federterra, which launched a major offensive against the brotherhoods in the summer "in order to compel them to enter the socialist organizations."[63]

Cavazza and Donini compounded these problems by delaying their promised reform of the *mezzadria* contracts. Two months after it had formally demanded new negotiations with agrarian employers, the Bolognese Federation of Brotherhoods protested in the fall of 1919 that "neither the landowners nor the state have been giving any attention to the reform of the contracts requested

[61] ASB, C6 F2, "Situazione delle organizzazioni delle classi medie (piccoli proprietari e coloni) della Provincia di Bologna, no date, 1919.

[62] See L. Arbizzani, "Lotte agrarie," p. 301.

[63] On the Socialist offensive against the independent peasants, see ASB, C6 F2, Police Chief to Prefect, May 5, 1919; *ibid.*, Minister of Interior to Prefect, May 27, 1919; *ibid.*, Police Chief to Prefect, June 30, 1919. By mid-July, the secretary of the Bolognese Federterra claimed that as a result of the leagues' recruitment campaign "another 15,000 day laborers and sharecroppers have enrolled in the last months." See *RdC*, July 19, 1919.

by the . . . peasants."[64] The apparent recalcitrance of the AAB in this sensitive area rekindled old antagonisms and made the independent unions increasingly hostile to any proposals for electoral collaboration. Voicing the discontent of his rank and file, Massimo Federici, the provincial secretary of the brotherhoods, bitterly attacked the AAB's program in late August:

> If you prize collaboration, continue to preach it; you will be doing valuable work, but preach it to the landowners. . . . Tell them that as long as there are those of their colleagues who refuse to discuss anything with their peasant associates, who respond to legitimate requests . . . by threatening eviction, who impose their interests with arrogance and force . . . who reject on principle any contractual changes that ease the financial burdens of the peasants . . . your collaboration will be a myth. . . . The laboring associate, who finds himself in trouble while his capitalist associate stands by enjoying the spectacle, loses the desire to remain in such an uncordial relationship and seeks collaboration elsewhere.[65]

In the province of Bologna, this "elsewhere" came to mean the Popular party. Founded in February 1919, the Bolognese branch of the Popular party not only drew prominent Catholic landowners away from the Liberal League but also became a magnet for more traditional and devout peasant cultivators, sharecroppers, and tenant farmers in the foothills and mountains of the province.[66] From the outset, the activities of Christian democratic organizers among the peasants before the war assured the new party a privileged relationship with the brotherhoods. The PPI took advantage of this legacy in 1919 by adopting a rural program that promised to defend the peasants from both the exploitation of the landowners and the pressures of the socialist leagues. The program's appeal in Bologna

[64] ASB, C7 F1, resolution of the Federazione della fratellanze coloniche, September 13, 1919.

[65] *Libertà Economica*, August 31, 1919.

[66] On the founding of the Bolognese branch of the Popular Party, see ASB, C5 F1, Police Report to Prefect, February 5, 1919. For the party's program, see A. Serpieri, *La guerra e le classi rurali*, pp. 310-312.

was evident by the summer of 1919, when the prefect reported that the brotherhoods, while having "constitutional political ideas," were becoming "supporters of . . . the clerical party."[67] The Popular party developed an especially strong following in the more isolated communes of the mountains, where in late August it claimed to have the support of eleven labor cooperatives, five associations of small proprietors, and six chapters of the Provincial Union of Shepherds.[68] In the fall, the brotherhoods and the PPI cemented their alliance with the selection of the two leading peasant spokesmen, Massimo Federici and Fulvio Miliani, to head the local party ticket. For the architects of agrarian political renewal, the Catholic peasant alliance marked a serious setback, since the PPI refused to participate in an antisocialist coalition and instead ran its own separate slate of candidates.[69]

With the countryside firmly in the hands of either the Socialists or the Popular party, the parties of order were forced to concentrate their attention on the city of Bologna. The large middle class population and highly organized political life in the provincial capital appeared to offer more favorable conditions for bloc politics. Accordingly, in mid-October the local chapter of the National Association of Combatants sponsored a meeting that attracted representatives from the Union of Economic Forces, the Bolognese Liberal League, and the Reformist Socialist, Radical, and Republican parties, who tentatively agreed on the need for a united front against the Socialists. In the following days, the list of prospective participants in the coalition grew to include the Nationalist Group, the Union of Shopkeepers, the Industrial Union, the Association of Landlords, and the AAB.[70]

When actual negotiations began, however, it quickly became

[67] ASB, C7 F1, Prefect to Ministry of Interior, May 20, 1919.

[68] ASB, C5 F1, Consociazione Popolare Costituzionale pel bene della Montagna to Prefect, August 23, 1919.

[69] See A. De Benedictis, "Note su classe operaia," pp. 97-98.

[70] For an account of the meeting, see ASB, C7 F1, Police Chief to Prefect, October 13, 1919. On the position of the Nationalists, see resolution cited in ASB, C5 F1, Police Chief to Prefect, October 21, 1919. The AAB's presented in its position in *Libertà Economica*, October 31, 1919. On the other groups, see D. Donati, "Aspetti dell'organizzazione," p. 426.

apparent that the memories of the "radiant May" of 1915, patriotic rhetoric, and antisocialist slogans were an inadequate formula for uniting such a heterogeneous collection of economic and political interests. The contrasting aims and expectations that divided the agrarians from other groups in the coalition soon found expression in sharp disagreements between the Bolognese Liberal League and the Association of Combatants over questions of candidates and programs. Under pressure from the big commercial farmers, the Liberal League advanced the candidacy of Calisto Paglia, one of the directors of the AAB, to represent "the class of farmers" and to encourage "a greater fusion of the city and the countryside."[71] This attempt at explicit interest representation met with strong opposition from the veterans who took Marchese Tanari at his word and expected the coalition to stand above private ambitions and the pressures of special interest groups. As a result, the veterans rejected Paglia and proposed a litmus test of combat experience for all candidates of the coalition. The veto of Paglia's candidacy and the refusal of Count Gualtiero Isolani, an officer in the army during the war, to accept a place on the ticket put the agrarians in an extremely difficult position since, as Tanari lamented, "we did not have a veteran-farmer."[72]

Additional disagreements arose over the coalition's political platform. While agrarian notables and the employer associations favored a narrow program that stressed a conservative defense of the established order, the veterans wanted to give the platform a decidedly reformist cast more in tune with popular expectations in 1919. In particular, they demanded the inclusion of a plank, calling for a "constituent assembly" to carry out a sweeping, if undefined, reform of the Italian political system. Certain pragmatic businessmen like Frank De Morsier displayed a willingness to accept the plank, "given the necessity of an alliance for the approaching elections." But old-fashioned conservatives in the Liberal League and the AAB reacted with alarm at the very mention

[71] See Tanari's account in *Libertà Economica*, October 31, 1919.
[72] *Ibid.*

of a constituent assembly. Marchese Tanari, for one, asserted that he "could not accept the word 'constituent' " because he had sworn "allegiance to the Monarchy."[73]

Far from encouraging compromises and mutual concessions, the seeming invincibility of the Socialist electoral machine in Bologna intensified doctrinaire rigidity and ideological conflict within the nonsocialist camp. After a week and a half of negotiations had failed to produce an agreement on candidates and platform planks, the Bolognese Liberal League broke off talks with the veterans on October 23 and voted to present its own separate electoral slate.[74] The next day the Association of Combatants followed suit, charging that the Liberal League was concerned "only with names and colleges to conquer, while the veterans want to have a noble battle of ideas."[75]

With the open break between the two groups, the antisocialist bloc disintegrated as the various parties and associations hastened to join one or the other of the competing tickets. The more democratic and reform-oriented parties tended to align with the veterans. A week after the rupture, the Radical party voted to support the candidates of the Association of Combatants, and in the following weeks the Reformist Socialists and Republicans took similar stands.[76] Other organizations like the Bolognese Nationalist Group decided "to remain separate from and above the parties" and to use the electoral campaign exclusively to disseminate its own propaganda.[77]

In the absence of an alliance with the veterans, the Bolognese Liberal League lost much of its populist and patriotic appeal, and became little more than the political mouthpiece of the economic elites. Not surprisingly, the Union of Economic Forces threw its

[73] For the debate within the Liberal League on this issue, see ASB, C5 F1, Police Chief to Prefect, October 15, 1919.

[74] ASB, C5 F1, Police Chief to Prefect, October 23, 1919.

[75] *Ibid.*, Police Chief to Prefect, October 24, 1919.

[76] ASB, C5 F1, Police Chief to Prefect, October 29, 1919.

[77] See resolution of the Bolognese Nationalist Group in ASB, C5 F1, Police Chief to Prefect, October 26, 1919.

support to the Liberal League on the grounds that its "candidates would be sincere and valid defenders of the productive forces, commercial and agricultural."[78] Likewise, the Liberal slate won the backing of the associations of shopkeepers, manufacturers, landlords, and agrarians. The Liberal League's electoral platform registered these changes in its base of support. In the final weeks before the elections, a new antidemocratic and antiunion rhetoric characterized the speeches of its candidates, who denounced the eight-hour day and the right to strike, and spoke ominously of "the producer classes' lack of faith in the parliamentary system."[79] Such ideological consistency came at a high price. On the eve of the elections, it was apparent that little had changed in the camp of the parties of order since the previous spring, when the prefect had depicted them as small, isolated groups "looked upon by the mass of the population with diffidence and skepticism."[80]

The situation in Bologna reflected the fragmentation and divisiveness of the constitutional parties throughout much of the Italian peninsula. In many constituencies a five-party campaign developed, involving the PSI, the Popular party, Giolittians, conservative interventionists, and veterans. An electoral race of this nature favored the two disciplined mass parties, who received an additional boost from Nitti's decision to conduct the campaign without the usual prefectoral intervention.[81] The outcome of the elections of November 16, the freest in the history of unified Italy, put an end to the parliamentary dominance of the old liberal political class. The constitutional parties won less than a quarter of the popular vote in the north and center, and saw their representation in the Chamber of Deputies fall dramatically from 410 to 193 seats. The PSI emerged as the largest single party in the Chamber, capturing 32.4 percent of the ballots and increasing its representation from 52 to 156 seats. Significantly, the Socialists

[78] *Libertà Economica*, October 31, 1919.

[79] See D. Donati, "Aspetti dell'organizzazione," p. 427.

[80] ASB, C7 F1, Prefect to Ministry of Interior, April 3, 1919.

[81] C. Seton-Watson, *Italy from Liberalism*, p. 549; C. Maier, *Recasting Bourgeois Europe*, pp. 126-128.

were especially strong in the key regions of Piedmont, Lombardy, Emilia, Tuscany, and Umbria, where their share of the vote ranged from 40 to 60 percent. Only an impressive showing by the Popular party, which took 20.5 percent of the vote and 100 parliamentary seats, forestalled a complete Socialist landslide.[82]

Nowhere was the defeat of the parties of order or the triumph of the Socialists more overwhelming than in the province of Bologna. In the capital city, a traditional stronghold of the elite, the PSI amassed 22,044 votes or 63 percent of the total, the Liberal League a mere 4,494. The defeat of the parties of order was even more complete in the countryside, where nearly three-quarters of the electorate cast ballots for the Socialist slate. Overall, the Liberal ticket won only 7.8 percent of the popular vote and came in a distant third behind both the Socialists and the Popular party. With the PSI capturing seven seats and the Catholics one, the Bolognese propertied classes found themselves totally excluded from the Chamber of Deputies for the first time.[83]

Local notables and the agrarian press interpreted the size of the PSI's victory less as proof of Socialist invincibility than as the result of the utter collapse of the conservative political opposition. Alberto Giovannini, one of the candidates of the Bolognese Liberal League, concluded that the elections had brutally demonstrated to the propertied classes "not only [their] lack of organization, but the absence of any contact with the great masses." In its own editorial post-mortem, *Il Resto del Carlino* concentrated its harshest criticisms on the parties of order: "More than a victory for the Socialists . . . the elections in Bologna have been marked by the total defeat of the moderates. . . . While the entire world was being transformed, the [Liberal League] has continued to subsist on miserable personal ambitions and malignant antisocialist grudges."[84]

[82] *Ibid.*; Jens Petersen, "Elettorato e base sociale del fascismo italiano negli anni venti," *Studi Storici*, XVI, no. 3 (1975), pp. 636-638.

[83] ASB, C5 F1, "Risultato votazione in Bologna città," November 17, 1919; *RdC*, November 22, 1919; *ibid.*, November 23, 1919.

[84] *Libertà Economica*, November 30, 1919; *RdC*, November 19, 1919.

The elections of November also had consequences in Rome that greatly accentuated the plight of the propertied classes at the provincial level. Far from clarifying the political situation, the results produced a state of parliamentary paralysis that precluded the formation of any stable government. Under the leadership of the maximalists, the PSI refused to participate in or support a coalition government, if only to preserve its own fragile unity. As a consequence, the success of any cabinet depended on the votes of the politically inexperienced and divided Popular party, which hedged its support with innumerable conditions and reservations. The self-imposed withdrawal of the Socialists and the refusal of the Popular party to assume responsibility for the formation of a government meant that ministerial duties fell once again to the old liberal politicians, who were themselves bitterly divided by old feuds and new rivalries. These circumstances not only led to frustrating delays in legislation, but also deprived the government of the necessary authority to administer effectively the country. In the province of Bologna, the resultant weakness and uncertainty of the prefecture and the police contributed substantially to a breakdown of law and order, which initially exaggerated both the power of the Socialists and the vulnerability of the propertied classes.[85]

3. *The Battle for Control of the Farms: The Strikes of 1920*

As in other provinces of the Po Valley, political developments in Bologna after the war were inseparably linked to the ongoing struggle in the countryside between the socialist leagues and agrarian employers. Indeed, the leagues' victorious strikes and boycotts during the spring and summer of 1919 had given the left's electoral campaign a tremendous boost by demoralizing the parties of order and by promoting a massive influx of new members into the socialist organizations. The stunning success of the PSI at the ballot box in November greatly increased, in turn, the numerical

[85] See note 12 in this chapter.

strength of the Bolognese leagues. One month after the elections, the Bolognese Federterra informed the prefect that it now represented some forty thousand agricultural workers and nine thousand sharecropping families or, in its own words, "the totality of day laborers and the overwhelming majority of peasants in the province."[86]

More importantly, the electoral results of November encouraged local labor leaders to formulate a program of their own which was considerably more radical in its objectives than that adopted by the fifth National Congress of the Federterra in June 1919. The program approved by the congress had avoided any concerted attack on the commercial farming interests of the Po Valley, and had concentrated instead on the "socialization" of state, Church, and uncultivated lands.[87] Appropriate perhaps for conditions in central and southern Italy, this cautious national program had little relevance to the situation in Bologna where most of the arable land was in the hands of private proprietors. Consequently, the Bolognese Federterra decided in the winter of 1919-1920 to launch a campaign that directly challenged the economic position and managerial authority of the large commercial farmers.[88]

The chief architect of the new campaign was Giuseppe Massarenti, the controversial labor leader from Molinella. In fact, the tactics and objectives pursued by the Molinellese leagues in the summer of 1919 provided the model for the policies the Federterra proposed to advance at the provincial level in 1920. After his acquittal on charges stemming from the "Guarda Massacre" of 1914, Massarenti resumed command of the leagues and cooperatives in Molinella in June. As his first act in office, he presented local employers with a set of nonnegotiable demands. Apart from substantial wage increases, he demanded that they evict the share-

[86] ASB, C16 F1, Federterra to Prefect, December 16, 1919.

[87] See *Avanti!*, June 14, 15, and 16, 1919; R. Zangheri, *Lotte agrarie in Italia. La federazione nazionale dei lavoratori della terra, 1901-1926* (Milan, 1960), pp. 373-374.

[88] ASB, C7 F1, "Decisione del Tribunale penale di Bologna," June 10, 1919. On Massarenti's demands, see L. Arbizzani, "Lotte agrarie," p. 302.

croppers hired after October 1914, cancel all nonunion contracts, and pay a fine of 500,000 lire "as an indemnity for the damages suffered by the laborers in 1914." But the most important innovations introduced by Massarenti were procedural rather than substantive: the refusal to recognize the AAB as a bargaining agent and the insistence that the employers accept his demands on an individual basis. In this fashion, he aimed not only to win immediate concessions from the growers, but also to break permanently the power of the AAB and preclude any future organized resistance to the leagues.[89]

With the enthusiastic support of the rank and file, Massarenti called a work stoppage early in July that brought all agricultural activity in the commune to a halt. The third week of the month the press reported that "the strike in Molinella is total: the fields are deserted; the sharecroppers, day laborers, and contract workers [*obbligati*] have joined together; the livestock has been abandoned."[90] Despite financial assistance from the Union of Economic Forces, agrarian unity rapidly disintegrated in the face of such a broad and compact labor front. By the end of July, all resistance from the landowners had collapsed, nonunion laborers had been enrolled in the leagues, and the major commercial farmers had agreed to give the prefect the sum of 270,000 lire "for all construction of infant schools . . . under the care of the labor organizations."[91]

The success of the Molinella strike, together with the enormous expansion of the Bolognese Federterra in 1919, led Massarenti to propose a more ambitious strategy for the entire province the

[89] Writing to the prefect in mid-July, Calisto Paglia, the vice-president of the AAB protested how "no request—either before or during the strike—has been presented by the leagues of Molinella . . . [who] are refusing to negotiate with the association." See ASB, C6 F2, July 12, 1919.

[90] *Il Secolo*, July 26, 1919, in ASB, C6 F2, 1919.

[91] ASB, C6 F2, Police Report to Prefect, July 21, 1919; *ibid.*, Inspector General of Public Security to Prefect, July 21, 1919; *ibid.*, Prefect to President of the Congregazione di Carità, July 31, 1919. For the terms of the agreement, see *RdC*, August 1, 1919; on the unsuccessful intervention of the Union of Economic Forces, see *ibid.*, July 31, 1919.

following year. Capitalizing on the Federterra's near total control of the agricultural labor force, he formulated a set of uniform and interlocking contracts for all categories of farm labor that entailed a drastic transformation of the traditional economic hierarchies in the countryside. The contract for the day laborers, in particular, imposed severe restrictions on the managerial prerogatives of the farmers and gave the leagues an unprecedented role in the selection of crops, machines, and methods of cultivation. To eliminate perennial conflicts between sharecroppers and day laborers, his *mezzadria* contract transformed the peasant from an associate of the landlord into a simple supplier of labor. Under its terms, the sharecropper was to receive a substantially larger share of the harvest and a guaranteed minimum income, while the landlord was made responsible for the costs of all supplies, tools, and additional hired hands.[92] Both the wage scales and the crop shares were made intentionally excessive in order to induce profound structural changes in the prevailing systems of land tenure and ownership. By sharply reducing the income landowners and leaseholders derived from agriculture, Massarenti sought to compel them to cede their farms to the leagues in the form of collective leases—the first step toward the eventual "socialization of the land."[93]

The revolutionary implications of Massarenti's strategy were evident not only in the contracts themselves, but also in the procedures for their implementation, which made the employers little more than obedient executors of league decisions. Above all, the Molinellese labor leader insisted that all contracts be presented at the same time so that the entire work force would be mobilized and the employers could not change their crops, methods of cultivation, or tenure arrangements to circumvent the demands of a specific category of laborers. Moreover, he required unconditional acceptance of the contracts. To ensure that conventional labor-management bargaining did not dilute or modify their demands,

[92] L. Arbizzani, "Lotte agrarie," p. 307; L. Preti, *Lotte agrarie nella valle padana*, pp. 430-431.

[93] L. Arbizzani, "Lotte agrarie," p. 308; I. Barbadoro, *Storia del sindacalismo italiano*, vol. I, p. 363.

the leagues refused to recognize or negotiate with the AAB and its representatives. Instead, each employer had to go to the nearest league office and sign an individual contract.[94]

The publication of the Federterra's contractual demands in December 1919 provoked a predictable reaction of panic and outrage from the propertied classes. Filippo Cavazza immediately protested to the minister of agriculture that "the leagues intend to destroy completely the sharecropping system, having declared it an obstacle to the realization of their communist ideas," and warned of imminent conflicts that would be "politically dangerous [and] extremely harmful to production."[95] Virtually all factions of the provincial elite shared Cavazza's alarm, as police officials indicated in the spring of 1920: "Before the peasant contracts had been published in full, it was generally assumed that the landowners, including the members of the Agrarian Association, would accept the new agreements without discussion because of the impossibility of resisting the leagues. . . . But with the full publication of the contracts, the landowners—perhaps too late—hastened to form a coalition of their own and many enrolled in the Agrarian Association, seeing in the demands of the Federterra the systematic destruction of private property and a social revolution."[96]

The reaction of the propertied classes to the leagues' demands greatly accelerated the pace of agrarian reorganization mapped out by Cavazza earlier in the fall of 1919. In December the AAB was officially disbanded and replaced by a new organization, the Provincial Association of Agriculturalists (APA), which proposed "to embrace the great family of farmers" and pursue productivist aims that "extend beyond the narrow limits of class interests."[97] From its inception, the APA relied upon the widespread fear of social revolution to rally the support of all agrarian employers from the big commercial farmers to the small peasant proprietors. Its prop-

[94] See ASB, C16 F1, Subprefect of Imola to Prefect, March 28, 1920.

[95] ASB, C16 F1, letter, Count Filippo Cavazza to Ministry of Agriculture, December 19, 1919.

[96] *Ibid.*, Police Report to Prefect, May 16, 1920.

[97] On the founding of the APA, see *Libertà Economica*, January 13, 1920.

aganda leaflets warned them that "your property rights are in danger and the fruits of your land could be lost in a short time [unless] you unite with the other landowners for the preparation of a common defense." Such a message found a highly receptive audience in the first half of 1920. Numbering fewer than two hundred at the beginning of January, the association had doubled its membership at the end of one month. The influx of frightened and angry landowners and farmers continued through the spring, and by June the APA claimed to represent some two thousand employers.[98]

Under the leadership of its new president, Calisto Paglia, the APA set out to blunt the radical thrust of the Federterra and divide the peasant classes by advancing a program that offered material concessions and individual incentives as an alternative to the sweeping structural changes demanded by the leagues. Paglia directed his appeals to the sharecroppers in particular. In January he announced the APA's proposed revision of the *mezzadria* contracts, which called for the greater "collaboration of the peasant in the management of the farms and in the ownership of the livestock." To broaden the entrepreneurial role of the sharecroppers, he extended the duration of the contracts from one to three years, and promised them special awards and prizes for the quality and quantity of their production as well as financial compensation for "improvements made on the farms." The contract also involved the formation of a new arbitration commission, composed of two sharecroppers, two landowners, and the president of the Bolognese Appeals Court, to mediate any disputes or disagreements.[99] Nor did the APA neglect the day laborers, who were offered a wage settlement more generous than that sought by the Federterra. In the event of a long and exhausting strike, agrarian leaders calculated that these mon-

[98] For an example of the APA's propaganda, see the pamphlet of the Comitato di preparazione, dated February 6, 1920, in ASB, C7 F1. On the growth of the association, see ASB, C7 F1, Royal Commissioner to Prefect, February 20, 1920; ASB, C16 F1, Paglia to Prefect, February 8, 1920; *Il Progresso*, June 5, 1920.

[99] See *Intorno alla vertenza agraria bolognese del 1920. Relazione della Associazione Provinciale degli Agricoltori Bolognesi* (Bologna, 1921), pp. 24-26.

etary concessions would encourage rank and file discontent within the leagues. As Cavazza wrote to Paglia, "if the wage rates are somewhat . . . higher than those demanded by the local leagues, they will inescapably effect the spirit of the laborers . . . who will be driven to question why the strike continues."[100]

At the same time, the APA adopted extraordinary measures to ensure the discipline of its members and the uniform implementation of its policies throughout the province. Emergency legal and press committees were set up, the former to deal with legal and political matters, the latter to prepare a weekly bulletin to help the members "maintain their unity and their lively interest in what is happening in other areas of the province during this exceptional period."[101] In preparation for a long and bitter struggle with the leagues, Paglia vested the most extensive powers in a new disciplinary committee, which exacted written pledges from each branch of the association "to abstain from any independent action or negotiations with the labor organizations."[102]

During the spring of 1920, the APA also took steps to influence public opinion in its favor and rally the support of other employer organizations in the country. For these purposes, agrarian interests purchased the Bolognese daily, *Il Progresso*, in April which became the self-proclaimed "voice of national production" and the "organ of the producers and the agrarians." In the following months, *Il Progresso* distinguished itself as the most outspoken defender of the APA and as a relentless critic of government "absenteeism" and the supposed excesses of the socialist "anti-state."[103] Outside the province, the APA pursued and gained the backing of the other

[100] ASB, C16 F1, Filippo Cavazza to Paglia, April 12, 1920.

[101] ASB, C16 F1, *Bollettino dell'Associazione Provinciale di Agricoltori*, no. 1, March 3, 1920.

[102] *Ibid.*, no. 2, March 10; no. 6, April 6; no. 8, April 21, 1920.

[103] *Il Progresso*, April 20, 1920. The director of the paper was Attilo Fontana, who had also been elected to parliament as a "representative of the Agrarian Party." See Nazario Sauro Onofri, *I giornali bolognesi nel ventennio fascista* (Bologna, 1972), p. 124. For examples of the paper's partisan stance, see *Il Progresso*, July 16 and 29, 1920.

agrarian associations of the Po Valley; their representatives elected Paglia president of the Interprovinciale in April.[104]

The APA had barely begun its preparations when the agricultural workers of Medicina left the farms in January 1920, setting in motion a labor offensive that soon engulfed the major farming regions of Italy. From the rice fields of Piedmont to the plains of Apulia, over one million laborers, sharecroppers, and tenant farmers went out on strike to gain wage increases, contractual reforms, union hiring halls, and guaranteed employment.[105] The size of the strikes and the militancy of the laborers quickly compelled agrarian employers in most provinces to give in. A mere tenth of the strikers returned to work with less than a halfway settlement. Even the battle-hardened agrarian association of Ferrara was only able to hold out against the strikers for two weeks before conceding defeat and granting all the demands of the leagues.[106]

The well-organized and disciplined resistance of the APA, however, precluded any rapid or easy victory for the Federterra in Bologna. In contrast to their colleagues in neighboring provinces, the Bolognese agrarians displayed an exceptional determination to resist and were prepared, government officials reported, "even to lose the harvest rather than give in to what they see as oppression."[107] The economic importance of the province, the radical demands of the leagues, and the tenacity of the APA all combined to draw national attention to the Bolognese strike. Indeed, it be-

[104] See *Bollettino dell'Associazione Provinciale di Agricoltori*, no. 8, April 21, 1920. For his part, the Bolognese prefect seemed well disposed toward the association, ordering his staff in February to give "the promoters of the new organization all possible encouragement so that it can assume a vital role." ASB, C7 F1, Prefect to Subprefects, February 10, 1920.

[105] Riccardo Bachi, *L'Italia economica nel 1920* (Città di Castello, 1921), pp. 356-360, provides a description of the strikes and the demands of the laborers. For strike statistics, see C. Seton-Watson, *Italy from Liberalism*, p. 521. The number of strikers in agriculture was nearly double that of 1919 and four times higher than the prewar record of 1907 (254,000).

[106] On the situation in Ferrara, see Paul Corner, *Fascism in Ferrara 1915-1925* (London, 1975), pp. 88-89; A. Serpieri, *La guerra e le classi rurali*, p. 279, evaluates the success of the strikes.

[107] ASB, C16 F1, Royal Commissioner to Prefect, no date, 1920.

came the focal point of what was widely perceived as a life and death struggle in which the fate of Italian rural socialism and private property hanged in the balance.[108]

The provincial conflict escalated in February when striking day laborers were joined by the sharecroppers, who rejected the contract offered by the APA. Paglia retaliated by ordering his members to initiate procedures for the dismissal of the nine thousand peasant families involved, a decision that proved to be a tactical error for the landlords. In accordance with the old contracts, the departing sharecroppers cultivated only their share of the crops. As a result, the landlords' share was left untended, since the APA could not find hired hands or new tenants willing to incur the wrath of the leagues.[109] Strike leaders took advantage of the situation and instructed their rank and file to occupy the deserted farms, claiming that otherwise "the harvests will be endangered because of the conflict between capital and labor."[110] Angry agrarian spokesmen denounced the occupations as part of a "revolutionary movement" and demanded that the prefecture take "energetic action to reestablish order and defend the rights of property." But given the parliamentary situation and the general turbulence in the country during the spring of 1920, the Nitti government was slow to respond to the APA's entreaties. It was not until late May, a month and a half after the first occupations in Bologna, that the minister of agriculture finally revised the controversial Visocchi Decree to exclude all land seizures carried out without the owners' consent, and in June the crops were once again abandoned in the fields.[111]

As the strike dragged on through the spring and into the summer, it began to strain the internal cohesion of both the APA and

[108] See L. Preti, *Lotte agrarie nella valle padana*, p. 427.

[109] See *ibid.*, p. 433; R. Bachi, *L'Italia economica 1920*, p. 532.

[110] ASB, C16 F1, Federation of Cooperatives to Prime Minister, March 29, 1920; *RdC*, March 30; May 27, 28, 1920; L. Arbizzani, "Lotte agrarie," p. 315. The communes in which the land occupations took place were Medicina, Bologna, Castelmaggiore, Castel d'Argile, Ozzano, Bentivoglio, Calderara di Reno, Zola Predosa, and Bazzano.

[111] ASB, C16 F1, resolution of the APA, April 17, 1920; L. Arbizzani, "Lotte agrarie," p. 317; C. Seton-Watson, *Italy from Liberalism*, p. 552.

the Federterra. Already in April a group of some forty small proprietors and leaseholders broke ranks and signed contracts with the leagues. The same month also saw the first signs of conflicts within the ruling council of the APA.[112] By midsummer the total loss of the rice, wheat, hemp, sugar beet, and forage crops appeared imminent. A growing number of farmers, faced with serious financial losses and subjected to the relentless pressure of the leagues, withdrew from the APA. Despite Paglia's efforts to maintain morale and discipline, the prefect reported at the end of July how a "sizeable group of landowners, especially the smaller ones, have accepted the contract proposed by the Federterra."[113]

Behind its seemingly monolithic facade, the Federterra also began to experience its own disciplinary problems, particularly among the more traditional sharecroppers in the district of Imola, where the independent peasant brotherhoods had enjoyed a strong following prior to the war. These problems stemmed largely from a profound divergence of views on the aims and objectives of the strike. While leaders of the Federterra considered their extreme contractual demands as a way to eliminate the *mezzadria* system and "proletarianize" the peasantry, many sharecroppers saw them as a means of individual advancement that would lead ultimately to the purchase of their own farms.[114] The fragile allegiance of these peasants to the program and strategy of the leagues was increasingly evident as the complete loss of the harvests became a real possibility. As early as May, a small nucleus of discontented sharecroppers resigned from the Federterra, accepted the APA's contract, and formed an independent union whose membership grew steadily during the summer.[115] More importantly, those peas-

[112] On the defection of the small proprietors, see *RdC*, April 18, 1920; for the internal conflicts, see ASB, C16 F1, no. 2, published attack by Cesare Fornaciari on March 30, 1920, "Sul contegno dell'Ufficio di Presidenza dell'Associazione Agricoltori Bolognesi e per il decoro degli agricoltori e della loro organizzazione," and Paglia's reply in a letter to the prefect, April 2, 1920.

[113] ASB, C16 F1, Prefect to Ministry of Interior, July 30, 1920.

[114] See L. Arbizzani, "Lotte agrarie," p. 307.

[115] See *ibid.*, p. 317; ASB, C16 F1, Subprefect, July 12, 1920. Unfortunately there were few indications of who these dissident sharecroppers actually were.

ants who remained in the leagues often ignored the orders of the strike committee, as the subprefect indicated in June: "The peasant sharecroppers enrolled in the red leagues in the district of Imola do not approve, in large part, of the policies of the provincial Federterra so that, for example, the hay even of the red peasants has been largely mowed. Also the leaders of the local leagues have had to allow the peasants to harvest the entire peach crop. . . . As regards the letter notifying the landowners of the new contract imposed by the Federterra, many peasants in the red leagues . . . have informed their bosses that they are prepared to negotiate and to take no account of the letter."[116]

The leagues dealt with dissident sharecroppers in much the same fashion as they dealt with recalcitrant landowners, using boycotts, threats, and violence against property and person to compel obedience. With the complete support of the Socialist municipal administrations, the special tribunals of the leagues employed boycotts indiscriminately against anyone who did not join the strike. The victims of such boycotts faced virtually total isolation. A subsequent parliamentary commission reported that "the boycotted peasants were not only denied any manual labor, but they could not purchase food or clothing, they could not sell their produce, and in some cases . . . they and their families were denied medical assistance."[117] In a few areas dissident sharecroppers attempted to combat the boycotts by mounting their own boycotts. The independent peasant union in the commune of Dozza, for instance, voted in mid-June to boycott the local village inhabitants, "depriving them of milk, eggs, fresh cheese, [and] greens."[118]

Emilio Sereni, in his study *La questione agraria nella rinascita nazionale italiana* (Turin, 1975), pp. 117-119, argues that these future recruits of fascism were, for the most part, wealthier sharecroppers who had greatly advanced their economic position during the war and who were therefore ill-disposed toward the Federterra's program for the socialization of the land.

[116] ASB, C16 F1, Subprefect of Imola to Prefect, June 19, 1920.

[117] ASB, C7 F1, "Novembre," "Commissione parlamentare per i fatti di Bologna," 1921.

[118] ASB, C6 F2, no. 3, Subprefect of Imola to Prefect, June 17, 1920. Two days later, the same group of peasants pledged mutual assistance for the grain harvest. See *ibid.*, no. 1, Subprefect to Prefect, June 19, 1920.

Any efforts at resistance met with violent retaliation from the strikers. In late July the prefect informed his superiors of a dramatic rise in "attacks against persons, ferocious boycotts of dissidents, arson, and damages . . . to private property." During the previous month and a half alone, the police reported sixteen cases of arson, four cases of assault and battery, two instances of mob violence, and one assault on a policeman.[119] Violence by striking laborers reached a peak in August, leading spokesmen for the independent union to protest to the prefect "the attacks of fanatics, the threats of death, the destruction, and the arson committed by the red leagues."[120] Nor did the problems of uncooperative peasants necessarily end when they capitulated to these pressures; often they also had to pay a stiff punitive fine to the local socialist labor leader in order to gain admission or readmission into the leagues.

In much of the countryside, the leagues effectively supplanted the police and prefectoral officials as the real authorities. Government absenteeism and inadequate law enforcement ranked highest among the complaints of landowners and proprietors. One agrarian notable, Count Aldobrandino Malvezzi, gave a graphic indication of how the propertied classes perceived the pervasiveness of socialist power in the province in a letter to the minister of finance in April:

> It is not a mere phrase when I write that the province of Bologna today is only nominally a part of the kingdom of Italy. . . . The Chamber of Labor rules and no one dares disobey its orders because everyone has become convinced that the government will not help anyone who takes the initiative in resisting the socialist tyranny. . . . Open and ever more frequent violations

[119] ASB, C16 F1, Prefect to Ministry of Interior, July 30, 1920; *ibid.*, Police Report to Prefect, August 23, 1920. In addition, see ASB, C16 F1, no. 1, 1920 for a series of reports and letters recounting violence suffered by peasants who had left the leagues. After the strike, police reported the following statistics: 190 cases of arson or crop damage; 40 violations of the right to work; 20 injuries or deaths; 16 thefts; 15 cases of embezzlement. See ASB, C7 F1, "Novembre," 1921.

[120] ASB, C16 F1, petition to Prefect, August 11, 1920. The same month the subprefect of Imola reported that "the red unionists are attempting to prevent the boycotted peasants from doing any work." *ibid.*, August 23, 1920.

> of prefectoral ordinances go unpunished—be it by the city administration or by the Chamber of Labor. . . . The authority of this anonymous socialist government is increasingly reinforced and in fact is the only one recognized in the province.[121]

Such complaints seemed to fall on deaf ears in Rome. With their weak coalition governments, neither Nitti nor his successor Giolitti were prepared to take any strong action against the leagues. Giolitti, in particular, preferred to rely on his old prewar method of allowing the strikes to run their course and then arranging a compromise settlement. Passivity at the top of the state apparatus in Rome tended to translate into appeasement of the Socialists by authorities at the provincial level. During the strike in Bologna, the actions of the politically sensitive prefect appeared to be guided primarily by the desire to avoid confrontations or conflicts with the leagues that "could have regrettable consequences." For their part, local police officials denied any responsibility for the growing violence, insisting that their forces were "inadequate for the control of the situation."[122]

In the absence of forceful intervention by the government, the prolongation of the strike favored the leagues. Their boycotts and violence were devastatingly effective in the short run, despite claims by prefectoral officials that these tactics would not produce "a stable and organic success, since in large part it is a question of extorted enlistments and is therefore devoid of any cordial consensus on principles and methods of struggle."[123] After the Federterra rejected a compromise proposed by a special government commission of agricultural technicians in mid-September, agrarian resistance began to collapse. During the following month, the number of deserters from the ranks of the APA swelled dramatically: over

[121] ACS, Carte Schanzer, B22, letter Malvezzi to Schanzer, April 10, 1920, quoted in C. Maier, *Recasting Bourgeois Europe*, p. 178.

[122] On the attitude of the Bolognese prefect, see ASB, C16 F1, no. 1, Prefect to S. E. Sottosegretario di Stato, July 30, 1920; for the police, see ASB, C16 F1, Police Chief to Prefect, August 17, 1920.

[123] ASB, C7 F1, "Novembre," Subprefect to Prefect, August 18, 1920.

eighteen hundred landowners signed pledges accepting the Federterra's *mezzadria* contract, some sixteen hundred stipulated individual labor contracts with the employment offices of the leagues.[124] Paglia managed to avoid the total collapse of his organization only by coming to terms with Alberto Calda, the Federterra's chief representative. Their agreement officially ended the strike on October 25, 1920.

The agrarian leader portrayed the final settlement as a victory of principle for the APA, since the leagues had implicitly recognized him as the contractual agent of the remaining members of the association. On the whole, however, the outcome of the strike seemed to represent an overwhelming triumph for the Federterra. The Paglia-Calda agreement required landowners to provide their sharecroppers with sanitary housing, family gardens, and a guaranteed income in years when the harvests were insufficient. The peasant's share of the crops now rose from the traditional 50 percent to 60 percent for cereals and 65 percent for sugar beets and hemp. The day laborers also won major concessions. In addition to substantial wage increases, the APA gave the leagues complete control of agricultural hiring in the province and guaranteed their laborers employment in a series of jobs and land reclamation projects that had previously been reserved for the sharecroppers.[125]

A moral victory on the issue of organizational representation did little to compensate commercial farmers for the substantial material losses they had suffered. As a result of the strike, a third of the hay, a fifth of the grain harvest, and a quarter of the grapes had been lost, an estimated financial sacrifice of 120 million lire. Especially hardhit were the big rice growers of the lower plains who had to reduce the area devoted to their crop from four thou-

[124] *La Squilla*, October 23, 1920. During the last weeks of the strike, the Socialist daily published the names of all the landowners who had signed the Federterra's contract. On the unsuccessful efforts of the government to mediate the strike, see L. Arbizzani, "Lotte agrarie," pp. 318-320.

[125] Federterra, *Capitolato colonico per la provincia di Bologna, 1920* quoted in L. Arbizzani, "Lotte agrarie," pp. 324-326; see *ibid.* for the concessions won by the day laborers.

sand acres to seventeen hundred.[126] Even Paglia had to recognize the disastrous economic impact of the strike. As the head manager of a large commercial farm in Bentivoglio, he reported a 53 percent fall in net income for the agricultural year 1920-21, a loss he attributed chiefly to the "agrarian struggle . . . unleashed in the province."[127]

The collapse of the hemp market in the second half of 1920 compounded the negative effects of the strike and the new burdens imposed by the leagues. Between early 1919 and the summer of 1920, the price per quintal of hemp had doubled, encouraging growers to expand their acreage in the expectation of windfall profits.[128] But after July, these favorable conditions began to disappear. The revival of production elsewhere in Europe reduced foreign demand and led to a drop in exports. By the middle of the fall, there were increasingly ominous signs of serious stagnation and declining prices in the hemp markets of Emilia. Thus, precisely at a time when the Paglia-Calda agreement had saddled them with considerably higher labor costs and restricted their ability to respond to changing market conditions, local growers faced the prospect of much lower profits from the sale of their hemp crop.[129]

The municipal elections at the beginning of November added political insult to the economic injuries of the strike. The propertied classes entered the electoral campaigns discouraged and disorganized. In the district of Vergato, the subprefect reported that the parties of order were "composed of disheartened and tired men . . . divided by old interests and grudges [who] can exercise little

126 On the general crop losses, see L. Preti, *Lotte agrarie nella valle padana*, p. 438; for the plight of the rice growers, see ASB, C6 F2, 1921, "Statistica del tornaturato di coltivazione umida 1911 al 1921."

127 See Calisto Paglia, *Donazione Pizzardi. Relazione sul modo di gestire la tenuta di Bentivoglio*, Vol. I (Bologna, 1923), p. 6 in ACS, Presidenza del Consiglio dei Ministri, F3 SF1-1, 1924.

128 For information on the hemp market in this period, see *Bollettino del Sindacato Agricoltori di Bazzano*, no. 4-5, September 1924; *RdC*, January 3, 1924. In the first half of 1920, hemp exports doubled.

129 See V. Peglion's article in *Il Giornale Agrario*, April 16, 1921 as well as P. Corner, *Fascism in Ferrara*, p. 110.

influence on the electorate." Likewise, the subprefect of Imola noted that in his district "the parties of order are completely disorganized and without any hope of victory in the electoral contests."[130] The outcome of the voting more than justified the pessimism of the subprefects. Socialist slates captured fifty-four of the sixty-one municipal councils; of the remaining seven, the Popular party controlled six, the parties of order only one.[131]

By the fall of 1920, Bologna's men of wealth and property felt threatened in many areas. In the countryside their once unchallenged authority over the land had now been severely circumscribed by Socialist labor leaders who were seemingly determined to exclude them altogether from the productive process. In the city of Bologna, the frequent strikes and demonstrations not only disrupted their commercial activities, but also underscored their humiliating subservience to the arbitrary dictates of the all-powerful Chamber of Labor. From elective office to honorary positions in the municipal institutions, most of the prizes and distinctions of public life had been lost to the Socialists. Even their simplest pleasures—strolls through the arcaded streets of the urban center, dinners in Bologna's elegant restaurants, or shopping trips in Via Rizzoli—seemed to depend on the good will of the new provincial rulers. With the possible exception of nearby Ferrara, nowhere else on the peninsula did the propertied classes appear to confront a more drastic decline in wealth, power, and prestige than in Bologna.[132]

[130] ASB, C5 F1, Subprefect of Vergato to Prefect, September 7, 1920; *ibid.*, Subprefect of Imola to Prefect, September 22, 1920.

[131] For the results of the municipal elections, see *La Squilla*, November 28, 1920. In addition, the socialists transformed their prewar majority on the Provincial Administrative Council into a near total monopoly, capturing forty-seven of the fifty available seats.

[132] On the situation in Ferrara, see P. Corner, *Fascism in Ferrara*, pp. 104-112; perhaps the most eloquent description of the agrarians' seeming plight is that of Angelo Tasca's in *The Rise of Italian Fascism* (New York, 1966), p. 95.

VII. THE RISE OF AGRARIAN FASCISM IN BOLOGNA, 1920-1921

During the first nine months of 1920, the Italian peninsula appeared to be in the throes of a revolutionary crisis. With the Chamber of Deputies paralyzed by bitter political divisions and the economy plagued by soaring inflation, the government's authority seemed to collapse in the face of the most prolonged and intense period of social upheaval since 1898.[1] Beginning with railroad and postal strikes in January, a record number of over two million industrial, agricultural, and public service workers engaged in more than two thousand strikes and countless political demonstrations. Growing labor militancy led to violence: between April 1919 and September 1920, some one hundred and forty conflicts involving demonstrators and police resulted in over three hundred and twenty deaths.[2] As the strikes gained momentum, a massive influx of new recruits poured into the socialist unions: the General Confederation of Labor grew from 321,000 in 1914 to 2,200,000 by the end of 1920, while membership in the national Federterra

[1] Commercial farmers in Bologna certainly seemed to take the threat of revolution seriously. In April 1920, their daily paper proclaimed that "the bourgeoisie, besieged by lunatics and delinquents, sees its very existence endangered." See *Il Progresso*, April 21, 1920.

[2] Maurice F. Neufeld, *Italy, School for Awakening Countries* (Ithaca, 1961), p. 379; Paolo Alatri, *Le origini del fascismo* (Bologna, 1962), p. 61.

jumped from 100,000 in 1918 to over 800,000 at the beginning of 1921.[3] Industrialists and landowners were alarmed less by the size and violence of the strikes than by the radical demands of the strikers. At the same time that peasant leagues in the Po Valley were imposing a compulsory system of manpower obligations on landowners, in Turin factory councils were being set up to prepare for "the expropriation of industries in favor of the proletariat." Behind the calls for factory councils and monopolistic hiring offices, economic leaders perceived not only a threat to their authority in the work place, but also a revolutionary challenge to the basic hierarchies of wealth, power, and status in the society.[4] By September this challenge seemed to become a reality when the government remained passive while five hundred thousand metalworkers seized and organized production in plants throughout the peninsula. Spreading rapidly from the "industrial triangle," the factory occupation movement made its impact felt even in primarily agricultural provinces such as Bologna, where four thousand workers took over some sixty metallurgical plants.[5]

The maximalist leadership of the Socialist party did little to calm the inflated expectations of its rank-and-file or the fears of the propertied classes. Hailing all strikes as manifestations of revolutionary spirit, the maximalists denounced any cooperation with

[3] For the industrial union statistics, see Angelo Tasca, *The Rise of Italian Fascism* (New York, 1966), p. 73; for those of agriculture, see Renato Zangheri, *Lotte agrarie in Italia. La federazione nazionale dei lavoratori della terra, 1901-1926* (Milan, 1960), p. 371.

[4] Charles Maier, *Recasting Bourgeois Europe* (Princeton, 1975), pp. 136ff., provides a general discussion of the European elites' perception of postwar unrest. On the factory councils, see Francesco Magri, *Controllo operaio e consigli d'azienda in Italia e all'estero, 1916-1947* (Milan, 1947), p. 188ff.; on developments in the countryside, see R. Zangheri, *Lotte agrarie in Italia*, pp. xxxviii-xxxix, and Idomeneo Barbadoro, *Storia del sindacalismo dalla nascita al fascismo*, Vol. 1, *La Federterra* (Florence, 1973), chap. 4, *passim*.

[5] On the factory occupation movement in Italy, see Paolo Spriano, *L'occupazione delle fabbriche* (Turin, 1964); the occupations in Bologna are discussed in Brunella Dalla Casa, "Il movimento operaio e socialista a Bologna dall'occupazione delle fabbriche al Patto di pacificazione" in Deputazione Emilia-Romagna, per la storia della Resistenza, *Movimento operaio e fascismo nell'Emilia-Romagna 1919-1923* (Bologna, 1973), pp. 3-12.

non-socialist parties and exhorted their followers to use force "to conquer power and consolidate revolutionary conquests."[6] Not all factions of the party, however, shared the euphoria or easy optimism of the maximalists. Already in March 1920, the reformist leader, Claudio Treves, had pessimistically declared to the Nitti government: "This is the crux of the present tragic situation: you can no longer maintain your existing social order and we are not yet strong enough to impose the one we want." Cautionary voices could also be heard on the left wing of the party. In the summer of 1920, the future Communist leader, Antonio Gramsci, warned the national council of the party of the potential dangers at hand:

> The current phase of the class struggle in Italy is the phase that precedes either the conquest of political power by the revolutionary proletariat . . . or a tremendous reaction by the propertied class and the government caste. No violence will be overlooked in order to subjugate the industrial and agricultural proletariat; they will attempt to shatter ruthlessly the working class's organizations of political struggle (the Socialist party) and to incorporate the organizations of economic resistance (the unions and cooperatives) into the cogs of the bourgeois state.[7]

Despite persistent disorders in the country, the political initiative was beginning to shift from the left to the right even as Gramsci uttered these prophetic words. As early as June, the fall of the Nitti ministry and Giolitti's accession to power reflected how a unifying concern with social unrest had now replaced earlier political divisions over interventionism within the ranks of the constitutional parties.[8] Additional signs of a conservative revival came in the fall with the reorganization of industrial pressure groups and the municipal elections. Under the pressures of the factory

[6] M. Neufeld, *Italy*, p. 262.

[7] For Treves' comments, see A. Tasca, *The Rise of Italian Fascism*, p. 73; for Gramsci's, see Antonio Gramsci, *Sul Fascismo: L'analisi del fenomeno fascista negli scritti più significati Antonio Gramsci*, ed. Enzo Santarelli (Rome, 1973), p. 78.

[8] See Renzo De Felice, *Mussolini il rivoluzionario* (Turin, 1965), pp. 600-601.

occupations, businessmen temporarily put aside their sectoral differences to construct a cohesive and militant organization on an industry-wide basis in order to combat the labor movement.[9] Electoral returns from the municipalities in late October and early November indicated a similar trend. Overcoming the fragmentation that had prevailed in 1919, the parties of order forged coalitions that successfully recaptured all the major cities, with the exception of Milan and Bologna.[10]

The conservative revival was facilitated by increasing conflicts and declining morale on the left. Although technically the metal workers and rural laborers had emerged victorious from the strikes of 1920, the actual conquests fell far short of the sweeping social revolution they expected. With few visible changes in the patterns of daily work, disillusionment replaced the enthusiasm and militancy that had characterized the union rank-and-file during the previous two years. The onset of a recession in the late fall of 1920, with its accompanying layoffs and weakened bargaining power for the unions, further demoralized workers while enabling employers to undermine and restrict earlier concessions. The inconclusive outcome of the strikes also sharpened long standing ideological conflicts within the Socialist party between reformists, maximalists, and communists without moderating the party's parliamentary intransigence. These internal conflicts would shortly culminate in January 1921 when the extreme left withdrew to form the Communist party of Italy.[11]

To a certain extent, developments on the Italian peninsula in the fall of 1920 reflected a more general receding of the revolutionary tide throughout Europe after the defeat of the Red Army

[9] Mario Abrate, *La lotta sindacale nella industrializzazione in Italia, 1906-1926* (Turin, 1966), pp. 297ff.

[10] For a summary of the electoral returns, see C. Maier, *Recasting Bourgeois Europe*, p. 189.

[11] On the economic recession, see R. Bachi, *L'Italia economica nel 1920* (Città di Castello, 1921) pp. vii-viii. For tensions and divisions within the Socialist party, see Christopher Seton-Watson, *Italy from Liberalism to Fascism* (London, 1967), pp. 575-576.

outside of Warsaw. Not only in Italy, but also in France and Germany new possibilities appeared for a revived conservative equilibrium based on a coalition of elites and the middle classes.[12] For a substantial portion of Italy's propertied classes, however, the victories of the fall were either too veiled or had come too late to restore their confidence in the liberal parliamentary institutions or to quench their thirst for revenge. In the wake of the moderate strike settlements and electoral successes, employers appeared to recall only the passivity of the government and their own humiliations and violated property rights. Perhaps nowhere were these feelings more widespread than among the commercial farmers and industrialists in the province of Bologna.

1. *The Rising Tide of Agrarian Reaction*

The seeming invincibility of the local socialist movement and the government's unwillingness to intervene energetically in the agricultural strikes of 1920 rapidly undermined the confidence of Bolognese landowners and commercial farmers in conventional methods of social bargaining; increasingly they were drawn to seek out more coercive substitutes for the legal authorities in the province. Angered by land seizures and government inaction, agrarians were already talking about taking matters into their own hands in March. Late that month, the president of the APA called upon the prefect to evict the leagues from the farms they had forceably occupied in the commune of Medicina and cautioned that "many of our members are exasperated and want to react." A week later, Paglia repeated these demands, intimating that a substantial number of growers did not "intend to accept passively the oppression and the invasions."[13] When Nitti still refused to act, local spokesmen of the APA escalated the belligerency of their protests. In late April, for instance, the head of the organized agrarians in the commune of Bazzano, Julo Fornaciari, threatened that, in the ab-

[12] See C. Maier, *Recasting Bourgeois Europe*, p. 191.

[13] ASB, C16 F1, Calisto Paglia to Prefect, March 26 and April 2, 1920.

sence of state action, "the agriculturalists will have to defend themselves directly."[14]

The first organized reaction of the provincial elites, however, came less in response to problems in the countryside than to perceived threats to their privileged status and way of life as residents in the provincial capital. Early in April, a three-day strike called by the Chamber of Labor to protest police violence not only closed factories and shops but halted all transportation, power, and postal services. The unprecedented scale and intensity of the strike terrified and mobilized all factions of the elite, for it appeared to expose the extent of their abandonment, isolation, and weakness. With the security forces of the Chamber of Labor controlling all movement and traffic in the city, the mood of leading businessmen and landed interests was dramatically reflected in the pages of the agrarian daily, *Il Progresso*, which denounced the strike as "the product of a campaign of hatred and ferocity . . . against the nation and its citizens" and called upon the "bourgeoisie to prepare for defense and struggle."[15] Class solidarity immediately, if temporarily, superceded sectoral and political divisions of the provincial elites. On the last day of the strike, Count Filippo Cavazza joined with such eminent prewar moderates as Enrico Pini and Count Carlo Malvezzi to organize a meeting of "urban notables and persons from the world of commerce and industry" that led directly to the formation of the Bolognese Association of Social Defense.[16] According to its hastily composed charter, the association had the task of organizing squads of vigilantes, the *volontario civile*, who were to employ "whatever means necessary" in order to defend "the most elementary liberties." Sponsors of the association made no secret of their commitment to violent action, warning the prefect

[14] ASB, C16 F1, Julo Fornaciari to Prefect, April 30, 1920.

[15] *Il Progresso*, April 9, 1920.

[16] *RdC*, April 9, 1920. The presence of Enrico Pini at the meeting was particularly noteworthy; previously he had been a moderate supporter of Giolitti. In the same period, he resigned from the board of directors of *Il Resto del Carlino* to protest what he considered its sympathetic treatment of the leagues.

that they were prepared to take measures which "until now . . . we have entrusted to the laws of the state."[17]

Agrarian spokesmen took the lead in organizing and promoting the Bolognese Association of Social Defense and its program of armed vigilante action in the capital. Count Filippo Cavazza and the prominent Catholic landowner Carlo Ballerini assumed the leadership of the association, while *Il Progresso* became the most strident advocate of its policies. In sharp contrast to *Il Resto del Carlino,* which viewed the vigilante squads with open disapproval, the agrarian daily repeatedly insisted that responsible citizens had not merely the right but "the duty to resist and fight to the bitter end."[18] In a similar vein, propagandists of the APA exhorted members to participate in all initiatives of the association that aimed "to restore social discipline."[19]

The new willingness of Bologna's elites to experiment with their own violent remedies for the ills of the "red tyranny" provided the basis for collaboration with the Fascio di Combattimento, a movement that had led only a marginal existence in the province until the spring of 1920. On the national level, the first *fascio* had been set up in Milan by Benito Mussolini and a tiny gathering of ex-socialists, syndicalists, and war veterans in March 1919. Initially, Mussolini designed the *fasci* to express and embody not a precise political project but rather a state of mind, a pervasive mood of postwar discontent and undirected revolt. With their informal structure and highly flexible program, the fasci spread from Milan to some seventy other cities and towns of Italy, where they served as a point of reference for a small and heterogeneous mix of revolutionary interventionists, exservicemen, petty bourgeois employees, and a few men of property.[20]

[17] *AP,* Commissione parlamentare, "Memoriale della Camera di Commercio e Industria di Bologna," pp. 137-139 as cited in L. Arbizzani, "L'Avvento del fascismo nel Bolognese, 1920-1922," *Movimento Operaia e Socialista,* 1964, p. 85.

[18] *Il Progresso,* April 21, 1920; for the critical view of *Il Resto del Carlino,* see the issue of April 18, 1920.

[19] ASB, C16 F1, *Bollettino dell'Associazione Provinciale di Agricoltori,* no. 11, May 12, 1920.

[20] On the early fascist movement, see Renzo De Felice, *Mussolini il rivoluzio-*

The Fascist movement made its inauspicious entrance on to the political scene in Bologna the second week of April 1919, immediately falling prey to the conflicts that were disrupting all the local parties of order. At the founding meeting, two militant Republican exofficers, Guido and Mario Bergamo won control of the fascio and sought to give it a decidedly radical subversive direction, epitomized in their slogan: "Neither with the bolsheviks nor with the monarchists, but for the revolution." Already in the second meeting of the fascio, police reported that the Bergamo brothers' insistence on an ill-defined "revolutionary program" aroused strong opposition from conservative nationalist elements led by Dino Zanetti and Cesare Tumedei, who asserted that "they and their friends could not continue to belong to a fascio whose political program is openly opposed to the glorious House of Savoy." This political contrast became an open split less than two weeks after the founding of the fascio, when Zanetti and Tumedei led an exodus of monarchists and Nationalists out of the movement and into the Anti-Bolshevik League.[21] The fascio over which the Bergamo brothers came to preside thus included a small group of some seventy young officers and soldiers who shared their republican principles. Harassed by the Socialists and distrusted by provincial authorities as an ostensibly subversive organization, the fascio steadily declined in membership during the summer of 1919 and lapsed into inactivity. By late August, fifteen men remained in the fascio and, as one discouraged member informed the central committee in Milan, the city of Bologna had become a "completely apathetic center" for the Fascist movement.[22]

In the spring of 1920, however, the Bolognese fascio gained a new lease on life after the Bergamo brothers resigned in protest against the policies of the central committee, which they claimed

---

nario, 1883-1920 (Turin, 1965), chap. 12; Roberto Vivarelli, *Il dopoguerra in Italia e l'avvento del fascismo* (Naples, 1967), pp. 277-298; Adrian Lyttelton, *The Seizure of Power: Fascism in Italy, 1919-1929* (New York, 1973), pp. 42-52.

[21] For the evolution of internal conflicts within the Bolognese fascio, see ASB, C7 F1, Police Chief to Prefect, May 13, 1919.

[22] See ACS, Mostra della rivoluzione fascista, B100, letters of Garibaldo Pedrini to Pasella, August 16 and 22, 1919.

did not "conform to the basic conditions of the current national situation nor to the common interests of the nation." Like many left-wing Fascists elsewhere in the country, the Bergamo brothers were repelled by Mussolini's ties to wealthy business interests, the growing militarization of the movement, and its increasingly single-minded emphasis on violent resistance to bolshevism.[23] No such concerns appeared to trouble the former railway worker, prewar anarchist and revolutionary interventionist, Leandro Arpinati, who took over the leadership of the Bolognese fascio in April. Above all, Arpinati and his motley crew of supporters, which included a dishwasher, a butcher, another railway worker as well as a few students, veterans, and local merchants, did not share their republican predecessors' intransigent hostility toward the older forces of order in the city.[24]

Following the general strike, Arpinati quickly responded to overtures from the Association for Social Defense, recognizing that the sudden enthusiasm of the propertied classes for vigilante squads was bringing them "into our field of action." Practical considerations dictated collaboration as the Fascist leader made clear in a letter to the political secretary in Milan: "It is certainly true that these Bolognese bourgeois (and to say Bolognese is to say apathetic and cowardly) never made a move until, with the last strike, they felt themselves menaced in their own security and their own pockets; but should we for this reason not accept the money-arm which is so necessary for our battle and which these bourgeois (granted from fear alone) are offering us at this moment."[25] The immediate results of collaboration seemed to confirm the correctness of Ar-

[23] ACS, Mostra della rivoluzione fascista, B100, letter of Bergamo to Pasella, March 4, 1920. On the changing character of the Fascist movement, see A. Lyttelton, *The Seizure of Power*, pp. 50-53.

[24] On the group around Arpinati, see Pier Paolo D'Attore, "Agrari e fascismo. La formazione del regime reazionario di massa," (Tesi di laurea, University of Bologna, 1976) pp. 11-12. On Arpinati, in particular, see G. Cantamessa Arpinati, *Arpinati mio padre* (Rome, 1968).

[25] ACS, Mostra della rivoluzione fascista, B100, report of Arpinati to Pasella, April 26, 1920; also see A. Lyttelton, *The Seizure of Power*, p. 58.

pinati's judgments. With the financial backing of the Association of Social Defense, the Fascist squads put on their first major display of strength on the left's most prized holiday, May first, parading through the main avenues of Bologna, singing the movement hymn, "Giovinezza," and vilifying the socialists. For Arpinati, the parades represented an unqualified success. Not only had they enabled the fascio to absorb all other vigilante groups, but they had also attracted a crowd of young veterans, "ready to put up solid resistance to possible socialist violence." More importantly, Arpinati claimed that his squads had destroyed the myth of Socialist invincibility in the public squares of the city: "The local Socialists showed an exasperating calm; their headquarters (the Chamber of Labor) remained hermetically sealed for the entire day. I am convinced that they will never make the revolution."[26]

Arpinati's optimistic assessment of the fascio's strength in the city was premature. The end of the school year quickly revealed the dependence of Bolognese fascism on student enthusiasts, for with the departure of the students from the city for summer vacation, the fascio once again lapsed into inactivity. As the central committee learned in August, Bologna was the only major center that "in this period of rebirth and tremendous fascist activity does not give any sign of life." For his part, Arpinati withdrew temporarily from the movement, preferring to await "the return of the students to Bologna."[27] At the same time, the support given the Fascist squads by the Association of Social Defense in May did not signify that the provincial elites had completely rejected traditional channels of political influence or that they had made any firm commitment to extralegal action in the province. On the contrary, the fall of the Nitti government in June encouraged agrarian leaders to shift their attention to developments in Rome. Despite old animosities, the return of Giolitti to power revived conservative hopes throughout the country in a restoration of law

[26] ACS, Mostra della rivoluzione fascista, B100, Arpinati to Pasella, May 5, 1920.

[27] ACS, Mostra della rivoluzione fascista, B100, August 26, 1920; A. Lyttelton, *The Seizure of Power*, p. 60.

and order under government auspices.[28] Initially, Giolitti appeared to warrant such hopes in the province of Bologna; in July he ordered the requisition of all crops endangered by the strike and set up a special government committee of experts to arbitrate the conflict between the leagues and the growers. With the new possibilities for a negotiated settlement of the strike, agrarian enthusiasm for the methods of the Association of Social Defense and the fascio rapidly diminished. The association took no real initiatives during the summer and, according to the prefect, was "nearly forgotten because of the inertia of its leaders."[29]

Expectations of a quick return to normalcy proved to be shortlived. The Federterra's rejection of government mediation and the prime minister's refusal to take stronger measures against the factory occupations or league boycotts in the fall of 1920 rekindled interest in extremist proposals among the landowners and leaseholders, who now faced the imminent loss of their harvests. Agrarian spokesmen articulated the desperation and rage of their rank-and-file in no uncertain terms at a regional agricultural congress in late August. The vice-president of the APA, Luigi Neri, denounced the government for its "connivance with the bolsheviks," while Giacobbe Manzoni of Imola demanded the adoption of "the methods necessary to oppose the avalanche, which is burying the rights of property." Alberto Donini employed even more incendiary rhetoric, proclaiming his readiness to go "into ten provinces and unchain a violent rebellion."[30]

[28] For the initial response of the agrarians to the new government of Giolitti, see *Il Giornale Agrario*, June 17, 1920. The favorable response of the Italian bourgeoisie in general is discussed in R. De Felice, *Mussolini il rivoluzionario*, pp. 600-601, and in C. Maier, *Recasting Bourgeois Europe*, p. 181.

[29] ASB, C7 F1, *Novembre*, Prefect to Parliamentary Commission of Investigation, January 24, 1921. For the details of government intervention in the Bolognese strike, see L. Arbizzani, "Lotte agrarie in provincia di Bologna nel primo dopoguerra," in R. Zangheri, ed., *Le campagne emiliane nell'epoca moderna* (Milan, 1957), pp. 318-319.

[30] *Il Giornale Agrario*, September 9, 1920; *RdC*, August 31, 1920; *La Squilla*, September 4, 1920. On the conference itself, see "Le origini dello squadrismo. Il convegno agrario di Rimini," *Emilia*, July-August 1951, pp. 232-236.

By October renewed agrarian militancy led to sharp polarization within the APA. While Calisto Paglia remained committed to the path of compromise and legality, his authority was now challenged by a faction of "nationalist" agrarians, led by Giorgio Ghigi, who favored a definitive confrontation with the leagues and the government. The strength of the nationalist faction was sufficient to provoke prefectoral concern over "a sizeable group . . . disposed toward the armed defense of property rights."[31] The failure of nationalist efforts to sabotage the Paglia-Calda agreements did not discourage militant agrarians or reflect any broad acceptance of what seemed to be the new status quo in the countryside. On the contrary, in the weeks after the strike had officially ended, a growing number of commercial farmers simply resigned from the APA and disavowed the commitments made by Paglia.[32] Prefiguring the strategy that would prevail the following year in the province, militant agrarian leaders began to establish new ties with dissident sharecroppers so that, as Ghigi expressed it, "the landowner will join together with the peasant in the defense of the right to work."[33]

The fall of 1920 also witnessed a new convergence of interests between militant agrarians and powerful industrial groups in the provincial capital. With the spread of the factory occupation movement in late August, earlier sectoral divisions over tariff and tax questions gave way to a unifying concern with the workers' challenge to managerial authority in the factories and on the farms. The common concern of the propertied classes found clear expression in a telegram that Alessandro Calzoni, the local machine manufacturer and representative of the Consorzio Metalmeccanico Emiliano Romagnolo, sent to Giolitti in mid-September. Echoing the views of agrarian spokesmen, Calzoni accused the government of being "an accomplice of the . . . revolutionaries who want to

[31] ASB, C16 F1, marginal notes of prefect, October 16, 1920; *ibid.*, Prefect to Ministry of Interior, October 24, 1920.

[32] ASB, C7 F1, Subprefect to Prefect, November 10, 1920; ASB C16 F1, Federterra to Prefect, November 18, 1920; *ibid.*, APA to Prefect, November 23, 1920; *La Squilla*, December 18, 1920.

[33] *Il Giornale Agrario*, September 9, 1920; *Il Progresso*, October 13 and 28, 1920.

ruin Italy" and concluded with the ultimatum: "Either you intervene or we will act on our own."[34] Only two days after the factory occupations had begun, the APA sent a message of support to the besieged industrialists, affirming that the occupations had the same political objectives as the league boycotts "since by different paths communism . . . is attempting . . . to overthrow private property."[35] From such exchanges of mutual moral support, agrarian-industrial collaboration evolved into concrete action the third week in September, when the various employer associations joined forces to revive the Association of Social Defense.

The following month both agrarian and industrial interests merged with a more general antisocialist reaction, which began to assume an organized political form as the municipal elections approached. The first sign of this political resurgence came from the Bolognese Fascists who launched an appeal in early October to "all associations and political groups in the city that are fighting for the nation" to unite in a single electoral bloc in order "to oppose the demagogy of the extremists, whether red or black."[36] The Fascist appeal did not go unheeded. On the evening of October 20, the leaders of the fascio met with representatives from several political and patriotic associations and worked out a plan, the provincial police chief subsequently reported, "to reconstitute the Fascio di Combattimento on a broader base, with the principal aim of forming a strong organization capable of opposing the violence that the extremists of the Socialist party and the anarchists were committing in the city and in the province."[37]

The key to fascism's rapid emergence as a major political force in Bologna, this effective merger between the fascio and the older conservative groups reflected a decisive shift in aims and roles, both for the elites and for the local Fascists. For the big commercial

[34] ACS, Ministry of Interior, B74, Calzoni to Giolitti, September 11, 1920, as cited in B. Dalla Casa, "Il movimento operaio," p. 12.

[35] ASB, C16 F1, *Bollettino dell'Associazione Provinciale di Agricoltori*, no. 26, August 21, 1920.

[36] ASB, C5 F1, Police Chief to Prefect, October 7, 1920.

[37] ASB, C7 F1, "I fascisti," Police Chief to Prefect, February 3, 1921.

farmers and the business community, the merger reflected their firm commitment to a coercive and extralegal solution to the socialist threat, as Marchese Giuseppe Tanari made explicit in a letter to Giolitti's lieutenant, Luigi Facta: "I ask myself, if we are abandoned by the government, should we not enroll in the fasci. They are violent and impulsive, but they are also idealists and bring us some fresh air; and if there will have to be a civil war, old as I am, I will fight with them."[38] Such words from the scion of one of Bologna's most illustrious families, a man who had served as mayor, parliamentary deputy, and senator, gave eloquent testimony to the mood of alienation and desperation among the propertied classes by the fall of 1920.

Within the fascio itself, the reorganization in October entailed fundamental changes in structure and function. The radicalism, national concerns, and informal camaraderie of the 1919 Fascists "of the first hour" were gradually deemphasized and a new stress was placed on expanded recruitment, a more disciplined organization, and above all on the preparation and training of paramilitary squads, for the purpose of combatting violently the socialist movement. Continuity of Fascist rhetoric masked to a certain extent the significance of the internal changes and the related alliance with "the best section of the citizens." Despite their ties with local notables, Arpinati and other Fascist spokesmen continued to launch verbal attacks on the old political and economic leaders and to stress both the pragmatic character of the alliance and the complete independence of the fascio.[39] But the logic of collaboration was not lost on some of the more idealistic Fascists, who began to withdraw from the fascio because, as one of them put it, "I do not want to become a white guard."[40] Alarmed by reports from dissident Fas-

[38] Letter of Tanari to Facta, October 27, 1920; published in *Il Progresso*, February 10, 1921.

[39] On the shifting orientation of the fascio, see A. Lyttelton, *The Seizure of Power*, p. 60. For an example of Arpinati's rhetoric, see *AP, Camera dei Deputati*, Leg. xxv, 1919-21, Commissione parlamentare di inchiesta, cited in G. A. Chiurco, *Storia della rivoluzione fascista*, 5 vols. (Florence, 1929), vol. iii, p. 49.

[40] For example of internal opposition to Arpinati's new course, see ACS, Mostra

cists, the central committee in Milan sent Arpinati a stern warning at the end of October: "Precisely because it has grown so suddenly as to become obese, your fascio is carrying out its functions in a confused manner and many recent converts are Fascists like I am a country priest. It is not enough to enroll in a *fascio di combattimento* to be a good Fascist, but rather it is necessary to understand the spirit of our program. . . . I know that the Fascists have been placing themselves too completely in the service of the retrograde elements in Bologna, which could be politically damaging to the fascio."[41] Neither such warnings from Milan nor the departure of some of the original Fascists appeared to have much effect on the policies of the Bolognese fascio. Collaboration with the elites now made Arpinati financially independent of the national Fascist leadership, while the fascio's new paramilitary mission opened up unprecedented opportunities for violent action that could not be ignored, since they promised to increase greatly the movement's popularity, power, and prestige in the city. Far from being unique, the transformation of the Bolognese fascio in the fall of 1920 provided the model for "a chaotic ensemble of local reactions" that would soon sweep through the Po Valley, Tuscany, and Apulia in the following months and transform fascism into a mass movement.[42]

The first initiative of the fledgling antisocialist alliance in Bologna came twelve days before the municipal elections with the founding of the citizens' committee "Peace, Liberty, Work" to promote a slate of candidates drawn from the Liberal party, the Radical Association, the Nationalist Group, the Veterans' Association, and the industrial and agrarian organizations of the province.[43] Appropriately labeled "the bloc of fear" by the Catholic daily, *L'Avvenire d'Italia*, the committee's slate mounted a cam-

della rivoluzione fascista, B100, letter of exlegionnaire Leone Nanni Castelli to the Central Committee in Milan, November 11, 1920.

[41] ACS, Mostra della rivoluzione fascista, B100, Pasella to Arpinati, October 29, 1920.

[42] A. Lyttelton, *The Seizure of Power*, p. 54.

[43] L. Arbizzani, "L'Avvento," p. 95.

paign marked by exceptionally violent and inflammatory slogans. Voters were repeatedly incited to oppose the "barbarians" of the left, to combat the "nihilistic bolshevik madness," and to bring down "the dictatorship of an asiatic stamp that has sought to destroy peace, liberty, and work."[44] The verbal violence of the committee found a fitting complement in the physical violence of the newly emboldened Fascists who made increasingly frequent forays out into public squares and main streets of the city to challenge and provoke clashes with socialist sympathizers.[45]

The hastily organized campaign of the citizens' committee did little to change the outcome of the elections, from which the Socialist party emerged once again victorious. But in comparison to the elections of 1919, the results of the voting in the city revealed the new unity and growing strength of the antisocialist forces. While the Socialists saw their share of the vote decline by 5 percent, the slate backed by the citizens' committee captured 26 percent of the votes, doubling its share and substantially outdistancing the Popular party. More importantly, defeat at the polls in November 1920 did not lead to renewed political disarray and demoralization within the antisocialist camp. On the contrary, for the provincial elites, the defeat only confirmed the inefficacy of electoral politics as a means of defending their interests, and consequently, they felt more than ever the need for the increasing violence of the Fascist squads. The Bolognese fascio did not disappoint its wealthy allies; four days after the voting, Fascists and other patriotic groups held a new rally that culminated in the first tentative assault on the headquarters of the Chamber of Labor.[46] The political initiative now began to shift decisively out of the offices of the Socialist

[44] See the pamphlets of the committee: "La conquista della libertà per tutti," October 27, 1920; "Il comunista è il nemico da abbattere ad ogni costo," October 30, 1920; see also editorials in *Il Progresso*, October 28 and 29, 1920.

[45] On these exploits of the Fascists, see G. A. Chiurco, *Rivoluzione Fascista*, vol. II, p. 192; L. Arbizzani, "L'Avvento," p. 94; PSI, *Fascismo: Inchiesta socialista sulle gesta dei fascisti in Italia* (Milan, 1963), p. 266. This report was first published by *Avanti* in the summer of 1921.

[46] PSI, *Fascismo: Inchiesta socialista*, pp. 266-268.

party, Chamber of Labor, and municipal council and into the streets and public squares of the city.

2. *Fascism Takes the Offensive: The Battle of Palazzo D'Accursio*

Already on the eve of the municipal elections, the Bolognese Fascists had clearly affirmed their intention to ignore the results of the voting. Addressing a rally on October 31, a spokesman from the fascio served notice that, regardless of the vote, "the red flag will not be unfurled from Palazzo D'Accursio," Bologna's city hall.[47] As the leaders of the fascio recognized, the flying of the red flag from the tower of city hall provided an ideal issue for rallying public opinion behind any initiatives that it might take. Indeed, for many students, shopkeepers, businessmen, and professional people, the red flag had come to symbolize some of the most feared and hated aspects of socialist rule: antipatriotism, the coercive strikes and boycotts, the continual threat of social revolution.

The Socialist party gave the Fascists the pretext that they needed by calling a mass demonstration in front of Palazzo D'Accursio for the evening of November 21 to celebrate the electoral victory and the official installation of the new municipal council. After a press campaign of the agrarian daily, *Il Progresso*, had prepared the ground, the fascio distributed a leaflet throughout the city on November 20, proclaiming its declaration of war: "Citizens, the maximalist reds, routed and defeated in the piazzas and streets of the city, are bringing the rural masses to the municipal palace. We will never tolerate this insult! It is an insult to the Patria and to every Italian citizen who wants to have nothing to do with Lenin and bolshevism. Sunday, women and all those people who love peace and tranquility stay at home and if you value the Patria display the Italian Tricolor from your windows. On the streets of Bologna, Sunday there should be only Fascists and bolsheviks.

[47] *RdC*, October 31, 1920.

This will be the trial! The great trial in the name of Italy."[48] In response to this Fascist ultimatum, the Socialists began to prepare their own defense of city hall, mobilizing the "red guards" and stocking the Palazzo with cases of bombs. By the afternoon of November 21, the city had become an armed camp.[49]

As the crowds of Socialist supporters gathered that evening for the celebration, armed squads of Fascists took up positions at the corners of the central piazza that faced on Palazzo D'Accursio. When the newly elected mayor, Ennio Gnudi, stepped out on the balcony of the palazzo to greet the rally, the Fascists opened fire on the crowd. In the ensuing panic and confusion, Fascist bullets and Socialist bombs accounted for several dozen casualties and nine deaths in the piazza, while within the council chambers, unidentified men fired indiscriminately into the small group of non-Socialist councilors, fatally wounding the lawyer, war veteran, and Nationalist Giuliano Giordani.[50]

Despite the large number of Socialist victims, it was Giordani's death that captured public attention and triggered a massive reaction of indignation and revulsion against the Socialist party, which the Bolognese fascio and its respectable allies were quick to exploit and catalyze. Elevating Giordani to the status of an heroic martyr, "cowardly assassinated by the cut-throats of the municipal bolshevik majority," the fascio proclaimed two days after the battle: "Our anguish makes us deaf to every word of calm and peace."[51] The Fascists now dropped their defensive posture and began a counteroffensive against the socialist movement that would steadily gain momentum in the following months. In the first weeks after the battle of Palazzo D'Accursio, the fascio unleashed its violence primarily on the most visible leaders. On November 26,

[48] Cited in G. Salvemini, *Scritti sul fascismo*, Vol. I, ed. R. Vivarelli (Milan, 1961), p. 35.

[49] A. Tasca, *The Rise of Italian Fascism*, p. 100.

[50] For accounts of the battle, see *ibid.*, p. 101; G. Salvemini, *Scritti sul fascismo*, vol. I, p. 36; L. Arbizzani, "L'Avvento," pp. 99-100.

[51] See letter dated November 23, 1920, published in *Il Progresso*, November 24, 1920.

for instance, a Socialist city councilor, Enrico Leone, was jumped, beaten, and spit upon; two weeks later, a similar reception awaited two Socialist parliamentary deputies, Bentini and Nicolai, in front of the municipal court house. On a more informal basis, groups of Fascists circulated through the streets and in the meeting places of the city to ensure that "anyone who was or even *seemed* a Socialist was beaten, vilified, insulted."[52] Spokesmen for the fascio proudly claimed full responsibility for these attacks and made very clear that the Fascist squads "will not disarm, but will instead react violently against the responsible spokesmen of the *Pus*."[53]

In the wake of the battle of Palazzo D'Accursio, the violent exploits of the squads rapidly transformed the fascio into the most important political force in the city. Yet the successful violence of the Fascists both reflected and depended upon public support and official tolerance. Indeed, as a special parliamentary commission concluded in January 1921: "The fascio would not have the great importance which it has acquired in the city of Bologna in the last months if it had not attracted the sympathy and consensus of a majority of the citizens. The movement of anti-socialist reaction, which has its most aggressive expression in fascism, is composed of various elements. It is like a river into which flow different currents."[54] Years of Socialist rule had left a legacy of bitter resentments that, in conjunction with the murder of Giordani, created an exceptional climate, in which Fascist assaults could appear as a legitimate reaction to leftist excesses and a noble defense of wounded patriots. The same climate of opinion affected local authorities as well: as early as November 26, the provincial police chief warned his superiors that he could not count on his men to repress "demonstrations of whatever nature by Fascist or nationalist veterans, especially when they are directed against the syn-

[52] PSI, *Fascismo: Inchiesta socialista*, pp. 271-272; B. Dalla Casa, "Il movimento operaio," pp. 26-27.

[53] *RdC*, December 19, 1920. *Pus* was the pejorative term used by the fascists to refer to the Socialist party.

[54] ASB, C7 F1, Commissione parlamentare di inchiesta; see also G. A. Chiurco, *Rivoluzione fascista*, vol. III, pp. 48-49.

dicalists and anarchists." Having borne the brunt of the strikes and worker protests of the previous two years, police officials tended increasingly to look upon the unlawful activities of the squads with benevolent neutrality or even outright approval.[55]

While both prefectoral and parliamentary reports stressed fascism's broad support in the city, they attributed the most crucial supportive role to the local elites in the weeks after November 21. The Bolognese prefect provided a clear and succinct description of this role in a report to the Ministry of Interior: "The bourgeoisie and the Fascists were almost fused in a single intent: to demolish the arrogance of the Socialist party."[56] Virtually all important groups of landowners and commercial farmers immediately became enthusiastic proponents of Fascist violence. Only four days after the battle of Palazzo D'Accursio, the chief agrarian organ, *Il Progresso*, came out with a front page editorial, glorifying the Fascists as "brave and audacious youths who have generated a healthy revolt against maximalist domination in our city" and exhorting them "to break off the claws of the assassins—executors and instigators of the crime—who are attempting to reestablish themselves in Bologna."[57] The paper greeted the attacks on Socialist leaders with unqualified approval and called upon all responsible citizens to "promote this reaction of common sense and introduce it to the people." By the first week in December, the APA had joined the major commercial and industrial associations of the capital in public support of the fascio and its initiatives.[58] Similarly, the Catholic daily, *L'Avvenire d'Italia*, took a decidedly profascist position after November and agrarian leaders of the local Popular party organization, such as Carlo Ballerini, praised the Fascists for

[55] R. De Felice, *Mussolini il rivoluzionario*, p. 657n.

[56] ASB, C7 F1, "Novembre," Prefect to Ministry of Interior, no date, 1921.

[57] *Il Progresso*, November 25, 1920. Two days after Giordani's death, Count Filippo Cavazza declared that the martyr's blood had "to fall not only on the assassins and their instigators, but also on all those . . . who attempt to devalue every idealistic impulse." *ibid.*, November 24, 1920.

[58] *Ibid.*, December 5, 1920. For the agrarian daily's support of Fascist violence, see, for example, the issues of December 21, 1920, January 9 and 27, 1921.

their ostensible resistance to "socialist violence."[59] By the end of December, it was clear that the provincial elites were paying more than lip service to the Fascists. According to the police chief, "many wealthy citizens of the city" were collecting and offering the fascio substantial sums of money to facilitate its endeavors.[60]

With the encouragement and backing from the most influential sectors of the urban population, the Fascists stepped up their attacks in December and early January, striking indiscriminately against all levels of the socialist movement. Moreover, the attacks began to extend outside of the city and now assumed the form of well-organized military expeditions, as in the assaults on the league headquarters of Castel San Pietro and Monterenzio, which were carried out by heavily armed squads, transported by trucks from the city. The appeal and popularity of the fascio increased steadily with every successful punitive expedition. From fewer than one hundred activists in early November, the fascio's membership climbed to over five thousand men by March 1921.[61]

The repercussions of the battle of Palazzo D'Accursio, however, extended well beyond the borders of the province of Bologna. Indeed, more than any other single event, the battle and its impact in the city provided the inspiration and spark igniting a tremendous terrorist offensive of the Fascist movement throughout northern and central Italy. From the dramatic clash of November 21 to the public reaction and Fascist punitive expeditions supported by local authorities and elites, the Bolognese situation set a precedent and a pattern that other towns and cities in the Po Valley soon followed.[62] After personally witnessing the battle in Bologna, Fer-

[59] On the position of *L'Avvenire d'Italia*, see N. S. Onofri, *I giornali bolognesi nel ventennio fascista* (Bologna, 1972), chap. 3, *passim*. Representatives of the Bolognese branch of the Popular party told the parliamentary committee: "Fascism here represents, more than the ranks of official fascism, the phenomenon of reaction against the socialist violence." See L. Arbizzani, "L'Avvento," p. 259.

[60] ASB, C7 F1, 1921, Police Chief to Prefect, December 28, 1920.

[61] On the punitive expeditions, see *Fascismo: Inchiesta socialista*, pp. 273-274; for the growing membership of the fascio, see statistics in R. De Felice, *Mussolini il fascista*, Vol. I (Turin, 1966), p. 8.

[62] As Tasca has written, "The events of the Palazzo d'Accursio precipitated in

rarese Fascists returned to their provincial capital, where they intensified pressures on the local Socialists. Much like their comrades in Bologna, the Socialists of Ferrara wound up playing into the hands of the fascio. On December 20, a bloody clash in the main square of the city provoked a sudden public outcry against the Socialist party and signaled the beginning of a vicious Fascist counteroffensive under conditions that were virtually identical to those in Bologna.[63] In the wake of successes in Bologna and Ferrara, the movement of provincial fascism, with its military organization, armed squads, and punitive expeditions, spread rapidly to other zones of Emilia, Lombardy, Veneto, Piedmont, Tuscany, and Apulia. Within the span of a few months, this wave of essentially local reactions would propel the Fascist movement and a surprised Benito Mussolini to sudden political prominence on the national level.[64]

In Bologna as elsewhere, the Socialist movement was thrown into a panic and unexpectedly put on the defensive by the events of November 21 and their immediate aftermath. Already on the evening of the battle, Socialist uncertainty and confusion were reflected in the decision of the Chamber of Labor to avoid any immediate general strike of protest against the Fascist assault. Far from unifying the movement, the Fascist offensive only sharpened preexisting ideological and policy conflicts between reformists, maximalists, and communists. Reformist socialists on the city council attempted to resign in order to disassociate themselves from the

---

Bologna, Emilia, and throughout Italy an outburst of accumulated hate and violence. . . . The era of violence, reprisals, and 'punitive expeditions' had begun." A. Tasca, *The Rise of Italian Fascism*, p. 101.

[63] Paul Corner, *Fascism in Ferrara, 1915-1925* (London, 1975), pp. 116-117.

[64] For the development of provincial fascism, see A. Tasca, *The Rise of Italian Fascism*, pp. 101-123 as well as the local studies; P. Corner, *Fascism in Ferrara*; Alessandro Roveri, *Le origini del fascismo a Ferrara, 1918-1921* (Milan, 1974); Rolando Cavandoli, *Le origini del fascismo a Reggio Emilia 1919-1923* (Rome, 1972); Mario Vaini, *Le origini del fascismo a Mantova* (Rome, 1961); Francesco Piva, *Lotte contadine e origini del fascismo: Padova-Venezia, 1919-1922* (Venice, 1977); Carla Ronchi Bettarini, "Note sui rapporti tra fascismo 'cittadino' e fascismo 'agrario' in Toscana," in Unione Regionale delle Provincie Toscane, *La Toscana nell'Italia unita* (Florence, 1962); Simona Colarizi, *Dopoguerra e fascismo in Puglia, 1919-1926* (Bari, 1971).

killing of Giordani, thereby giving additional credence to the Fascist account of the battle. Maximalist and communist spokesmen had scant opportunity to defend themselves as a result of arrest warrants that put them in jail or forced them to flee the province.[65] Accustomed to exercising unchallenged authority in the city, the Socialist party and the Chamber of Labor now found that they lacked the internal unity, strategy, and military organization to oppose effectively the Fascist raids. Despite its resounding victory the previous month, the left suddenly withdrew as an active force on the local political scene. In the weeks after the battle, no real effort was made to stem the tide of reaction by mobilizing the party's substantial mass base in public demonstrations or in measures for defense against the Fascist squads. Whether the product of Fascist intimidation or of a genuine desire to avoid further blood baths, the end result of Socialist passivity was to reinforce the image of Fascist invincibility and to strengthen the illusion that public opinion had shifted overwhelmingly to the right.[66]

The landowners and leaseholders quickly capitalized on the disarray created in the labor movement by the fascist offensive. As the Socialist daily, *La Squilla*, recognized, fascism had given the agrarians "hope in the advent of a miraculous force that would give them the means to attack the proletarians . . . and repudiate the agreements."[67] In the first weeks of December, local authorities received reports that a growing number of growers were repudiating the contracts signed by Calisto Paglia two months earlier. On December 2, for instance, the Federterra protested that none of the members of the APA in Castel San Pietro were willing to sign the new agreements; the following day, the subprefect of Vergato wrote that in his district the majority of large landowners now "opposed acceptance of the contracts."[68] The similar treatment

[65] B. Dalla Casa, "Il movimento operaio" pp. 26-27.

[66] *Ibid.*

[67] *La Squilla*, December 28, 1920.

[68] ASB, C16 F1, Federterra to Prefect, December 2, 1920; ASB, C7 F1, Subprefect to Prefect, December 3, 1920; ASB, C16 F1, Nicola Carbone to Prefect, January 5, 1921. For additional information on violations of the contracts by landowners, see

of Catholic peasant brotherhoods indicated the essentially economic thrust of this renewed agrarian intransigence. Less than two weeks after the battle of Palazzo D'Accursio, the prefect learned that the landowners had also begun to assume "an openly hostile attitude" toward the sharecropping contract signed by the APA with the brotherhoods. By mid-January, the provincial secretary of the brotherhoods appealed to the prefect for his intervention in four communes where, he claimed, "the landowners refuse to concede those just reforms that have been recognized by their own employer organizations."[69]

Such actions revealed not only the agrarians' intention to reverse their earlier defeats, but also the collapsing authority of the APA. As early as December 7, the provincial secretary of the Federterra angrily noted that the agrarian association "has been incapable of making its members respect the laws of honor."[70] With his name and honor attached to the agreements of October, Calisto Paglia tendered his resignation as president of the APA in mid-December because of what he described as "the hostile attitude of many members . . . to the policies of the ruling council." Although Paglia finally received a begrudging vote of confidence at the end of the month, it had little concrete significance, since each day more and more landowners and commercial farmers refused to recognize the association's authority.[71] Irrevocably compromised and discredited by the humiliating settlement of October, the APA continued, for the most part, to exist in name only, while effective power and influence shifted steadily to local groups of agrarians and individual landowners.

La Squilla, January 15, 1921; ASB, C16 F1, Employment Office of Medicina to Mayor, March 24, 1921; *Ibid*, League of Braccianti of Minerbio to Calda, April 16, 1921.

[69] See ASB, C16 F1, Massimo Federici to Prefect, January 19, 1921; *ibid.*, Prefect to Ministry of Interior, February 19, 1921.

[70] Report of Mario Piazza, secretary of the Bolognese Federterra to congress, published in *La Squilla*, December 8, 1920.

[71] *Il Progresso*, December 18, 1920; *ibid.*, December 30, 1920. Unfortunately, there is virtually no information on who voted in support of Paglia and what their motives were for doing so.

Complementary as they were, the economic reaction of the landowners and the political violence of the Fascists in the winter of 1920-21 did not yet constitute a unified or systematic offensive against the Socialist movement. Despite its phenomenal growth in the months between November and March, Bolognese fascism remained primarily an urban movement with the overwhelming majority of its membership in the city of Bologna. As late as March 1, only six fasci, with a total membership of 595, existed outside of the capital.[72] Moreover, in this early phase of expansion, the program of the local Fascists did not extend far beyond the most visceral antisocialism. In its report on the Bolognese fascio in January 1921, the parliamentary investigative commission concluded that "the political program and policies of these youths are not well-developed and perhaps not even clearly defined" and tended to oscillate "from a vague humanitarianism, resembling socialism, to an advanced and pugnacious nationalism."[73] During this period, the APA and the agrarian press actively supported the fascio and wealthy propertied interests helped finance its expeditions, but few prominent landowners or leaseholders actually enrolled in the movement. Most agrarians were seemingly content to reap the immediate economic advantages that fascism indirectly offered them through its violent disruption of the socialist movement.[74]

Improvisation and informal cooperation ended, however, in the spring of 1921 with the transformation of Bolognese fascism into a mass movement. As the fasci spread into the countryside in the months after March, a gradual but profound change took place in

[72] For information on membership, see ASB, C7 F1, *Fascismo*, October 22, 1921.

[73] *AP*, *Camera dei Deputati*, Leg. xxv, 1919-21, Commissione di inchiesta, cited in G. A. Chiurco, *Rivoluzione fascista*, vol. iii, p. 49. For a similar vision see Dino Grandi's article, "Il nostro posto," in *L'Assalto*, December 11, 1920.

[74] On the financial role of the agrarians, see the report of the parliamentary commission cited in L. Arbizzani, "L'Avvento," p. 254. Ignazio Benelli's son took part in the attack on the Socialist deputies, Bentini and Nicolai, while Giacobbe Manzoni later claimed to "have been the first Fascist in Imola." For Manzoni, see his pamphlet, "Responsabilità di persone, di classi, e di partiti di fronte ai problemi della produzione, della bonifica agraria e della disoccupazione," ASB, C16 F1, November 30, 1922.

the ideology, program, leadership, and social base of the provincial movement. Such changes were inextricably linked to simultaneous emergence of an organized agrarian-Fascist offensive against both the Socialist and Catholic labor organizations.

3. *Agrarians and the Transformation of Fascism into a Mass Movement*

During the spring and summer of 1921, Bolognese fascism ceased to be an organization of displaced war veterans and professional adventurers and became instead a powerful mass movement. To a great extent, this transformation drew its inspiration and models from earlier developments in the neighboring province of Ferrara. Through a combination of terror, skillful propaganda, and innovative organizational measures, the Ferrarese Fascists achieved one of the first and most impressive triumphs of any provincial fascio in the entire country. After the events of December 20, the movement in Ferrara entered into a period of expansion that far surpassed Bologna's; from a mere five nuclei in mid-December, it grew to forty by mid-January. Membership increased at an equally rapid pace so that at the end of March the province had the second most numerous fascio on the peninsula with nearly two thousand more members than the Bolognese movement.[75] The key to the success of the Ferrarese fascio lay in its lightning conquest of the countryside, formerly the stronghold of the Socialists. In the span of a few weeks, the seemingly invincible Socialist leagues collapsed and the loyalties of substantial numbers of rural workers appeared to shift to the Fascists. By the elections of May, the fasci polled nearly fifty thousand votes and could claim to control over forty thousand workers in the overwhelmingly agricultural province.[76] A number of factors contributed to the extraordinary success of the Ferrarese Fascists. The violence of Italo Balbo's squads drove away the leaders and demoralized the rank and file of the leagues,

[75] P. Corner, *Fascism in Ferrara*, pp. 120-121.
[76] *Ibid.*, p. 138.

while agrarian employers used various forms of economic pressure to break the Socialist monopoly of labor. To prevent any reconstitution of the perennially resilient leagues, the Fascists and landowners collaborated in the sponsoring of "independent syndicates" that served to regiment the workers who had left the leagues. The conquest of the Ferrarese countryside, however, depended on more than violence and economic coercion. In addition, the Fascists proposed schemes for land redistribution and a more open land market that initially drew enthusiastic support from certain groups of day laborers, sharecroppers, and small peasant proprietors. The syndicates came to control the majority of the laborers and by the summer of 1921 represented the real mass base of fascism in the province.[77]

Similar but more gradual trends became evident in Bologna in April 1921, with the spread of the Fascist movement from its urban base to the small towns and hamlets of the province (Maps 7-10). The first week of that month alone saw the founding of fasci in ten different communes.[78] By the end of May, twenty-three new fasci were operating in the countryside, while total membership had nearly doubled to 10,280 men. Expansion continued without respite throughout the summer and fall of 1921. At the end of October, Bolognese fascism had replaced its Ferrarese neighbor as the second largest provincial movement in the country, with forty-four nuclei and nearly twelve thousand members.[79] In sheer numbers, the original city fascio continued to be the most important organizational component; its five thousand members were divided into four companies, each operating its own action squad. Not surprisingly, the other large fasci were located in the district capitals of Imola and Vergato, which had a combined membership of fifteen hundred blackshirts. Membership in the other fasci was considerably smaller, ranging from as few as thirty to as many as two hundred fifty men. Regardless of their size, all the fasci dis-

[77] *Ibid.*, pp. 137-169.
[78] *L'Assalto*, April 10, 1921.
[79] See R. De Felice, *Mussolini il fascista*, I, pp. 8-9.

played a relatively uniform internal structure, characterized by a functional division of labor: half the members, usually younger men or so-called *principali*, belonged to the action squads, while the other half, the "old men," handled problems of information, financing, and transportation. Within each fascio, power tended to concentrate in the hands of a single leader, typically the commander of the squads who ruled through a blend of personal charisma, fear, and intimidation.[80]

As elsewhere in northern and central Italy during 1921 and 1922, the Fascist expansion in Bologna relied on local conditions and initiatives. The earliest nuclei outside of the city of Bologna were often the product of a few isolated individuals who bore some particularly intense grudge against the Socialists or who hoped to gain certain economic or political benefits from their defeat. As a rule these enthusiasts first appealed to the urban fascio for its punitive intervention in their communes. After the squads from the city had carried out one or more expeditions against the municipal Socialist leaders or the league offices, local exponents could play on a range of long-standing resentments and rancors to build up a core group of Fascist supporters. The actual founding of the fascio took place in a formal ceremony in the main square of the designated town or hamlet. Before a crowd, swelled by the presence of blackshirts from the city, the top Fascist leaders in the province would give stirring speeches and then officially consign the *gagliardetto*, or banner, to the new fascio. In communes where the Socialist party had ruled supreme for more than a generation, the very fact that the Fascists held their ceremony in the main square of the town left a tremendous impression on the population and greatly increased the prestige and appeal of the fascio. Even after their founding, the earliest rural fasci did not necessarily lead a comfortable existence. Depending on the tenacity of the Socialist organizations and the abilities of the local Fascist organizers, ad-

[80] For a breakdown of the membership by fascio, see ASB, C7 F1, "I fascisti," October 22, 1921; on the structure of the fasci, see ASB, C7 F1, Partiti Politici, September 28, 1922. The growing authoritarian character of life within the fasci is discussed in A. Lyttelton, *The Seizure of Power*, p. 67.

Map 7
Spread of Fascist Nuclei in Bologna, December 1920.

Map 8
Spread of Fascist Nuclei in Bologna, January-February, 1921.

Map 9
Spread of Fascist Nuclei in Bologna, March-April 1921.

Map 10
Spread of Fascist Nuclei in Bologna, May-June, 1921.

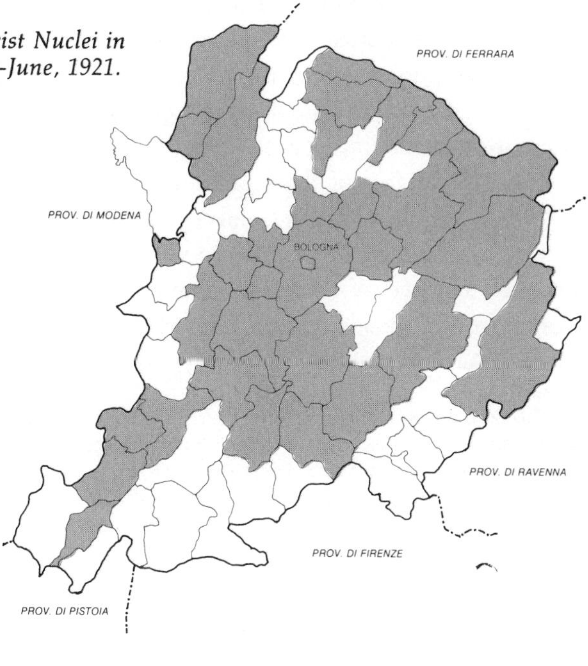

ditional incursions by squads from the city or Ferrara might be required. But once the fascio had established a solid base of support in the commune, its squads could begin to spread their missionary activities to other communes, where the same process would be repeated. Thus, the Fascist movement spread as a series of local initiatives and reactions, encouraged but in no sense controlled by the main fascio in the capital. In the short run, the local roots and parochial focus of rural fascism proved to be significant assets, for they allowed each fascio to tailor its appeals and policies to fit the particular needs and concerns of its immediate constituents.[81]

With the arrival of fascism in the Bolognese countryside, important changes took place in the social base of the movement. The misfits, restless veterans, and students who comprised the Fascists "of the first hour" were now joined by men drawn from a wide range of political backgrounds, occupations, and professions. The evidence available on membership is scanty, but it suggests the decidedly interclass character of the rural fasci. The fascio of San Giorgio di Piano was perhaps typical: of its 141 members, there were ten landowners or leaseholders, eighteen professional people, four merchants or manufacturers, seven white-collar employees, five public service workers, fifteen factory workers, and eighty-two day laborers and sharecroppers.[82] The equally scanty information on the make-up of the action squads reveals a similar heterogeneity. Most of the squad members, the *squadristi,* were students, public employees, shopkeepers, farm managers, or landowners; virtually all of them were young men between the ages of sixteen and twenty-three.[83] The new rank-and-file of the Bolognese fasci and squads corresponded closely to nationwide trends in the social composition of the Fascist movement as they are

[81] This portrait represents an impressionistic synthesis of numerous reports that appeared in the local press and prefecture during the spring of 1921.

[82] ACS, Mostra della rivoluzione fascista, B105, no date, 1921.

[83] This conclusion is based on only ten men profiled by local authorities in Imola and Bagni di Poretta. See ASB, C7 F1, police report, August 9, 1921; *ibid.*, Subprefect to Prefect, June 10, 1921.

revealed by data that the national secretariat made public in the fall of 1921.[84]

Among the first occupational categories to go over to the Fascist movement in Bologna were the public employees. In the immediate aftermath of November 21, the teachers' union as well as large groups of municipal and provincial workers employed in white-collar jobs resigned in mass from the Socialist Chamber of Labor.[85] In the countryside the numerically most important component of the fasci came from the ranks of small peasant proprietors and sharecroppers. Significantly, this peasant nucleus resulted less from Fascist coercion than from voluntary and often enthusiastic conversion. Much as in Ferrara and other provinces of Emilia, Fascist organizers in the Bolognese countryside were the chief beneficiaries of a special set of postwar economic and political conditions.[86] On the one hand, favorable trends in agricultural prices, contracts, and taxes had increased the number of relatively prosperous peasants, anxious to invest their new savings in land. On the other hand, the agricultural strikes of 1920 had opened up the land market, especially in the low plains where panic and fear led many old landowners to sell their land at extremely low prices. As census data revealed, by 1921 the extraordinary convergence of supply and demand in the local land markets had begun to have a significant impact on the structure of property holdings in the province. The number of peasant proprietors, which had fallen in the first decade of the century, more than doubled between 1911 and 1921, with much of the increase taking place in 1920-21.[87] Well before fascism arrived in the countryside, the new small landowners had provided some of the most tenacious resistance to the Federterra and often had borne the brunt of the leagues' boycotts and violence. Under these circumstances, peasant entrepreneurs

[84] A. Tasca, *Nascita e avvento del fascismo*, vol. I, p. 257.

[85] B. Dalla Casa, "Movimento operaio," p. 28.

[86] For the situation in Ferrara, see P. Corner, *Fascism in Ferrara*, pp. 151-157.

[87] See Arrigo Serpieri, *La guerra e classi rurali italiane* (Bari, 1930), pp. 360-361; Osvaldo Passerini, *Inchiesta sulla piccola proprietà coltivatrice formatosi nel dopoguerra*, Vol. VII, *Emilia e Marche* (Milan, 1932), p. 25.

Map 11
Distribution of New Small Properties in Bologna, 1919-1926.

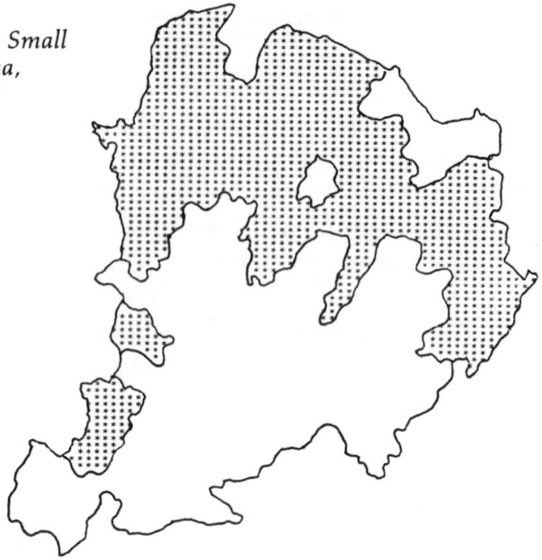

were drawn to a movement such as fascism that promised to defend their recently acquired propertied status and to liberate them from the economic restrictions and burdens imposed by the Socialist leagues. Through their assault on the Federterra and their promotion of unfettered private initiative, the rural fasci did appear to open up substantial opportunities to new or aspiring proprietors for individual advancement. Indeed, the spread of the Fascist movement into the countryside in the spring of 1921 ushered in a period of unprecedented growth in the number of small landowners, above all in the plains (Map 11). In the five communes of the plains for which precise statistics are available, the number of peasant proprietors more than tripled between 1920 and 1928, increasing from 228 to 738.[88] In a similar manner, the fasci attracted ambitious

[88] These statistics cover the communes of San Giovanni in Persiceto, Calderara di Reno, Crevalcore, Sant'Agata Bolognese, and Sala Bolognese. During this period, the average size of holdings declined from 7.02 hectares to 5.5 hectares. See O. Passerini, *Inchiesta piccola proprietà*, vol. VII, p. 36.

sharecroppers who were eager to exploit the advantageous contractual and price conditions in order to improve their own positions, free from the obligations and controls of the Federterra. As early as February 1921, provincial authorities were reporting on the entrance into the movement of "some young peasants [who] hope, with the help of the fasci di combattimento, to escape altogether the influence and demands of the other categories of laborers."[89]

The size of this peasant nucleus, however, was relatively modest. As the total membership figures for the rural fasci clearly indicated, the early peasant Fascists did not constitute a mass movement in any sense comparable to the Socialist leagues. Moreover, analysis of the social composition of the rank-and-file sheds little light on the policies or changing power relations within the increasingly hierarchical and authoritarian fasci. Of considerably greater importance in this regard was the growing involvement of prominent landowners and leaseholders, who began to play a key role in the expansion of fascism into the countryside.

Developments in the province of Ferrara early in 1921 demonstrated to local agrarians the ways in which a rural-based fascism could serve to eliminate costly contracts, break the Socialist control of the labor force, and reconsolidate entrepreneurial authority in the countryside.[90] In April they began to follow the example of their Ferrarese colleagues. Financial support of the fasci, which had been largely informal and spontaneous in the winter, gave way to formal agreements between local agrarian groups and Fascist leaders that stipulated the exact sums which each landowner or leaseholder would contribute "to pay the expenses of [the] fascio for propaganda and activities."[91] At the same time, a growing number of commercial farmers served as more than paymasters, becoming promoters and organizers of the new fasci. Direct agrar-

[89] ASB, C7 F1, "Novembre," Subprefect to Prefect, February 5, 1921.

[90] See P. Corner, *Fascism in Ferrara*, pp. 163-168.

[91] For examples of these formal agreements, see ASB, C7 F1, "I fascisti," letter of the Crevalcore fascio to landowners, August 30, 1921; circular to landowners of Castel San Pietro, no date, 1921.

ian involvement was most dramatically evident in the commune of Molinella where the aggressive young leaseholder Augusto Regazzi and Arturo Pedrelli, former representative of the APA and large estate manager, organized a fascio in April. Both men had long been bitter foes of the leagues and were drawn to fascism for essentially economic motives. In the spring of 1921, Regazzi stood on the brink of bankruptcy because of his own financial mismanagement and love of "gambling, women, and parties." To improve his desperate economic position, he became an early and enthusiastic exponent of Fascist violence against the leagues. Already in March, police officials began to report from Molinella that Regazzi was attempting to exploit "the labor organizations' fear of the Fascists . . . in the hope of being reimbursed for all the wage increases he has already paid out."[92] Likewise, for Pedrelli fascism appeared to signify primarily liberation from the controls and demands of the leagues and the opportunity to reap financial rewards through the use of cheap nonunion labor.[93] Predictably, agrarians dominated the Fascist nucleus in Molinella from its inception. While Pedrelli soon emerged as the head of the local movement, the ruling council of the fascio also included such prominent commercial farmers as Giuseppe Bolognesi and Federico Rossi. Regazzi quickly developed an infamous reputation for violence as a squad boss and by the fall of 1921, he had become, according to the prefect, "one of the most active exponents of the agrarian Fascist movement in the plains zone of the province."[94]

The fascio of Molinella did not represent an isolated case. The founding of a fascio the same month in San Giovanni in Persiceto resulted primarily from the efforts of Alfonso Funi, Giovanni Lodini, and Alfredo Zambonelli, three of the largest leaseholders in

[92] On Regazzi's background and activities, see ASB, C7 F1, police report, March 3, 1921.

[93] Pedrelli is discussed in ASB, C7 F1, police reports of April 8 and 24, 1921.

[94] ASB, C7 F1, Prefect to Ministry of Interior, October 6, 1921; on the influential role of the commercial farmers see ASB, C7 F1, police reports of August 12, October 6, 22, 27, 1921.

the commune. This trend toward increasing agrarian control of the rural movement continued through the summer and fall. By the end of October, influential growers or their agents presided over the fasci of Malalbergo, Castenaso, Castel San Pietro, Medicina, and Galliera, while the large landowners, Marchese Ruggero Benadelli and Bruno Caliceti were, in the words of the prefect, "the most influential members" of the fasci in Casalecchio and San Giorgio di Piano.[95]

The growth of agrarian fascism came in large part at the expense of the APA. In April the entire Imolese chapter of the association, under the leadership of the agrarian Fascists Giacobbe Manzoni and Count Alessandro Ginnasi, formally withdrew from the APA and disavowed all labor and sharecropper agreements made the previous fall.[96] Other groups of landowners and leaseholders soon followed suit, leading the attorney of the Federterra to protest bitterly to Calisto Paglia about the "huge number of violations committed by your associates of the agreements made last November." Angered by what he called "the bad faith of the few reinforced by the apathy of the majority," Paglia resigned his post as president of the association in late May.[97] A caretaker staff headed by Count Gualtiero Isolani did little to halt the progressive disintegration of the APA. In a communique to the members two months after its installation, the staff presented a grim picture of the situation within the association: "For some time now the worst evil that can hit an organization has noticeably increased: *absenteeism*. Last week, for example, two meetings of great importance were called. . . . Both meetings had only two, we say two, members present." Count Isolani himself established close contacts with

[95] L. Scagliarini, "Proprietari e contadini a San Giovanni in Persiceto, 1919-1924," in Deputazione Emilia-Romagna per la Storia della Resistenza, *Movimento operaio e fascismo nell'Emilia-Romagna, 1919-1923* (Rome, 1973), p. 160; ASB, C7 F1, "Fasci di combattimento della Provincia," October 22, 1921.

[96] ASB, C5 F2, Subprefect to Prefect, April 22, 1921; *ibid.*, C16 F1, Resolution passed by APA, April 23, 1921.

[97] ASB, C16 F1, Nicola Carbone to Calisto Paglia, May 7, 1921; *ibid.* for Paglia's letter of resignation.

Fascist leaders, so that by the fall of 1921 the power and influence of the provincial elites had definitely shifted away from the old APA to the new rural fasci.[98]

Agrarian involvement in the fasci of Bologna and Ferrara reflected a more general pattern that became increasingly evident throughout the Po Valley as well as in Tuscany and Apulia during 1921. With minor local variations, agrarian interests in province after province began to take the lead in promoting, organizing, and directing the various Fascist nuclei. In Reggio Emilia, for example, the founder of the provincial Fascist movement, Ottavio Corgini was also president of the Chamber of Agriculture, while the commander of the action squads and the secretary of the Fascist federation were both large landowners. In other provinces such as Alessandria and Pavia, where no fasci had existed prior to the winter of 1920-21, the agrarian associations themselves directly founded Fascist organizations. Like their colleagues in Emilia, agrarian representatives in Tuscany began in the summer of 1921 to resign from their old organizations and to enroll in the fasci, in order to be "exclusively Fascists." During the same period, the fasci in Apulia developed primarily as instruments of agrarian power, continuing and expanding prewar methods of landlord intimidation.[99]

The rapid growth of agrarian fascism coincided with significant ideological and programmatic changes in Mussolini's movement. The evolution of national Fascist agricultural policy in the course of 1921 clearly indicated the new influence and importance of the large commercial growers. The initial program of agricultural reform, presented by Gaetano Polverelli in *Il Popolo d'Italia* in January, directed its appeal to land-hungry peasant sharecroppers, tenant farmers, and day laborers, with the slogan: "To every peas-

[98] On internal problems of APA, see *Il Giornale Agrario*, August 6, 1921. For Count Isolani's close ties to the Fascists, see Chapter IX.

[99] For developments outside of Bologna and Ferrara, see R. Cavandoli, *Fascismo a Reggio Emilia*, p. 130; M. Vaini, *Fascismo a Mantova*, p. 137; A. Lyttelton, *The Seizure of Power*, p. 70; C. Ronchi Bettarini, "Note sui rapporti," p. 365; S. Colarizi, *Dopoguerra e fascismo in Puglia*, pp. 135-136. A. Tasca, *The Rise of Italian Fascism*, pp. 113-114 provides a general account of the situation in Lombardy.

ant his land! To every peasant the entire fruit of his sacred work."[100] As agrarians expanded their role in the rural fasci, however, Fascist leaders began to add major qualifications to Polverelli's populist proposals. Under pressure from various landowner associations, Mussolini affirmed in early April that, in giving land to the peasants, it would be "necessary to take account of the diverse conditions of time, place, [and] the moral and technical preparation of the agricultural laboring masses." In accordance with this new meritocratic emphasis, the defense of the large scale commercial farm assumed a special importance for Fascist leaders, who now insisted that its elimination would be "the worst agricultural disaster imaginable."[101] A revised agricultural program, which appeared in June 1921, openly proclaimed fascism's intent to favor northern agrarian entrepreneurs: "The large commercial farms are generally sound. Only the ignorant could confuse them with the *latifondo*. The large farm . . . requires minimum costs and affords maximum profits. It could not be divided up without increasing costs and diminishing profits, with serious social consequences. In addition, the large farm permits the cultivation of outlying land [and] the utilization of . . . female and child labor. Also here as in the case of the factories, it is a question of efficiency. Technical skills cannot be improvised."[102] Although the movement continued to pay lip service to the ideas of land redistribution and "agrarian democracy" after June, their implementation was indefinitely postponed and no longer constituted any serious threat to the large capitalist growers of the Po Valley.

4. *Agrarians and Power Struggles within Fascism*

The tremendous influx of landowners and commercial farmers and the related changes in Fascist agricultural policy did

[100] Cited in Franco Catalano, *Potere economico e fascismo. La crisi del dopoguerra 1919-1921* (Milan, 1964), p. 239.

[101] *Ibid.*, pp. 244-245.

[102] "Programma agrario fascista del 1921," reprinted in R. De Felice, *Mussolini il fascista*, vol. I, app. 2, p. 737.

not occur without provoking serious tensions and conflicts within the movement, both locally and on the national level. Indeed, by the summer of 1921, acute political observers like Antonio Gramsci began to speak of two distinct and conflicting fascisms: one associated with the original urban nuclei and composed chiefly of veterans, students, and middle class followers; the other associated with the rural fasci and composed of landlords, leaseholders, and peasants.[103] On the provincial level, the rise of agrarian-controlled fasci in the countryside aroused strong resentments among Fascists "of the first hour" in the cities and led to increasingly bitter power struggles. While the urban and rural Fascists shared an aggressive antisocialist orientation, their motives and objectives were often sharply divergent. For many Fascists in the provincial capitals, violence against the Socialists had been linked, at least in part, to an intense patriotism and a vague rebellion against all authority. As a result, they tended to view the growing involvement of the propertied classes, with their crude economic objectives, not only as a threat to the prestige and influence of the city fasci, but also as a corruption and distortion of fascism's mission of national redemption.[104] Developments during the winter of 1920-21 in Ferrara, where agrarians achieved their earliest and most complete dominance of the movement, prefigured the type of internal difficulties that came to beset most provincial organizations in the following two years. As early as December 1920, spokesmen for the city fascio in Ferrara attacked the increasing influence of the agrarian association, charging that the local Fascist movement had become "no more nor less than the bodyguard of the profiteers."[105] Such accusations marked the opening salvo in a prolonged struggle within Ferrarese fascism, characterized by mutual recriminations, angry resignations, dissident factions, and frequent reshufflings of

[103] See Gramsci's article, "I due fascismi," *L'Ordine Nuovo*, August 25, 1921. For similar judgments, see sources cited in R. De Felice, *Mussolini il fascista*, I, p. 12n.

[104] See A. Lyttelton, *The Seizure of Power*, p. 62.

[105] ACS, Mostra della rivoluzione fascista, B102, fascio Ferrara, I, Gaggioli letter, December 29, 1920 as cited in *ibid*.

the local directorate, that culminated in the final defeat of the city fascio in the fall of 1922.[106]

Divisions over the issue of relations with the provincial elites emerged within the Bolognese fascio even prior to the spread of the movement into the countryside. Already in January 1921, the founder of the city fascio, Leandro Arpinati affirmed the need for the movement "to cut all contacts with the conservatives and the various . . . factions of the bourgeoisie" so that it could become a truly independent force, representing "the interests of all the people."[107] Since Arpinati had been the chief architect of the merger between the fascio and the employer associations and old parties of order the previous fall, his sudden hostility to collaboration was not simply a matter of principle, but also a response to challenges to his personal authority from new leaders such as Dino Grandi, who had closer political and social ties with prominent commercial and agrarian interests in the province. A handsome and ambitious twenty-five year old lawyer and journalist from a rural family in the district of Imola, Grandi had entered political life as a propagandist for the Nationalist Association and the interventionist cause while still a teenager in 1914-15. After serving as an officer in the Italian army during the war, Grandi had been actively involved with the old moderate political clubs in the unsuccessful attempt to forge a unified antisocialist electoral bloc in the fall of 1919. Although a relative latecomer who joined the fascio of Bologna in September 1920, he rapidly rose to prominence in the movement. In contrast to Arpinati, the tough man of action who preferred to command the squads, Grandi built up his following as a major fund-raiser and director of the Fascist daily, *L'Assalto*.[108]

The first signs of a personal and ideological rivalry between the two men came in early January over the question of the fascio's

[106] P. Corner, *Fascism in Ferrara*, chap. 8, *passim*.

[107] Cited in G. Pesce, *La marcia dei rurali* (Rome, 1929), p. 112.

[108] On Grandi's background, see ACS, Segretaria Particolare del Duce, cart. ris. B13 letter of Grandi to Mussolini, June 23, 1932; Richard Webster, *Industrial Imperialism in Italy, 1908-1915* (Berkeley, 1975), pp. 349-350; Chapter VI, note 46.

political direction. To reassert the movement's autonomy and to purge it of conservative contamination, Arpinati and his supporters in the directorate proposed to give the fascio "a political character with openly republican aims." Significantly, Grandi not only led the opposition that defeated Arpinati's proposal, but also formulated the victorious counterproposal, proclaiming the political neutrality of the fascio "as an indispensable condition for keeping the members of divergent political opinions united in the common opposition to the bolshevism of the maximalists."[109] In effect, the decision to keep the movement "above" politics paved the way for the consolidation of closer ties with agrarian interests and facilitated the Fascist expansion into the countryside during the spring and summer of 1921. Mutual antagonism increased after the national elections of May, which saw Grandi's triumph and Arpinati's defeat in their bids for parliamentary seats. In the ensuing weeks, Grandi began to accuse the city boss of financial and organizational mismanagement, while Arpinati countered with charges that Grandi and his followers were opportunists who had "never taken part in the punitive expeditions."[110]

The evolution of this personal rivalry closely paralleled the gradual shift of power from the urban fascio to the new agrarian Fascist movement. Much as in Ferrara, agrarian influence in Bologna grew steadily with the spread of the rural fasci and the founding of the provincial Fascist federation, which supplanted the city fascio at the helm of the local movement.[111] With Grandi increasingly involved in political affairs in Rome, the chief beneficiary of this power shift was Gino Baroncini, a young surveyor from Imola who quickly distinguished himself both as an able organizer and as a fiery polemicist. Unlike Arpinati, he appeared to have few qualms about allying with the large landowners and leaseholders, having once been an employee of the Bolognese Agrarian Association in Imola. Backed by agrarian interests and Grandi, Ba-

[109] ASB, C7 F1, Police Chief to Prefect, January 4, 1921.
[110] ASB, C7 F1, no date, 1921, cited in N. S. Onofri, *I giornali bolognesi*, p. 147.
[111] See A. Lyttelton, *The Seizure of Power*, p. 66.

roncini became the first secretary of the provincial federation and by the summer of 1921 had emerged as the foremost exponent of the view that "fascism must decisively support the agrarians and direct all its forces against the employment offices of the leagues."[112] Through his control of the federation and his success in organizing new fasci, Baroncini gradually built up a position in the Po Valley second only to Roberto Farinacci among the *ras* or paramilitary bosses of provincial fascism.[113] The rise of the Bolognese *ras* to prominence came in large part at the expense of Arpinati whose prestige and influence declined during 1921, despite his continued hold on the city fascio. By late October, the police were reporting that of the two opposing factions within Bolognese fascism, "the one commanded by Arpinati" now had "few followers" in contrast to "the one commanded by Grandi and Baroncini." Embittered by the attacks of his rivals, Arpinati actually withdrew from the movement in the winter of 1921-22, returning only after a direct personal appeal by Mussolini.[114]

Local rivalries and power struggles in Bologna and other strongholds of provincial fascism foreshadowed a far more serious conflict on the national level in the summer of 1921 between Mussolini and the agrarian Fascists of the Po Valley. In the late spring, Mussolini and the central committee in Milan began to recognize that the stunning expansion of the movement in the provinces represented a mixed blessing. While the violence of the rural squads had made a major contribution to the popularity and power of fascism in the entire country, it also had created new problems for the continued advance of the movement as a coherent and unified political force. Responsive to local rather than national imperatives

[112] *La Squilla*, June 11, 1921. According to the prefect, the faction "headed by Baroncini . . . represented the agrarian conception of violence as a necessity for the defense of the farmers' interests." Cited in N. S. Onofri, *I giornali bolognesi*, p. 148. For Baroncini's prewar services in the AAB, see ASB, C6 F2, Subprefect of Imola to Ministry of Interior, January 28, 1913.

[113] A. Lyttelton, *The Seizure of Power*, p. 185.

[114] ASB, C7 F1, "I fascisti," Police Chief to Prefect, October 22, 1921; for Arpinati's temporary withdrawal, see N. S. Onofri, *I giornali bolognesi*, p. 148n.

and directly subsidized by their immediate supporters, the provincial fasci tended increasingly to escape any effective control by Mussolini. After the Fascist electoral success of May, the relative autonomy and chaotic violence of these fasci threatened not only to reduce the Duce's margins for parliamentary maneuver in Rome, but also to undermine his personal authority over the movement. In order to consolidate the political gains of the previous half year and to reimpose his control over the local *ras*, Mussolini took a drastic step in the summer of 1921. With the support of the majority of Fascist deputies, he launched a proposal for a "pact of pacification" with the Socialist party. Unofficial negotiations began in July and by the first week in August, an agreement had been signed, committing both sides to end violence immediately and to respect each other's economic organizations.[115]

From its earliest mention, the idea of a peace treaty with the Socialists aroused strong opposition from the provincial fasci of the Po Valley. The first week in July, the prefect in Bologna reported that "the local Fascists, and especially the agrarian elements, are hostile to a truce because they still consider violence and intimidation necessary to their work of penetration into the countryside."[116] Bologna quickly became the storm center of opposition to the pact of pacification: on July 4, the provincial federation approved Baroncini's resolution, denouncing the inopportunity of "any negotiations with the Socialist party"; the following day Grandi organized an emergency meeting of regional leaders that issued a stern warning to the Fascist deputies and the central committee "not to commit themselves to any definitive agreements without taking account of the particular conditions of the provinces of Emilia and Romagna."[117] For a variety of reasons, nearly all components of the provincial movement were hostile to the truce. The *ras* and municipal bosses like Augusto Regazzi had an obvious vested interest in maintaining the climate of violence and illegality

[115] See C. Seton-Watson, *Italy from Liberalism*, pp. 592-593; A. Lyttelton, *The Seizure of Power*, pp. 54-55.

[116] ASB, C7 F1, "I fascisti," Prefect to Ministry of Interior, July 4, 1921.

[117] See N. S. Onofri, *I giornali bolognesi*, p. 142.

that had brought them to power and legitimized their rule. Similarly, the rank-and-file in the squads recognized that a genuine truce would deprive them of their chief functions in the province, the punitive expeditions and assaults on the Socialists. While Mussolini might view violence as a limited instrument to achieve precise political objectives, for most *squadristi* violence was an end in itself, the essence of their group existence and the main source of their *esprit de corps*. Even in the city fascio, the pact of pacification did not encounter much support. Despite their feuds with the agrarian Fascists, Arpinati and his followers opposed in principle any parliamentary negotiations as a betrayal of fascism's original patriotic and redemptive mission.[118]

As the reports of the prefect revealed, agrarian interests provided the backbone of support for Grandi and Baroncini. Such support reflected in part the local concern of large landowners and leaseholders that the truce would benefit exclusively the Socialist leagues. At the same time, opposition to the pact also reflected agrarian hostility toward the national government and the political status quo in Rome. The same week that Fascist deputies began negotiations with the Socialists, the government announced, without prior consultation with agricultural spokesmen, new tariff schedules that were highly favorable to the steel, machine, and chemical sectors. For commercial farming groups who had been lobbying for advantageous export agreements as well as access to cheaper imported agricultural machines, the decree appeared to signify a complete betrayal of their interests. Agrarian representatives in the Chamber of Deputies and the various agricultural associations angrily denounced the industrial tariffs and accused the government of "sacrificing the interests of agricultural production to those of the steel manufacturers and other financial groups."[119] In this

[118] ACS, Mostra della rivoluzione fascista, B100, Arpinati to Pasella, August 19, 1921.

[119] For the reaction of northern commercial farmers to the tariffs, see Agostino Lanzillo, *Le rivoluzioni del dopoguerra* (Città di Castello, 1922), pp. 197-205; Vincenzo Poni, *La tariffa doganale del 1 luglio 1921 e gli interessi dell'agricoltura* (Piacenza, 1923).

context, agrarian intransigence on the issue of the pact aimed to achieve two separate objectives: the continuation of the antisocialist crusade in the countryside and the obstruction of any political stabilization on the national level inimical to the interests of commercial farmers.

After signing the pact of pacification in August, Mussolini moved to bring his followers into line, attacking the dissident leaders as defenders of the agrarians, "the most exclusive, sordid, and despicable classes that exist in Italy."[120] Unintimidated by these accusations, the provincial movements in the Po Valley closed ranks behind Grandi, Italo Balbo of Ferrara, and Roberto Farinacci of Cremona. In mid-August, representatives of some six hundred fasci from Emilia, Romagna, Lombardy, and the Veneto gathered in Bologna and publicly repudiated the agreements made by the central committee with the Socialist party. In an impressive display of their independent power, the following month Grandi and Balbo organized a "March on Ravenna" by some two thousand blackshirts, ostensibly to celebrate Dante's seventh centennial.[121] By the time of the National Fascist Congress in November, Mussolini had little choice but to accept a compromise with Grandi and the agrarian Fascists. In exchange for his tacit disavowal of the pact with the Socialists, Mussolini received Grandi's support for the transformation of the Fascist movement into a political party, the National Fascist party (PNF), with a formal program and a defined hierarchical structure. As the Duce himself expressed it, the pact of pacification now "belonged to the past, [and] was nothing more than a retrospective episode."[122]

In no sense did the agreements of November put an end to all internal rivalries, local feuds, and conflicts between provincial bosses and national leaders, which continued to plague fascism well into the 1920s. However, the congressional compromise between Mussolini and the *ras* did resolve what would prove to be the most

[120] Quoted in A. Tasca, *The Rise of Italian Fascism*, p. 233.

[121] For the meeting in Bologna, see *RdC*, August 17, 1921; on the March on Ravenna, see R. De Felice, *Mussolini il fascista*, vol. I, pp. 178-179.

[122] See A. Tasca, *The Rise of Italian Fascism*, p. 248.

serious internal crisis of the movement. Significantly, in the following months the military and political forces of fascism united once again in a campaign that would bring the Duce to power in October 1922. For the various *ras* and their agrarian backers, the congress not only confirmed their power within the national movement, but also assured them, at least implicitly, that they would have a free hand to operate independently within the confines of their respective provinces.

5. *The Consolidation of an Agrarian-Fascist Program in Bologna*

Neither local rivalries nor tense relations with the central committee prevented Bolognese Fascist leaders from developing, in collaboration with agrarian spokesmen, their own agricultural program for the province in the spring of 1921. With its emphasis on mechanization, productivity, and rural solidarity, the program exposed by Grandi and Baroncini was, in many respects, a virtual carbon copy of the proposals advocated by Count Filippo Cavazza and the AAB in 1919. Embracing Cavazza's vision of a new role for agrarian interests in the rationalization of agricultural production, Grandi insisted on "the right of property, not as an absolute hereditary right, but as a social force whose character varies with the changing times." Contractual reforms, spearheaded by "socially conscious" landowners were to provide the foundation for "the industrialization of agriculture . . . in the general interest of the nation."[123] Like Cavazza, the two Fascist bosses emphasized in particular the need for profit-sharing contracts that transformed the rural laborers into partners and associates of the growers in the processes of farm production.[124] Such contracts would in turn favor the growth of a class of stable and socially conservative peasant proprietors. In what could have been a page from one of

[123] Dino Grandi, "Il programma agrario dei fascisti," *Il Progresso*, April 10, 1921; *L'Assalto*, April 9, 1921.

[124] *Ibid.*

Count Cavazza's articles two years earlier, Grandi wrote in the summer of 1921: "We want to transform . . . the day laborer into the sharecropper, the sharecropper into the tenant farmer, and ultimately the sharecropper into the small landowner. This program will lead to the elimination of the day laborers who are the social calamity of the countryside, it will encourage saving, [and] will morally elevate the agricultural laborer. . . . Fascism will seek to favor the small private landowner [and] . . . will implement profit-sharing contracts . . . and tenancy."[125] As these quotations suggest, Fascist plans and proposals for the countryside responded to the same imperatives as the AAB's program of 1919: the need to break the power of the Federterra, to reduce agrarian dependence on the politically explosive day laborers, and to link the large growers with the small peasant proprietors in a cohesive and unified rural bloc.

If the program advocated by Grandi and Baroncini clearly reflected the continuity of commercial agrarian concerns in the postwar period, it also included certain innovative organizational initiatives and methods of implementation. In contrast to the AAB, which had had to rely on various forms of economic coercion and the uncertain support of the state in its dealings with the leagues, the agrarian Fascists had the means to impose their will through direct violence. The paramilitary squads provided a powerful weapon in the rural communes for breaking up the leagues and terrorizing the mass of day laborers into submission. As the Ferrarese Fascists had already demonstrated early in 1921, the squads could accomplish what economic strings alone had failed to achieve, carrying out political conversion at the point of a gun.[126] At the same time, Grandi and the more astute agrarian spokesmen recognized the limits of violence; to consolidate their conquests and to prevent any resurrection of the Socialist leagues, alternative labor organizations had to be created in order to control and regiment the newly "liberated" agricultural workers.

[125] *L'Assalto*, June 11, 1921.

[126] P. Corner, *Fascism in Ferrara*, p. 165.

Undoubtedly inspired by the successes of the Ferrarese Fascists in this area of activity, Grandi and Baroncini began to promote and organize autonomous unions and employment offices in the spring of 1921. With the support of the established parties of order and "local patriotic associations," the Bolognese fascio announced the founding of a Syndical Chamber of Labor, composed of "apolitical" syndicates of sharecroppers, day laborers, and transportation workers on March 1, 1921.[127] Stressing nonpartisanship and productive collaboration between capital and labor, the statutes of the new syndicates echoed the familiar ideals and aims of their agrarian Fascist sponsors. In general terms, they proposed to defend both labor and production, integrating and harmonizing "manual labor with the labor of the mind" so that "the interests of the various social classes are in harmony with those of the nation."[128] In pursuit of these goals, the syndicates advocated a program that, in its promotion of profit-sharing contracts and "the progressive economic and moral ascension of the laborers," coincided with identical pronouncements in the Fascist press.[129] More specifically, they proposed to provide legal services to members and contractual reforms as well as various consumer and producer cooperatives.

Despite their claims to political neutrality, the autonomous unions relied primarily on the essentially negative appeal of opposition to the Socialists, proclaiming themselves resolute opponents of the "tyranny of the leagues." In their speeches and propaganda, Fascist promoters incessantly played on the resentments, antagonisms, and discordant ambitions within the rural labor force engendered by the bitter strikes of the previous year. Dissident sharecroppers, for instance, were guaranteed protection from Socialist boycotts and reprisals and were promised restitution of all fines that they had paid to the league bosses. Similarly, dissident day laborers were assured of a new hiring office, located in the headquarters of the fascio, where they could find employment "without having to

[127] *RdC*, March 1, 1921.
[128] *Ibid.*, March 9, 1921.
[129] *Ibid.*, April 9, 1921; *L'Assalto*, April 9, 1921.

resort to the Socialist leagues."[130] Regardless of the initial intentions of the Fascist organizers, such a pronounced antisocialist orientation had unavoidable consequences in a province like Bologna where for decades the dominant social conflicts had been between the leagues and the organized landowners. Much as in Ferrara, any attacks on the Socialists in the Bolognese countryside could not take place without necessarily strengthening the position of the large landowners and commercial farmers. Even those Fascist syndicalists who genuinely wanted the unions to defend the interests of their adherents dared not alienate the large growers, whose support in the forms of material aid and preferential hiring was essential to the success of the entire unionizing campaign.[131]

From the outset, agrarian spokesmen had little difficulty supporting unions with a program that proposed to do exactly what they had been advocating since the end of the war. Most landowners and leaseholders saw the immediate utility of the syndicates as instruments to break the Federterra's monopoly of organized labor and to reintroduce forms of interunion competition that could only work to their advantage as rural employers. With the chronic unemployment in the countryside, the very presence of an alternative labor organization enabled agrarians to dominate the job market, employing only compliant laborers and boycotting the leagues. Certain farsighted commercial farmers also viewed the syndicates as a crucial component of a more permanent solution to the problem of labor militancy in the rural communes. As prewar developments had shown, economic coercion and intermittent political repression did not provide any enduring social peace, since after every local defeat the leagues always managed to reorganize the laborers. The autonomous unions offered the means to prevent a repetition of this pattern by institutionalizing the immediate gains achieved by the squads. Once Fascist violence, economic pressures, or personal ambition had convinced rural workers to desert the leagues, the syndicates could reorganize and control

[130] *L'Assalto*, March 26, 1921.

[131] On this problem in Ferrara, see P. Corner, *Fascism in Ferrara*, p. 134.

them and thereby ensure agrarian supremacy over the labor force on a more lasting basis.[132] For these various reasons, landowners and leaseholders soon came to play a direct and decisive role in the autonomous unions. By the summer of 1921, the prefect was reporting that in the plain all the syndicates were "under the leadership of the fasci [and] the agrarians," a situation that was also evident in the district of Imola where the police claimed "the syndicate is only a direct emanation of the agrarian association and the fascio."[133]

Together with the Fascist squads, these autonomous unions became the basic weapons in a new systematic offensive against the Socialist party and labor movement in the course of 1921 and 1922. Beginning in the spring of 1921, the Bolognese Fascists, in collaboration with the large landowners and leaseholders, unleashed a three-pronged assault on the Socialist municipal administrations, cooperatives, and union organizations. In contrast to the random and spontaneous violence of the previous winter, the punitive expeditions were now directed at strategic targets in the countryside, with the objective of destroying the vital organizational and leadership links of the socialist movement. Selective terror and violence became skillfully coordinated with a campaign by the fasci and their agrarian allies to regiment day laborers and sharecroppers into the autonomous unions. Both the growth of fascism as a mass movement and the consolidation of an agrarian Fascist alliance were inseparably bound to the success of this terrorist offensive.

[132] Such thinking was by no means limited to Bolognese agrarians; see *ibid.*, pp. 164-168.

[133] ASB, C7 F1, Police report to Prefect, September 28, 1921; ASB, C7 F1, "I fascisti," Prefect to Ministry of Labor, July 13, 1921.

VIII. THE AGRARIAN FASCIST CONQUEST OF THE COUNTRYSIDE

Beginning in the spring of 1921, Bologna was shaken by an explosion of violence and destruction without precedent in the modern history of the province. The mountains of police and prefectoral reports from this period eloquently testified to both the dimensions and brutality of what soon emerged as a unilateral civil war against the institutions and personnel of the Socialist labor movement. Scarcely a day would pass without new reports of Fascist violence: punitive expeditions, beatings, shootings, arson, devastated union halls and party headquarters. Between March and May alone, squads of blackshirts ravaged over thirty-five newspaper offices, chambers of labor, peasant leagues, cooperatives, and workers' social clubs, destroying the fruits of some three decades of Socialist organizational work. The situation in Bologna was far from unique; in the same months, nearly two hundred and fifty labor institutions elsewhere in the Po Valley suffered an identical fate.[1] Impossible to quantify but perhaps equally important were the innumerable accounts of minor fights, assaults, and threats against socialist sympathizers that deluged the offices of the prefecture and the police chiefs throughout 1921 and 1922. Such

[1] For a provincial breakdown of these statistics, see Angelo Tasca, *The Rise of Italian Fascism* (New York, 1966), p. 120.

Fascist violence, supplemented by the economic pressure of rural employers and the partisan justice of state authorities, proved to be remarkably effective. Indeed, months before the March on Rome, this blend of terror and coercion had drastically transformed political life and labor relations in the province.

Despite its seemingly chaotic and improvised character, Fascist violence in the rural communes conformed to a relatively consistent plan of action, clearly inspired by the extraordinary success of Italo Balbo and his squads in Ferrara. Like other provincial movements in the Po Valley, the Bolognese Fascists patterned their organizations, policies, and methods after the pace-setting Ferrarese fascio.[2] The actual process of Fascist conquest in Bologna, however, was not a simple repetition of the Ferrarese experience. On the contrary, the offensive in the Bolognese countryside encountered greater difficulties and developed at a far slower pace than the movement in the neighboring province. If fascism seized power in Ferrara as a result of a dazzling blitzkrieg campaign, in Bologna its victory came only after a prolonged war of attrition.

The electoral results of May 1921 and the size of the "independent" unions by the summer of that year attested to the speed and completeness with which the Ferrarese Fascists destroyed the peasant leagues and developed into a substantial mass movement. In what had been one of the premier "red" provinces of the Po Valley where the Socialist party had captured nearly three-quarters of the vote in 1919, the Fascist organization and coercion engineered a complete reversal in 1921. While the electoral strength of the Socialists collapsed, the vote of the National Bloc increased eight-fold with the support of the Fascists; Balbo's squads were particularly effective in the rural communes where the bloc increased its vote from four thousand to nearly thirty-seven thousand.[3] Similarly, the Fascist unions in Ferrara, which had begun

[2] On the development of the Fascist movement in Ferrara, see Paul Corner, *Fascism in Ferrara, 1915-1925* (London, 1975) and Alessandro Roveri, *Le origini del fascismo a Ferrara, 1918-1921* (Milan, 1974).

[3] P. Corner, *Fascism in Ferrara*, p. 179; Charles Maier, *Recasting Bourgeois Europe* (Princeton, 1975), p. 327.

from scratch in February, could boast a membership of over forty thousand day laborers by June 1921.[4] In Bologna, on the other hand, Fascist achievements were considerably more modest. Here, six months of punitive expeditions did not succeed in substantially altering mass political loyalties. Although the National Bloc expanded its share of the vote from 13.4 to 27.1 percent in May, the Socialist and Communist left remained the dominant electoral force in the province, capturing nearly 58 percent of the vote.[5] Likewise, the Bolognese independent unions were hardly an overnight success. To conceal the comparative weakness of the syndicates, union organizers steadfastly refused to provide precise figures on membership throughout 1921. Only in January 1922 did they give any clear indication of the unions' numerical strength. At the founding congress of the Provincial Federation of National Syndicates that month, Baroncini reported a membership of twenty-five thousand, a figure that included not only day laborers, but also sharecroppers, white-collar employees, and technicians.[6] Placed next to the earlier achievements of the Federterra, which had seventy-three thousand members in the summer of 1920, the syndicates appeared to have a relatively small following in the countryside and, under no circumstances, constituted a mass base of support for fascism comparable to that of the Ferrarese unions, at least until the fall of 1922.[7]

The contrasting experiences of the Bolognese and Ferrarese Fascist movements reflected important differences in the rural labor

[4] P. Corner, *Fascism in Ferrara*, p. 167.

[5] Luigi Arbizzani, "L'avvento del fascismo nel Bolognese, 1920-1922," *Movimento Operaio e Socialista*, 1964, p. 264; Brunella Dalla Casa, "Il movimento operaio a Bologna dall'occupazione delle fabbriche al patto di pacificazione," in Deputazione Emilia-Romagna per la Storia della Resistenza, *Movimento operaio e fascismo nell'Emilia-Romagna* (Rome, 1973), p. 66.

[6] See *RdC*, January 19, 1922.

[7] L. Arbizzani, "Lotte agrarie in provincia di Bologna nel primo dopoguerra," in R. Zangheri, ed., *Le campagne emiliane nell'epoca moderna* (Milan, 1957), p. 298 provides information on the size of the Bolognese Federterra. For the strength of the Fascist syndicates in the fall of 1922, see ASB, C7 F1, Prefect to Ministry of Interior, September 28, 1922.

forces and Socialist organizations of the two provinces. As a result of natural terrain and large-scale land reclamation, the overwhelming mass of the work force in the Ferrarese countryside consisted of landless day laborers who found seasonal work on the large capitalist farms. Already in 1900, this vast army of marginally employed workers represented nearly 60 percent of the rural population and had become "the overriding feature of provincial life."[8] Control of these agricultural workers was the key to political and social power in Ferrara, as the Socialists had demonstrated in 1919-20. In the context of 1921, the relative homogeneity of the agricultural labor force worked to the advantage of Fascist organizers. Balbo and his squads were able to focus their efforts on a single class of laborers, an economically vulnerable class for whom chronic unemployment was a basic feature of daily life. With the leagues in disarray, the desperate need to find work took precedence over political allegiances and contributed greatly to the passage of the day laborers from the Socialist organizations to the autonomous unions.[9] The province of Bologna, on the other hand, had a tremendous variety of agricultural systems, forms of land tenure, and categories of rural laborers as one moved from the low plain to the foothills and mountainous zones. Apart from its landless day laborers, Bologna also had a large population of sharecroppers with divided political loyalties and economic interests.[10] Not only did this heterogeneous work force preclude any rapid and sweeping triumphs in the province but it also forced Fascists to evolve gradually a number of different strategies to meet the highly varied social and economic conditions in the countryside.

At the same time, Bolognese Fascists faced a far more tenacious and disciplined socialist labor movement than their Ferrarese colleagues. From their founding, the peasant leagues in Ferrara had been distinguished by a pronounced instability, frequently hovering between reformism, maximalist socialism, and revolutionary

[8] P. Corner, *Fascism in Ferrara*, p. 3.
[9] *Ibid.*, p. 164.
[10] See Chapter I, Section 1.

syndicalism; throughout the prewar period, it was not uncommon for the mass of laborers to shift from one group of leaders to another.[11] Such instability tended to inhibit the development of firm organizational loyalties or a coherent political commitment among the laborers and, as Angelo Tasca noted, made them "an easy prey to demagogues, to the friends and collaborators of Mussolini."[12] Conversely, the Bolognese Federterra had the largest and most stable rural labor organizations of any province in the entire country. Despite occasional setbacks, the leagues in Bologna had grown steadily and remained firmly in the hands of reformist leaders who were able to create a rich organizational life for both day laborers and sharecroppers. Continuity of leadership and organization over nearly three decades enabled the Federterra to sink deep roots in the Bolognese countryside. By 1921, the great majority of the rural work force had long been integrated into a network of Socialist institutions that included not only unions, but also cooperatives, social clubs, and electoral schools. In contrast to their Ferrarese comrades, the day laborers and a large portion of the sharecroppers in Bologna had thus acquired strong political and personal loyalties to the Socialist organizations, loyalties that proved to be surprisingly resistant to Fascist demagoguery and coercion.[13]

This combination of social and political circumstances shaped both the forms and pace of the Fascist advance in the Bolognese countryside. In particular, the limited effectiveness of propaganda and demagogic appeals slowed the advance and compelled the local fasci to rely more on violence, intimidation, and agrarian economic pressures to achieve their objectives. Moreover, unlike in Ferrara, victories on the municipal level were often tenuous and required constant vigilance and repeated doses of coercion to avoid a revival of socialist influence among the workers. Nonetheless, all these

[11] P. Corner, *Fascism in Ferrara*, p. 167.

[12] A. Tasca, *The Rise of Italian Fascism*, p. 102.

[13] On the distinctive features of Bologna's socialist labor movement, see Giovanni Procacci, *La lotta di classe in Italia agli inizi del secolo XX* (Rome, 1970), pp. 112-113, 308-311.

factors only delayed and complicated the Fascist conquest in Bologna; they did not prevent it. By the early fall of 1922, agrarian fascism had all but eliminated its Socialist adversaries and replaced the "red baronies" with a new "state within the state."

As in other provinces of the Po Valley, the victorious Fascist offensive in Bologna was directed simultaneously against the Socialist municipal governments and the leagues of sharecroppers and day laborers. In this offensive, the relationship between Fascist violence and agrarian interests was complex; the squads cannot be simply dismissed as a white guard of agrarian reaction. A wide variety of political aspirations and psychological needs appear to have motivated the rank-and-file in the squads: some blackshirts saw themselves as genuine revolutionaries, building a new and ideal society or at least destroying an old and decadent one; others were rebelling against all forms of authority or simply enjoyed the male camaraderie of the squads; yet others found in the violent exploits of the fasci an outlet for individual aggression or the fulfillment of youthful fantasies of heroism and adventure.[14] Such subjective intentions and motives ultimately led to bitter disputes within the movement, but they did not fundamentally alter the objective consequences of the Fascist offensive: the destruction of a strong and effective labor movement and the reestablishment of agrarian supremacy in the Bolognese countryside.

The convergence of Fascist violence and elite interests was clearly evident in the joint crusade of the squads and agrarians against the Socialist municipal governments. Although carried out simultaneously with attacks on other Socialist institutions in the province, the campaign against the municipalities was, in many respects, a precondition for a more general offensive against the leagues. For decades the red municipalities had played a vital supportive role for the laborers in the leagues, providing them with employment in public works projects, economic subsidies in the winter months, social programs, and channels of political influence.

[14] See Edward Tannenbaum, "The Goals of Italian Fascism," *The American Historical Review*, LXXIV, no. 4 (April 1969), pp. 1183-1191.

Apart from their support of the leagues, landowners and commercial farmers had an additional reason for seeking the elimination of the red municipal administrations. As the prefect reported in February 1921, the Socialist mayors were seeking to "push their expenses to the highest possible level in order to . . . abolish private property by absorbing all profits through taxation." On the eve of the Fascist offensive, many growers were convinced that certain municipalities intended to raise the land taxes as much as 200 percent above the official value of the properties.[15] The pressing need of propertied interests to block these tax proposals, together with the wider political and social objectives of the fasci, provided more than enough fuel for the devastating campaign that the agrarian Fascists proceeded to unleash throughout the province in the spring of 1921. Within the span of a year and a half, only a few isolated Socialist municipalities were left standing, the last remnants of what had once been the Socialist party's most impressive provincial "satrapy."[16]

1. *Beatings and Boycotts: The Fall of the Socialist Municipalities*

As the municipal councilors in the commune of Crevalcore sat down for their weekly meeting in the town hall one evening in late April, a frightening spectacle suddenly unfolded before their eyes: "Fascists broke in with clubs and hammers, demanding the immediate resignation of the entire Socialist administration." Within days all the Socialist councilors had tendered their resignations because of what they claimed was "the unprecedented violence of

[15] In February 1921, the prefect wrote to the ministry of interior that the "Socialist municipal administrations are seeking to push their expenses to the highest possible level in order to . . . abolish private property by absorbing all the profits through taxation." ASB, C4 F1, February 25, 1921.

[16] Both agrarian spokesmen and Fascist propagandists used the term "satrapy" to characterize the local structures of power created by such Socialist leaders as Giuseppe Massarenti.

the Fascists."[17] Far from being an isolated incident, the Crevalcore expedition became the model for similar raids throughout the province and particularly in those communes where the Socialists were most firmly entrenched. In Molinella, for example, the *squadristi* destroyed the offices of Giuseppe Massarenti, mayor of the commune and the leading Socialist organizer in the lower plain. Harassment of Massarenti reached such intensity that in June Giolitti himself intervened, ordering the prefects of both Bologna and Ferrara to insure "Massarenti is protected from any violence."[18] Socialist administrators in other communes of the plain were less fortunate than their Molinellese comrade. At the end of September, the mayor of Budrio informed the prefect that his municipal council had been compelled to resign, being unable to carry out its most essential functions in the "climate of violence and intimidation created here" by the Fascists.[19] Similarly, the Socialist municipal council in San Giovanni in Persiceto was unable to hold a single business meeting from early September until October 24, when all the councilors resigned after they had received a series of threats and exemplary beatings at the hands of the squads.[20] Punitive expeditions against the Socialist town halls in the rural communes continued throughout the winter of 1921-22 and reached a peak in the summer of 1922, when a general Fascist mobilization forced the resignation of seven municipal councils in a period of less than a week.[21] The Fascist squads did not restrict their violent pressures on Socialist administrators to the council chambers of the town halls. Writing on behalf of his municipal comrades, the Socialist deputy, Luigi Fabbri, protested to the prefect in October 1921 that

[17] PSI, *Fascismo: Inchiesta socialista sulle gesta dei fascisti in Italia* (Milan, 1963), pp. 286-288.

[18] ASB, C7 F1, Giolitti to the prefects of Bologna and Ferrara, June 1921

[19] ASB, C7 F1, Mayor of Budrio to Prefect, September 20, 1921.

[20] See L. Scagliarini, "Proprietari e contadini a San Giovanni in Persiceto, 1919-1924," in Deputazione Emilia-Romagna per la Storia della Resistenza, *Movimento operaio e fascismo nell'Emilia-Romagna, 1919-1923* (Rome, 1973), p. 161.

[21] ACS, Ministero dell'Interno, Dir. Gen. P. S., Prefect, June 23, 1922. The communes involved were Castel D'Argile, Castenaso, Pianoro, Castelmaggiore, San Giorgio di Piano, San Lazzaro di Savena, and Casalecchio.

"all our activities . . . even as simple citizens are completely paralyzed by Fascist threats and violence."[22] Insults, threats, menacing letters, visits in the middle of the night, and brutal assaults became a common, but no less terrifying, experience for local Socialist officials. The secretary of the Socialist section in Castenaso, Emilio Avon, could certainly testify to the character and effectiveness of the Fascist methods. At the end of March, Avon received a note from the fascio that read: "You are the secretary of the Socialist section. We want to test your courage." Late the following night a truckload of masked Fascists arrived at the home of the sleeping Avon. Breaking down the front door and brandishing pistols, the *squadristi* dragged Avon outside. Amid the screams of his wife and three children, the unfortunate official was clubbed into unconsciousness and "invited to leave town within fifteen days on pain of death," an offer that Avon found hard to refuse.[23] Such incidents, which occurred in commune after commune, were bound to take their toll on the local cadre of the Socialist party. Isolated in their crumbling rural bastions, deprived of police protection, and lacking the organizational apparatus to defend themselves from the well-armed and highly mobile squads, growing numbers of Socialist administrators and officials chose to withdraw from public life.[24]

To reinforce and at the same time exploit this Fascist terrorism, leading landowners and leaseholders organized a separate but complementary campaign to deprive the Socialist municipalities of tax revenues. While agrarian opposition to the municipal land tax had been evident prior to the war, the most immediate precedent for some form of radical antifiscal action came in the summer of 1920. Angered by the strikes and the inertia of local authorities, the agrarian association of Imola threatened to "suspend the payment of taxes until the government energetically intervened," a proposal that failed to win broad support within the APA and was never

[22] ASB, C7 F1, Luigi Fabbri to Prefect, October 5, 1921.

[23] PSI, *Fascismo: Inchiesta socialista*, pp. 284-285.

[24] See A. Tasca, *The Rise of Italian Fascism*, pp. 123-128.

put into effect.[25] With the spread of fascism into the countryside the following year, militant agrarian opposition to the Socialist municipalities reemerged. Already in March, for instance, the subprefect in the district of Vergato reported that local landowners were banding together in "hostile demonstrations" against the municipal councils and their plan to pass a sharp hike in the land tax.[26]

These isolated local initiatives mushroomed into a major interprovincial crusade in the fall of 1921. At the end of August, the Federation of Agriculturalists of Modena launched a proposal for a convention of agrarian representatives from northern and central Italy to coordinate a common strategy "to counteract the extremely serious situation created in agricultural industry by the excessive burdens of the municipal and provincial taxes."[27] Held in Bologna in late September, the convention attracted all the prominent agrarian spokesmen of the Po Valley: Cavazza, Donini, Paglia, Lino Carrara, and Attilo Fontana. Fontana, a former director of *Il Progresso* and the agrarian leader in parliament, reflected the decisively antisocialist thrust of the convention, attributing the excessive fiscal burdens of the growers to the red municipalities which, in his view, were seeking the "progressive spoliation of the wealthy in favor of their own clientele through a sectarian application of the tax laws." To combat this project, Fontana proposed two remedies that the convention unanimously approved: "The first is that of performing the necessary formalities stipulated in the laws and regulations in order to obtain the modification of illegal tax increases. The second is the refusal to pay taxes, a remedy which has been called a fiscal strike, but which is really a matter of legitimate defense when certain conditions exist." Capturing the prevailing militancy of the gathering, Carrara closed the convention with a ringing declaration that at long last the landowners

[25] ASB, C16 F1, Subprefect to Prefect, June 9, 1920.
[26] ASB, C7 F1, Novembre, Subprefect to Prefect, March 15, 1921.
[27] *RdC*, August 30, 1921.

and commercial farmers were ready to react aggressively "with any means against illegality."[28]

Bolognese agrarians did not delay in implementing the first method of antitax action. Following the Provincial Council's approval of the Molinellese budget in December, Adolfo Rossi, a well-known agrarian Fascist from the commune, presented a formal appeal to governmental authorities on behalf of all the landowning taxpayers. Despite the heated protests and accusations of the Socialist daily, *La Squilla*, the appeal received a sympathetic hearing in Rome. Two days before Christmas, the higher authorities overruled the Bolognese provincial council and recognized, in the view of the profascist press, the complete right of the taxpayers to defend against "systems . . . that lead to real expropriation."[29]

Emboldened by this initial success, agrarian leaders escalated their campaign against the Socialist municipalities in the first months of 1922. In February an assembly of taxpayers from all the communes of the province elected a fiscal strike committee, headed by Count Gualtiero Isolani and Giacobbe Manzoni, which in turn founded the Provincial League of Taxpayers. From its inception, the league was an obvious brainchild of the landowners. The entire executive council as well as the local representatives were all prominent agrarian spokesmen, while the employer associations gave unqualified support to the new organization.[30] Significantly, the Bolognese fasci also strongly backed the league and its initiatives in the first half of 1922. In fact provincial Fascist leaders issued orders to their members in March "to participate in the formation of municipal antitax committees and facilitate in every way . . . this serious undertaking."[31]

The Provincial League of Taxpayers represented far more than

[28] See *ibid.*, September 25, 1921.

[29] *La Squilla*, December 3, 1921; *RdC*, December 30, 1921.

[30] ASB, C6 F2, *Bollettino ufficiale della Lega provinciale dei Contribuenti*, May 1, 1922; *Giornale Agrario*, June 18, 1922. The executive committee included such prominent agrarian spokesmen as Raffaele Stagni, Cesare Baroni, Roberto Cremonini, and Luigi Calori.

[31] *RdC*, March 16, 1922; ASB, C6 F2, Police Chief to Prefect, no date, 1922.

an antitax movement as prefectoral reports clearly revealed. For the subprefect of Imola, the league was "more than anything else an organ of the agrarians . . . to organize the mass of taxpayers in a united rebellion against the payment of local taxes, presenting itself to them as a liberator from tax pressures in order to shape them into a vast and compact bloc for the next administrative elections." Highlighting the intimate connection between the Fascist expeditions and the tax strikes, the same official reported in the summer that the league was seeking to extend its control over the municipal governments "by organizing committees for the reconstitution of municipal councils that have resigned or been closed down."[32] In this fashion, the league became an instrument for capitalizing on the Fascist offensive against the Socialist administrators and reestablishing agrarian political power on the local level.

The first important undertaking of the league came in April in the form of a "fiscal strike," designed in the words of Calisto Paglia to force the municipalities to recognize "their duties toward the larger economy."[33] On April 7, an assembly of taxpayers in Budrio voted to withhold their contributions and refused to recognize debts incurred by the Socialist administrators the previous year "unless the municipal budget [was] brought within legitimate limits." From Budrio, the strike spread rapidly to the rest of the province, leading its promoters to claim an overwhelming success.[34] Giacobbe Manzoni boasted to an assembly of Imolese agrarians at the end of April that "the vast majority of taxpayers have not appeared at the windows of the tax office . . . not only in the commune of Imola, but in all fifty-four communes of the province that have already joined the protest."[35] The prefect confirmed Manzoni's claim; in a report to the Ministry of Finance, he wrote that as a result of the League's activities, "tax contributions have been scarce,

[32] ASB, C6 F2, Subprefect to Prefect, March 9, 18, and July 23, 1922.
[33] *Giornale Agrario*, May 7, 1922.
[34] *RdC*, April 7, 1922; ASB, C6 F2, Prefect to Ministry of Interior, no date, 1922.
[35] See ASB, C6 F2, above cited bulletin of the Taxpayers' League.

in some zones virtually nil and in others limited to only small taxpayers."[36]

While this blend of Fascist violence and agrarian economic pressure could not match the achievements of the Ferrarese Fascists, who had eliminated almost all the Socialist municipalities in their province during April 1921, it did reach its main objectives in Bologna by the fall of the following year. With their communes on the brink of bankruptcy and their administrators harassed and intimidated, only the most powerful and well-organized municipal strongholds of the Socialist party survived the summer of 1922.[37] Much as in Ferrara, the collapse of the Socialist administrations signified for the agrarians and Fascists more than an end to the political "red tyranny" on the local level. Not only were the Socialists removed from power, but they were often replaced by prefectoral commissioners who did little, effectively allowing the fasci to control their respective communes. For the large commercial farmers and landowners, the new situation in the municipalities brought both economic and political rewards. As a rule, the appointed commissioners reduced their tax contributions and eliminated the costly social programs favored by the Socialists. Subsequent administrative elections, carried out under the vigilant eye of the fasci, enabled prominent landowners to recapture the mayors' office and key posts on the municipal councils.[38] More importantly, the fall of the red municipalities was instrumental to the concurrent agrarian Fascist offensive against the Socialist labor movement. Deprived of the public works, subsidies, and political support that the Socialist municipalities had provided them in the past, the leagues and cooperatives of the day laborers and share-

[36] ASB, C6 F2, Prefect to Ministry of Interior, April 13, 1922.

[37] See in particular the case of Molinella; L. Arbizzani, "L'Avvento," p. 275; Giacomo Matteotti, "The Conquest of Molinella," in his *The Fascisti Exposed: A Year of Fascist Domination* (New York, 1969; 1st English ed. 1924), pp. 103-119.

[38] See, for example, the description of the situation in San Giovanni in Persiceto, in L. Scagliarini, "Proprietari e contadini," p. 162; for comparable developments in Ferrara, see P. Corner, *Fascism in Ferrara*, pp. 176-177.

croppers were all the more vulnerable to coercion from the Fascist squads and the agrarian employers.

2. *A Small Carrot and a Big Stick: Agrarian Fascism and the Red Sharecroppers' Unions*

The new sharecropping contract signed by Calda and Paglia in October represented the crowning achievement of the Bolognese Federterra in 1920. Not only did the contract give sharecroppers substantial economic benefits, but it also enhanced the strength and unity of the entire rural labor movement by granting special privileges to the Socialist cooperatives and employment offices, while severely restricting the profits and managerial prerogatives of the landowners. According to its terms, both the sharecroppers and day laborers were bound by reciprocal rights and responsibilities that were designed to minimize conflicts of interest between the two categories and bring them together in their dealings with agrarian employers.[39] Thus, it was not surprising that the sabotage and revision of this contract would be a top priority for agrarian Fascists in the spring of 1921. Indeed, the division and conquest of the agricultural work force, the advance of the independent unions, and the reassertion of entrepreneurial authority in the countryside all depended on their success in obstructing and ultimately destroying the Paglia-Calda agreements.

The problems encountered by Fascist syndicalists in organizing new unions of sharecroppers clearly underscored the central importance of the contractual issue. As developments in the winter of 1920-21 had revealed, the independent unions found a ready-made constituency among the dissident sharecroppers, who had suffered at the hands of the league bosses and were anxious to get revenge and advance their personal positions in the new climate created by the action squads. Fascist organizers exploited the rancors and hatreds of the previous year's strikes in order to encourage the voluntary passage of sharecroppers from the leagues to the

[39] L. Arbizzani, "Lotte agrarie," pp. 324-327.

independent unions. Throughout the spring of 1921, the Fascist daily, *L'Assalto*, repeatedly urged dissident peasants to go to their local fascio and denounce the fines, abuses of power, and violence that they had suffered at the hands of the leagues.[40] Upon receipt of such denunciations, the squads would proceed to extract from the leagues the sums supposedly "extorted" from the sharecroppers and return them to their rightful owners when they entered the syndicates. The actual restitution of the fines often provided the occasion for well-publicized celebrations to demonstrate the growing strength of the independent unions and to encourage additional denunciations and political conversions.[41]

Fascist syndicalists supplemented this essentially negative appeal with promises of peaceful collaboration and land for all peasants who would join the new unions. Beginning in March, agrarian spokesmen and syndicalist representatives held a series of promotional meetings in a number of communes in the province to publicize their program. A leaflet distributed to the sharecroppers of Molinella reflected the type of appeal made in these meetings: "We intend to develop our program of organization, certain that the results will demonstrate its superiority over those of our adversaries, results that will be obtained not by impositions, boycotts, and monopolies, but through the free development of the energies of labor, harmonizing the interests of the different categories of labor with the superior criterion based on increased production and the just distribution of the benefits that derive from it."[42] Following the lead of their Ferrarese colleagues, local agrarian associations made certain exemplary economic concessions to the syndicates. In mid-July, for example, the landowners of San Pietro in Casale signed an agreement with the peasant syndicates for the leasing of an undetermined amount of land to the sharecroppers, an agreement that both Fascist leaders and agrarian spokesmen claimed would also have value in other zones of the province.[43]

[40] L. Arbizzani, "L'Avvento," p. 258; L. Scagliarini, "Proprietari e contadini," p. 159.

[41] See, for example, the account of one such celebration in *RdC*, March 22, 1921.

[42] *Ibid*. For text of leaflet, see *La Squilla*, September 3, 1921.

[43] *RdC*, July 20, 1921.

By itself, this campaign for the voluntary passage of sharecroppers from the red leagues to the Fascist unions achieved only modest results. The syndicates made the most headway in communes where the Socialist leagues were new and relatively weak or where tensions between sharecroppers and day laborers were particularly sharp. In the district of Imola, a prewar stronghold of the peasant brotherhoods and the scene of bitter conflicts within the peasant classes in 1920, police officials reported in late March that approximately six hundred sharecroppers intended "to resign from the Chamber of Labor [and] many others are prepared to negotiate directly with their employers."[44] Elsewhere, however, Fascist syndicalists encountered little enthusiasm among the sharecroppers. Decades of socialist propaganda and struggles with the landowners had given the majority of peasants a clear sense of their own interests and made them profoundly skeptical about agrarian promises of collaboration, especially when such collaboration entailed the sacrifice of their recent contractual gains. From the outset, the determination of the landowners and large commercial farmers to destroy the Paglia-Calda contracts and reassert their old economic and managerial prerogatives placed severe limits on the program and mass appeal of the syndicates. Since the organizational disarray of the Bolognese propertied classes prevented the formulation of a provincial land program comparable to the one sponsored by the Ferrarese agrarian federation, the local syndicates could offer only vague future promises and immediate sacrifices to the peasants. Apart from their political and organizational loyalties to the leagues, few sharecroppers were prepared to give up voluntarily the new Socialist contracts and return to the older and less favorable arrangements. In striking contrast to Ferrara, the agrarian policies of the Bolognese fasci did not persuade a large number of sharecroppers to embrace the cause of fascism.[45]

As a consequence, agrarian Fascists in Bologna had to rely primarily on violence and intimidation to weaken the red leagues, obstruct the Paglia-Calda contracts, and insure what amounted to

[44] ASB, C16 F1, Police Report to Prefect, March 29, 1921.

[45] On the situation in Ferrara, see P. Corner, *Fascism in Ferrara*, pp. 160-163.

the forced passage of sharecroppers to the syndicates. Like their comrades in the municipal administrations, the leaders of the Socialist sharecroppers' unions became prime targets of the blackshirts in the spring of 1921. A typical case of Fascist methods of physical persuasion occurred in the commune of Monteveglio in late March where the squads took the secretary of the local union captive and compelled him to sign a statement denouncing the Federterra's contract, "under the barrel of a gun."[46] Occasionally, intimidation of the leadership produced the desired rippling effect on the rank-and-file of the leagues. In June, for instance, the league boss of San Giovanni in Persiceto capitulated to Fascist pressures and called upon an assembly of his followers to enroll in the "apolitical syndicates" sponsored by the fascio; after the meeting, the majority of peasants proceeded to abandon the Socialist Chamber of Labor.[47] On other occasions, the fasci were not adverse to the use of indiscriminate terror, as the Socialist sharecroppers in Santa Maria in Duno discovered in April. During a meeting of peasants called to discuss the implementation of the new contracts, "a group of masked men, brandishing clubs and pistols, suddenly broke into the hall . . . [and] opened fire indiscriminately." After killing one of the peasants and wounding nine others, the squad sacked the league offices and burned every portable object including the peasants' bicycles.[48]

In their campaign against the socialist labor leaders, the Fascists received substantial assistance from state prosecutors and courts. Swept up in the general climate of antisocialist reaction, the provincial tribunals and appeals courts began in the winter of 1920-21 to treat the boycotts and fines imposed during the agricultural strikes as acts of criminal extortion.[49] A series of legal processes brought by government authorities in the first six months of 1921

[46] PSI, *Fascismo: Inchiesta socialista*, p. 283.

[47] L. Scagliarini, "Proprietari e contadini," p. 159.

[48] For a fuller account of the incident, see ASB, C7 F1, Mayor of Bentivoglio to Prefect, April 30, 1921.

[49] See Guido Neppi Modona, *Sciopero, potere politico e magistratura, 1870-1922* (Bari, 1973), pp. 246-247.

effectively decimated the leadership of the peasant leagues in several communes. In February, the entire leadership of the red league of sharecroppers in Crevalcore, including the treasurer and president, were arrested and prosecuted "for assaults and extortion committed against those who did not belong to the red leagues"; in June a similar fate befell all the members of the executive committee of the union of tenant farmers and sharecroppers in Granarolo.[50]

Fascist violence and legal repression against the league bosses greatly strengthened the position and bargaining power of agrarian employers. Summarizing developments in the Bolognese countryside during the first six months of 1921, the prefect stressed how "large numbers of agrarians are profitting from . . . the intimidating presence of the fasci to evade the agreements and contracts [and] to go back to formulas that are by now outdated."[51] In its annual report, the general council of the provincial Federterra echoed these charges, denouncing local landowners for "systematic and general infractions of the general provincial agreement, . . . the refusal to give the peasants obligatory credits, and above all the refusal . . . to advance the necessary supplies as sanctioned in the agreements and in the contracts."[52] While there had been reports of contractual violations as early as the winter of 1920-21, the first organized agrarian rebellion against the Calda-Paglia agreements took place in April in the district of Imola. Under the leadership of the agrarian Fascist Giacobbe Manzoni, the Imolese landowners voted early that month to compile "written contracts different from the general contract of the Federterra." True to their word, the landowners proceeded to sign a new contract with the sharecroppers' syndicate two months later that Manzoni arbitrarily designated as the only contract to be recognized as valid in the district.[53]

[50] G. A. Chiurco, *Storia della rivoluzione fascista* (Florence, 1929), Vol. II, p. 298.

[51] ASB, C16 F1, Prefect to Ministry of Interior, August 21, 1921.

[52] *La Squilla*, December 17, 1921.

[53] ASB, C16 F1, Police Report to Prefect, March 29, 1921; *ibid.*, resolution of

Landowners in other communes of the province began to emulate the Imolese agrarians in the ensuing months, refusing to advance the prescribed money and supplies to their red sharecroppers and unilaterally reducing the peasants' share of the harvest.[54]

With the arrival of the major summer agricultural works, these local initiatives gave way to a more systematic and broader campaign by agrarian Fascists to deprive sharecroppers of the right, sanctioned in the Paglia-Calda agreements, to select the machines for the annual threshing. Since the sharecroppers in the Socialist unions intended to use the threshing machines of their own cooperatives, which were manned by workers from the red leagues, this campaign represented more than a simple attack on the Federterra's sharecropping contract. By dictating the choice of machines, Fascist syndicalists could sever a vital institutional link between the unions and cooperatives, reduce the financial independence of the Socialist labor movement, and gain control of a substantial number of jobs in the countryside. Similarly, for agrarian interests who had long been involved in the profitable business of leasing farm machinery, control of the selection process was crucial not only because it gave them invaluable economic leverage in their dealings with the sharecroppers, but also because it could be used to eliminate dangerous competition from the Socialist machine cooperatives.[55]

Depending on the relative strength of the syndicates and the intensity of Socialist resistance, the fasci and landowners employed different methods and policies to attain their objectives. In the district of Imola, where the syndicates already had a sizeable membership and the landowners were well-organized, local Fascists

the association included in the report of the Subprefect of Imola to Prefect, April 6, 1921; see also the *Giornale Agrario,* April 9, 1921.

[54] See ASB, C7 F1, Royal Commissioner to Prefect, August 22, 1921; *ibid.*, petition to Prefect, October 15, 1921; *ibid.*, Police Chief to Prefect, November 2, 1921.

[55] See *La Squilla,* July 2, 1921. Sharecroppers could rent the threshing machines of their own cooperatives at a lower rate than those owned by the landowners or the agrarian association.

relied primarily on a boycott of the Socialist cooperatives in order to establish what they described as a "new equilibrium of forces" in the countryside. After meeting with representatives of the agrarian association the first week in July, the secretary of the fascio and boss of the Imolese syndicates, Mansueto Cantoni, announced that "all peasants enrolled in the syndicates would use the machines leased by the syndicates." With good reason, the agrarian association enthusiastically supported this policy, since the syndicates leased all their machines from its subsidiary, the Farm Machine Cooperatives.[56] While the fascio claimed to be defending the right to work, the landowners attempted to impose the syndicates' machines on all their sharecroppers, regardless of their political and organizational affiliations. Representing the sharecroppers' unions and the cooperatives, the Imolese Chamber of Labor tenaciously resisted agrarian Fascist demands throughout the summer of 1921, despite intensified violence from the squads and a growing number of desertions from its ranks. After the prefect intervened in the dispute in early September, however, Socialist resistance collapsed and the Chamber of Labor formally disavowed important features of the Federterra's contract. In an agreement signed on September 8 with the agrarian association, the Socialist leaders granted the machines of the syndicates 40 percent of the work in the district and guaranteed a 50 percent share of the harvest to the landowners instead of the 40 percent previously stipulated.[57]

On the other hand, in the communes of the plain where the syndicates existed in name only, the agrarian Fascists had to rely primarily on intimidation and violence to gain compliance from the sharecroppers. Occasionally, the fasci sought to impose themselves as middlemen between the cooperatives and the sharecroppers. In Castel San Pietro, for instance, a "neutral committee" headed by Augusto Alvisi, a former official of the APA and secretary of the fascio, demanded that the Socialist cooperatives lease

[56] *RdC*, July 8 and 9, 1921.

[57] *Ibid.*, September 9, 1921; ASB, C16 F1, Federterra to Prefect, September 3 and 5, 1921.

eight threshing machines directly to it at substantially reduced prices, warning that otherwise "the machines will not leave the garages."[58] Wherever a large number of private machine owners belonged to the fascio, the squads were mobilized to insure that "the Socialist agricultural machines would not leave the garages for love or money," while the landowners used verbal threats to encourage the peasants to relinquish their right of selection.[59] A typical case of such threats can be found in a letter sent by one landowner to his recalcitrant sharecroppers in Castelfranco, in which he wrote: "I must warn you that while leaving you free to use the machines of your choice, you will be held responsible for any damages that could possibly result from repressive action taken against you and your families and I reserve the right to terminate the sharecropping contract in the event that the present situation deteriorates further."[60]

The Fascist squads gave substance to these agrarian threats by employing their own distinctive brand of physical persuasion. Protesting to the prefect in July, the Chamber of Labor described a scenario that became a daily occurrence in the summer and fall of 1921: "The Fascists visit the peasants and in a few words give them this warning: 'the choice of the machines for this year belongs to the landowner; he has chosen the one belonging to the fascio and if you refuse it there will be thrashings and you will be held responsible for whatever else might happen.' "[61] Once the thresh-

[58] See ASB, C7 F1, Consorzio provinciale delle Cooperative agricole to Prefect, July 6, 1921. Similar methods were used in Budrio, Medicina, and San Giovanni in Persiceto.

[59] ASB, C7 F1, letter to Police Chief quoted in his report to the Prefect, July 7, 1922; *ibid.*, Police Chief to Prefect, July 4, 1921.

[60] ASB, C16 F1, Police Report to Prefect, September 26, 1921. In a similar vein, the League of Peasants and Tenant Farmers of Budrio protested to the prefect in July that certain wealthy landowners "with threatening words and actions, are attempting at all costs to prevent . . . the peasants . . . from choosing the machines for the threshing of the grain, which by right they acquired with legally registered contracts." See ASB, C7 F1, July 12, 1921.

[61] ASB, C7 F1, Molinella, Camera Confederale di Lavoro to Prefect, July 7, 1921. Recipients of these threats included the sharecroppers of big landowners and leaseholders like Count Antonio Malvasia, Antonio Bonora, Saltarelli, and Zaniboni.

ing or harvesting had begun, the squads went around the countryside, watching the fields to guarantee that their orders were obeyed. Throughout the peak agricultural season, the prefect received numerous reports of blackshirts halting the field work and forcing sharecroppers to remove machines that they had leased from their local Socialist cooperatives.[62]

Although provincial authorities were well aware of the events taking place in the countryside, they did little to protect the red sharecroppers or to punish the violent excesses of the *squadristi*. As in most other provinces of the Po Valley, a compound of partiality and fear dictated such passivity in Bologna. On the municipal level, sympathetic police officials turned a blind eye to Fascist assaults and refused in general to intervene in the confusing and complex contractual disputes, claiming in the words of the provincial police chief that it was not legitimate "to compel [specific] agrarians to allow the peasants to work with the machines of their choice, because of the absolute refusal of all the landowners to accept the Calda-Paglia agreements."[63] Unlike the vast majority of his professional colleagues who feared that strong action against the Fascists might endanger their careers, the tough new Bolognese prefect, Cesare Mori, arrived in the spring of 1921, determined to restore impartial law and order in the province. By the fall, however, Mori had discovered that he had little effective control over his subordinates. Writing to a commander of the Carabinieri in October, he vented his frustration, complaining that "despite my repeated recommendations and instruction . . . the authors of this violence, all well known and pointed out by me on various occasions, have never been arrested."[64] If Mori's devotion to duty was

[62] See, for example, ASB, C7 F1, Police Report to Prefect, July 20, 1921. *La Squilla*, July 2, 1921, charged that "terrorist squads are going around the countryside intimidating the peasants not to use the threshing machines of their cooperatives."

[63] ASB, C7 F1, Police Chief to Prefect, September 10, 1921. For case of police indifference see *ibid.*, Secretary of the peasant leagues of Crespellano to Royal Commissioner, August 25, 1921.

[64] ASB, C7 F1, Prefect to Commandante Sez. RR.CC., Crespellano, October 17, 1921.

somewhat unusual among Italian prefects, his dilemma was not, for it reflected not only local conditions, but also the gradual disintegration of state authority at all levels in the prevailing climate of governmental instability and parliamentary paralysis in Rome.[65]

The fragmentary evidence available suggests that Fascist coercion, agrarian economic policies, and legal repression had greatly eroded the strength of the red sharecroppers' unions by the end of 1921. In a wave of innumerable local agreements, peasants capitulated, either individually or collectively, to the fasci on the issue of the machines, paving the way for additional agrarian demands that only further emasculated the Federterra's contract. For many sharecroppers who had been suddenly deprived of their old union leaders and forced to relinquish recently acquired contractual rights, the Fascist syndicates came increasingly to represent the only possible source of economic security and protection. Indeed, the growth of the syndicates in the course of 1921 amply testified to the effectiveness of the agrarian Fascist campaign. From an initial nucleus of one hundred sixty families, membership in the peasant syndicates rose to more than three thousand by December.[66] Yet, despite these impressive statistics, the victory of the squads and landowners remained only partial at the end of 1921. Even after nearly a year of intimidation and punitive expeditions, a bloc of some two thousand sharecroppers still refused to desert the organizations of the Federterra and continued to insist on the "complete and faithful application" of the Calda-Paglia agreements in early 1922.[67]

The remarkable tenacity of the Bolognese red unions forced local agrarians to take more extreme legal measures in the winter of 1921-22. By the beginning of February, virtually all the remaining Socialist sharecroppers had received eviction notices from their respective landlords. Although of dubious legality, the notices succeeded in creating a climate of fear and panic that agrarians ex-

[65] See Adrian Lyttelton, *The Seizure of Power: Fascism in Italy, 1919-1929* (New York, 1973), pp. 40-41.

[66] *RdC*, December 18, 1921.

[67] *Ibid.*, February 10, 1922.

ploited to promote a new and revised sharecropping contract, compiled by the Agrarian Committee.[68] Seemingly faced with a choice between losing their farms and accepting a revised contract, the overwhelming majority of peasants opted for the latter. During the spring, the entire membership of the peasant unions in communes like Crespellano and Calderara di Reno transferred in mass to the syndicates; in July the last organized stronghold of Socialist sharecroppers in the district of Imola folded and following the example of their comrades elsewhere "the mass of peasants . . . enrolled in the syndicate."[69] By the end of the summer, only Massarenti's organizations in Molinella continued to hold out, but they were now effectively isolated, existing as little more than oases in a countryside dominated by the fasci and their agrarian allies.

The character of the new sharecropping contract, which replaced that of the Federterra, clearly demonstrated who were the real victors in the Fascist offensive against the red peasant unions. Based primarily on a contract compiled in 1905, it systematically eliminated nearly all the important reforms won during the strike of 1920. According to its terms, the landlords regained exclusive control over farm management and an equal share in the division of the products, while the peasants had to pay all the costs of farm repairs and transportation. As the Socialist press bitterly observed, contractual revision created a situation in which the landlord once again became "the arbiter of the [peasant's] existence and economy."[70] More immediately, the elimination of the red unions and the forced enrollment of sharecroppers into the syndicates greatly enhanced the simultaneous offensive against the agricultural work-

[68] *Ibid.* For additional information on the evictions, see *La Squilla*, December 10, 1921 and February 11, 1922.

[69] For developments in Crespellano and Calderara di Reno, see ASB, C7 F1, Police Reports of June 28, 1922; on the collapse of the union in Sesto Imolese, see ASB, C6 F2, Subprefect to Prefect, June 28 and July 5, 1922; *ibid.*, Police Report to Prefect, July 24, 1922.

[70] *La Squilla*, December 31, 1921. On the contract, see *ibid.*, October 19, 1922; for a comparison between the Federterra contract and that of the agrarian Fascists, see C. Schmidt, *The Sword and the Plow* (New York, 1938), p. 134.

ers. For with the gradual passage of sharecroppers into the syndicates, the agrarian Fascists not only weakened the labor alliance forged by the Federterra over the previous twenty years, but also gained additional instruments to break the resistance of the landless day laborers, the backbone of the Socialist movement in the Bolognese countryside.

3. *The Politics of Employment: Agrarian Fascism and the Agricultural Proletariat*

The all-powerful leagues of landless day laborers seemed to represent the most formidable obstacle to the advance of the Bolognese Fascist movement into the rural areas of the province at the beginning of 1921. Unlike the sharecroppers who were dispersed throughout the countryside on relatively isolated farms, the day laborers had long been concentrated in the rural towns and hamlets of the plain where they often constituted the bulk of the population. Residential patterns, the uniformity of their work, and common problems and needs had all combined to give this mass of impoverished workers an exceptional sense of collective solidarity as well as an aggressive militancy.[71] Indeed, from the 1890s when Socialist organizers set up the first leagues, they had provided the Federterra with its most important social and political strength. Nearly three decades of strikes, blacklists, lockouts, and police repression had given the laborers ample opportunity to display their fighting spirit, discipline, and unwavering loyalty to their leagues. On their shoulders, able Socialist leaders had constructed the largest and most effective rural labor organization in the entire country.

Despite its impressive achievements and imposing facade, the Bolognese Federterra, like the labor organizations in other agricultural provinces of the Po Delta, was far from invulnerable, however. In a region where chronic unemployment was a permanent feature of rural life, the total monopoly and rigid control

[71] See Chapter I, Section 1.

of the agricultural labor force achieved by the leagues in 1920 was not simply the crowning achievement of years of struggle, but a vital necessity. For the Federterra's elaborate system of employment offices and rotating work schedules to function at all, it had to be universally applied, since as Angelo Tasca has noted, "any breach of its terms brought other workers to starvation."[72] With only a few months of work available each year, even a small number of independent laborers could trigger a chaotic and desperate scramble for jobs and bring down the entire organizational edifice. To prevent such an occurrence, the leagues had built up an arsenal of weapons over the years; peer pressure, boycotts, fines, and violence had been used to discourage strikebreakers and to incorporate all categories of workers into the Socialist labor movement. These methods of recruitment required permanent vigilance to be successful, so that in the last analysis the whole system depended on the unhampered authority of the league leaders and their ability to enforce strictly all rules and regulations.[73]

By combining their resources and coordinating their policies, the fasci and agrarian employers were in an excellent position to exploit this weakness in the spring of 1921. Events in Ferrara had already shown them how a judicious blend of violence, unionizing activity, and discriminatory hiring practices could neutralize the league leaders and set in motion a process that the mechanism of the labor market would bring to completion.[74] At the same time, the first tentative forays by the urban squads into rural areas during the winter had revealed both the vulnerability of league offices and personnel to mobile raids and the sizeable support for Fascist actions among the local police. The free and unfettered use of violence was the crucial precondition of Fascist success in the plain, the stronghold of the red laborers where the mass of the population was resolutely hostile. For the squads could do what agrarian entrepreneurs with all their economic might had been unable to

[72] A. Tasca, *The Rise of Italian Fascism*, p. 92.
[73] *Ibid.*, pp. 92-93.
[74] See P. Corner, *Fascism in Ferrara*, p. 167.

achieve: to disarm the Socialist bosses and prevent them from enforcing the rigid observance of league policies. Once the leadership had been put out of commission and the meeting halls destroyed, landowners and commercial farmers could employ more conventional tactics to encourage desertions and to discriminate against the leagues.

Significantly, it was the league leaders, more than any other group of Socialist officials, who bore the brunt of Fascist violence in the spring of 1921. Beginning in mid-February when the secretary of the league in San Giorgio di Piano was attacked and beaten by a squad of blackshirts, relentless persecution became the dominant feature of daily life for local labor leaders in the plain. The provincial press clearly attested to the regularity and unconcealed nature of this persecution. Reporting on the events of a typical Saturday in March, *Il Resto del Carlino,* for example, wrote: "Yesterday was a day dominated by the activity of the Fascists who, as happens every Saturday, went hunting for league bosses in the province."[75] As a rule, the destruction of league offices, chambers of labor, and hiring halls accompanied the exemplary assaults on Socialist cadre. The month of April alone saw search-and-destroy missions by the squads in over twelve different communes.[76] Despite the seemingly random pattern of these punitive expeditions that were often the result of separate decisions by local squad commanders, the Federterra could not fail to grasp how the various strands of the "violent and bestial offensive" all converged to prevent the leagues "from carrying out their noble task of distributing manual labor."[77]

Following closely in the steps of the squads, Fascist syndicalists set up new independent unions, modeled on those in the Ferrarese countryside. Initially, organizers directed their appeals primarily

[75] *RdC,* March 7, 1921. That day a number of league representatives in Monte San Pietro, San Pietro in Casale, Altedo, and Praduro e Sasso received a taste of the "sacred club" or *santo manganello.*

[76] PSI, *Fascismo: Inchiesta socialista,* pp. 284-287.

[77] See the resolution voted by the General Council of the Federterra, published in *La Squilla,* December 17, 1921.

to the categories of permanent hired hands, many of whom had been deprived of their privileged position and forcibly recruited by the leagues the previous year. Propaganda leaflets distributed by the Fascist unions skillfully played on both the resentments and aspirations of these categories, by attacking the Federterra's program of "equality in common misery" and promising preferential hiring, steady work, and a return to special individual contracts for workers who deserted the leagues.[78] In this fashion, union organizers began with the limited objective of breaching the solidarity of the labor movement through the creation of what *La Squilla* described as a "vile minority of privileged workers."[79] In the circumstances of Bologna, even a small nucleus of independent workers was sufficient to give the landowners and leaseholders a powerful weapon in their dealings with the leagues.

As their program clearly indicated, the Fascist unions depended to a very large extent on financial support and favorable treatment from agrarian employers. While union leaders attempted to maintain at least the facade of independence, the prefect noted almost immediately that "behind the Fascist syndicates stand the agrarians . . . who are seeking above all to profit from the situation in order to destroy the [Socialist] organizations."[80] In fact the relationship between the agrarian interests and syndicates was one of mutual dependence, since the syndicates played a central role in the system of rewards and punishments which commercial farmers began to employ in the spring of 1921 to undermine the Federterra.

The first signs of an agrarian offensive against the leagues appeared in March. Recounting a conversation he had with a group of landowners in Castenaso, the police chief reported: "They told me that . . . they do not intend to subject themselves to any monopoly of the leagues or to request from them any manual labor. If the local laborers put aside the odious methods they have adopted in the past and apply directly to the landowners, they will

[78] See the flyer of the syndicate of Molinella, reprinted in *La Squilla*, July 23, 1921 as well as ASB, C7 F1, Subprefect of Imola to Prefect, October 19, 1921.

[79] *La Squilla*, July 23, 1921.

[80] ASB, C6 F2, Prefect to Ministry of Interior, March 18, 1921.

almost certainly be employed."[81] The same month, the fifteen largest agrarian employers in Medicina and Minerbio repudiated their labor contracts with the leagues and hired independent laborers for their spring work.[82] With the league leaders unable to retaliate against the workers who deserted, the Federterra and the Socialists could do little more than verbally protest these contractual violations. In response to league protests and prefectoral inquiries, growers justified such actions as necessary adjustments to the new labor situation created in their communes by the Fascist squads and syndicates. The policies of the farm company, Imprese e Conduzioni Agricole, in Galliera graphically illustrated the close interaction between commercial agrarians and the Fascists. After a number of punitive expeditions in the commune, a government commissioner wrote in June that the head agent of the company's estate had "succeeded with underhanded maneuvers in inducing a group of day laborers to abandon the league in order to have a way of violating a regular labor contract that the landowner Gino Lisi had signed." Lisi, a high official of the company, justified his contractual change of heart in a letter to *Il Resto del Carlino*: "The disappearance of the leaders, the closing of the leagues, . . . the resignation of the league bosses, [and] other well-known political and economic developments have led the laborers of my estate to desert the red flag and enroll in the syndicates. I gave them no orders or advice, but everyone will have to admit it was no longer possible for me to rely solely on organizations that have disappeared. Therefore, in the interests of the property and the laborers, I accepted all laborers of the zone, regardless of their political faith."[83] The largest leaseholder in the commune of Budrio, Alfredo

[81] ASB, C7 F1, Police Chief to Prefect, March 18, 1921.

[82] ASB, C16 F1, Employment Office to Mayor of Medicina, March 24, 1921; *ibid.*, League of braccianti of Minerbio to Calda, April 6, 1921. The employers involved were Giuseppe Menarini, Giuseppe Mainetti, Cesare Baroni, Alfredo Serra, Luigi Filipetti, Serafino Cazzani, Giuseppe Santi, Augusto Lenzi, the Società Agricola Fiorentina, the Società San Antonio Cremonini-Cavazza, Pietro Poggi, Count Gualtiero Isolani, Pietro Pirotti, and the Cataldi family.

[83] ASB, C6 F2, Prefectoral Commissioner to Prefect, July 9, 1921; *RdC*, July 17, 1921.

Benni adopted a similar stance on the issues of hiring and contracts. In the wake of charges by a Socialist deputy that he had "broken the pledges made to the leagues and was employing only personnel who were not enrolled in our organizations," Benni informed the police that some three hundred laborers had left the leagues and joined the fascio and as a result "the staff of the fascio of Budrio put heavy pressures on him to employ [these laborers] on . . . his estates."[84]

During the spring, the limited demand for labor on the farms made it relatively easy for growers to hire independent workers and ignore the Socialist employment offices. The harvest season in the late summer represented a very different situation for agrarian employers. For a brief span of weeks every year, landowners and leaseholders had a virtually inexhaustable need for hired hands; any labor shortages or strikes in this period could cause them to lose not only the output of a few weeks, but that of an entire year since the crops would rot if not collected. The advantages that the leagues ordinarily drew from this market situation, however, were not without countervailing pressures on their rank and file who desperately needed the earnings from the harvest work to survive the long months of enforced idleness during the rest of the year; "what was for the owners only a question of extra profits was a matter of life and death to the workers."[85] With the beginning of the harvest work in the summer of 1921, the agrarian Fascists ruthlessly exploited this point of vulnerability, convinced that the need for employment would prove stronger than any political or union loyalties.

Depending on the relative strength of the Socialist organizations, the employers and fasci used a range of methods to complete the harvest and dominate the labor market without recourse to the leagues. In the foothills and mountains of the province where the leagues were a recent phenomenon and the demand for labor was

[84] ASB, C7 F1, Fabbri to Prefect, July 15, 1921, *ibid.*, Police Chief to Prefect, July 22, 1921.

[85] A. Tasca, *The Rise of Italian Fascism*, p. 91.

less pressing, the landowners relied primarily on discriminatory hiring practices to achieve these objectives. Reporting on the progress of the grape harvest in the commune of Monteveglio, for instance, the police noted that "women enrolled in the syndicates which the Fascist elements control" were doing most of the work, while the majority of Socialist workers remained unemployed.[86] In other communes like Ozzano Emilia, where the independent unions had enough members, the landowners simply signed a new agreement with them and fired the laborers from the leagues. Once the red laborers had lost their jobs, they became highly susceptible to the appeals of the fascio, which according to the police was "working actively to tear the laboring masses away from the social-communist organizations by promising them steady employment." The same officials also stressed the crucial supportive role of the large landowners who "gladly take part in the activities of the Fascists, granting without difficulty the requests of the [syndicates], while rejecting those that come from other organizations."[87]

In the most important agricultural areas of the province, however, Fascist violence and agrarian pressures, unlike in Ferrara, had not significantly weakened the allegiance of the mass of day laborers to the leagues by the summer of 1921, so that the local syndicates were too small and too few in number to insure employers a sufficient supply of labor for the harvest. In the district of Imola, the leagues claimed that the Fascist syndicates "did not and do not count a single adherent in our zone"; similarly, in Molinella the fascio with its eighty members was dwarfed by the leagues who still represented forty-five hundred laborers in mid-August.[88] Yet despite their imposing numerical strength and solidarity, the Bolognese leagues' power was limited by the fact that their authority did not extend beyond the borders of the province. This provincialism of structure, an important weakness of the Italian labor movement in general, worked decisively to the advantage

[86] ASB, C7 F1, Police Chief to Prefect, August 27, 1921.

[87] ASB, C7 F1, Communes O-Z, Police Chief to Prefect, November 16, 1921.

[88] For Imola, see ASB, C7 F1, Chamber of Labor to Subprefect, December 17, 1921; on Molinella, *ibid.*, Vice-Mayor to Ministry of Interior, August 12, 1921.

of agrarian employers in 1921, for they were now able to tap sources of labor elsewhere in the region of Emilia where the fascists ruled supreme.[89]

Already in the first week of July, the propaganda of the syndicates indicated the policies that the landowners and fasci were prepared to take in order to neutralize the bargaining power of the leagues in the plains and Imola. In a series of speeches and pamphlets, Fascist spokesmen promised steady work to all those who passed from the leagues to the syndicates, threatening "to complete the harvest with imported laborers" if the workers ignored their offer.[90] The carrying out of such a threat had actually begun a month earlier in Molinella, where police reported in mid-June that nearly two hundred laborers from Ferrara were working on the farms, "sent in by the fasci with the tacit consent of the landowners who use them to smash the earlier labor contracts signed with the local leagues." A few weeks later, the Federterra described a similar situation in San Giorgio di Piano, charging that the landowners, with the help of Fascist enforcers, were employing "a system of assigning to the laborers of Ferrara the work normally given to the local population of agricultural workers."[91] To maximize the impact of what amounted to a boycott of the leagues and their hiring halls, landowners also put pressure on their sharecroppers to use the machines of the agrarian company, Moto Agricola, and to hire only personnel enrolled in the Bolognese and Ferrarese syndicates. For their part, the Fascist syndicates of sharecroppers followed the lead of their sponsors and ordered their members to deny any work to Socialist laborers.[92]

The general economic slump that hit Italian agriculture in 1921

[89] See A. Lyttelton, "Italian Fascism," in Walter Laquer, ed., *Fascism, a Reader's Guide* (Berkeley, 1978), p. 130.

[90] ASB, C7 F1, Prefect to Ministry of Interior, November 13, 1921; *ibid.*, Police Chief to Prefect, July 7, 1921.

[91] ASB, C6 F2, 3, Police Report to Prefect, June 20, 1921; ASB, C7 F1, Communes O-Z, Federterra to Prefect, July 10, 1921. For identical situation in Castel d'Argile, see ASB, C7 F1, Police Chief to Prefect, August 6, 1921.

[92] *RdC*, July 8, 1921; ASB, C7 F1, Communes O-Z, Employment Office and League of San Giorgio di Piano to Prefect, July 8, 1921; letter of protest from the socialist unions in Molinella, published in *La Squilla*, September 3, 1921.

greatly enhanced these agrarian Fascist policies. The return to more normal conditions of foreign trade, transportation, and food production led that year to a pronounced drop in the level of agricultural prices without a corresponding reduction in the costs of production for commercial farmers. This new deflationary trend affected in particular the key industrial crops of Bologna and Emilia. In decline since the previous summer, the price of hemp, for instance, fell by almost two-thirds in the course of 1921.[93] Growers in Bologna and other zones of the Po Valley responded to the falling prices by reducing their planting and production costs. In an emergency meeting called by the Interprovinciale in February, the hemp growers of Emilia and the Veneto voted "to limit as much as possible the cultivation of hemp in order to reduce by one half the yield of 1920." Later in the year, a committee of rice growers notified the Ministry of Interior that many Bolognese farmers had decided to abandon the cultivation, while in the key rice-growing commune of Medicina, the acreage devoted to the crop in 1921 remained well below the levels of 1918 and 1919.[94] At the same time, growers took steps to reduce their costs of production by imposing *compartecipazione* or crop-sharing contracts that required smaller capital investments and allowed for the more intense exploitation of the laborers. Augusto Lenzi, president of the agrarian association in Medicina, led the way in this direction: in the early fall, the Socialist Chamber of Labor alleged that he had broken his old contract with the leagues and "compelled the laborers to accept *compartecipazione* contracts" as a precondition for escaping "the continual violence and coercion of the Fascists."[95]

[93] On economic conditions, see R. Bachi, *L'Italia economica nell'anno 1921* (Città di Castello, 1922), pp. 177-178; *Libertà Economica*, July 10, 1922; *Giornale Agrario*, June 11, 1921.

[94] For full text of hemp growers' resolution, see *RdC*, February 15, 1921; on rice growers, see ASB, C16 F1, letter to Ministry of Interior, December 14, 1921. For statistics on rice cultivation, see ASB, C6 F2, "Statistica del tornaturato di coltivazione umida 1911 al 1921."

[95] ASB, C7 F1, Camera Confederale di Lavoro to Prefect, October 5, 1921. On the economic advantages of this type of response to deflationary recessions, see

These antirecessionary policies, by reducing production and consequently the demand for hired hands, served to strengthen the bargaining power of the commercial farmers at the expense of the Federterra. With fewer jobs available, the leagues became all the more vulnerable to employer boycotts and the competition of local and Ferrarese syndicates. The situation in the commune of Galliera reflected the plight of the leagues throughout the plain in the late summer of 1921. Here, provincial authorities noted in August, ordinarily one of the peak hiring months, that all the laborers belonging to the Fascist unions had jobs, while those enrolled in the red leagues were unemployed "because of the shortage of jobs."[96] By December, *Il Resto del Carlino* reported that twenty thousand of the seventy thousand day laborers in the province were completely unemployed, a grim situation that did not improve in the spring of 1922 when the number of jobless rose to thirty thousand.[97]

Commercial growers and landowners had learned from past experiences, however, that the leagues could weather boycotts and unemployment in the private agricultural sector by providing work for their rank and file in the land reclamation projects subsidized by the state. Two of these projects, the Renana and the Crevalcorese, were of special importance, since they covered a territory of over one hundred twenty thousand hectares in the provinces of Bologna, Ferrara, Ravenna, and Mantua and created thousands of jobs. During the period of Socialist dominance, the Federterra had gained recognition as the exclusive supplier of manual labor in the two projects that it channeled through a central employment office and three local hiring halls.[98] For the larger of the two projects, the Renana, the leagues had signed a longterm contract with the managing consortium in 1919 that appeared to work satisfactorily

---

P. Corner, "Rapporti tra agricoltura e industria durante il fascismo," *Problemi del Socialismo*, 1972, no. 11-12, pp. 725-727.

[96] ASB, C7 F1, Provincial Employment Office to Prefect, August 5, 1921.

[97] *RdC*, December 8, 1921; L. Arbizzani, "L'Avvento," p. 272.

[98] Idomeneo Barbadoro, *Storia del sindacalismo dalla nascita al fascismo*, Vol. I, *La Federterra* (Florence, 1973), pp. 241-242.

for all parties concerned. As late as July 1921, a director of the consortium imformed the prefect that the Federterra's employment offices had "always functioned efficiently in the development of the work as well as in the settlement of disputes."[99]

Both the advancement of their political goals and the interest of their syndicates made it imperative that Bolognese and Ferrarese Fascists challenge the Socialist monopoly in the Renana project. Under the existing contract, the leagues were able to maintain control in important rural communes like Molinella and to resist successfully the fasci and agrarian employers. At the same time, Fascist syndicalists needed to gain access to jobs in the project in order to keep the allegiance of their own workers who were also suffering the effects of the agricultural recession. Consequently, in May 1921 the fasci on the borders of the two provinces began to demand that workers from the syndicates be hired directly, without going through the Socialist hiring halls, and set up a permanent armed guard around the project to encourage laborers "to enroll in the syndicates."[100] These local initiatives grew into a major campaign in the fall when spokesmen for some forty fasci and syndicates from Bologna and Ferrara formally requested that the Renana consortium recognize the Fascist employment office in Traghetto (Ferrara) and no longer make deductions from the workers' salaries to finance the Federterra's hiring halls, warning that otherwise they would "take actions that they considered necessary."[101]

In their campaign to eliminate the Socialist monopoly and gain control of the jobs on the project, the Fascists found a powerful ally in the board of directors of the Renana consortium. Since the project was managed and partially financed by a group of local landowners and businessmen, the members of the board represented the cream of the Bolognese and Ferrarese agrarian elites.[102]

[99] ASB, C6 F2, Pasini to Prefect, July 1, 1921. On the contract between the Renana and the Federterra, see *RdC*, September 25, 1921.

[100] *RdC*, August 7, 1921.

[101] *Ibid.*, September 20, 1921.

[102] ASB, C6 F2, 3, "Personale del Consorzio della Bonifica Renana," 1922. Board

A combination of political sympathies and economic interests shaped the ostensibly neutral policies taken by the board in the dispute, as the police chief made clear in a report to the prefect:

> The board of directors, which is composed in large part of Fascists and Fascist sympathizers, would quite happily agree to the demand of the syndicates. . . . In fact Brunetti has declared that the consortium does not intend to enter into the merits of the dispute and will pay whoever loads and unloads the materials. From this it is easy to anticipate a simple agreement between it and the syndicate; an agreement designed to put the Socialist organizations in an inferior position. . . . The consortium, while not being directly involved and not compromising itself, will obtain its goal of replacing the Socialist laborers with those of the syndicates and then will be in the position of declaring the old contract null and void.[103]

The minutes of one board meeting in early October revealed the intention of the directors to extend the hiring practices they had used on their own farms to the project itself. During the meeting, Count Venturoli-Mattei argued that the large numbers of workers who had always found employment in the project could not "be excluded from the jobs or in any way harassed . . . solely because they no longer belong to the Socialist organizations." On the contrary, he insisted that the board must take account of "the concrete new conditions of local manual labor" and reevaluate its established hiring policies to see "if it might be appropriate to cancel the agreement signed when all the laborers were enrolled in one single organization in order to assure the participation in the project of all laborers who seek employment." After analogous observations by other directors, the board adopted the position that "it would be unjust to deny the new labor organizations of the fasci the same right that in the past have been conceded to the

---

members included Ignazio Benelli, Ubaldo Monari, Count Francesco Cavazza, Roberto Cremonini, Count Isolani, Agostino Ramponi, Count Mario Venturoli-Mattei and Ugo Bernaroli.

[103] ASB, C7 F1, Police Chief to Prefect, December 15, 1921.

Socialist leagues."[104] On the basis of such arguments, the chairman of the board, Ignazio Benelli, announced a new set of hiring procedures in January 1922 which he claimed would eliminate "partisanship and political bias," by allowing each organization to select representatives who would determine the distribution of available jobs.[105]

Once the Federterra's exclusive contract had been broken, it became relatively easy for the consortium to favor the syndicates. Indeed, not only did the directors refuse to recognize the government commissioner, sent to arrange a fair distribution of the labor, but they gave covert support to a Fascist strike early in 1922 by providing the armed squads with the keys to the project.[106] By the midspring, it had become patently evident to both the Federterra and the prefect that the board of the Renana project was deliberately seeking to break the Socialist organizations. The charges of the Federterra that the consortium was making "employment in the project an instrument of repression" found confirmation in the reports of the prefect who observed that the board "in evident agreement with agrarians and Fascists, has done everything possible . . . to encourage the clandestine importation of the syndicates' laborers into the project."[107] Nonetheless, the leagues could do little more than protest these practices, since any stronger action such as a strike would have allowed the consortium to sever all ties with the Federterra and fill its job quota with laborers from the syndicates.[108]

The weaknesses and inefficacy of the leagues' protests against the Renana consortium only reflected the more general plight of the Socialists in 1921 and 1922. Much as in Ferrara, the impossibility of combating the Fascist squads on their own terrain of

[104] ASB, C6 F1, 3 (1922) Minutes of board meeting of October 10, 1921.

[105] ASB, C6 F2, 3, Ignazio Benelli to syndical chambers of labor in Bologna and Ferrara, January 3, 1922.

[106] ASB, C6 F2, 3, Federterra to Prefect, March 9, 1921. See also, P. Corner, *Fascism in Ferrara*, p. 212.

[107] See ASB, C6 F2, 1, Prefect to Ministry of Interior, March 26, 1922.

[108] P. Corner, *Fascism in Ferrara*, p. 213.

violence led Bolognese leaders to pursue a policy of passive resistance to the punitive expeditions, lockouts, and new unions. The overwhelming majority of league leaders followed the lead set by Giuseppe Massarenti and his organizations in Molinella. After the first expeditions of blackshirts into the commune in March 1921, Massarenti and his colleages approved a resolution, affirming the principle that the working class "must not descend, whatever the costs and sacrifices, to the level of individual violence and bloody factional struggles that would mark the failure of any civilized society and the ruin of the country."[109] Noble as these sentiments were, they offered Socialist cadre and sympathizers little comfort or protection from the Fascist campaign of terror and destruction. Some laborers, in the absence of strong leadership from their bosses, made isolated and sporadic attempts to mount an armed resistance to the Fascists. In the commune of Budrio, for instance, *arditi del popolo* were formed in the fall of 1921, but after a violent clash with the squads in early September, in which one blackshirt was killed, the police immediately arrested thirty-two *arditi* and broke up the nascent resistance movement.[110] Such cases, however, were rare and the mass of the workers in the leagues obeyed the strategy of passive resistance at a terrible cost to themselves and their organizations. At the end of 1921, the Bolognese Chamber of Labor summarized the material and human costs of Fascist violence. In addition to the destruction of social clubs, chambers of labor, cooperatives, and league offices, 557 laborers had been arrested, 1,936 injured by guns and clubs, and 19 killed.[111]

The unimpeded violence of the Fascists, the passivity of the leagues, and economic deprivation led inexorably to demoralization and defeatism within the ranks of the Socialists. While it is impossible to measure in precise terms the extent of the Federterra's

[109] See L. Arbizzani, "L'Avvento," p. 261; for a comparable situation in the neighboring province, see P. Corner, *Fascism in Ferrara*, pp. 142-143.

[110] *RdC*, September 7, 1921; G. Chiurco, *Rivoluzione fascista*, vol. III, p. 514. On the hostile attitude taken by both the Socialist and Communist parties toward the Arditi del popolo, see A. Tasca, *The Rise of Italian Fascism*, pp. 156-157.

[111] See L. Arbizzani, "Lotte agrarie," p. 331.

defeat, local police and press reports in the fall of 1921 showed that the agrarian Fascists and their syndicates had made substantial headway even in communes of the plain where the league leaders had ruled for decades. In September *Il Resto del Carlino* announced that the league of Budrio, with over one thousand members, voted to leave the Socialist Chamber of Labor and reconstitute itself as a syndicate. Similarly, the following month, the subprefect reported that in Medicina "the passage of the laborers from the Socialist organizations was continuing."[112] The territorial concentration of squad activities in the late spring of 1922 provided additional evidence of Fascist success in the Bolognese countryside. In contrast to the previous year when reports of Fascist violence came from all over the province, in 1922 punitive expeditions were for the most part limited to the communes of Molinella and Medicina, the last two strongholds of the red leagues.

With the beginning of the major agricultural work in May, the agrarian Fascists mobilized their squads and syndicates in Bologna and Ferrara for a second and more massive offensive against the leagues of Molinella and Medicina. Already in the middle of that month, the police warned the prefect of plans for "a large-scale importation of manual laborers" into the two communes. As the police predicted, large blocs of Fascist laborers began to pour into these areas from other zones of the province and from Ferrara in June, while the squads visited local peasants and compelled them to sign written requests for hired hands from the syndicates.[113] The Molinellese agrarian association, headed by Giuseppe Magli, strongly supported the fasci, calling a "lockout against the Socialist manual laborers" and ordering its members to employ "only those enrolled in the national syndicates."[114] The completion of the har-

[112] *RdC*, September 18, 1921; ASB, C7 F1, Subprefect of Imola to Prefect, October 27, 1921.

[113] On the importation of Fascist laborers, see ASB, C6 F2, Police Chief to Prefect, May 13, 1922; ASB, C6 F2, 1, Prefect to Ministry of Labor, May 18, 1922; ASB, C7 F1, Prefect to Subprefects, June 24, 1922; ASB, C6 F2, 1, Federterra to Prefect, May 16, 1922.

[114] ASB, C7 F1, Resolution of Associazione Agricola di Molinella, August 20, 1922; *ibid.*, Police Chief to Prefect, August 22, 1922. The police chief characterized the lockout as "an act of repression," noting how "more than two hundred Socialist

vest did not lead to any relaxation of Fascist pressures. In mid-September the squads sacked and burned the headquarters of the municipal Socialist committee and the local employment office; a few weeks later the same fate befell the consumer and machine cooperatives and league leaders were given "forty-eight hours to leave town."[115]

The agrarian Fascist offensive in Molinella did not achieve its immediate objective of destroying the leagues in 1922. On the contrary, the red laborers of this commune held out against the fasci and commercial farmers until the mid-1920s.[116] Yet the heroic resistance of the Molinella leagues only underscored how complete the Socialist defeat and Fascist conquest were in the rest of the province. Despite their solid organization, discipline, and the intense loyalty of their rank-and-file that contrasted sharply with the Ferrarese red unions, virtually all the Bolognese leagues disintegrated under the impact of fascism's relentless war of attrition. Apart from memories, little remained of the great edifice, constructed by the Socialists in Bologna, at the end of the summer of 1922.

4. *The New State Within the State*

From the earliest punitive expeditions in various cities and towns of the Po Valley in the fall of 1920, provincial fascism had developed not only as an extreme reaction to the Socialist movement, but also as a revolt against the liberal state that local propertied elites were no longer prepared to entrust with the maintenance of law and order or the defense of their interests. As Dino Grandi proclaimed early in January 1921, the Fascists "in the face of a servile, cowardly state authority, rotten to the core, are rising to their feet with arms in hand in order to create a new authority

laborers have been fired . . . and replaced by day laborers of the syndicates of Molinella and surrounding communes."

[115] See *RdC*, October 14, 1922.

[116] See A. Colombi, *Pagine di storia del movimento operaio* (Rome, 1951), pp. 212-213.

and a new discipline; in order to create a NEW STATE."[117] Initially, however, fascism's antisocialist thrust obscured the extent to which its illegality and violence represented a challenge to state authorities. In the winter of 1920-21, parliamentary considerations and the desire to teach the Socialists a lesson encouraged Giolitti's government to tolerate the movement's excesses, while on the provincial level prefects and police officials openly sympathized with the blackshirts' campaign against the hated Socialist bosses. For his part, Giolitti was confident that he could use the Fascists to soften the resistance of the PSI and the Popular party and then oversee the movement's disappearance or absorption into the parliamentary system.[118]

The first indications that the Fascist squads posed a direct threat to governmental authorities came at the end of January 1921. Alarmed by the rising level of violence in the Po Delta, Giolitti ordered his prefects in Bologna, Ferrara, and Modena to revoke all permits to bear arms and to ban temporarily any public rallies, meetings, or caravans. When the Bolognese prefect, Visconti, announced these measures on January 25, he triggered an immediate rebellion in his province. Within days, a revived Association of Social Defense attacked the prefectoral decrees as "illegal, unconstitutional, [and] revolutionary" and voted to oppose with all possible means the implementation of "such an insidious ordinance."[119] After analogous declarations by the APA, an *ad hoc* Committee of Action against Disarmament, composed of Bologna's most prominent citizens, visited the prefect to inform him of "the irremovable decision of all the patriotic, political, and economic associations to not hand over their arms."[120] Under these circumstances, the Bolognese fascio confidently proclaimed in early Feb-

[117] *L'Assalto*, January 8, 1921.

[118] See R. De Felice, *Mussolini il fascista*, Vol. I (Turin, 1966), pp. 50-86.

[119] *RdC*, January 28, 1921. For the text of the prefectoral decree, see *ibid.*, January 26, 1921.

[120] *Ibid.*, February 3, 1921. The committee included Frank de Morsier, Giuseppe Franchi, and Carlo Ballerini. On the resolution of the APA, see *Il Progresso*, January 30, 1921.

ruary its intention to resist violently any efforts by provincial officials to enforce the bans. Faced with the disobedience not only of the Fascists but of virtually all the local elites, Visconti capitulated. Although the decrees remained in effect, he did little to see that they were enforced in the province. Indeed, the following months saw a sharp rise in the number of Fascist expeditions and acts of terrorism.[121]

The inability of Visconti and his police chief to restore law and order in Bologna led Giolitti to replace them the second week of February with a more resolute prefect, Cesare Mori. Unlike his predecessor or most of his colleagues in other provinces, Mori displayed a real determination to control the action squads and reassert the authority of his office. The limited success he achieved in these endeavors was particularly significant, for it exposed not only the seriousness of the Fascists' challenge to the government, but also the extent to which the movement had eroded discipline and hierarchical controls within the state apparatus itself. Throughout the spring and summer of 1921, he repeatedly pressured the police commanders in the countryside to intensify their vigilance "in order to prevent [and] impede violence, assaults, damages, and to repress them when necessary with speed and energy."[122] To a certain degree, Mori's tough administration seemed to produce results. Statistics compiled by the Ministry of Interior in May revealed that more Fascists had been arrested or had outstanding warrants in Bologna than in any other province in the entire country.[123] But often Fascist protests, partisan judges, and the disobedience of his own subordinates neutralized the prefect's initiatives. After Arpinati's arrest in March on charges of murder, for instance, stormy demonstrations by blackshirts in the center of

[121] A. Tasca, *The Rise of Italian Fascism*, pp. 107-108; for the position of the fascio, see *RdC*, February 3, 1921.

[122] See for example, ASB, C7 F1, Prefect to Questore and Commanders, July 29, 1921. On Mori's appointment, see *RdC*, February 9, 1921.

[123] ACS, Ministero dell'Interno, Dir. Gen. P. S., 1925 B96 in R. De Felice, *Mussolini il fascista*, vol. I, pp. 35-39. During this period, eighty-four fascists had been arrested, forty had outstanding warrants.

Bologna resulted in his speedy release from jail. Even when magistrates were not subjected to such pressures, they tended to view Fascist illegality with a sympathy that sharply contrasted with their harsh treatment of Socialist offenders.[124] At the same time, Mori's own reports eloquently testified to the difficulties he encountered in attempting to eliminate fraternization between police and *squadristi* and to have his orders actually carried out on the local level. Nor did he find the prefects of other provinces any more cooperative than his own subordinates. When the government, in an attempt to curb the punitive expeditions, placed Mori in charge of the whole region of Emilia in the fall of 1921, he was unable to exercise any effective control over the squads because the other prefects failed to collaborate with him.[125] Mori's difficulties in 1921 paled, however, in comparison to the problems he encountered in his second year in the Bolognese prefecture.

By the spring of 1922, the fasci had largely defeated the Socialist leagues and replaced them as the *de facto* rulers of the province. Much as in Ferrara, the very success of the Fascist offensive against the Socialists unavoidably altered the terms of struggle in Bologna. Increasingly, the original battle against the "red tyranny" evolved into a clear confrontation between fascism and the authority of the state, the only force still capable of challenging the local dictatorships of the *ras*.[126] In this confrontation, two circumstances favored the Fascists: the extreme weakness of Facta's caretaker government in Rome that provided the prefect with little support and the growing tendency of the provincial *ras* to collaborate in huge mass mobilizations not only to destroy remaining Socialist strongholds, but also to intimidate or remove local government officials.[127] Already in January, after an incident in which police

[124] A. Tasca, *The Rise of Italian Fascism*, p. 108; G. Neppi Modona, *Sciopero, potere politico e magistratura*, pp. 250-263.

[125] P. Corner, *Fascism in Ferrara*, p. 205; on Mori's problems with his subordinates, see ASB, C7 F1, Ministry of Interior to Prefect, July 29, 1921; *ibid.*, Prefect to Questore and Commanders, July 29, 1921.

[126] P. Corner, *Fascism in Ferrara*, pp. 209-210.

[127] A. Lyttelton, *The Seizure of Power*, pp. 78-80.

had opened fire on a squad that was storming a chamber of labor, the Ferrarese boss Italo Balbo threatened to mobilize ten thousand armed Fascists, warning Mori: "What would happen if I were not to succeed in restraining the squads in their desire for reprisals."[128]

Mori's steadfast refusal to bend to Fascist pressures set the stage for an open, and what proved to be definitive, confrontation in the summer of 1922. In response to the serious unemployment and mounting danger of labor conflicts, the Facta government ordered the prefects of Bologna, Ferrara, and Modena late in May to prevent the Fascist syndicates from importing laborers into the lower plain and called upon Mori, in particular, to stop the movement of workers within his province that did not "correspond to the actual needs of the agricultural work." With his usual dispatch, Mori immediately issued an emergency decree, forbidding the transfer of outside laborers into the communes of Medicina, Molinella, Budrio, and Sesto Imolese.[129]

The agrarian Fascists of Emilia quickly seized upon the prefectoral decrees as a pretext for a campaign to force the removal of the detested prefect. While agrarian leaders ordered employers "not to tolerate the impositions" of Mori, the secretary of the National Fascist Party, Michele Bianchi, sent messages to the fasci of Ferrara and Modena, urging them to prepare a massive display in Bologna of "the most immediate and tangible fraternal solidarity of all the Fascists of the Po Valley."[130] Count Gualtiero Isolani, Lino Carrara, and other leading business and commercial figures showed their support of the fasci by informing the government of their intention "to break off all relations with the local prefectoral authority."[131] On May 29, squads from Bologna and surrounding provinces, under the leadership of Balbo, began to occupy the capital city and demand the transfer of Mori out of the province.

[128] I. Balbo, *Diario 1922* (Milan, 1932), p. 25, cited in P. Corner, *Fascism in Ferrara*, p. 215.

[129] ASB, C6 F2, 1, Ministry of Interior to Prefects, May 21, 1922. For the full text of the decree, see *ibid.*, May 22, 1922.

[130] *Ibid.*, proclamation of the FPSA, May 26, 1922; *RdC*, May 28, 1922.

[131] *RdC*, May 28, 1922.

By June 1, *Il Resto del Carlino* estimated that some fifty to sixty thousand blackshirts had descended upon the city and had been greeted enthusiastically by local commercial farmers, industrialists, merchants, and shopkeepers who called a general strike that closed all the stores and factories.[132] The following day Facta chose the path of least resistance: Mori was called to Rome for consultations and the commander of the Bolognese garrison arranged a truce with the Fascists. In the wake of the occupation, the prefect became an outcast and a virtual prisoner in his own headquarters, as a government inspector reported in early July:

> Mori is in a very difficult and painful situation. He is isolated, removed from any contact with the citizens, if one excepts a few conversations with Socialist or Popolari supporters; he cannot leave the prefectural palace and travel on the city streets since at the least he certainly would be insulted and booed. [The citizens] follow the will and the initiatives of the Fascists entirely; hence among the class of businessmen, industrialists, and the bourgeoisie in general, including the 'better society' of Bologna, no one intends to maintain any relations with Mori; no one ascends the steps of the prefecture.[133]

The government finally gave in to the provincial elites and the fasci in August and transferred Mori to Apulia, a move that, in the words of Balbo, "crowned victoriously the battle of Bologna."[134]

Because of Mori's reputation and the central importance of the province, his difficulties and ultimate removal attracted national attention. For in removing its most able and resolute prefect, the government had given dramatic proof that fascism, and not the

[132] *Ibid.*, June 2, 1922.

[133] ACS, Ministero dell'Interno Dir. Gen. P. S., B43, F "Bologna," SF "Agitazione contro fisco," prefectural report of July 20, 1922 cited in C. Maier, *Recasting Bourgeois Europe*, p. 320.

[134] See L. Arbizzani, "L'Avvento," pp. 273-274; A. Lyttelton, *The Seizure of Power*, p. 80.

state, was the real ruler in a large part of Italy.[135] Locally, the fall of Mori cleared away the last major obstacle to the fasci's unchallenged control in the province. The new prefect, Aphel placed himself more or less at the disposal of the Fascist leaders who were now able to wield enormous power within the borders of Bologna. Reporting to the Ministry of Interior in September 1922, Aphel provided a graphic picture of the movement's strength. According to the prefect, the Provincial Fascist Federation commanded some one hundred fasci, one for each commune and in some communes one for every hamlet. The total membership at the time was approximately twenty thousand, half of whom belong to the action squads. Buttressing this political organization was a network of Fascist syndicates that controlled nearly eighty thousand workers, peasants, employees, and technicians. Apart from their own organizational strength, the prefect claimed that the *ras* could count on a climate of public opinion that was "favorably disposed toward the Fascist movement."[136] Thus months before the much-publicized March on Rome, Bolognese fascism had already supplanted the liberal state as the effective authority on the provincial level, a situation that received official recognition with Mussolini's ascension to the prime minister's office in October.

The municipal elections in the winter of 1922-23 appeared to confirm the prefect's claims. The general trend in voting became apparent in early December, when the subprefect of Castel San Pietro reported that in his district all the constitutional parties and employer associations had united behind the local fascio, which as a consequence "obtained a magnificent victory."[137] In the ensuing weeks, electoral returns from the former Socialist strongholds in the plain, from the district of Imola, and from the mountainous communes of Vergato all told the same story: the triumph of Fascist slates, often with 70 to 80 percent of the vote. When the

[135] C. Seton-Watson, *Italy from Liberalism*, p. 606; A. Lyttelton, *The Seizure of Power*, p. 80. On the national attention drawn to Bologna, see for instance *Il Corriere della Sera*, June 2, 1922.

[136] ASB, C7 F1, P. P., Prefect to Ministry of Interior, September 28, 1922.

[137] ASB, C5 F1, Subprefect to Prefect, December 12, 1922.

final results had been tallied, Fascist municipal governments controlled fifty-five communes, while in the remainder the party dominated coalitions with Liberal and Catholic elements.[138]

The very success of the Bolognese Fascists in destroying the Socialist movement and challenging the authority of the state, however, created in turn a host of new problems. For provincial fascism, whether in Bologna or other provinces of the Po Valley, had achieved its extraordinary unity primarily in its struggle against the Socialists rather than through a program of shared political and economic aspirations. As a result, victory over the external enemy removed the main source of cohesiveness at the same time that it forced the fasci to make creative policy choices that were bound to expose the profound conflicts of interest within the heterogeneous movement. Beginning with the first Fascist conquests on the local level in the fall of 1921, increasingly bitter internal rivalries and power struggles went hand in hand with each victory over the leagues.

[138] For electoral results see: in Imola, *ibid.*, December 21, 1922; in the plains, *ibid.*, Prefect to Ministry of Interior, January 14, 1923, *ibid.*, Police Chief to Prefect, January 22, 1923; in Vergato, ASB, C7 F1, Subprefect to Prefect, December 11, 1923. For general results, see ASB, C4 F1, Prefect to Mussolini, July 27, 1923.

IX. FROM MOVEMENT TO REGIME: BOLOGNESE FASCISM, 1921-1926

Most historians, in studying the rapid growth of agrarian fascism, have focused primarily on its dramatic initial phase of terroristic reaction. Comparatively little attention has been given to the more prosaic but perhaps equally important second phase of Fascist institutional consolidation in the countryside.[1] The transition from movement to regime proved to be a prolonged and arduous process that required the resolution or repression of bitter political rivalries and profound social conflicts within fascism. For agrarian interests in particular, the creation of a stable new power structure in the former red provinces involved four separate but interrelated tasks: the establishment of organizational control over the agricultural sector, the regimentation of labor, the domesti-

[1] For examples of this circumscribed treatment of agrarian fascism, see Luigi Salvatorelli and Giovanni Mira, *Storia d'Italia nel periodo fascista* (Turin, 1964), pp. 166-175; Renzo De Felice, *Mussolini, il fascista*, Vol. I (Turin, 1966), pp. 3-100; Angelo Tasca, *The Rise of Italian Fascism* (New York, 1966), pp. 82-130. A significant exception to this trend is Adrian Lyttelton, *The Seizure of Power: Fascism in Italy, 1919-1929* (New York, 1973), which provides a brief and fragmented, but highly insightful analysis of Fascist consolidation in the countryside. Though concerned with provincial fascism rather than the agrarians, per se, Paul Corner, *Fascism in Ferrara, 1915-1925* (London, 1975) and Simona Colarizi, *Dopoguerra e fascismo in Puglia, 1919-1926* (Bari, 1971) also pursue developments after the phase of violent reaction.

cation of Fascist syndicalism, and finally the development of secure channels of political influence, both locally and in Rome.

Fascist terror and coercion left a number of problems unresolved. Many of these problems stemmed from the movement's original success in forging a broad coalition of divergent political and social groups. From its inception, provincial fascism in the Po Valley had developed chiefly as a movement of opposition, first to the Socialists and subsequently to the authority of the liberal state. The movement's appeal was essentially negative, resting upon a convergence, rather than an identity, of interests among the local propertied classes, peasant proprietors, urban commercial elements, students, and war veterans, who for different reasons were prepared to collaborate in the destruction of the Socialist "baronies." As long as the red leagues remained strong, the immediate demands of the struggle necessitated a degree of solidarity that obscured the lack of common goals and aspirations. With the defeat of the Socialists, however, this unifying concern with battle plans gave way to the far more divisive issue of what direction the victorious fasci would now take.

The violence of the squads had largely destroyed the organizations of the Socialist labor movement, but it had not eliminated the structural roots of class conflict in the countryside. Demographic pressures, seasonal unemployment, and the special working and living conditions in the plains, which had fueled labor discontent and militancy in the past, all persisted. In the absence of the leagues, these problems reemerged in the form of growing tensions and conflicts between agrarian employers and the Fascist labor syndicates over hiring practices, wage schedules, and work hours. While landowners and leaseholders had strongly supported the syndicates as weapons in the battle against the leagues, their support had always been conditional. Once fascism had broken the Socialist "monopoly" of organized labor, they had little incentive to favor or protect the workers in the syndicates, who in any case no longer constituted a small and easily employable portion of the labor force. On the contrary, it was often in the short term interest of the employers to maintain competition between the weakened leagues and the Fascist syndicates, since in this way they could virtually dictate the terms of employment on their farms. Such practices aroused the alarm and anger of Fascist syndicalists whose organizations were to a large extent held together by the promise of preferential hiring. The reluctance of growers to implement labor contracts or fulfill hiring quotas not only weakened the syndicalists' control over the workers, but also directly endangered their recently acquired positions of power within the movement. As early as the fall of 1921, they began to put mounting pressures on the employers to hire all the laborers in the syndicates, pressures that naturally led to increasing resistance from the employers.[2]

In the province of Bologna, the struggle between the agrarians and the labor syndicates was conditioned by rivalries for power and prestige both on the municipal level and within the Provincial Fascist Federation. Despite the authoritarian and hierarchical structure of the federation, effective power was highly fragmented. In contrast to developments in many of the small provinces, no single leader had succeeded in imposing his authority on the entire Bolognese Fascist movement prior to the March on Rome.[3] Apart from the local roots of the fasci themselves, the size of the province, its strong traditions of municipal particularism, and its political and economic heterogeneity all contributed to the growth of various competing centers of power. Gino Baroncini, patron of the syndicates and leader of the rural fasci, appeared to be the most influential *ras*, but his power remained circumscribed by Leandro Arpinati, who continued to control the huge urban fascio, and by Dino Grandi, with his independent base of support in Imola, his immense personal prestige, and his national prominence. At the same time, these provincial leaders had to recognize the autonomous influence of certain squad commanders who exercised virtually unchecked power in their respective communes. As in many other provinces, the struggle for political power in Bologna gave

[2] See A. Lyttelton, *The Seizure of Power*, pp. 218-219.
[3] *Ibid.*, p. 168.

all relations an extraordinary and confusing fluidity; allies in one dispute became adversaries when other issues arose in the unstable and rapidly changing local and national settings.

The evolution of relations between agrarians, workers, syndicalists, and *ras* at the provincial level was conditioned in turn by the political and economic choices made by Mussolini and the Fascist government in Rome. Significantly, the presence of fascism in the government after October 1922 intensified local power struggles. As prime minister rather than head of an opposition party, the Duce confronted a host of new pressures from political allies and powerful economic groups that often clashed with the aspirations of hardliners and syndicalist elements within the PNF. The consolidation of his personal power and the preservation of parliamentary support for his coalition government made it imperative that Mussolini curb the excesses of his blackshirted followers and reestablish law and order in the country. The restoration of state authority, however, ran counter to the aims of the provincial Fascist bosses and *squadristi* who had a vested interest in maintaining the climate of violence and illegality that legitimized their positions and activities. Mussolini could not ignore Fascist dissidents or take drastic action to reduce the power of the *ras,* since in the multiparty system that remained after the March on Rome his own political power still depended upon the support of the PNF cadre and rank and file. As a result, in the period from 1923 to 1925, he charted a zig-zag course between the opposing groups and interests, both within and outside of fascism, a course that kept his options open but increased confusion and instability at the provincial level. Anxious to defend acquired positions and to gain leverage in Rome, Fascist bosses moved to tighten their hold on local power bases by attacking and, if possible, eliminating rival factions within the movement.[4]

Agrarian interests in Bologna and the Po Valley had to learn to

[4] A. Lyttelton, "Fascism in Italy: The Second Wave" in Walter Laqueur and George L. Mosse, ed., *International Fascism 1920-1945* (New York, 1966), pp. 76-78.

navigate in the turbulent waters of Fascist politics. The economic pressures of the syndicates, the political ambitions of insecure Fascist bosses, and the restless activism of the squads all represented potential threats that required continued agrarian intervention. The formulation of unified responses to these threats was complicated by the reemergence of divisions within the propertied classes themselves. As soon as the specter of "red tyranny" had dissipated, the antisocialist consensus of the agrarians began to break down into sectoral and factional disputes over labor policies, economic programs, and relations with fascism. The gradual consolidation of a new structure of agrarian political influence and economic power in the years between 1921 and 1927 thus involved not only the containment of rival forces within the Fascist movement, but also the resolution or repression of conflicts within the propertied classes.

1. *Beyond Reaction: The Drive for Control of the Agricultural Sector, 1921-1926*

With the destruction of the red leagues and the emergence of fascism as a major new force in the provinces and on the national political scene, agrarian interests throughout northern and central Italy began to seek ways of strengthening and institutionalizing the sizeable influence they had gained within the movement during the antisocialist reaction. By the March on Rome, three distinct strategies had been developed to achieve this objective. In provinces like Reggio Emilia and Parma, where the old farmers' associations remained the main centers of local economic power, agrarian leaders preferred to retain organizational independence from the fasci and relied primarily on their own resources as well as their close ties to banks and marketing consortia to condition Fascist policies and counterbalance the influence of the syndicates and troublesome *ras*. Already in the summer of 1921, spokesmen for the Provincial Chamber of Agriculture in Reggio Emilia were advocating a sharp division of labor between the agrarian associations and the fasci, with the former taking charge of economic affairs while the latter concentrated on strictly political matters.[5]

The General Confederation of Agriculture (CGA) pursued a similar strategy on the national level, seeking to exploit the favorable conditions created by the Fascist offensive to advance sectoral interests of the landowners and bolster its own power and influence. Although the confederation applauded the "healthy" reaction of the blackshirts against the Socialist and Catholic unions, its leaders were careful not to identify fully their corporative and professional concerns with such an unstable and equivocal political movement as fascism. Rather they maintained policies of external and selective collaboration with the fasci that were designed to allow for maximum influence without tying the agrarian associations to party discipline or to the uncertain fortunes of the movement. Above all, the CGA refused to entrust the Fascists with any formal or exclusive responsibilities for agrarian political representation. Precisely when the terrorist offensive of the squads was gaining momentum in the spring of 1921, the confederation sponsored the Agrarian Group in the Chamber of Deputies as its own direct parliamentary agency and began to promote the idea of a national agrarian party to unite all classes involved in agricultural production, independently from the Fascist movement.[6]

A different strategy was pursued in the provinces of Ferrara, Piacenza, Forli, Ravenna, and Padua where the old agrarian associations withdrew from the CGA and gradually merged with the local Fascist federations in a way that enabled them to preserve both their organizational structure and the dominant position of their leaders. This strategy found its clearest expression in Ferrara. Here the agrarian association merely changed its name in January 1923 and relied on its privileged relationship with Italo Balbo to

[5] See the article, "Agricoltori e fascismo" by Ennio Muratori in *Il Progresso*, May 31, 1921. For the situation in Reggio Emilia and Parma, see Rolando Cavandoli, *Le origini del fascismo a Reggio Emilia 1919-1923* (Rome, 1972), pp. 149-155, and A. Lyttelton, *The Seizure of Power*, p. 225.

[6] For the CGA and the partito agrario, see *Il Giornale Agrario*, January 9, April 2, November 19, and December 11, 1921.

maintain separate squads, ignore labor contracts, and dominate the Fascist labor syndicates, which became little more than instruments for the control and regimentation of the agricultural workers.[7]

In the province of Bologna, however, the near total organizational disarray of the agrarians and the absence of a single dominant Fascist boss precluded the implementation of either of these strategies. The humiliating capitulation of the Provincial Association of Agriculturalists (APA) in the fall of 1920 and the subsequent exodus of its membership meant that there was no agrarian association in the province with the authority to exert external pressure on the fasci. At the same time, the fragmentation of power within the Bolognese Fascist Federation prevented growers from establishing any exclusive alliance comparable to the one between Balbo and Vico Mantovani, the agrarian leader in Ferrara. Consequently, local agrarians confronted much earlier than elsewhere the problem of their longterm relationship with fascism and were forced to develop their own distinctive organizational strategy. Representing a blend of immediate imperatives and long range objectives, this Bolognese strategy not only shaped the course of agrarian-Fascist relations in the province, but it also was to have a major impact on the development of agrarian interest-group politics in the Po Valley and in Rome.

Initially, the weakness of the APA proved advantageous to agrarian interests and the Fascist, for it facilitated the assault on the Calda-Paglia agreements of 1920 and freed growers to arrange informal alliances with the fasci at the local level. But by the fall of 1921, the lack of an effective employers' organization was becoming more of a liability than an asset for both parties, especially in those areas where the Fascist labor syndicates had achieved their greatest successes. As membership in the syndicates grew, Fascist leaders came under mounting pressure from their rank and file to fulfill their pledge of steady employment and to enforce the new labor contracts. In the absence of a disciplined agrarian association, their efforts met with little cooperation from the landowners and

[7] See P. Corner, *Fascism in Ferrara*, pp. 192-195, 242, 243.

leaseholders, who exploited the renewed competition for jobs to ignore all contractual agreements, reduce wages, and lengthen work hours.[8] By the spring of 1922, the problem of "agrarian egotism" was a source of growing concern to Fascist syndicalists, who warned that the disorganization of the employers and the wage cuts could provoke "a desperate reaction from the working classes and even from those elements in the syndicates."[9] Developments in the number of communes seemed to justify their alarm. In Castelfranco, for instance, police reported that the laborers who had enrolled in the Fascist unions were "now returning to the Socialist leagues because of the failure of the syndicates to provide employment," while another police report from Crevalcore noted that the Socialists had "reorganized . . . [and] consequently the Fascist syndicate had been disbanded."[10]

Despite the immediate economic benefits they derived from this situation, the more astute commercial farmers began to find that the weakness of the APA was jeopardizing their longterm interests by prolonging instability in the countryside and by endangering their privileged relationship with the fasci. In particular, they recognized that, even with their sons and stewards holding key positions within the movement, the lack of a strong organization prevented any systematic interest representation and left individual farmers vulnerable to pressures from the syndicates and Fascist bosses. Their judgment appeared to find confirmation in the increasingly hostile rhetoric of Gino Baroncini. Although the leading rural *ras* had collaborated closely with agrarian employers in the destruction of the Socialist leagues, his own interests began to diverge from theirs in the fall of 1921. Baroncini saw the agrarians' unrestrained pursuit of profits as a menace to his own position of

[8] On agrarian labor practices in this period, see *RdC*, August 3, September 23, October 15, 1921; ASB, C7 F1, Police Chief to Prefect, October 13, 1921; ASB, C7 F1, Police Chief to Prefect, March 1, 1922.

[9] See ASB, C7 F1, Comizi, Police Chief to Prefect, April 13, 1922; on the matter of 'agrarian egotism' see *L'Assalto*, January 15, 1921 and A. Lyttelton, *The Seizure of Power*, p. 223.

[10] ASB, C7 F1, 2, Police Chief to Prefect, March 20 and April 20, 1922.

authority in the province, which rested upon his patronage and control of the mass movement organized in the syndicates. When the problem of unemployment in the syndicates became particularly acute in the winter, Baroncini went so far as to threaten the employers, warning landowners "who have not fulfilled their duties to our laborers that, if the '*santo manganello*' was good for the league leaders, it could be even better for them."[11]

In order to eliminate "the state of disorganization in which the employers find themselves," two young agrarian Fascists, Gino Cacciari and Julo Fornaciari, set up committees of landowners and leaseholders in the winter of 1921-22 to negotiate directly with the Fascist labor syndicates. By the beginning of March, the committees were functioning in nine of the major communes of the plains. Encouraged by their initial success, Cacciari and Fornaciari transformed the committees that month into official Fascist "Agrarian Syndicates" under the direction of a Provincial Federation of Farmers' Syndicates (FPSA).[12] Their initiative received strong backing from both Baroncini and the Fascist union organizers. For Baroncini, the agrarian syndicates appeared as an ideal instrument to curb the independence of the employers and to assert his control over them, since once they had been brought into the Fascist organizational structure, they would be subject, at least in theory, to the discipline of the Provincial Fascist Federation. The syndicalists looked to the new organizations to provide disciplined compliance with the labor contract that they had already had to impose on their own rank and file.[13]

[11] *L'Assalto*, November 26, 1921. Earlier in the fall, Baroncini wrote: "It is undeniable that many agrarians . . . are deluded by the false belief . . . that we might be the jealous custodians of the present social order and are disposed to support them in any struggle in defense of their selfish interests. These gentlemen, if they have not yet learned, will have to learn very quickly. The economic situation in the country this winter will require sacrifices from everyone and therefore also from the agrarians." *ibid.*, October 12, 1921.

[12] On the origins of the FPSA, see ASB, C7 F1, Prefectoral Commissioner to Prefect, December 12, 1921; *L'Assalto*, February 11, 1922; *Il Giornale Agrario*, March 12, 1922; Giovanni Pesce, *La marcia dei rurali* (Rome, 1929), p. 120.

[13] See *L'Assalto*, April 15, 1922, and A. Lyttelton, *The Seizure of Power*, p. 222.

The agrarian syndicates, however, were not simply an attempt by the Fascists "to subject all interest groups to a process of totalitarian coordination" as some historians have suggested.[14] On the contrary, both in its leadership and program, the FPSA reflected the dominant influence of large commercial farming interests in alliance with a new generation of agricultural technicians. While its two founders were relatively new faces on the provincial scene, neither was hostile or alien to the inner circles of the Bolognese elite. Cacciari came from an agrarian family in Medicina and was an agricultural technician with a degree in agronomy from the University of Bologna; Fornaciari had been the head of the APA branch office in Bazzano and was already emerging as an important spokesman for the local sugar beet growers by 1921.[15] Moreover, behind these "new men" stood some of the most influential commercial farmers in the province. Count Gualtiero Isolani, caretaker president of the APA, Raffaele Stagni, prewar leader of the militant Bolognese Agrarian Association, Alfredo Benni, Augusto Lenzi, and Francesco Neri—to mention only the most prominent figures—were all charter members of the FPSA and quickly assumed important positions within its organizational network.[16]

The program of the agrarian syndicates responded to immediate political imperatives as well as to the long-range interests of the

[14] *Ibid.*, p. 221. Likewise, Ferdinando Cordova, *Le origini dei sindacati fascisti 1918-1926* (Bari, 1974) argues that the agrarian syndicates came largely as a result of initiatives taken by Edmondo Rossoni to extend his control over agrarian employers. See pp. 132-133.

[15] On the backgrounds of Cacciari and Fornaciari, see G. Pesce, *Marcia dei rurali*, pp. 114-115; A. Lyttelton, *The Seizure of Power*, p. 476; for Fornaciari's role in the APA, see ASB, C16 F1, Julo Fornaciari to Prefect, April 30, 1920. On his role as an organizer of sugar beet growers, see his article, "La Federazione nazionale bieticultori" in *L'Italia Agricola*, March 1932, pp. 235-236.

[16] See *Il Giornale Agrario*, March 12, 1922 for leaders of the FPSA. The smooth transfer of power from the old association to the federation indicated that the agrarian syndicates were not imposed upon the major growers. In mid-September, Count Isolani, whom the Fascist press praised as "a man of clear intellect and strong will whom the farmers know and love," officially disbanded the APA, claiming that the problems of the Bolognese agrarians had been "happily resolved" with the founding of the FPSA. See *Il Giornale Agrario*, September 21, 1922 and *L'Assalto*, October 14, 1923.

big commercial growers. In the short run, the FPSA provided a much needed organizational presence within the Provincial Fascist Federation to counterbalance the labor syndicates and insure that they did not impose measures which infringed upon managerial prerogatives or profits. Cacciari strongly advocated an alliance of all rural producers "to stimulate the greatest possible production by harmonizing and mobilizing all the forces that take part in it," a position that appeared to coincide with Baroncini's own plans for "integral syndicalism" or the creation of corporations in which employers and laborers were represented on an equal basis.[17] Cacciari also moved to eliminate one of the main concerns of provincial Fascist leaders by promising that the FPSA would guarantee the application of all labor agreements, sharecropping contracts, and wage rates that it negotiated with the labor syndicates.[18] Subsequent developments would show that the agrarian syndicates interpreted the ideas of class collaboration and productivism in a somewhat different manner than Baroncini and the Fascist labor organizers. But in the period prior to the March on Rome, these differences were concealed by the more pressing need to establish the FPSA in the province.

At the same time, the agrarian syndicates allowed a small group of commercial growers to use the coercive might of fascism to extend their control over the mass of small and medium landowners and peasant farmers. Cacciari openly affirmed the intention of his federation to "unite in the same syndicate landowning farmers, absentee landlords, leaseholders, peasant cultivators, and sharecroppers." Playing down the contrasting needs and interests of these groups, he stressed their common concern with the efficient operation of their farms, which in his view was "a technical problem that must be solved by technicians" who had to be left "to work in peace."[19] Despite their ostensibly neutral technocratic

[17] See the Statute of the FPSA, Article II, published in *Il Giornale Agrario,* August 6, 1922; on Baroncini and integral syndicalism, see A. Lyttelton, *The Seizure of Power,* pp. 221-222; F. Cordova, *Le origini dei sindacati,* pp. 132-133.

[18] *Il Giornale Agrario,* June 25, 1922, interview with Cacciari.

[19] *Ibid.*

rhetoric, the leaders of the FPSA conceived it essentially as an agency for the expansion of capitalist agriculture in the province. Through participation in the agrarian syndicates, all rural producers were to be integrated into a network of economic institutions in which the large commercial farmers were heavily involved: rural banks, machine-leasing businesses, insurance companies, and refining and processing industries. In this fashion, the FPSA aimed to blend the political imperatives of fascism with the economic interests of its promoters by encouraging the rise of small proprietors locally while insuring the enhanced control of the large growers at the level of supplying and marketing.[20]

As its leadership and program suggest, the FPSA marked a new stage in the longterm shift of power within the Bolognese elite, away from the traditional agrarian leadership toward a younger group of commercial farmers with close ties to the rural banks and marketing consortia. The agrarian syndicates claimed to speak for a "new elite of farmers" who stood at the pinnacle of the fascist "hierarchy of merit and expertise." Without mentioning any names, their spokesmen boasted how "the liberals who used to direct the agrarian association were increasingly isolated . . . and deprived of the authority and personal influence their offices and social position had previously assured them."[21] In fact, the old guard of absentee landlords, who had founded the first employers' associations, headed the liberal clubs, and served as the mayors and deputies in Bologna for decades, were distinguished by their absence from the ruling council of the FPSA. Notables like Marchese Giuseppe Tanari, Count Francesco Cavazza, and Enrico Pini continued to be treated with respect, but they appear to have played at best only a marginal role in the agrarian syndicates.

Initially, the FPSA did not receive an enthusiastic reception from all segments of the propertied classes in the province. The fragmentary evidence available precludes any precise or systematic profile of the agrarians who resisted or opposed the syndicates.

[20] *Ibid.*, August 6, 1922.

[21] G. Pesce, *Marcia dei rurali*, p. 106, 127, 134.

For the most part, Fascist leaders spoke in vague terms of "old, retrograde, or apathetic landowners" who considered "private property an hereditary privilege . . . [and] their wealth a right that has no duties."[22] The few recalcitrant agrarians specifically mentioned by name in *L'Assalto* or prefectoral reports were medium-scale landowners, with holdings that ranged from 48 to 156 hectares, or else minor aristocrats like Marchese del Turco of Imola who refused to recognize any hiring quotas and arbitrarily reduced wages. In certain areas, the FPSA's plans for heavy capital investments and large-scale land reclamation alarmed groups of small proprietors who sought refuge in the Popular party.[23] As a rule though, opposition to the agrarian syndicates did not assume an organized form and reflected less the idealism than the shortsighted individualism of the more old-fashioned landowners. Much like its predecessors, the FPSA had to overcome the "clear lack of interest and collective consciousness among the landowners."[24]

But unlike its predecessors, the FPSA had a new and more potent instrument to shake the landowners out of their apathy and indifference. Gino Baroncini and his squads proved to be the most persuasive recruiters for the syndicates. When the FPSA ran into

[22] *L'Assalto*, August 26, October 21, 1922.

[23] On the small proprietors and the Popular party, see ASB, C16 F1, Subprefect to Prefect, November 21, 1921; for the names of uncooperative landowners, see *L'Assalto*, April 20, 1922 and ASB C7 F1, 3, Subprefect to Prefect, May 10, 1922. Information on their property holdings is from the Catasto dei Terreni. Registro delle partite, 1924-25 in the Ufficio Tecnico Erariale di Bologna, communes of Budrio and Imola.

[24] *L'Assalto*, October 7, 1922, report of Aurelio Manaresi to the Provincial Fascist Federation. Only in the district of Imola did the FPSA encounter any organized opposition. Here, the ambitious agrarian leader Giacobbe Manzoni had succeeded in independently reorganizing the old employers' association after the strikes of 1920 and had used the Fascist offensive against the red leagues to bolster his personal power and influence. As president of the Chamber of Agriculture of Imola and the Provincial Taxpayers Union, he achieved a certain prominence in the spring of 1922 and managed to exert sizeable influence on the policies of the Imolese Fascists. In particular, he allegedly utilized the weapon of a tax boycott against the local fasci and labor syndicates "to dominate them [and] bring them into line with . . . the wishes and interests of the agrarians." See ASB, C6 F2, 1, Subprefect to Prefect, July 23, 1922 and *ibid.*, C16 F1, Subprefect to Prefect, September 21, 1922.

difficulties from landowners in Castelfranco, Casalecchio di Reno, and Budrio in the spring of 1922, Baroncini intervened, warning that "now is the time to use violence against all these bourgeois who are concerned only with their own interests; now is the time to react and react violently against all those who continue to view property as a hereditary privilege."[25] The agrarian syndicates took advantage of the squads' menacing presence to distribute circulars in the countryside that, in the view of the prefect, constituted "clear threats and intimidations." In those cases where warnings proved insufficient, the squads actually carried out a few punitive expeditions, the prefect reported, "against farmers who have not followed the directives of the fasci."[26]

With the support of the big commercial farmers, the political backing of the fasci, and the coercion of the squads, the FPSA had largely achieved its organizational objectives months before the March on Rome. At the end of August, Cacciari and Fornaciari claimed to have organized "the majority of farmers in the province" in fourteen syndicates, each with its own office and resident technician. That month they called upon the prefect to recognize their federation as the exclusive representative of the Bolognese

[25] *L'Assalto*, "Due cazzotti agli agrari," May 12, 1922.

[26] ASB, C7 F1, 4, Prefect to Police Chief, May 18, 1922. For a report on the beating of one landowner, Francesco Cesari of Budrio, see ASB, C7 F1, Police Chief to Prefect, October 12, 1922. Baroncini also played an important role in the defeat of Giacobbe Manzoni. Late in July, he launched a campaign against Manzoni, publicly attacking him for his failure to insure that his members "kept faith with their pledges and carried out their social duties" and denouncing him as "a man incapable of leading the agrarian organization of Imola with modern criteria." In quick succession, the Provincial Fascist Federation, the FPSA, and the labor syndicates withdrew their support from the League of Taxpayers, which soon ceased to play an important role in the province. Promoters of the agrarian syndicates proceeded to ally with Manzoni's rivals within the Chamber of Agriculture to force his resignation from the presidency in mid-September. Two months later, a newly elected council, headed by three big commercial farmers, transformed the chamber into an agrarian syndicate, entering "completely into the orbit of the Fascist movement." See *L'Assalto*, July 22, 1922; ASB, C6 F2, 1, Subprefect to Prefect, July 23, 1922; *Il Giornale Agrario*, August 25, September 2, 1922; ASB, C16 F1, Subprefect to Prefect, September 21, 1922.

agrarian employers. When the FPSA finally released its official membership figures a year later, they revealed a constituency of some 3,650 farmers who accounted for approximately 85 percent of the farm land in the province.[27]

After the March on Rome, Cacciari and Fornaciari immediately set out to implement their program of economic integration in the province. Beginning in the spring of 1923, the FPSA absorbed the existing commodity organizations of sugar beet and hemp growers, and founded new consortia for rice and tobacco farmers. Under the direction of the major farmers, these cartels attempted to unite all producers of a particular crop, negotiate collective agreements with their respective processing sectors, and control the quantity and quality of production in accordance with market conditions.[28] Not surprisingly, the sugar beet growers' consortium achieved the most immediate results, since it represented a comparatively small and cohesive group of highly capitalized farmers and already enjoyed the backing of a national federation.[29]

[27] ASB, C7 F1, FPSA to Prefect August 31, 1922; for membership statistics, see *RdC*, October 27, 1923 and ASB, C7 F1, 2, FPSA memorandum, no date 1923. The membership list of the agrarian syndicate for the district of Minerbio, the only one to find its way into the hands of the prefect in 1922, seemed to justify the FPSA's claims. Apart from ten large landowners and leaseholders who dominated the syndicate, the list also included 22 absentee landlords, 63 middle and small proprietors, and nearly 130 small tenant farmers. See ASB, C6 F2, "Elenco dei soci divisi per categoria" 1922.

[28] For the founding and development of the Fascist commodity associations in Bologna, see ASB, C16 F1, *Bollettino Sindacato degli Agricoltori di Bazzano*, no. 4, June 6, 1923; *RdC*, September 2, 1924; *L'Agricoltore d'Italia*, IV, no. 37, November 28, 1925. The board of directors of the sugar beet consortium included Fornaciari, Cacciari, and Giuseppe Magli; that of the hemp growers included Count Isolani, Francesco Neri, Bruno Caliceti, Cesare Bonora, Marcello Serrazanetti, Enrico Masetti, and Guido Gardi.

[29] In 1923 and 1924, the sugar beet growers consortium managed to win highly favorable contracts for its members. In addition it also played an active role in various projects for the "industrialization of local agriculture." In 1923, for example, it took the lead in promoting the construction of a sugar refinery in the commune of Molinella to stimulate production and reduce transportation costs. Despite opposition from factions within the municipal fascio, the project made rapid headway and with the support of the FPSA and the Bolognese prefecture, the

In its campaign to organize and regulate agricultural production and marketing at the provincial level, the FPSA received substantial assistance from the leading local bank, the Cassa di Risparmio. Headed by Count Isolani and a group of stockholders that included the most prominent farmers and industrialists, the bank took advantage of Fascist legislation and state funding in 1923 to greatly expand its activities in the countryside.[30] In collaboration with the commodity associations it helped finance, the Cassa di Risparmio funded the construction of silos for wheat, hemp, and rice growers, and provided special credit arrangements to aid in the pooling of crops and the purchasing of high yield seeds, agricultural machines, and chemical fertilizers.[31] Economic integration was further facilitated by the creation of provincial economic councils in 1925. Although the minister of the national economy, Giuseppe Belluzzo, viewed the councils as mechanisms for the transmission of central directives from Rome, the one in Bologna also served to advance the interests of local groups. An amalgam of the old agrarian council and the Chamber of Commerce, the Bolognese Provincial Economic Council provided an institutional setting in which industrial leaders like Frank De Morsier could meet agrarian spokes-

refinery began operations in the fall of the following year. Significantly, the new plant helped transform the zone around Molinella into the most important sugar beet area in the province, both in terms of yields and productivity, by the late 1920s. See *RdC*, February 27, 1923; *Bollettino Sindacato degli Agricoltori di Bazzano*, no. 10-11, November 23, 1923; *ibid.*, no. 2-3, March 28, 1924 for contracts. On the sugar refinery, see *RdC*, September 6, 1923; ASB, C6 F2, Gulinelli to Prefect, April 30, 1924; *ibid.*, C7 F1, 3, Royal Commissioner to Prefect, May 13, 1923; *ibid.*, C6 F2, Prefect to Mussolini, July 6, 1924; *ibid.*, C7 F1, 3, Fornaciari to Sindacato Molinella, December 22, 1924. For the importance of the refinery in the late 1920s, see J. Fornaciari, *Attività e problemi dell'organizzazione dei bieticultori* (Bologna, 1934), tables 1 and 4.

[30] See Cassa di Risparmio, *La Cassa di Risparmio in Bologna nei suoi primi cento anni* (Bologna, 1937), pp. 317-319 for list of directors and stockholders. On the role of Count Isolani and Enrico Masetti in particular, see Agostino Bignardi, *Costruttori di terra* (Bologna, 1958), pp. 20-21, 25-26.

[31] On the activities of the Cassa, see *Cassa di Risparmio*, pp. 253-261; A. Bignardi, *Costruttori di terra*, p. 25; Pier Paolo D'Attore, "Agrari e fascismo. La formazione del Regime reazionario di massa (Bologna negli anni venti)" (Tesi di Laurea, University of Bologna, 1976) pp. 50-51.

men such as Count Isolani and Julo Fornaciari to coordinate their activities and prepared joint commercial undertakings.[32]

Through a network of institutions that included the commodity associations, the Bolognese Agrarian Consortium, the Cassa di Risparmio, and the Provincial Economic Council, a relatively small group of commercial farmers, together with the leading industrial and banking interests of the city, were able to extend their control over agricultural activity during a period when the division of many large estates and the growth of small property holdings would have seemingly favored the fragmentation of economic power in the Bolognese countryside.[33] Despite their recently acquired property status, small proprietors found themselves even more dependent on the big growers after 1922. Virtually all local farmers who wished to make a living from their land were gradually forced to turn to the main commercial organizations in the province: the rural banks offered them much needed credit; the agrarian consortium sold the cheapest machines and fertilizers; the Società Bolognese Produttori Sementi had the highest quality seed; the

[32] For Belluzzo's views, see A. Lyttelton, *The Seizure of Power*, p. 322. On the Bolognese Provincial Economic Council, see P. P. D'Attore, "Agrari e fascismo," p. 64; Frank De Morsier, *Dalla Camera di Commercio al Consiglio provinciale dell'Economia di Bologna* (Bologna, 1928), pp. 1-10; *L'Agricoltore d'Italia*, v, no. 14, April 3, 1926 and no. 31, July 31, 1926. The convergence of interests on the council found its clearest expression in the project for a central *borsa delle merce* or produce exchange in the capital city. First proposed in 1926, the exchange aimed to remedy the shortcomings of the agricultural markets in Emilia where, according to De Morsier, the movement of goods "from one square to the next" no longer corresponded to "modern business practices." By opening up more profitable and secure outlets, the exchange promised to give "the most vigorous impulse" to the production and marketing of hemp, rice, grain, and seed, while its efficient functioning would entail the increased "standardization" of all the products. At the same time, De Morsier insisted that the larger and more rapid flow of goods would give a tremendous advantage to "the merchants and industrialists of the city and province."

[33] On the growth of small property in the province between 1920 and 1928, see Consiglio Provinciale dell'Economia Corporativa, *La provincia di Bologna nell'anno decimo. Monografia statistica-economica* (Bologna, 1932), p. 513. Data on the five communes, for which there is information, indicates that the number of landowners rose from 228 to 738, while the average size of each holding fell from 7.02 to 5.5 hectares.

commodity associations controlled the most profitable outlets for their crops. In this fashion, the power of the commercial farmers came to rest not only on the competitive superiority of their farms, but also on their increasing control of marketing outlets, agricultural credit, and supplies of seed, fertilizers, and farm machines.[34]

As Cacciari and Fornaciari clearly recognized, however, the success of these provincial initiatives depended upon the existence of a more broadly based organization capable of coordinating agrarian interests throughout the Po Valley and lobbying for favorable government legislation in Rome.[35] With this goal in mind, the two Bolognese leaders launched a new national organization in December 1922, the Italian Federation of Farmers' Syndicates (FISA), to replace the old General Confederation of Agriculture and insert the representatives of northern commercial agriculture directly into the emerging power structure of the Fascist regime. Like its provincial progenitor, the FISA, which formally adopted the program of integral syndicalism, benefited from the energetic support of the Fascist *ras* and labor leaders who viewed it primarily as a means of controlling the agrarians and guaranteeing the application of contracts.[36] With their backing, the new federation made rapid progress in those areas where commercial agriculture predominated and the pressure from the Fascist labor syndicates was the greatest. Despite resistance from the old independent agrarian associations in Parma and Reggio Emilia, the FISA managed to win over the majority of employers in most provinces of northern and central Italy in 1923. By the end of the year, it claimed over two hundred twenty-five branches in forty-five provinces, largely concentrated in the Po Valley or, as one Fascist leader expressed it, "in those

[34] See P. P. D'Attore, "Agrari e fascismo," pp. 50-51.

[35] This was especially true in the case of the commodity associations which required a larger national organization in order to hold their own in dealings with the big industrial processors and refiners.

[36] For the founding and program of the FISA, see ASB, C7 F1, Police Chief to Prefect, December 28, 1922; ACS, Presidenza del Consiglio dei Ministri, F3, no. 1-2, Prefectoral report, January 5, 1923; *RdC*, January 6, 1923; G. Pesce, *Marcia dei rurali*, p. 85, 87, 95; A. Lyttelton, *The Seizure of Power*, p. 225.

parts of Italy that truly constitute the agricultural wealth of the nation."[37]

The FISA encountered more serious obstacles in its attempt to subordinate traditional landed groups in the south to the interests of northern commercial farmers. The large southern landowners, who derived a good income from leasing their lands at exorbitant rents, had little interest in Cacciari's plans for production controls and the industrialization of agriculture.[38] Moreover, they had few of the labor problems that beset farmers in the Po Valley and consequently had less need for an organization to counteract the influence of the workers' syndicates within fascism. These traditional propertied groups considered the FISA a trojan horse of the "barbarians of the north" and sought refuge in the independent General Confederation of Agriculture (CGA), which remained a surprisingly strong rival of the agrarian syndicates in the south and the capital after the March on Rome.[39] Following the example of the nonfascist parties in the government, the CGA leaders used their established position and contacts in Rome to resist absorption. Their strategy was fairly effective in the short run because of the relative weakness of the PNF in the south and the Duce's continued need for conservative political support.[40]

The refusal of the CGA to disband forced the FISA to engage in a bitter jurisdictional dispute that split agrarian employers into two mutually opposed regional blocs. In the dispute the openly Fascist commitment of the FISA proved to be a mixed blessing. Initially, it appeared to give the syndicates the upper hand. In January 1923, the party directorate decided that all members of

[37] ASB, C7 F1, 1, FISA leaflet, January 11, 1924. On resistance of the old agrarian associations, see G. Pesce, *Marcia dei rurali*, pp. 94-95; F. Cordova, *Le origini dei sindacati*, p. 136; R. Cavandoli, *Fascimo a Reggio Emilia*, pp. 254-257.

[38] A. Lyttelton, *The Seizure of Power*, pp. 350-351.

[39] G. Pesce, *Marcia dei rurali*, p. 112, 83-84; F. Cordova, *Le origini dei sindacati*, p. 136. Until the summer of 1923, the CGA had a powerful ally in the undersecretary for agriculture, Ottavio Corgini.

[40] See G. Pesce, *Marcia dei rurali*, p. 89; F. Cordova, *Le origini dei sindacati*, pp. 153-160; A. Lyttelton, *The Seizure of Power*, pp. 224-225.

the PNF must belong to Fascist professional organizations.[41] This decision facilitated the spread of the syndicates in the Po Valley, but it did not immediately increase the FISA's influence within the Roman bureaucracy. Later in the spring, for instance, the government consulted the CGA rather than the FISA on the revision of land tax assessment. Prompt demands from Cacciari that the "Fascist government listen to the voice of the Fascist farmers" soon led to the FISA's inclusion in the preparations, but then only as a regional pressure group. In that capacity, it was quite successful, for the final redistribution of the tax burden grossly favored the regions of the north at the expense of the south, Sicily, and Sardinia.[42]

The FISA's lack of political independence, however, became a major liability the following year precisely when the old confederation seemed to be on the brink of surrender. Concerned that the struggle between the two employer organizations might hurt the government in the upcoming parliamentary elections, Mussolini intervened in February 1924, imposing a merger on terms that gave the leaders of the CGA important positions in the FISA and integrated the old provincial associations without altering their structure or leadership. Such a politically expedient merger marked a serious setback for the organizational ambitions of the Bolognese spokesmen, since it left unresolved the underlying economic and regional conflicts, which soon reappeared in the form of paralyzing factional disputes within the newly expanded federation. In the wake of the merger, the FISA did not function as a unified national agrarian lobby, a situation that remained unchanged throughout 1924 as a result of the Matteotti affair and the ensuing crisis of fascism.[43]

Only after the defeat of the antifascist opposition and the consolidation of Mussolini's dictatorship in 1925, did commercial farming interests regain the upper hand. The preparation of a law on col-

[41] A. Lyttelton, *The Seizure of Power*, p. 225.

[42] *Ibid.*, pp. 225-226; G. Pesce, *Marcia dei rurali*, pp. 96-98.

[43] G. Pesce, *Marcia dei rurali*, pp. 113-125.

lective labor relations and official recognition of the Fascist syndicates provided Cacciari with the pretext to challenge the former leaders of the CGA. When the plan for such a law became known in the fall of 1925, it aroused strong opposition from older, more traditional agrarian spokesmen, who charged that it would mean "the militarization of the farmers."[44] The Bolognese leaders not only defended the proposed law, but demanded that it be preceded by a purge of the FISA so that "legal recognition might be given to a truly Fascist organization." Their view prevailed; in December the government pressured the old directorate of the federation to resign and appointed Cacciari "Extraordinary Commissioner" with sweeping powers to reorganize the FISA. Cacciari proceeded in the spring of 1926 to purge "agrarian incrustations" from both the federation and the local employer associations, and to appoint his own loyal commissioners in nearly every province of the south. In this way, the "fascistization" of the FISA served primarily to enhance the power and influence of northern commercial farmers at the expense of the southern *latifondisti*.[45]

With the promulgation of the Syndical Laws and the transformation of the FISA into the National Fascist Confederation of Farmers in the fall of 1926, agrarian leaders from Bologna and the Po Valley had largely established their organizational control over the national agricultural sector. Of course, such control was not absolute, especially in the south where landed notables continued to exercise independent influence through their local clientele groups and their connections within the Fascist hierarchy. Moreover, the agrarian confederation remained considerably more subservient than the industrialists' confederation to the political dictates of the regime.[46] Nonetheless, Cacciari and other northern spokesmen still dominated the only official organizational representative of Italian agricultural employers after 1926. As a result, commercial farming

[44] *Ibid.*, pp. 134-135.

[45] *Ibid.*, pp. 135-143.

[46] A. Lyttelton, *The Seizure of Power*, pp. 327-328; Fausto Pittigliani, *The Italian Corporative State* (London, 1933), pp. 162-163.

interests were assured a disproportionately large role in the institutionalized process of social bargaining created by the corporative state.[47]

2. *Beyond Reaction: Agrarians, Fascist Syndicates, and the Struggle to Regiment Agricultural Labor, 1923-1926*

The gradual consolidation of power within the propertied classes in the period from 1923 to 1926 coincided with a protracted struggle by agrarian interests at the provincial level to wipe out the remnants of Socialist resistance, to domesticate the Fascist labor syndicates, and to regiment the agricultural laborers. Fascist violence had not eliminated the "labor problem" in Bologna, nor did it guarantee the immediate and unhampered dominance of the large landowners and commercial farmers. For the destruction of the Socialist leagues had altered the form but not the content of class conflict in the countryside. Indeed, inflation, unemployment, and the decline in real wages all assured the persistence of labor unrest and militancy after the March on Rome; only now they found expression in new strains and tensions within the heterogeneous Bolognese Fascist movement.

An enormous gap existed between the rhetoric and reality of labor relations in the province in 1923. If one believed the statements of Gino Baroncini or the reports of the prefect, the terrorist offensive of the squads had ushered in a new era of social peace. Summarizing the situation in the summer of 1923, Baroncini boasted how there had "not been a single economic disturbance," since every dispute between capital and labor was "immediately and systematically resolved by the technical organs of the Fascist federation." Similarly, the prefect wrote later the same year that the harvest had taken place "in the most complete tranquility" thanks to "the application of labor contracts, inspired by the principles of

[47] A. Lyttelton, *The Seizure of Power*, pp. 349-363.

equity and production."[48] Conventional indicators of labor strife seemed to confirm these glowing reports. In 1923, government officials reported only one agricultural strike in the entire country, involving a mere 110 workers.[49]

The absence of strikes, however, concealed a considerably less harmonious situation in the Bolognese countryside. Both sharecroppers and day laborers saw their working and living conditions decline in the course of 1923. As the prefect conceded, the revised *mezzadria* contract imposed by the Fascists increased the obligations of the sharecroppers, while eliminating virtually all the advantages they had gained with the agreements that had ended the strikes of 1920. According to its terms, sharecroppers had to pay a larger portion of the property taxes and expenses for fertilizers and to accept a reduced share of the harvest and the livestock products. The new contracts were so unfavorable to the peasants that Fascist labor leaders felt compelled to demand special government legislation to invalidate legally the agreements of 1920, warning that otherwise "the sharecroppers who have enrolled in the national syndicates will desert and all the exhausting work completed up to now will be undone."[50]

The situation of the day laborers deteriorated even more dramatically in 1923. Although local agricultural markets began to show some signs of improvement from the recession of 1921-22, hemp prices still were half what they had been in 1920, and sugar beet and wheat growers complained that their revenues barely covered taxes and labor costs.[51] The burdens of this lingering recession fell primarily on the laborers. Already in May, police officials warned of growing "discontent among certain groups of workers

[48] For Baroncini's views, see his report to the executive council of the PNF, published in *RdC*, August 29, 1923; on the prefect's evaluation, see ASB, C7 F1, 2, Prefect to Ministry of Justice, November 29, 1923 and Prefect to Mussolini, November 5, 1923.

[49] See R. De Felice, *Mussolini il fascista*, vol. I, pp. 396-397.

[50] ASB, C16 F1, Prefect to Ministry of Interior, June 1, 1923.

[51] On the situation in the hemp markets, see Roberto Roversi, *Canapa ed autarchia* (Rome, 1939), p. 15; on sugar beet growers, see *L'Assalto*, January 26, 1924.

because of the current unemployment crisis." With the end of the harvest and the completion of most of the work on the Renana land reclamation project in the fall, unemployment reached very serious levels in the plains. During the month of October alone, the ranks of the jobless farm laborers more than doubled, and their numbers continued to grow in the winter of 1923-24.[52] Moreover, those laborers who did find work had to accept a smaller remuneration than in previous years. Nearly all the labor contracts signed in the region of Emilia in 1923 stipulated salary cuts of up to 10 percent, while individual employers, in the absence of any effective controls, unilaterally imposed even more drastic wage reductions.[53] Inflation compounded the effects of unemployment and falling wages by further reducing the real income of the farm laborers. From its base in July 1920, the cost-of-living index had risen some 16 percent by the summer of 1923 and showed no signs of leveling off.[54]

Despite its official advocacy of class collaboration, the FPSA did little to ameliorate the plight of the laborers. As Fascist labor leaders soon discovered, the growers organized in the agrarian syndicates viewed class collaboration exclusively in terms of the "superior interests of production," which in practice translated into economic benefits for themselves and continual sacrifices for agricultural laborers and sharecroppers. Such a one-sided vision of collaboration placed labor syndicalists in an especially difficult position, since they had built their organizations not only by coercion, but also on the basis of promises of wage increases and protection from unemployment. Their failure to deliver on these pledges in 1923 seriously damaged their credibility and threatened to provoke an explosive backlash of anger and resentment from their rank and file.[55]

[52] For statistics on unemployment among the day laborers, see ASB, C12 F2, 1924; the preoccupation of local authorities with labor unrest is evident in ASB, C7 F1, Police Chief to Prefect, May 10, 1923.

[53] See F. Cordova, *Le origini dei sindacati*, pp. 121-125.

[54] *Ibid.*, p. 126.

[55] See A. Lyttelton, *The Seizure of Power*, p. 310.

While similar difficulties plagued the labor syndicates in other provinces of Emilia, they were compounded in Bologna by continued pressure from the left, above all in the commune of Molinella. Socialist organizers in Giuseppe Massarenti's old stronghold demonstrated their mass support in March 1923 by sending Mussolini a secretly circulated petition signed by the majority of the local laborers, in which they repudiated the syndicates and reaffirmed their allegiance to the leagues even "at the cost of dying of hunger with their families."[56] By the summer, provincial authorities expressed fears that the example of the Molinellese laborers and the growing discontent within the syndicates might favor a revival of the red leagues. In their evaluation of the unemployment situation in May, for instance, police officials went on to report that "the Socialists are intensifying their propaganda . . . for a vast movement of Socialist resurgence that could signal the beginning of a general offensive by the subversives."[57] Renewed repression prevented any organizational revival of the leagues in 1923, but it did not soften the passive resistance of the laborers in Molinella. In December, a special prefectoral commissioner underscored both the depth of Socialist loyalties and the limited efficacy of Fascist violence in the commune when he wrote: "Thirty long years of uninterrupted subversive propaganda . . . have created an unhealthy environment that it would be vain to hope to cleanse in a brief time; it will require a long and patient process of detoxification, carried out by the higher authorities with love and vigilant care, since the local [Fascist] forces are not up to the task."[58]

Agrarian indifference or opposition, however, effectively sabotaged nearly every initiative taken by the Fascist labor syndicates in 1923 to placate their membership and counteract the enduring appeal of the Socialists. When the peasant syndicates attempted to eliminate the prevailing contractual anarchy in the province by

[56] ASB, C7 F1, 3, Police Report, March 5, 1923 and Commissioner Molinella to Prefect, March 7, 1923.

[57] ASB, C7 F1, Police Chief to Prefect, May 10, 1923.

[58] ASB, C7 F1, 3, Prefectoral Commissioner to Prefect, December 12, 1923.

implementing their revised *mezzadria* contract in January, they received scant cooperation from many landowners, who imposed terms that did not conform to the Fascist contract or who refused to sign any written agreements with their sharecroppers.[59] Significantly, appeals to the agrarian syndicates proved fruitless. For the most part, the FPSA either ignored the appeals or else disavowed all responsibility for the recalcitrant landowners. By the summer of 1923, frustrated Fascist peasant leaders were denouncing publicly "the unjustified obstinancy of the agrarians" and threatening to engage "in a struggle that could endanger production" in order to force "the bosses to maintain their commitments."[60]

The same fate befell the labor syndicates' proposals that the commercial growers execute special projects on their farms to help alleviate the unemployment in the countryside. The FPSA made a great show of responding to the proposals, calling meetings of agrarian employers, drawing up plans for farm improvements, and establishing "municipal councils of production" to find work for the day laborers. But this whirl of activity produced little in the way of concrete measures on behalf of the unemployed.[61] Content to rely on the repressive apparatus of fascism to contain unrest, the big growers were unwilling to make "uneconomical sacrifices" to strengthen the syndicates, especially when their weakness enhanced agrarian control over the labor market. As one police official concluded, "the landowners are by temperament and political education opposed to any idea of improving the working classes; they consider fascism exclusively as an instrument for the protection of their private interests and they profit from it to reduce their concessions to the workers."[62]

Initially, the leaders of the labor syndicates looked to the Pro-

[59] For reports on agrarian contractual intransigence, see *L'Assalto*, February 17, May 5, September 8, October 6, and December 15, 1923.

[60] *Ibid.*, May 5, 1923.

[61] See, for example, the report on meetings held in Castelmaggiore to resolve the unemployment situation in *L'Assalto*, September 29, 1923.

[62] ASB, C7 F1, 2, Police Chief to Prefect, October 6, 1924.

vincial Fascist Federation to defend their interests and discipline uncooperative agrarian employers. With Gino Baroncini at the helm of the federation, these expectations did not seem unreasonable at first. Throughout most of 1923, the Fascist *ras* and leading patron of the syndicates denounced "agrarian egotism" and repeatedly vowed his determination to help the laborers and defend them from unjustified exploitation.[63] Although his demagogic rhetoric temporarily defused the issue, it did not translate into a systematic campaign to bring the employers into line. For Baroncini could not alter the fact that Bolognese fascism from its inception had been built upon the destruction of the agricultural workers' rights. Much as in the neighboring province of Ferrara, the defeat of the red leagues in Bologna unavoidably strengthened the position of the large commercial growers, both on their farms and within the federation itself. Without using the methods of the leagues, a political impossibility for the Fascists, Baroncini and the syndicalists could not alter this new balance of power or exert any real control over the employers.[64] Moreover, they lacked the support of national party leaders who had little interest in alienating those elements that had permitted the growth of provincial fascism. On the contrary, Mussolini's desire to normalize relations with the employers' federations in 1923 led him to reduce his support for integral syndicalism and the totalitarian claims of the Fascist syndicalists.[65]

Baroncini's sudden fall from power in December 1923 after a public clash with Grandi[66] left local syndicalists politically isolated and brought their long simmering resentment and frustration out into the open. Indeed, a number of them took part in a brief rebellion against the PNF and the provincial federation in February 1924. Early that month, Walter Squarzoni, provincial secretary of

[63] For an evaluation of Baroncini's activities, see ASB, C7 F1, 2, Prefect to Mussolini, December 3, 1923.

[64] On the situation in Ferrara, see P. Corner, *Fascism in Ferrara*, pp. 240-253.

[65] See A. Lyttelton, *The Seizure of Power*, p. 229.

[66] For a more detailed discussion of Baroncini's fall from power, see the next section in this chapter.

the rural labor syndicates, violently denounced party leaders, accusing them of being "more favorable to the employer classes" than to the laborers. After his dismissal on charges of indiscipline, Squarzoni organized a meeting of some thirty dissident Fascist labor organizers in mid-February to plan the launching of a new union organization independent from the Fascist corporations. His initiative provoked a quick reaction from the provincial federation that dispatched squadrists to break up the meeting and arrest the participants; the rebellion ended almost as soon as it began.[67]

The dismissals and punitive measures of February and the following months demonstrated that the Bolognese federation had the strength to check any rebellion but not to maintain discipline or remove the deeper sources of discontent within the syndicates. The problems of inflation and rural unemployment became even more pronounced during the first half of 1924. The prefect provided an alarming picture of economic conditions in the countryside and their impact on popular opinion in the spring: "In less than two months, the cost of living has risen approximately 30 percent, and basic necessities have undergone more sizeable increases. . . . The mood of the workers . . . is scarcely one of friendliness toward the local authorities and the government which, according to them, have done nothing to demonstrate their interest in halting the inflationary spiral."[68]

Under mounting pressure from their rank and file, various local Fascist labor organizers began to resort to more extreme measures against recalcitrant landowners and leaseholders. By the summer, the prefecture had received a number of petitions from agrarian employers, complaining of "the thousands of abuses, assaults, and tyrranical actions that used to be committed by the bolsheviks and

[67] On the abortive rebellion, see ACS, Ministero dell'Interno Finzi, B11, F118, Bocchini reports, February 2 and 13, 1924; ASB, C7 F1, 1, Bocchini to Mussolini, February 9, 1924.

[68] See ASB, C16 F1, 1924, quoted in P. P. D'Attore, "Agrari e fascismo," p. 21. On the dismissals and punitive measures, see ASB, C7 F1, 3, Police Chief to Prefect, August 6, 1924.

now by so-called Fascists."[69] Nor did the prompt removal of these militant syndicalists guarantee peace. In communes where Fascist union leaders remained passive, the laborers often took matters into their own hands. Several hundred laborers in Budrio, for instance, repudiated the leaders of the syndicate in May, set up their own committee, and demanded a meeting with the local fascio to plan "an immediate and energetic action to resolve the serious crisis."[70] A few months later, laborers in Malalbergo carried out a series of wildcat strikes against the orders of the syndicate and, police reported, were preparing "to exact reprisals at the opportune moment."[71]

Significantly, the disappearance and murder of Giacomo Matteotti in June appears to have had little direct impact on labor relations in the Bolognese countryside. In contrast to the major industrial centers, the sudden political crisis did not lead in Bologna to an upsurge in working-class militancy or a revival of the free unions.[72] Local police officials gave no indication of popular protests against the regime such as the commemorations to Matteotti and the antifascist leafleting that took place in nearby provinces; less than two weeks after the disappearance of the Socialist deputy, the prefect informed Mussolini that "the situation remains normal, the population calm." In a more ample report the following month, the prefect noted the opposition activities of small groups of Freemasons, students, and veterans in the city, but insisted that otherwise "life everywhere in the province is tranquil and normal; even the agricultural work, and particularly the threshing that in the past provoked unrest and serious incidents, is being completed in perfect tranquility."[73] If such reports were accurate, they graph-

[69] ACS, Ministero dell'Interno, B66, "alcuni agricoltori di comuni limitrofi alla città di Bologna" to Prefect, July 1, 1924.

[70] ASB, C7 F1, 2, Sindacato Braccianti Budrio, May 17, 1924.

[71] ASB, C7 F1, 2, Police Chief to Prefect, October 6, 1924.

[72] On the Matteotti crisis and working-class discontent, see A. Lyttelton, *The Seizure of Power*, pp. 310-311.

[73] ASB, C7 F1, 1925, Prefect to Mussolini, June 16, 1924; *ibid.*, Prefect to Ministry of Interior, July 16, 1924.

ically testified to the success of Bolognese fascism in eliminating the leadership and organizational structure of the old Socialist movement.

While the Matteotti crisis hardly threatened the basis of Fascist power in Bologna, it did prevent the provincial federation and its agrarian allies from taking strong measures to reduce the independence of the syndicalists and to restore discipline within the labor organizations. Far from unifying the Fascist camp, the events of the summer and fall sharpened tensions between the party and the syndicates throughout the Po Valley.[74] Moreover, the disaffection of the rank and file remained evident, even though it did not assume any organized form. As the police chief of Malalbergo observed in October:

> There exists in reality a general discontent, especially among the agricultural laborers, which finds expression privately in words of disdain for fascism and in proposals for retaliation. . . . Having examined the origins of this climate of opinion, I have to reveal that there has been a lack of efficacious organizational and propaganda work after the revolutionary phase of fascism to convince the masses to accept and recognize the new postulates of the party. As a result, while they belong to the national syndicates for reasons of convenience or out of fear of persecution, they have remained with all their baggage of Socialist principles and formulas.[75]

The uneasy calm that prevailed in the Bolognese countryside in the second half of the year came to an abrupt halt after the third of January. In the immediate aftermath of Mussolini's speech to the Chamber of Deputies, Fascist syndicalists gained a new freedom of action in their dealings with agrarian employers. Indeed, their demands for a major labor offensive in 1925 enjoyed, at least temporarily, the support of both the party and the Grand Council. Roberto Farinacci, new general secretary of the PNF, looked fa-

[74] A. Lyttelton, *The Seizure of Power*, pp. 311-312.
[75] ASB, C7 F1, 2, Police Chief to Prefect, October 6, 1924.

vorably upon a campaign that might limit the influence of local notables and help make the workers "an active part of the movement."[76] Likewise, the Grand Council indicated its support by passing a resolution at the end of January, in which it criticized intransigent employers and recognized the need for strike action. In February, the Bolognese prefect received instructions from the Ministry of Interior to take a sympathetic view of any initiatives by the syndicates and to encourage "the landowners and employers to observe faithfully the agreements concluded with the Fascist organizations."[77]

The Bolognese syndicates immediately capitalized on the new political situation. Less than a week after Mussolini's speech, they canceled their old contracts with the two major consortia for land reclamation, the Renana and the Crevalcorese, and demanded a wage hike to offset the rising cost of living. The refusal of the directors to grant the increases led to more drastic measures; in March and April work stoppages took place at various locations in the projects before the consortia finally accepted a compromise settlement.[78] During the same period, the syndicates increased their pressures on private landowners in a number of communes, threatening them with strikes unless they applied the Fascist contracts. Encouraged by their results, labor leaders announced in May an ambitious plan of reorganization within the syndicates to overcome "feelings of distrust" among the rank and file and to prepare for a sweeping revision of all labor contracts.[79]

The strikes in the spring of 1925, however, marked an end rather

[76] A. Lyttelton, *The Seizure of Power*, pp. 314-315.

[77] *Ibid.*; Charles Maier, *Recasting Bourgeois Europe* (Princeton, 1975), p. 557; ASB, C6 F2, Minister of Interior to Prefect, February 3, 1925.

[78] On the negotiations and strikes in the land reclamation projects, see ASB, C6 F2, Uff. Centr. Collocamento to Ministry of Public Works, January 7, 1925; ASB, C6 F2, 1926, Secretary Sindacato Provinciale degli Consorzi, February 7, 1925; *ibid.*, Benelli to Prefect, March 25, 1925; *ibid.*, Police Report to Prefect, April 13, 1925.

[79] See ASB, C6 F2, Police Report to Prefect, March 25, 1925; *RdC*, March 20, 1925; for the reorganization plans of the syndicalists, see *Il Lavoro d'Italia*, May 26, 1925, quoted in P. P. D'Attore, "Agrari e fascismo," pp. 21-22.

than a beginning; they were the last legal work stoppages in the province until the 1940s. Events outside Bologna sealed the fate of the local syndicalist revival. Government and party support for a labor offensive quickly vanished after the Fascist unions nearly lost control of a major national strike in the steel and engineering industries in March. The following month the Grand Council reversed its earlier position and took steps to curb the militancy and independence of the syndicates. In addition to requiring the approval of the central authorities for all future strikes, the Grand Council ordered a sweeping purge of the syndicalist cadre, and enlarged the role of the provincial party federations in the selection of union officials.[80]

The April meeting of the Grand Council signalled the opening of a new phase of centralization within the Fascist trade union movement that involved the imposition of rigid political controls at all levels. Beginning in August with the dismissal of Alberto Cuccoli, provincial secretary of the labor syndicates, the Bolognese Fascist Federation removed the remaining militant union leaders and replaced them with more reliable party hacks.[81] While at the national level the precise role of the syndicates in the regime was not determined until 1926-27 with the Legge sindacale and the Charter of Labor, the issue had been largely settled in Bologna during the summer and fall of 1925. By the end of the year, the local syndicates had lost all autonomy and had given up any serious pretense of defending the interests of labor. Much as in Ferrara, the syndicates in Bologna now became the obedient executors of government labor policies and "mechanisms for the regimentation of rural workers."[82]

The domestication of the Fascist syndicates was followed in 1926 by measures to eliminate the last pocket of organized Socialist resistance in Molinella. Despite repeated punitive expeditions,

[80] A. Lyttelton, *The Seizure of Power*, pp. 315-317.

[81] See P. P. D'Attore, "Agrari e fascismo," pp. 27-28 for the purge of the syndicates in Bologna. On general trends toward centralization, see C. Maier, *Recasting Bourgeois Europe*, pp. 558-559.

[82] See P. Corner, *Fascism in Ferrara*, p. 284.

blacklisting, and the loss of their old leaders, the mass of Molinellese laborers continued to resist Fascist penetration. Even after the prefect officially closed the provincial Chamber of Labor and its affiliated leagues in January 1925, the workers only reorganized under a different label, founding a Free Syndicate of Confederated Laborers.[83] Such an embarrassing thorn in the side of the provincial federation forced party leaders to take extraordinary action. In the summer of 1926, they ordered the eviction and compulsory emigration of all nonfascist laborers from their homes in the commune. Local growers expressed a certain concern at the loss of the "good manual labor, especially precious in periods of intense and unpostponeable agricultural work," but at least in this case political imperatives took precedence over economic interests. In the fall the red laborers were evicted and transported to Marzabotto and other remote areas of the province; workers from the neighboring provinces of Ferrara and Rovigo filled their places.[84]

The defeat of the syndicalist militants and the pacification of Molinella removed the last obstacles to the virtually unchallenged dominance of commercial farmers in the Bolognese countryside. Developments after 1926 clearly demonstrated the inability of the Fascist unions to win concessions or enforce agreements with agrarian employers. When the syndicates did intervene, it was to impose additional sacrifices on their members. In May 1927, for instance, *Il Popolo d'Italia* publicized a meeting of Fascist union representatives in Bologna, in which they decided "voluntarily" to slash all wages in the province by 10 percent, the first of many salary reductions that would take place under the regime.[85] A petition sent to the prefect the following year by a group of laborers provides a more personal testimonial to the weakness of the syndi-

[83] For order closing the Chamber of Labor, see ASB, C7 F1, 3, 1926, January 7, 1925. On the free syndicate in Molinella, see ASB, C7 F1, 3, Prefectoral decree, June 29, 1926.

[84] ASB, C7 F1, 3, Police Report to Prefect, August 7, 1926; P. P. D'Attore "Agrari e fascismo," pp. 30-31.

[85] See Gaetano Salvemini, *Under the Axe of Fascism* (New York, 1971), p. 183, 222-228.

cates: "After having made all the sacrifices asked of them . . . the workers have reached a point of having to struggle for their very survival which is threatened by misery, hunger, and disease. By now their rights no longer exist . . . only their duties to the employers, and when our representative goes to them to discuss our interests, he is ridiculed and ignored."[86] Moreover, the absence of a strong independent union movement allowed commercial farmers not only to cut wages, but also to expand their use of labor management techniques that intensified competition among the laborers and permitted a far greater exploitation of the work force. Above all, with the "Battle of the Lira" and the decline in farm prices in 1927, limited sharecropping contracts (*compartecipazione*) and piece rates allowed agrarian entrepreneurs to shift the burdens of the crisis on to the shoulders of their peasant laborers.[87]

The relative docility of the Fascist unions after 1926 did not mean that the regime had resolved or eliminated the "labor problem" in the countryside. Local syndicate officials conceded in 1930 that the familiar scourges of the agricultural work force in Bologna—seasonal unemployment, a low standard of living, and poor housing conditions—had become more pronounced. Their own statistics showed that in 1928-29 as much as three-quarters of the rural laborers were unemployed during the winter months, while even in the harvest season some five thousand laborers remained idle.[88] Not surprisingly, mass unemployment and brutal exploitation sparked periodic eruptions of labor unrest.[89] The short-term

[86] ASB, C16 F1, petition to Prefect, January 5, 1928.

[87] For a more ample discussion of labor management techniques, see P. Corner, "Fascist Agrarian Policy and the Italian Economy in the Inter-war Years" in John A. Davis, ed., *Gramsci and Italy's Passive Revolution* (London, 1979), pp. 245-249. On the use of limited sharecropping contracts and piece rates in the Bolognese countryside, see Confederazione Nazionale dei Sindacati Fascisti dell'Agricoltura, Unione provinciale di Bologna, *I nostri problemi. Un anno di attività* (Bologna, 1930), pp. 36-39, 92-93.

[88] CNSFA, *I nostri problemi*, pp. 84-87.

[89] In January 1927, some five hundred unemployed workers demonstrated for "bread and work" in the commune of Galliera, and in June farm laborers there staged a temporary work stoppage; after a summer of frequent clashes with police, women rice workers deserted the fields of Malalbergo and Minerbio in October of

economic interests of the propertied classes, however, did not require the resolution of the labor problem, merely the containment of its more disruptive social and political manifestations. As long as the repressive apparatus of fascism remained firm, these sporadic incidents of unrest, in themselves, constituted no great danger to the dominant position of the big landowners and leaseholders. Geographically isolated, deprived of any real political leadership and coordination, worker protests invariably collapsed in the face of economic pressures and police intervention.

In their capacity as employers of labor, Bolognese commercial farmers could look with obvious satisfaction on the provincial situation six years after the first punitive expeditions into the countryside. The violence and coercion of the squads had destroyed the Socialist "monopolies" that had loomed as such a serious menace to their profits, managerial prerogatives, and property rights in the immediate postwar period. More importantly, fascism had replaced the red leagues with subservient labor organizations that offered agrarian employers the best of both worlds by controlling worker discontent while leaving them relatively free to dictate the terms of employment in agriculture. At least in their dealings with the rural workers, the agrarians were, to paraphrase Angelo Tasca, once again "the cocks of the walk."[90]

3. *Agrarian Fascism and the Process of Political Stabilization in Bologna, 1923-1926*

In the period from 1923 to 1926, the gradual domestication and integration of the Fascist syndicates into the regime was inseparably linked to the development of a stable system of political authority in Rome and the provinces capable of restoring order and providing efficient administration. For a paramilitary move-

the following year; in 1930, there were reports of protests by sharecroppers on one of the large estates in Molinella; again the next year, rice workers in the commune of Medicina briefly went out on strike. See P. P. D'Attore, "Agrari e fascismo," p. 159.

[90] A. Tasca, *The Rise of Italian Fascism*, p. 95.

ment such as provincial fascism, which had thrived on illegal violence and found its unity in combat, the transition from disruptive opposition to the formal exercise of state power was especially difficult, since it brought into the open all the latent contradictions and contrasting aspirations of the movement. Indeed, after the March on Rome, competition for office sharpened tensions between party and state, Fascist moderates and militants, employers and syndicates, and led to a general increase in instability and confusion.[91] Two additional factors accentuated the problems of transition in Bologna: the lack of a single dominant leader, which split the movement into feuding factions, and the extraordinarily rapid absorption or repression of the nonfascist parties. The virtual absence of any significant organized opposition not only reduced the need for unified action by the Fascists, but also shifted the locus of all political conflict to the municipal fasci and the provincial federation.

Despite its overwhelming victory in the municipal elections, the Bolognese Fascist movement was in a state of chronic disarray and crisis throughout much of 1923 and 1924, with bitter factional disputes paralyzing activities at all levels of the provincial organization. In the district of Vergato, for instance, the subprefect reported in December 1923 that none of the Fascist administrations were able to function effectively because of old private feuds, rivalries between hamlets and towns, and "contrasts of interest between groups who . . . have not forgotten completely the class mentality they were taught by the subversive parties."[92] Nor was the situation in Vergato unique. Complaining that "disinterested commitment has been replaced by unsatisfied ambition," Dino Grandi reported in 1924 that the majority of fasci in the province did little more than engage in "sterile internal struggles that have wasted and divided their energies and aroused passions and bitterness."[93]

[91] See A. Lyttelton, *The Seizure of Power*, pp. 158-178; R. De Felice, *Mussolini il fascista*, vol. I, pp. 388-517.

[92] ASB, C7 F1, 3, Subprefect to Prefect, December 16, 1923.

[93] See *RdC*, August 1, 1924.

Economic conflicts between agrarian employers and the labor syndicates often underlay factional strife at the local level. As early as the summer of 1923, police officials in Castelfranco noted the presence of a "true and proper class struggle between the bosses and the workers," which they attributed to the fact that "certain farmers, who have the directorate of the fascio in their hands, refuse to apply the sharecropping contracts." Angered by the intransigence of the landowners on the issue of contracts, the secretary of the Castelfranco syndicates publicly attacked the employers as "exploiters of fascism" in May, triggering a crisis that disrupted the fascio for the remainder of the year.[94] In other areas, internal divisions and conflicts resulted from private and business rivalries between the major agrarian entrepreneurs. The struggle between Carlo Cremonini and Giuseppe Mainetti, the two biggest commercial farmers in Crevalcore, for control of the vast estate of Prince Torlonia, was primary cause for the frequent clashes between Fascists of the municipal center and squads from the outlying hamlet of Palata Pepoli. In their reports on the disturbances, the prefect and the police chief stressed how the fascio of Palata Pepolo supported Cremonini's campaign to unseat Mainetti as administrator of the Torlonia estate, while the Crevalcore Fascists, whose political secretary was Mainetti's chief foreman, defended the latter.[95]

The maneuvers of insecure squad commanders to preserve their independent power and political influence further contributed to dissension and turmoil within the local fasci. Tough municipal warlords like Augusto Regazzi of Molinella and Emilio Marchesini of Budrio, who had exercised virtually unchecked authority in their respective bailiwicks in 1922, found themselves in an increasingly anomalous position after the March on Rome. With the Socialists largely routed and the Fascists in the government, the police grad-

[94] ASB, C7 F1, 3, Police Chief to Prefect, July 15, 1923; ACS, Ministero dell'Interno, B50, Prefect to Ministry of Interior, December 3, 1923.

[95] ASB, C7 F1, 2, Police Chief to Prefect, May 15, 1922; ACS, Ministero dell'Interno, B29, Prefect to Ministry of Interior, July 1, 1923; ASB, C7 F1, 2, 1926, Police Chief to Prefect, June 8, 1925.

ually assumed their old functions, while Mussolini and the PNF moved to curb their freedom of action and absorb their squads into new state and party organizations.[96] These initiatives found support among local agrarian interests, who had previously financed the squadrists' violence against the red leagues, but now wished to reduce their influence within the fasci.

As their actions in 1923 and 1924 indicated, neither Regazzi nor Marchesini were prepared to go quietly into retirement. After Regazzi lost control of the Molinella fascio to the industrialist Francesco Furlani and a group of wealthy commercial growers, he formed a dissident faction of Fascists in Alberino, a hamlet that had a long tradition of bad relations with its municipal center. By skillfully exploiting this antagonism, Regazzi managed to disrupt the Molinella fascio and obstruct, at least temporarily, every initiative taken by Furlani in 1923, from boycotts against the red transport workers to projects for the construction of a sugar refinery in the commune.[97] Similarly, in his report on Marchesini, the prefect charged in 1924 that the squad commander from Budrio had refused to recognize how "the accession of fascism to the government imposed and imposes on all Fascists special duties of discipline and obedience to the laws," and instead had continued "to use violence indiscriminately against everyone, including Fascists." Marchesini's municipal enemies succeeded in having him jailed on charges of embezzlement and fraud for a brief period in the spring of 1924, but upon his release, he provoked a new crisis in the Budrio organization by linking up with dissident syndical elements to promote a strike by bricklayers opposed by the leaders of the fascio.[98]

Both local authorities and PNF observers traced the chronic prob-

[96] For efforts by the PNF and the government to demobilize the squads and control Fascist violence, see ASB, C7 F1, De Bono to Prefects, January 27, 31, March 27, 1923; *ibid.*, Mussolini to Prefect, June 13, 1923. On the general problem of the squad commanders, see A. Lyttelton, *The Seizure of Power*, pp. 168-169.

[97] ASB, C7 F1, 3, Royal Commissioner to Prefect, May 13, 1923.

[98] ASB, C7 F1, 1, Police Chief to Prefect, May 16, 1924; ACS, Finzi, B11, F118, Prefectoral Report, June 8, 1924.

lems of feuding and factionalism in the fasci to the weakness of the Provincial Fascist Federation and its failure to provide strong, decisive leadership. Without one dominant figure such as Balbo in Ferrara or Farinacci in Cremona, the federation lacked the unity and authority required to impose its policies uniformly throughout the province, resolve conflicts, and discipline dissident elements. Indeed, power struggles within the directorate of the federation itself fueled factional infighting at the local level by splitting the fasci into opposing camps which supported this or that Fascist chieftain. In the district of Imola, for instance, most of the fasci backed their native son, Dino Grandi, and in one fascio, that of Castel San Pietro, police officials warned in the winter of 1923-24 that even a visit by Gino Baroncini could lead to violent incidents. Conversely Baroncini's supporters controlled the majority of fasci in the district of Vergato, where Grandi could count on only three isolated municipal organizations.[99] As a result, political stabilization in Bologna, which the government, the PNF hierarchy, and agrarian interests all desired, presupposed the triumph of one of the rival leaders, who could then centralize and strengthen the authority of the provincial federation.

In the first half of 1923, Gino Baroncini appeared to be the most likely candidate for the job of bringing order to the house of Bolognese fascism. In addition to being the political secretary of the provincial federation and the highest ranking party official in Bologna, Baroncini controlled the Fascist daily, *L'Assalto*, had his man Umberto Baccolini in charge of the labor syndicates, and enjoyed the unqualified backing of the prefect Fausto Aphel. By the fall, his accomplishments in organizing fasci and syndicates in the province had won him a public tribute from the Grand Council and had earned him a position among the *ras* of the Po Valley second only to Roberto Farinacci.[100] During the same period, Baroncini also assumed a prominent role in national politics as the

[99] ASB, C7 F1, 1, Subprefect Imola to Prefect, December 21, 1923; *ibid.*, Subprefect Vergato to Prefect, December 21, 1923.
[100] See A. Lyttelton, *The Seizure of Power*, p. 185.

chief patron of the syndicates and as one of the foremost spokesmen for the intransigent Fascists who demanded new repressive legislation and an end to parliamentary government. Acting in concert with Farinacci, he helped orchestrate a campaign in the fall of 1923 to defeat Massimo Rocca and the moderate revisionist wing of the PNF that favored a conservative restoration of state authority at the expense of the *ras* and the squads.[101]

Baroncini's notoriety as an outspoken defender of provincial fascism, however, aroused the enmity of important government and party officials in Rome who wanted to reduce the power of the local bosses. Already in the summer of 1923, Aldo Finzi, Mussolini's undersecretary for domestic affairs, embarked on his own "holy crusade against the *ras*." Baroncini made himself a primary target of this crusade in August by attacking the undersecretary's efforts to arrange a compromise agreement with the Socialist cooperatives of Molinella. Beginning that month, Baroncini's name was included in police and ministerial reports of supposed "plots by dissident Fascists against the government," and his activities became the object of mounting public criticism in Rome.[102]

Significantly, Finzi's campaign had important support in Bologna where Baroncini's efforts to subordinate all interests to his personal control had begun to alarm other Fascist warlords as well as influential agrarian elements. In the summer of 1923, Baroncini came into open conflict with Dino Grandi and Italo Balbo when he sought to take over *Il Resto del Carlino*.[103] Moreover, his extremist rhetoric, his violent threats, and his zealous defense of the labor syndicates had antagonized and alienated influential agrarian interests. The big commercial farmers of the plains especially resented Baroncini's attempt to use the labor syndicates to limit entrepreneurial freedom and make himself an independent economic force in the countryside.[104]

[101] *Ibid.*, p. 181.

[102] *Ibid.*, p. 185; R. De Felice, *Mussolini il fascista*, vol. I, p. 414.

[103] N. S. Onofri, *I giornali bolognesi nel ventennio fascista* (Bologna, 1972), pp. 96-100, 128-129, 148; *RdC*, May 20, 1923, Baroncini letter.

[104] See A. Lyttelton, *The Seizure of Power*, p. 185, 470 (note 25).

Baroncini's own indiscretions provided his enemies in Rome and Bologna with the opportunity to bring him down in December 1923. Addressing a provincial conference of Fascist cadre early that month, Baroncini accused Grandi of being "a dishonest politician . . . [and] a traitor."[105] In response to demands from Grandi that the party's disciplinary court take action against his accuser, Mussolini relieved Baroncini of his official duties and placed a special PNF commissioner, Eduardo Rotigliano, temporarily in charge of the provincial federation. To prevent the dethroned *ras* from mobilizing his supporters, Rotigliano immediately muzzled *L'Assalto* and forbade any factional rallies or propaganda in the province. Finzi played his part in the drama by transferring the prefect Aphel out of Bologna and by apparently giving his replacement, Arturo Bocchini, orders to join in the campaign against Baroncini.[106] At the same time, certain local squad commanders joined with agrarian leaders to engineer a revolt by the Fascist unions of the plains against Umberto Baccolini, forcing him to resign as head of the federation of syndicates the third week of December. The speed and thoroughness of the campaign made it devastatingly effective. Stripped of his offices, silenced, and deprived of his old influence in the syndicates and prefecture, a stunned and embittered Baroncini formally resigned from the directorate of the federation at the end of the year and shortly thereafter left the party.[107]

The sudden demise of Baroncini resulted in a rather surprising shift of power within the Provincial Fascist Federation. While Grandi had been the man around whom the various currents of opposition had rallied in 1923, it was Leandro Arpinati, boss of the urban fascio, who emerged as the chief beneficiary from the events of

[105] ASB, C7 F1, 2, Prefect to Mussolini, December 3, 1923; *RdC*, December 3, 1923.

[106] *RdC*, December 13, 15, 22, 1923; ACS, Ministero dell'Interno, B50, December 9, 1923, "Verbali di riunione dei rappresentanti nella vertenza Grandi-Baroncini." For transfer of Aphel and the role of Bocchini, see A. Lyttelton, *The Seizure of Power*, p. 185.

[107] ASB, C7 F1, 1, Resolution of Sindacati Pianura, December 21, 1923; ACS, Ministero dell'Interno, B50, Bocchini report, December 21, 1923. For Baroncini's withdrawal, see N. S. Onofri, *I giornali bolognesi*, p. 129, n. 74.

December. The pressing need to restore unity to the strife-torn provincial movement militated against the selection of Grandi as the successor to Baroncini; Grandi's role as a central protagonist in the campaign had made him a controversial figure, especially among the still numerous followers of the defeated *ras*. In any case, Grandi's real ambitions lay in Rome rather than Bologna, and in the summer of 1924 he became undersecretary in the Ministry of Interior.[108]

Arpinati, on the other hand, had maintained a low profile in December and had not been linked publicly to either of the feuding factions within the federation. Although his personal base of support was in the city of Bologna, his solid reputation as a tough Fascist of "the first hour" helped make him more acceptable to the rural *squadristi* who had previously identified with Baroncini. Consequently, he was the only prominent leader capable of mediating the countless petty quarrels and rivalries in the various municipal fasci. Finally and perhaps most importantly, Arpinati was a personal friend of Mussolini who strongly backed his candidacy in order to have a reliable ally in command of one of the most important provincial federations in the country.[109] Early in January 1924, Arpinati took over the post of political secretary of the provincial federation and in March he received additional powers to enforce order and discipline within the local party organizations.[110]

At first glance, the return to prominence of a man who had been a harsh critic of the agrarian wing of the movement in 1921 appeared to mark a serious setback for the Bolognese propertied classes. New conditions in 1924, however, favored a convergence of interests between the city boss and commercial farmers. Charged with the difficult tasks of curbing factionalism and restoring order

[108] A. Lyttelton, *The Seizure of Power*, p. 185; on Grandi's move to Rome, see R. De Felice, *Mussolini il fascista*, vol. I, app. 12.

[109] Concerning relations between Mussolini and Arpinati, see A. Lyttelton, *The Seizure of Power*, pp. 185-186. On Arpinati's appointment, see *RdC*, March 11, 1924.

[110] *Ibid.*

within the fasci, Arpinati needed the support of the big growers to combat dissident elements in rural areas and to bolster his overall authority in the province. The growers were more than willing to give the political secretary this support, since they also had a vested interest in the restoration of political stability, threatened by militant syndicalists and unruly squadrists. Moreover, new channels of communication between the Fascist leader and the agrarians facilitated collaboration. By 1924 Arpinati had become the close friend of a number of young commercial farmers such as Marcello Serrazanetti and Enea Venturi, who began to act as his most trusted advisors on problems in the countryside.[111]

Developments in the first half of the year clearly demonstrated how Arpinati's political aims coincided with the economic interests of the commercial farmers. After crushing the revolt by disgrunted syndicalists in February, Arpinati initiated a campaign to weed out the more militant elements from the Fascist unions in the spring and summer of 1924.[112] To deal with the disruptive activities of the local squad commanders, he relied primarily on the intervention of the prefect and the police. When Emilio Marchesini, for instance, ignored directives from the provincial federation and called a protest rally by the labor syndicates in Budrio, Bocchini sent additional police units to the town and immediately hit Marchesini and his friends with arrest warrants.[113]

Agrarian interests demonstrated their satisfaction with the leadership and initiatives of Arpinati by enthusiastically supporting the PNF in the parliamentary elections of April. Marchese Tanari expressed the general view of the local propertied classes when he wrote a friend prior to the balloting: "I have been a convinced liberal, but now I feel toward liberal theory like that lover who has completely lost faith in his loved one. . . . If before going to the Creator, I will be able to see my country with 'hierarchy,

[111] For conflicts between Arpinati and agrarians in 1921, see Chapter VII, pp. 329-331. On the accommodations of 1924, see ACS, Segretario particolare del Duce, cart. ris., f. "Arpinati"; P. P. D'Attore, "Agrari e fascismo," pp. 24-26.

[112] See notes 67 and 68 in this chapter.

[113] ACS, Finzi, B11, F118, Bocchini report, June 8, 1924.

organization, and *discipline*' [and] with a little less freedom for those who seek to destroy it, I will not mourn over the replacement of theory by the new practice!"[114] During the campaign, the FPSA functioned as an electoral agency, deluging its members with leaflets that urged them to show their "trust in the head of the government and the Duce of fascism" while influential growers played an active role in organizing profascist rallies in the rural areas of the province.[115] Both Arpinati and the agrarians could be pleased with the results of their political collaboration; in Bologna the Fascist-dominated National List captured over 70 percent of the vote.[116]

Bolognese agrarians had little reason to withdraw their support from fascism even after the political crisis that rocked the country in June 1924. Indeed, the Matteotti affair appeared to strengthen the commitment of the big landowners and commercial farmers to Arpinati and the government. Despite the dramatic resignation of Aldo Oviglio, the leading Bolognese Fascist moderate, as minister of justice, the old parties of order displayed no signs of resurgence or opposition to Mussolini and the PNF.[117] Much as in Ferrara, the bulk of growers had backed and often instigated the violence of the squads in the past, and consequently lacked the reservations and scruples of middle-class Fascists in other areas of the country. For the most part, they were alarmed less by the brutal murder of the Socialist deputy than by the political instability and social unrest it had produced. Typical of their attitude was that of Carlo Ballerini, a prominent landowner and Catholic political figure. A long time sympathizer of fascism, Ballerini chose to enroll officially in the PNF shortly after the discovery of Mat-

114 Biblioteca Comunale di Bologna, MS Tanari, XL, 4, letter dated March 14, 1924.

115 On propaganda, see ASB, C5 F1, FPSA leaflet of April 2, 1924 and *Bollettino Sindacato degli Agricoltori di Bazzano*, no. 2-3, March 28, 1924. On the activities of the growers in the electoral committees, see *L'Assalto*, April 5, 1924.

116 *RdC*, April 8, 1924 reported that the National List won 111,112 votes, while the six other slates together polled less than 32,000.

117 See ASB, C7 F1, 1, Prefect to Ministry of Interior, July 16, 1924. On Oviglio's resignation, see R. De Felice, *Mussolini il fascista*, vol. I, p. 645.

teotti's body in August, a particularly difficult moment for Mussolini's government. In a letter to Arpinati, Ballerini attributed his decision to the fact that the Matteotti affair had "revived suddenly the dormant aspirations of political desperados."[118]

The wisdom of this course of action became evident after Mussolini's speech to the Chamber of Deputies on January 3. With the gradual consolidation of the Fascist dictatorship in 1925, the locus of power shifted definitively from the provinces to Rome, a shift that enhanced Arpinati's power as party *federale* in Bologna. Under instructions from Mussolini to restore discipline in the party, the Bolognese political secretary proceeded in the fall of 1925 to disband the squads and dissolve all those fasci in which there were continued disturbances. The general reorganization of the PNF along strictly hierarchical lines in 1926 further bolstered Arpinati's authority by eliminating elections within the party and by giving the *federali* responsibility for nominating the secretaries of the local organizations.[119]

Arpinati displayed a surprising discretion in the use of his new powers. In collaboration with the prefect and influential agrarian leaders, he employed a blend of punishments and rewards to remove his opponents and establish his control over the rural fasci. While he ruthlessly persecuted those bosses like Augusto Regazzi, who refused to renounce their municipal thrones, Arpinati also inserted many former dissident Fascists into comfortable, but politically harmless, positions in the state administration or the private sector. Both Baroncini and his old lieutenant Umberto Baccolini became executives of the agrarians' insurance company, Ramo Grandine, the former as a board member in Milan, the latter as an agent in Bologna. Likewise, Emilio Marchesini, the exsquad commander from Budrio, received a seat on the Provincial Council; in compensation for his dismissal as secretary of the labor syndicates, Alberto Cuccoli was appointed *podestà* of Castelfranco, the

[118] *L'Assalto*, n. 35, 1924, cited in N. S. Onofri, *I giornali bolognesi*, p. 66. For similar situation in Ferrara, see P. Corner, *Fascism in Ferrara*, pp. 272-273.

[119] See A. Lyttelton, *The Seizure of Power*, pp. 285-295.

administrative office that replaced elected municipal councils. In this way, potential troublemakers were not only disarmed and cut off from their local supporters, but also pacified by the lure of opportunities for personal advancement within the regime.[120]

By the end of 1926, the process of political stabilization in Bologna had been largely completed. As police officials reported the following year, the provincial federation had become "a strong and truly secure organism with a disciplined mass base." Not surprisingly, the new stability marked a personal triumph for Arpinati, who according to the same officials, enjoyed the "popularity, trust, and esteem of the great majority of the population" and was the "leader recognized by one and all."[121] Apart from his political clout as party *federale,* he exercised sweeping control over propaganda and leisure activities in the province as *podestà* of the capital city, administrative director of *Il Resto del Carlino,* and president of the Italian federations of soccer and track and field.[122]

The structure of political power in Bologna after 1926, however, was less a one-man dictatorship than a *de facto* partnership between Arpinati and the local propertied classes, which benefited enormously from the elimination of popular suffrage and free party competition. Indeed, they acquired a degree of political influence unparalleled since the late nineteenth century. Approximately half the *podestà* in the province were either prominent agrarians or their agents in the late 1920s.[123] A similar situation prevailed on the Provincial Council, where the seats once occupied by popularly elected Socialist representatives were now filled by the "natural

[120] On the persecution of Regazzi, see ACS, Segretario particolare del Duce, cart. ris., B45, F242r. For Baroncini and Baccolini, see *Ibid,* B79; on Cuccoli and Marchesini, see P. P. D'Attore, "Agrari e fascismo," p. 94. Such practices reflected more general trends within the PNF after 1926; see Lyttelton, p. 301.

[121] ACS, Segretario particolare del Duce, cart. ris., B75, "Arpinati," police report, October 6, 1927.

[122] On Arpinati's role in the management of *Il Resto del Carlino,* see N. S. Onofri, *I giornali bolognesi,* pp. 102-107; for his other activities, see P. P. D'Attore, "Agrari e fascismo," pp. 24-26; A. Lyttelton, *The Seizure of Power,* p. 303; documents included in the file cited in the previous footnote.

[123] For complete list, see ASB, C4 F1, June 2, 1926.

leaders" of the community. Presided over by Vittorio Peglion, director of the Superior School of Agriculture at the university, the Provincial Council included the leaders of the FPSA as well as a number of big commercial farmers, industrial entrepreneurs, and bankers. Finally, agrarian interests were well represented at the upper levels of the Provincial Fascist Federation by the young commercial farmers Marcello Serrazanetti, Enrico Cacciari, and Enea Venturi, who were among Arpinati's closest advisors and friends.[124]

Such arrangements though did not constitute a simple restoration or return to the past. Under the new regime, agrarian notables no longer had the type of direct control over political decisions they had once enjoyed through their local liberal and monarchist clubs. They might exercise sizeable influence through the *podestà*, prefecture, and provincial federation, but the actual decisions were now made by professional party bureaucrats and state officials in Rome rather than by informal understandings between landed gentlemen as in the late nineteenth century. Nor did fascism restore the largely unorganized "free for all" that had characterized social relations in the province prior to the advent of the Socialist leagues. In exchange for the strong government they had long sought, agrarian interests had to curb their traditional individualism and accept a certain level of organizational regimentation, even in their dealings with agricultural laborers. Despite the obvious weakness of the Fascist syndicates, landowners and commercial farmers still had to recognize them and at least go through the ritual of negotiating collective agreements with them.[125]

At the same time, the consolidation of the Fascist regime helped to institutionalize a shift in the balance of power within the Bolognese elite that had begun in the first decade of the century. While the propertied classes as a whole benefited from the triumph of

[124] See P. P. D'Attore, "Agrari e fascismo," p. 82, 89-90. Arpinati also had a farm at Malacappa which he received as a loan from his friend, the commercial farmer Enea Venturi. See N. S. Onofri, *I giornali bolognesi*, p. 133, n. 146.

[125] See C. Maier, *Recasting Bourgeois Europe*, pp. 572, 584.

fascism, it was a relatively new group of ambitious commercial farmers, and not the old guard of absentee landowners, who dominated the major centers of economic power and political influence in the province after 1926. The names of once prominent patrician families—Cavazza, Tanari, Salina, Malvezzi, Hercolani, Massei—had mostly disappeared from the roster of municipal and provincial councilors, *podestà*, and directors of banks, land reclamation companies, employers' associations, and commodity organizations. In their place appeared the names of men more attuned to the imperatives of capitalist agriculture: big prewar leaseholders like Alfredo Benni and Cesare Bonora, the sons of an earlier generation of commercial farmers, and young agricultural technicians such as Gino Cacciari and Julo Fornaciari. Those members of the old aristocracy like Count Gualtiero Isolani, who remained active in provincial affairs, did so as farmer-businessmen rather than as absentee landlords.[126]

The dominant position of commercial farming interests found expression not only in the control of key institutions, but also in the structure of property holdings in the Bolognese plains in the late 1920s. The provincial land registry of 1925, and subsequent additions to it, show that many of the most important noble families had given up their estates. Thus, for example, four of the largest aristocratic landowners in Bologna prior to the rise of fascism—Count Francesco Cavazza, Prince Luigi Napoleone Bonaparte, Prince don Antonio d'Orleans, and Marchese Giuseppe Tanari—had all sold their properties by 1927.[127] Significantly, the

[126] For information on Count Isolani, see A. Bignardi, *Costruttori di terra*, pp. 20-21. Enea Venturi, Marcello Serrazanetti, Anselmo Ramponi, and the Lenzi brothers were all sons of prominent commercial farmers.

[127] See Catasto dei terreni, communes of Molinella, Medicina, Minerbio, Budrio, San Giovanni in Persiceto, Galliera, and San Pietro in Casale. While twelve of the largest estates in Minerbio in 1902 were owned by old aristocratic families, in 1925 only four of them remained on the land registry, and the holdings of two of them had been reduced to less than one hundred hectares. Likewise, the estates of the Prince di Orleans, Count Marchetti, and Count Armandi Avogli Oratti in San Giovanni in Persiceto were divided up and sold between 1920 and 1924. See ASB, C6 F2, "Elenco dei detentori di terreno nel mandamento di Minerbio," 1902;

major buyers of land were either former leaseholders or new joint-stock farm companies. In 1925 the Bonora family owned nearly seven hundred hectares of the Ducato di Galliera, the estate it had previously leased from the Prince d'Orleans; two years later, Alfredo Benni bought virtually all the property of his landlord Prince Bonaparte, some eighteen hundred hectares of the most valuable farm land in Molinella, Minerbio, and Budrio.[128] The same period witnessed the rapid growth of farm companies. By 1928, three of these companies—the Società Anonima Agricola, the Società Agricola Portonovo, and the Imprese e Conduzioni Agricola—controlled over eight thousand hectares of prime farm land in the lower plains.[129]

As these trends in organizational leadership and property holding suggest, the consolidation of Fascist authority in the province of Bologna entailed more than the defeat of the rural working classes and the defense of inherited social position and political power. If fascism began as a disparate reaction of many social groups to the "red tyranny," its subsequent evolution betrayed the expectations not only of men "of the first hour" and militant syndicalists, but also of the agrarian old guard. Despite its rhetorical defense of small peasant property and its glorification of traditional rural values, the regime created a set of institutional arrangements that consistently favored the big landowners and

---

L. Scagliarini, "Proprietari e contadini a S. Giovanni in Persiceto (1919-1924)" in Deputazione Emilia-Romagna per la storia della Resistenza, *Movimento operaio e fascismo nell'Emilia-Romagna* (Rome, 1973), p. 164.

128 See Catasto dei terreni. Among the other big leaseholders who became major landowners were Roberto Cremonini, Giuseppe Bolognesi, Augusto Lenzi, Alessandro Dal Rio, Enea Venturi, Alfonso Funi, and Giuseppe Taddia.

129 *Ibid.* Under the direction of Roberto Cremonini, the Società Anonima Agricola purchased the estates of Count Francesco Cavazza, some three thousand hectares in the plains, in 1928. The Società Agricola Portonovo was founded by Ignazio Benelli in 1918, and owned over twenty-four hundred hectares in the commune of Medicina. Constituted in 1919 in Rome, the Imprese e Conduzioni Agricole owned 1,483 hectares in San Pietro in Casale, as well as a farm of 604 hectares in Galliera. For additional information, see Credito Italiano, *Società Italiane per azioni, 1920*, 3 vols. (Rome, 1921), vol. III, p. 2194 and 2198.

farmers over the little man after 1926.[130] More importantly, within the dominant classes, some groups gained more than others. For the transformation of the Bolognese fascist movement into an authoritarian system of power was above all the triumph of the well-organized, efficient, and ruthless protagonists of commercial agriculture.

[130] For general trends after 1926, see P. Corner, "Fascist Agrarian Policy," pp. 244-254.

EPILOGUE: THE RELATIVE REWARDS OF DICTATORSHIP

Although the basic framework of agrarian economic power and political influence had been largely institutionalized by the end of 1926, the advantages commercial farmers derived from it must be located in the context of developments after 1926. Indeed, the most important structural changes in relations between the agricultural sector, industry, and the Fascist regime took place in the late 1920s and the ensuing decade. On the whole these changes were decidedly unfavorable to agriculture, which suffered a severe and prolonged depression and saw its interests subordinated to those of heavy industry. Clearly 1927 marked the crucial turning point. The drastic revaluation of the lira the previous year provoked a catastrophic fall in farm exports, prices, and incomes. As Gino Cacciari, the top agrarian official in the regime, reported to the Fascist Grand Council, "the category of producers, which has felt most brutally the impact of the crisis created by the healthy deflationary policy, is that of the farmers. Anyone who has examined objectively the conditions of the farmers in certain provinces . . . can attest to this truth: more than the interests of individuals have been compromised; the productivity of the land has been compromised because the farmers lack the financial resources to hold out."[1]

[1] ACS, Segretario particolare, cart. ris., B27, Cacciari to Grand Council, November 7, 1928. On the effects of revaluation on agriculture, see Ruggero Grieco, "La

Far from being a temporary setback, the deflationary trends of 1927 continued into the 1930s. For the Battle of the Lira also contributed substantially to altering the terms of exchange between agriculture and industry. Both as a supplier of raw materials to industry and as a consumer of manufactured goods, the position of agriculture worsened during the 1930s. While farm prices fell 44 percent between 1928 and 1934, prices for the principal industrial products fell only 29 percent. Nor did the agricultural revival after 1933 close this "scissors crisis," since farm prices rose less rapidly than those of industry. By the beginning of World War II, the relative importance of agriculture in the national economy had declined significantly.[2]

To a certain extent, the difficulties of Italian farmers were the result of a worldwide crisis of agricultural production in the interwar decades. After World War I, a period in which European and American farmers had enjoyed high prices for their crops, the growth in food supplies, together with the general recession of 1921, led to a sharp drop in farm incomes. Except for a brief resurgence in 1924, agricultural prices remained at a low level throughout the 1920s. Efforts by growers to compensate for their reduced income per unit through increased output only accentuated the problems of overproduction by intensifying pressures on agricultural prices in the glutted world market. Moreover, much as in Italy, farmers elsewhere in Europe and in the United States were caught in an increasingly disastrous price scissors in their dealings with industry.[3] Even prior to the revaluation of the lira,

situazione agraria e contadina alla fine del 1927," *Lo Stato Operaio*, II, no. 3 (March 1928), pp. 89-97; Adrian Lyttelton, *The Seizure of Power: Fascism in Italy, 1919-1929* (New York, 1973), pp. 351-352.

[2] On the relationship between agricultural and industrial prices, see Ministero per la Costituente, *Rapporto della commissione economica*, Vol. II, *Industria—Relazione* (Rome, 1947), pp. 3-10; Ester Fano, "Problemi e vicende dell'agricoltura italiana tra le due guerre," *Quaderni Storici*, no. 29-30, May-December 1975, p. 484.

[3] See M. Tracy, *Agriculture in Western Europe: Crisis and Adaptation Since 1880* (London, 1946), pp. 117-120; Ingvar Svennilson, *Growth and Stagnation in the European Economy* (Geneva, 1954), pp. 82-89.

Italian growers of sugar beets and hemp began to feel the effects of this unfavorable international market situation. In 1924, for instance, renewed competition from Czechoslovakian sugar factories drove down prices on the home market, leading refiners to repudiate their agreements with the Sugar Beet Growers' Federation and suspend payments to the farmers.[4] Likewise, hemp growers were already in difficulty before 1927. After a short period of prosperity in the mid-1920s, when prices rose to over 1,000 lire per quintal and production expanded, the dumping of Russian hemp on European markets in 1926 cut foreign demand for Italian production; in the course of the year domestic hemp prices plummeted nearly 40 percent.[5]

In Italy, however, the policies of the Fascist regime strongly affected the timing and severity of the crisis in the countryside. By 1925 there were numerous indications that the Italian economy had become dangerously overheated: rising imports of raw materials and foodstuffs, the falling value of the lira on foreign exchanges, skyrocketing inflation.[6] In response to these alarming conditions, Mussolini adopted policies of selective protection and monetary deflation in order to reduce food imports, cut consumption, and encourage industrial concentration, savings, and foreign investment in Italy. The cumulative effect of such policies was to sacrifice the interests of agricultural producers to those of heavy industry, which produced for the domestic market and required cheap imported raw materials. While the high level of revaluation crippled agricultural exports by making them more expensive on foreign markets, the introduction of new duties on imported farm machines in 1926-27 pushed up the production costs of Italian growers. Even those programs ostensibly designed to aid agriculture—the "Battle of Wheat" and "Integral Land Reclamation"—

[4] A. Lyttelton, *The Seizure of Power*, p. 338.

[5] For the fluctuations in hemp prices, cultivation, and production, see Roberto Roversi, *Canapa ed autarchia* (Rome, 1939), pp. 15-16; Giovanni Proni, *La canapicoltura italiana nell'economia corporativa* (Rome, 1938), pp. 40-49; *L'Agricoltore d'Italia*, v, no. 15, April 10, 1926.

[6] A. Lyttelton, *The Seizure of Power*, p. 338.

were tailored to the needs of industry, since they aimed to expand the domestic market for chemical fertilizers, farm machines, and irrigation plants at a time when foreign demand had slackened.[7]

Structural differences between the largely competitive agricultural and monopolistic industrial sectors accentuated the negative effects of Fascist economic policies in the countryside. With their superior organization and dominance in their respective areas of production, giant corporations like FIAT, Montecatini, Eridania, and the Linoficio e Canapificio Nazionale were in a position to dictate the terms of exchange with their agrarian suppliers and buyers. Despite the serious crisis in agriculture, the declared profits of the sugar cartel nearly tripled from 1927 to 1930.[8] The same years also saw Montecatini extend its control over the production and marketing of chemical fertilizers in Italy. By the fall of 1931, Montecatini had effectively eliminated its foreign competitors and imposed an agreement on the Federconsorzi that enabled the company to regulate production of sulphuric acid and phosphates, and to set its own prices.[9]

The sacrifices resulting from this general subordination of agriculture to large-scale industry, however, were not shared equally by all the regions and classes of rural Italy. The new postwar class of small peasant proprietors, who had been among the earliest converts to fascism in the countryside, suffered most directly from the economic conditions that prevailed after 1926. In the absence of any protection from the regime, prices for vegetables, fruits, olive oil, and wine—the staples of the peasant economy especially

[7] On these functions of the programs, see C. Schmidt, *The Plough and the Sword* (New York, 1938), pp. 71-72; Andrea Marabini, "I risultati della battaglia del grano," *Lo Stato Operaio*, VIII, no. 5 (May 1934), pp. 392-406; Alessandra Staderini, "La politica cerealicola del regime: l'impostazione della battaglia del grano," *Storia Contemporanea*, IX, no. 5-6 (December 1978), pp. 1027-1079; E. Fano, "Problemi e vicende dell'agricoltura," pp. 484-485.

[8] See Paul Corner, *Fascism in Ferrara, 1915-1925* (London, 1975), p. 286.

[9] Angelo Ventura, "La Federconsorzi dall'età liberale al fascismo," *Quaderni Storici*, no. 36, December 1977, pp. 716-719; C. Schmidt, *The Plough and the Sword*, p. 71n.

in the south—declined dramatically.[10] At the same time that their incomes fell, the revaluation of the lira increased the burden of their debts, driving many small proprietors into bankruptcy or forcing them to sell their holdings precisely when land values were slipping. According to Sereni, the number of forced land sales for failure to pay taxes septupled between 1926 and 1936, while the number of expropriations in favor of creditors increased nearly ten-fold.[11] The ruthless elimination of these peasant strata from the productive process seriously undermined the claims of fascism to be a regime of the small property holder.

The large landowners and commercial farmers of the Po Valley fared considerably better, since the regime provided them with a range of mechanisms to protect their profit levels and escape the worst effects of the crisis. From the outset, the destruction of the Socialist labor movement and the creation of a powerful repressive apparatus in the countryside allowed the big growers to respond to the fall in farm prices by slashing wages or by returning to sharecropping and leasing arrangements that shifted a larger portion of the expenses and risks on to the peasant laborers. As a result of agreements between agrarian employers and the compliant Fascist unions, Salvemini estimated that agricultural workers lost from 50 to 70 percent of their earnings between 1926 and 1934.[12] The same period saw a sizeable growth in the number of sharecroppers and tenant farmers as well as a pronounced deterioration in the contractual terms they had to accept. In the prov-

[10] A. Cadeddu, S. Lepre, F. Socrate, "Ristagno e sviluppo nell'agricoltura italiana, 1918-1939," *Quaderni Storici*, no. 29-30, May-December 1975, pp. 505-507.

[11] E. Sereni, *La questione agraria nella rinascita nazionale italiana* (Rome, 1946), pp. 123-124. The plight of the small proprietors was recognized by the agricultural technicians of the regime, see Osvaldo Passerini, *Inchiesta sulla piccola proprietà coltivatrice formatasi nel dopoguerra*, Vol. VII, *Emilia e Le Marche* (Milan, 1932), pp. 45-48. Commenting on the situation in Bologna, the FPSFA reported to the prefect how the sharp drop in prices had "extremely serious repercussions in agricultural circles, especially among the small farmers who are awaiting their first harvest after an entire year of crisis that has left them deeply in debt." ASB, C16 F1, June 30, 1928.

[12] Gaetano Salvemini, *Under the Axe of Fascism* (New York, 1971), p. 228.

ince of Bologna, for instance, the *mezzadria* contract of 1929 not only increased the landlord's share of the harvest and gave him absolute control over crop selection, farming techniques, and marketing, but also transferred half the expenditures for fertilizers and insecticides, and all the costs of transportation and the maintenance of dikes, ditches, and drains to the sharecropper.[13] In this fashion, agrarian employers were able to lessen the impact of the crisis by intensifying their exploitation of labor in relation to costs. Such arrangements in the northern plains constituted more a temporary response to unfavorable market conditions than a permanent reversion to backward and less productive methods of farming. Corner's analysis of the 1931 and 1936 censuses in Bologna and Ferrara suggests that once agricultural prices began to rise in the mid-1930s the big growers reduced their reliance on sharecropping and returned to labor systems that employed large numbers of landless agricultural workers.[14]

The capitalist farmers of the Po Valley were also the chief beneficiaries of fascism's policies of grain protection and land reclamation, which greatly strengthened their position both as direct agricultural producers and as commercial and financial intermediaries in the countryside. In the summer of 1925, the regime launched the "Battle of Grain," instituting a series of measures to protect the price of wheat and encourage growers to increase the productivity of their farms. In addition to a new and quite high import duty designed to raise domestic wheat prices, a variety of subsidy devices were introduced to stimulate more intensive cultivation: reduced gasoline prices for farm machines, special railroad freight rates for chemical fertilizers, assistance in the distribution of select seeds, and funds for the construction of silos.[15]

With their rich farms, technical expertise, and access to invest-

[13] C. Schmidt, *The Plough and the Sword,* p. 134.

[14] P. Corner, "Considerazioni sull'agricoltura capitalistica durante il fascismo," *Quaderni Storici,* no. 29-30, May-December 1975, p. 528.

[15] C. Schmidt, *The Plough and the Sword,* pp. 49-50; G. Tattara, "Cerealicultura e politica agraria durante il fascismo," in G. Toniolo, ed., *Lo Sviluppo economico italiano, 1861-1940* (Bari, 1973), p. 377.

ment capital, the commercial growers of the Bolognese plains were ideally situated to take advantage of the regime's program. Both its price-support measures and its investment subsidies favored the more efficient farmers who had substantial quantities of wheat available for market.[16] The lending policies of the Cassa di Risparmio, an agency of the wheat campaign, clearly followed this pattern. Often only the large growers had access to the new forms of credit instituted by the bank. In the case of its pooling operations, for example, the bank restricted its monetary advances for pooled wheat to those farmers with over one hundred quintals of grain, a restriction that excluded most small peasant proprietors. Moreover, almost all the forty-five silos financed by the Cassa di Risparmio in the late 1920s and early 1930s were located in sixteen communes of the low plains.[17]

Such institutional arrangements produced predictable results. The bulk of new investments in seed, machines, and chemical fertilizers after 1925 appears to have been concentrated on the large farms of the plains. By 1932, 95 percent of the wheat-growing area in the plains was being sown with high-yield seed, in comparison to only 50 percent in the rest of the province.[18] The number of tractors in use in the plains rose by more than a third between 1925 and 1932, while in the foothills and mountains there remained few if any in operation. Likewise, the big farms of the plains were the major purchasers of nitrate fertilizers, the consumption of which doubled from 1926 to 1929.[19] Since the tariffs kept domestic wheat prices well above those on the world market, these invest-

[16] P. Corner, "Fascist Agrarian Policy and the Italian Economy in the Interwar Years," p. 251; G. Tattara, "Cerealicultura e politica agraria," p. 385.

[17] On the lending policies of the bank, see A. Marabini, "I risultati della battaglia del grano," pp. 196-197, for the financing and distribution of the silos, see Consiglio Provinciale dell'Economia Corporativa, *La provincia di Bologna nell'anno decimo. Monografia statistica-economica* (Bologna, 1932), pp. 498-502, and Cassa di Risparmio, *La Cassa di Risparmio in Bologna nei suoi primi cento anni* (Bologna, 1937), p. 295.

[18] Consiglio Provinciale, *La provincia di Bologna*, p. 593.

[19] *Ibid.*, pp. 553-563; UMA, *Quarant'anni di motorizzazione agricola in Italia 1928-1967* (Rome, 1968), pp. 16-17, 98-99, 238-239.

ments enabled commercial growers to prosper not only by expanding their output, but by increasing the productivity of their farms. Even during the worst years of the Great Depression, between 1930 and 1932, wheat harvests in the plains of Bologna more than doubled, production per hectare rose from 17.3 to over 37 quintals.[20]

At the same time, the Battle of Wheat encouraged a new fusion of public and private power that further consolidated the organizational control of capitalist agrarian interests over the local agricultural economy. In the years after 1925, the Bolognese Wheat Commission—together with established entities like the Agrarian Consortium, the Società Bolognese Produttori Sementi, and the Cassa di Risparmio—received extensive authority to administer the program at the provincial level. Through these semi-official agencies, in which they held the levers of power, a small group of commercial farmers were able to dominate the access of virtually all agricultural producers to credit, supplies of seed, machines, and fertilizers, and even the markets for the sale of their crops.[21] Mutually advantageous cooperation between the consortium, seed company, and bank led to their growing financial integration, so that in 1931, for instance, the Cassa di Risparmio became the majority stockholder in the Società Bolognese Produttori Sementi.[22]

The second major agricultural program of the fascist regime, Comprehensive Land Reclamation, provided similar advantages and

[20] Consiglio Provinciale dell'Economia Corporativa, *La provincia di Bologna*, p. 594. The national average yields in 1932 were 15.3 quintals per hectare. See C. Schmidt, *The Plough and the Sword*, p. 54.

[21] On the role of the FPSFA and the Bolognese Wheat Commission, see ASB, C16 F1, 1928, Federation to Syndicates and Technicians, September 12, 1925; *ibid.*, Federation to CNSFA, June 20, 1928; *L'Agricoltore d'Italia*, IV, no. 21 and 24, August 8 and 29, 1925. The membership of the commission included Count Gualtiero Isolani, Gino Cacciari, Alfredo Benni, Enea Venturi, Cesare Bonora, and Giuseppe Garagnani. See ASB, C16 F1, 1926, August 6, 1925. For the activities of the seed company and the rural bank, see *L'Agricoltore d'Italia*, V, no. 34, August 21, 1926; ASB, C16 F1, FPSFA to Prefect, June 2, 1928; Cassa di Risparmio, *Cassa di Risparmio in Bologna*, pp. 294-296.

[22] See *Cassa di Risparmio in Bologna*, pp. 294-296.

benefits. As conceived by its chief architect, Arrigo Serpieri, this program involved massive state intervention in the countryside to bring about a profound transformation of land usage and secure "the intensification of production in those regions where waste lands exist."[23] Government-sponsored consortia of landowners were to assume responsibility for the improvement of designated areas, carrying out all works that would increase agricultural output and raise productivity. Other features of the program aimed to force the modernization of underdeveloped areas of the country by opening them up to penetration by commercial farming interests. Thus, Serpieri proposed to make improvements in certain areas compulsory rather than voluntary, and stipulated that in cases of noncompliance the land could be expropriated in favor of outside consortia and private joint-stock companies that agreed to carry out the required work.[24]

If the actual achievements of Comprehensive Land Reclamation fell far short of Serpieri's aspirations because of the Depression and resistance from southern landowners, the program did serve to strengthen the strong in the Bolognese countryside.[25] After 1924 the two major private consortia for land reclamation—the Renana and the Crevalcorese—also became organs of the state, representing what Serpieri described as the "union between public and private elements." As such, they received substantial state funds, the authority to set work priorities and, with subsequent legislation in 1928, the power to compel proprietors to participate in the projects.[26] Moreover, much like the Battle of Wheat, Comprehen-

[23] Arrigo Serpieri, "La bonifica integrale," conference in September 1927, cited L. Villari, *Il capitalismo italiano del '900* (Bari, 1975), pp. 194-201.

[24] C. Schmidt, *The Plough and the Sword*, pp. 79-80; Jon S. Cohen, "Un esame statistico delle opere di bonifica intraprese durante il regime fascista," in G. Toniolo, ed., *Lo sviluppo economico italiano* (Bari, 1973), p. 354.

[25] On the shortcomings of the program, see A. Lyttelton, *The Seizing of Power*, pp. 350-351, in addition to the works cited in the previous note.

[26] A. Serpieri, "La bonifica integrale," p. 201. On the background of the consortia in Bologna, see *L'Agricoltore d'Italia*, v, no. 46, November 6, 1926; Consiglio Provinciale, *La provincia di Bologna*, pp. 420-431. For the board members of the Renana, see ASB, C6 F2, 3, "Personale del consorzio della Bonifica Renana," 1922,

sive Land Reclamation helped to enlarge the role of the rural banks in the countryside. Since the government provided only part of the necessary capital, the less affluent members of the consortia had to turn to local credit institutions like the Cassa di Risparmio which financed the reclamation initiatives.[27]

The large commercial farmers, who sat on the boards of the reclamation consortia and the rural banks, used the authority of the state and public funds to advance their private interests. The area of Bologna most affected by the project encompassed a zone of 111,640 hectares in the lower plains where the commercial farms already predominated.[28] By 1935 when the two consortia had largely completed their work, some 338 million lire had been invested in the construction of drainage systems, electrical plants, roads, and canals. As a result of these improvements, property values in the reclaimed areas tripled, while previously unproductive land now produced yields well above the national average.[29] In addition, the big farmers were able to exploit most fully the infrastructure created by the projects. Much of the agricultural machinery employed in reclamation passed into their hands by the mid-1930s. Similarly, the new power plants benefited almost exclusively a select group of growers who used them for the electrification of their farms.[30]

The same growers were also the direct beneficiaries of the privileged treatment the Fascist regime accorded to producers of sugar beets, rice, and hemp—the mainstays of commercial agriculture

---

and ACS, Presidenza del Consiglio dei Ministri, 1925, F3, 1-1, Benelli to Mussolini, June 30, 1925; for that of the Crevalcorese, see *L'Agricoltore d'Italia*, IV, no. 26, September 12, 1925.

[27] On the role of the bank, see *Cassa di Risparmio in Bologna*, p. 298. For the authority of the consortia, see J. Cohen, "Un esame statistico," p. 355.

[28] Giuseppe Tassinari, *La bonifica integrale nel decennale della legge Mussolini* (Rome, 1935), pp. 98-99; Consiglio Provinciale, *La provincia di Bologna*, pp. 420-431.

[29] See G. Tassinari, *La bonifica integrale*, pp. 88, 98-100, 119. In the province, 700 kilometers of canals, 164 kilometers of roads, and 20 power plants were constructed. For additional information, see Consiglio Provinciale *La provincia di Bologna*, p. 554, and FPSFA, *Relazione della presidenza 1932* (Bologna, 1932), p. 75.

[30] *Ibid.*

in the Po Valley. The regime intervened energetically in behalf of these crops, providing either protective tariffs or export subsidies, and advancing policies of cartellization, rationalization, and production controls. In the case of sugar beets, protectionism represented above all a mechanism to ensure "harmony" between conflicting economic groups by allowing them to reconcile their interests at the expense of the consumer.[31] The sharp drop in sugar prices in 1924 provoked a serious clash between growers and refiners. Despite the introduction of a moderate tariff at the end of the year, the refiners' union refused to negotiate a new agreement with the growers' federation, which retaliated by ordering its members to curtail their cultivation of sugar beets.[32] These conflicts did not prevent the two organizations from launching a common campaign in Rome for higher duties on sugar. In response to their pressures, the government formed a special tariff commission that included the head of the Sugar Beet Growers' Federation, the director of the FISA, and the president of the refiners' union. Since most of the members had "a direct and immediate interest in the reestablishment of the tariff," it was hardly surprising that the commission concluded its work with a strong recommendation that the government double the existing duties on imported sugar.[33] In the fall of 1925, the government granted the increase, the first of many that would assure producers a virtual monopoly of the domestic market and make Italy the country with the highest-priced sugar in Western Europe. Protection not only facilitated intersectoral

[31] A. Lyttelton, *The Seizure of Power*, p. 340.

[32] On the actions of the refiners, see *RdC*, February 1, 1925; *L'Agricoltore d'Italia*, IV, no. 2, March 28, 1925; L. Perdisa, *La bietola da zucchero nella economia italiana* (Rome, 1938), p. 255. For the reaction of the beet growers, see ASB, C16 F1, 1926, Resolution of FISA, March 29, 1925; ACS, Presidenza del Consiglio dei Ministri, 1925, F3 SF8, Bocchini to Ministero dell'Interno, April 7, 1925. The Bolognese Consortium alone managed to have the area devoted to beet cultivation reduced from 3,224 to 915 hectares. See ASB, C16 F1, 1926, statistics on sugar beet acreage for 1924-25.

[33] For an account of the commission's activities, see F. A. Repaci, "La relazione della commissione per il regime doganale delle bietole e dello zucchero in Italia," *Riforma Sociale*, 1925, pp. 523-537.

cooperation, but also bound the growers and refiners more closely to their respective cartels. In the years after 1925, the two cartels worked together to limit output and maintain prices by stipulating national contracts that fixed the quota of sugar beets for each factory and the acreage which each grower could devote to the crop.[34]

Local rice and hemp growers found the Fascist regime no less responsive to their needs and problems. During the 1920s, the regimentation of labor and favorable market conditions had encouraged Bolognese rice growers to double their production.[35] But rice, primarily an export crop, could not escape the effects of the Great Depression. Beginning in 1929, rice prices fell precipitously on world markets; by 1933 they were a third of what they had been prior to the crisis.[36] Lobbying by the National Consortium of Rice Growers and the National Fascist Confederation of Farmers led the government to intervene in the fall of 1931 with a complex system of "export dumping" and high import duties. To administer the system, the government founded the National Rice Agency which established minimum farm prices of rice and paid a bounty to exporters so that they could sell abroad below world prices.[37] Such arrangements worked decisively to the advantage of a select group of commercial farmers in Bologna, since they kept domestic prices well above those on world markets. Significantly, Bolognese growers increased their production of rice by 12.5 percent between 1929 and 1936.[38]

The Fascist regime also intervened in favor of hemp growers in 1931. Already in difficulty in 1926, producers of this crop saw

[34] A. Lyttelton, *The Seizure of Power*, p. 340; L. Perdisa, *La bietola da zucchero*, pp. 253–257.

[35] See FPSFA, *Relazione della presidenza 1932*, pp. 35-36; Consiglio Provinciale, *La provincia di Bologna*, pp. 608-609.

[36] C. Schmidt, *The Plough and the Sword*, p. 146.

[37] *Ibid.*; Ente Nazionale Risi, *L'opera del regime fascista attraverso l'Ente Nazionale Risi* (Milan, 1938), pp. 9-10.

[38] On rice production in Bologna, see Giorgio Stupazzoni, "Mezzo secolo d'agricoltura nel Bolognese," *La Mercanzia*, 1968, no. 6, p. 566.

prices fall by more than 50 percent between 1929 and 1931.[39] Voluntary measures by the National Consortium of Hemp Growers to reduce acreage and rationalize marketing operations met with little success largely because of tenacious opposition from the small cultivators. Consequently, the big growers who dominated the consortium turned to the state in 1930, demanding that it impose compulsory cartellization and centralize control of seed distribution, production, and marketing.[40] Their efforts were crowned in the summer of 1931 when the regime created the National Federation of Consortia for the Defense of Hemp Cultivation (Federcanapa). A series of decrees from 1932 to 1936 empowered the Federcanapa to issue licenses, standardize methods of cultivation, and set prices on the basis of agreements between farmers and processors. Although compulsory cartels and stockpiling primarily benefited the large processing companies, whose declared profits doubled from 1934 to 1939, they also strengthened the position of the big hemp growers by removing less fertile land from cultivation and excluding less productive farms from the markets.[41]

As this brief survey of farm policies and programs indicates, preferential treatment by the Fascist regime allowed commercial agrarian interests in Bologna and elsewhere in the Po Valley to turn adversity to their advantage. Protectionism, land reclamation, and export subsidies, which permitted the survival of economically inefficient estates and traditional social relations in the south, had very different consequences in the northern plains where they encouraged a process of agricultural modernization and rationalization. Significantly, the commercial farms of the Po Valley accounted for the bulk of new investments in tractors, chemical

[39] G. Proni, *La canapicoltura italiana*, p. 41.

[40] Despite the fall in prices, hemp production in Bologna declined only slightly, from 97,680 to 96,820 quintals between 1929 and 1930. See Consiglio Provinciale, *La provincia di Bologna*, p. 632. For the views of the Consortium, see Consorzio Nazionale Canapicultori, *Resoconto dell'adunanza del consiglio. Relazioni della presidenza* (Rome, 1930), pp. 30-35, 42-47.

[41] G. Proni, *La canapicoltura italiana*, p. 275. On the profits of the Linoficio e Canapificio Nazionale, see E. Sereni, *La questione agraria*, p. 263.

fertilizers, and land reclamation in the Italian countryside after 1926.[42] These investments translated into a qualitative and quantitative advance in northern agricultural production. During the early 1930s when producers of vegetable and fruit crops suffered a sharp drop in yields per hectare, sugar beet and rice growers were able to reduce total output and substantially increase the productivity of their farms. Similarly, wheat farmers in Emilia registered an increase in output per hectare that far outstripped that of any other regional group in the country from 1930 to 1934.[43] Moreover, the same period witnessed major changes in the organizational structure of northern agriculture with the growth of large farms and agrarian joint-stock companies, and the consolidation of cartels that limited competition, standardized production, and rationalized marketing operations.[44]

While it would be unwise to generalize about Fascist movements on the basis of a single local experience, the situation in Bologna after 1926, and the developments that led up to it, are not without a larger significance for historical debates on Italian fascism. Indeed, the pull of her example and the prominent role played by her spokesmen before and after World War I gave events in Bologna a wider national importance. To begin with, they underscore the difficulties of applying at the provincial level the distinction drawn by Renzo De Felice between the "true Fascists" of the movement and the "flankers" from the old ruling classes who sabotaged the original revolutionary project.[45] Apart from the problem of locating a cohesive group of "true Fascists" with a

[42] See Domenico Preti, "La politica agraria del fascismo: note introduttive," *Studi Storici*, XIV (1973), no. 4, pp. 858-859; P. Corner, "Considerazioni sull'agricoltura capitalistica," p. 526; P. Corner, "Fascist Agrarian Policy and the Italian Economy in the Inter-war Years," in John A. Davis, ed., *Gramsci and Italy's Passive Revolution* (London, 1979), p. 253.

[43] See A. Cadeddu, S. Lepre, F. Socrate, "Ristagno e sviluppo nell'agricoltura italiana," pp. 511-513.

[44] On the growth of large farms and joint-stock companies, see E. Sereni, *La questione agraria*, p. 195 and J. Cohen, "Rapporti agricoltura-industria e sviluppo agricolo," P. Ciocca and G. Toniolo, eds., *L'economia italiana nel periodo fascista* (Bologna, 1976), p. 403.

[45] See R. De Felice, *Fascism, An Informal Introduction to Its Theory and Practice* (New Brunswick, 1977), pp. 44-54.

coherent revolutionary project, such a distinction obscures the extent to which the propertied classes had entered into the organizational structure of provincial fascism well before the March on Rome. Much like their colleagues elsewhere in the Po Valley, Bolognese commercial farmers were no mere external supporters or "flankers" of fascism; they were actively involved at all levels of the movement and had a crucial part in the formulation of rural strategy as well as in the creation of new Fascist nuclei in the countryside. In this respect, the situation in Bologna supports the findings of Paul Corner in Ferrara and the more general conclusions of Valerio Castronovo, who have both stressed the instrumental character of fascism in the hands of Italian elites.[46]

The new structure of power and distribution of rewards and sacrifices in Bologna after 1926 also suggest the need to reconsider those interpretations that have portrayed Fascist movements as antimodernist revolts and Mussolini's regime, in particular, as a bulwark of reactionary and economically retrograde *latifondisti.*[47] The men who helped organize and ultimately controlled the Fascist movement in Bologna scarcely fit the image of died-in-the-wool reactionaries bent on preserving an archaic rural order. On the contrary, they were in the vanguard of capitalist agricultural development, the men who ran the most modern commercial farms, set up the new credit and marketing arrangements, and facilitated the integration of agricultural and industrial interests in the countryside. Nor was their influence limited to the province of Bologna, since they founded and led the new organizations that came to enjoy a virtual monopoly of agrarian interest representation during the Fascist era. The special protection and encouragement commercial farmers received under fascism does not fit the image of

[46] P. Corner, *Fascism in Ferrara*, pp. 282-288; V. Castronovo, "Il potere economico e il fascismo," in Guido Quazza, ed., *Fascismo e società italiana* (Turin, 1973), pp. 47-88.

[47] For a general statement of the 'anti-modernist' thesis, see H. A. Turner, Jr., "Fascism and Modernization," *World Politics*, XXIV, July 1972, pp. 547-564. On the Italian case, see E. Sereni, "La politica agraria del regime fascista," in Comitato promotore, *Fascismo e antifascismo (1918-1936). Lezioni e testimonianze* (Milan, 1972), pp. 298-304; P. Corner, "Rapporti tra agricoltura e industria durante il fascismo," *Problemi del Socialismo*, 1972, no. 11-12, pp. 721-722.

a regime that supposedly sacrificed industrial growth and the interests of capitalist agriculture in order to preserve anachronistic positions of privilege in the countryside. As Corner has argued, the fact that the big farms of the Po Valley increased their share of the value of agricultural production during the Fascist period implies the opposite, namely that "the *latifondista* of the South emerged from fascism in a position relatively weaker with respect to the capitalist areas of the North than he had been at the beginning of the regime."[48]

The reinforcement of commercial farming interests within the agricultural sector, however, should not be taken as evidence for the thesis advanced by A. James Gregor that Italian fascism was one of a number of twentieth-century "developmental regimes bent on the modernization and industrialization of their respective national communities."[49] To place fascism in the same category with bolshevism, maoism, and castroism distorts not only the intentions and achievements of Mussolini's regime, but also its relations with the Italian propertied classes. Above all, such an approach obscures the decisive new fusion of public and private power that allowed special interest groups to consolidate their positions within the national economy.[50] The historian Ester Fano has more aptly depicted the Italian economy under fascism as one of "growth without development."[51] For the regime's responsiveness to the immediate interests of strategic industrial and agrarian groups often came at the expense of longterm developmental needs of the economy. Wage and tariff policies that defended established profits and

[48] P. Corner, "Fascist Agrarian Policy," pp. 253-254.

[49] A. James Gregor, *Italian Fascism and Developmental Dictatorship* (Princeton, 1979), pp. 303-318; "Fascism and Modernization: Some Addenda," *World Politics*, XXIV (1972), pp. 370-384.

[50] In his work, *Interpretations of Fascism* (Morristown, N. J., 1974), pp. 202-203, Gregor argues that fascism "used the possessing class as repositories of investment capital" and that "in the last analysis, it was Fascism and not the coalition of propertied elites that came to control the political and economic system." For a more general discussion of the fusion of public and private power, see Roland Sarti, "Fascist Modernization in Italy: Traditional or Reactionary?" *The American Historical Review*, LXXV, April 1970, pp. 1043-1045.

[51] E. Fano, "Problemi e vicende dell'agricoltura," p. 493.

eased balance-of-payments difficulties served to accentuate the perennial inadequacy of the domestic market by reducing incomes and compressing consumer demand. The Battle of Wheat, in particular, created as many problems as it resolved, since it intensified regional imbalances, damaged livestock production, and retarded the growth of crops better suited to Italian climate and soil. Likewise, the proliferation of cartels and intersectoral agreements on prices and production discouraged innovation, mobility, and dynamism, acting thereby as a "powerful brake on the entire economy."[52]

On a more general level, the history of Bologna in the first three decades of the twentieth century raises certain questions about the connection drawn by Barrington Moore Jr. between commercial agriculture, based on a system of hired farm laborers, and the growth of Western democratic institutions. According to Moore, the emergence of fascism was linked to an institutional complex characterized by "labor-repressive agrarian systems" that relied upon strong political mechanisms rather than the workings of the labor market to ensure an adequate work force and profitability.[53] In the case of Italy, however, the Fascist movement found its first and greatest rural stronghold not in the regions of the south that traditionally used these mechanisms, but in the most advanced areas of capitalist agriculture in the Po Valley. The Bolognese experience suggests a quite different analysis of the problem of fascism and agrarian structure in Italy, one that emphasizes the central importance of commercial farming and agricultural wage labor in shaping the latent civil war that led to the movement as well as the policies the regime subsequently pursued in the countryside.

At the same time, the course of events in Bologna provides a concrete demonstration of Charles Maier's thesis that "rescuing bourgeois Europe meant recasting bourgeois Europe." Both before

[52] R. Sarti, *Fascism and the Industrial Leadership in Italy, 1919-1940* (Berkeley, 1971), p. 102; on the problems created by the Battle of Grain, see C. Schmidt, *The Plough and the Sword*, pp. 59-65.

[53] Barrington Moore Jr., *Social Origins of Dictatorship and Democracy* (Boston, 1966), pp. 433-435.

and after World War I, developments in the province reflected various larger European patterns: the growing influence of working class organizations, the gradual shift from parliamentary parties to organized interest groups, the desperate search for stability in the face of mass radicalization. More specifically, the increasingly antagonistic relations between agrarian interest groups of the Po Valley and the old liberal political class underscores the significance that Maier has attributed to Italy's failure "to replace her antique parliamentary and party structure."[54] Likewise, the situation in Bologna after 1926 illustrates how the achievement of stability meant considerably more than the restoration of prewar society. It involved not only new institutional arrangements and a new agrarian leadership, but also a fundamental restructuring of power relations within the propertied classes.

Fascism, as Maier has argued, was distinguished less by its economic policies, which often paralleled those of the parliamentary regions of the West, than by its reliance on dictatorial methods. Economic consolidation and modernization of corporate organization in Mussolini's Italy was largely the result of political coercion and the authoritarian regimentation of labor.[55] In the countryside peasant laborers paid for the advance of commercial agriculture in the form of increased exploitation and a diminished standard of living. Policies that crudely rewarded the rich and penalized the weak precluded any genuine social peace and required the presence of a permanent repressive apparatus. When that apparatus finally collapsed under the burdens of military defeat, Nazi occupation, and civil war, some of the foremost luminaries of agrarian fascism in Bologna would pay the ultimate price for the advantages they had enjoyed under the regime.[56]

[54] Charles Maier, *Recasting Bourgeois Europe* (Princeton, 1975), p. 592.

[55] *Ibid.*, pp. 577-578. For surveys of the responses of various European governments to the crisis in agriculture, see the sources cited in note 3.

[56] On the hardships and violence suffered by some of the most prominent commercial farmers in Bologna after 1943, see A. Bignardi, *Costruttori di terra* (Bologna, 1958).

References

Unpublished Documents

The major part of the documents that I have consulted are from the Archivio di Stato di Bologna, Gabinetto Riservato di Prefettura. For the period from 1901 to 1928, the materials are organized according to subject for each year in the following categories:

(1) Categoria 4, Fascicoli 1 and 2: "Sindaci, amministrazioni comunali e provinciali"
(2) Categoria 5, Fascicoli 1 and 2: "Elezioni politiche e amministrative"
(3) Categoria 6, Fascicolo 2: "Agitazioni operaie, disoccupazione, scioperi, dimostrazioni, congressi"
(4) Categoria 7, Fascicolo 1: "Partiti politici e associazioni"
(5) Categoria 16, Fascicolo 1: "Agitazioni agrarie, agricoltura" (1919-28)

The Gabinetto Riservato includes these special categories for the indicated years:

(1) Categoria 6: "Agitazioni operaie a Molinella" (1914)
(2) Categoria 6, Fascicolo 1: "Avvenimenti straordinari" (1915)
(3) Categoria 7, Fascicolo 1: "Ordine pubblico" (1919-22)
(4) Categoria 7: "I fascisti" (1921)
(5) Categoria 7: "Fatti del 21 novembre 1920, avvenimenti inerenti a fatti politici" (1921)

The Archivio di Stato di Bologna also contains a number of institutional and family archives. The following have been consulted:

(1) Archivio della Camera di Commercio
(2) Carte di amministrazione del Ducato di Galliera
(3) Archivio Privato Malvezzi de' Medici
(4) Archivio De' Bosdari, "Circolo Cavour: 1890-1910"

For the years from 1917 to 1928, the following series of documents were consulted at the Archivio Centrale dello Stato in Rome:

(1) Ministero dell'Interno
  Direzione Generale di Pubblica Sicurezza, Affari Generali e Riservati (1922-24)
  Gabinetto Finzi (1922-24)

(2) Ministero delle Armi e Munizioni (1917)

(3) Segretaria Particolare del Duce, Carteggio Riservato

(4) Mostra della Rivoluzione Fascista

(5) Presidenza del Consiglio dei Ministri (1923-26)

In addition, I have consulted the family archive of Marchese Giuseppe Tanari in the Biblioteca Comunale di Bologna. The documents, which include Tanari's correspondence, speeches, and position papers, are organized as follows:

(1) Carteggio XXXIX, 2: "Scioperi e boicottagi, polemiche"
  3: "Atteggiamenti del Tanari all'inizio della guerra europea, 1914-16"

(2) Carteggio XL, 4: "Azione contro-bolscevica e altre questioni politiche"

Information concerning the structure of landownership in the plains was drawn from the Catasto dei Terreni, Registro delle partite in the Ufficio Tecnico Erariale di Bologna. The Catasto, which was compiled in 1924 and 1925, lists all the landowners by commune, the extent of their holdings, and their taxable value. Moreover, it registers all changes in ownership from 1925 to 1945. I have made use of the Catasto for the communes of San Pietro in Casale, Sant' Agata Bolognese, Baricella, Bentivoglio, Budrio, Galliera, Malalbergo, Medicina, Molinella, Sala Bolognese, San Giovanni in Persiceto, Crevalcore, Minerbio, Sasso Marconi, San Giorgio di Piano, Ozzano Emilia, Imola, and Bazzano.

Printed and Published Governmental Publications

Atti Parlamentari, Camera dei Deputati, Discussioni, Rome, 1893, 1901, 1908.

Atti Parlamentari, Senato del Regno, Discussioni, Rome, 1901.

Atti della Giunta per la inchiesta agraria sulle condizioni della classe agricola, Vol. III, *Relazione del commissario, Marchese Luigi Tanari*. Rome, 1881.

Bollettino dell'Ufficio del Lavoro. 1901-14.

Bollettino del Lavoro e della Previdenza Sociale. 1923.

La città e provincia di Bologna descritta nei suoi rapporti storici, statistici, topografici, e commerciali. Bologna, 1889.

Ministero di Agricoltura, Industria e Commercio, Direzione Generale della Statistica. *Annuario statistico italiano.* Rome, 1900, 1904, 1911, 1913, 1917-18, 1919-20.

———. *Censimento della popolazione del Regno d'Italia 1901,* Vol. III. Rome, 1902.

———. *Statistica delle organizzazioni padronali,* Vol. I, *Le agrarie.* Rome, 1912.

Ministero per la Costituente. *Rapporto della commissione economica presentato all'assemblea costituente,* Vol. I, *Agricoltura,* and Vol. II, *Industria.* Rome, 1947.

Agrarian Publications

1. Periodicals

L'Agraria Bolognese. 1911-13 (organ of the Bolognese Agrarian Association).

L'Agraria. 1915-18 (monthly journal of the National Agrarian Confederation.

L'Agricolture d'Italia. 1923-26 (organ of the FISA).

L'Agricoltura Bolognese. 1901-22 (monthly technical journal).

Annali dell'Osservatorio di Economia Agraria di Bologna. 1928-32 (publication of the Istituto Nazionale di Economia Agraria).

Annali della Società Agraria Provinciale di Bologna. 1892-1910.

Annali dell'Ufficio provinciale per l'Agricoltura ed Atti del Comizio Agrario di Bologna. 1900-1904.

Bollettino dell'Associazione Provinciale degli Agricoltori Bolognesi. Spring-Summer 1920.

Bollettino dell'Associazione Agraria Parmense. Nov. 1907.

Bollettino della Società degli Agricoltori Italiani. 1901-1902, 1905, 1907-1908.

Bollettino del Sindacato Agricoltori di Bazzano. 1923-25.

Bollettino Federale Agrario. 1908-12 (publication of the Interprovincial Agrarian Federation).

Bollettino Mensile del Consorzio Agrario Bolognese. 1901-15.

Giornale Agrario. 1919-22 (weekly publication of the National Agricultural Secretariat and National Confederation of Agriculture).

Italia Agricola. 1926-32 (publication of Federconsorzi).

Italia Industriale e Agraria. 1913-15.

La Tribuna Agraria. 1908 (organ of the Agrarian Society of Imola).

2. Books and Pamphlets

Associazione Agraria Bolognese. *La questione Zerbini. Un agitazione agraria rivelata nelle sue cause, nel suo scopo, e nelle sue responsabilità.* Bologna, 1912.

———. *Per la Mobilitazione Agricola. Memoriale presentato a S.E. Ministro dell'Agricoltura.* Bologna, 1917.

Associazione Provinciale degli Agricoltori Bolognesi. *Intorno alla vertenza bolognese.* Bologna, 1921.

Bizzozero, Antonio. *Diciotto anni di cooperazione agraria 1893-1910.* Parma, 1911.

Camera di Commercio. *Appunti per gli studi sulle industrie locali nei riguardi dell 'dopoguerra.'* Bologna, 1918.

Cavazza, Count Filippo. *La compartecipazione ai prodotti agricoli in rapporto all'elevazione economica dei lavoratori della terra e all'incremento della produzione.* Bologna, 1919.

——— and Donini, Alberto. *Produzione agricola e mano d'opera.* Bologna, 1918.

Coletti, Francesco. *Le associazioni agrarie in Italia dalla metà del secolo XVIII alla fine del XIX.* Rome, 1901.

Comizio Agrario di Bologna. *Monografia del podere bolognese.* Bologna, 1884.

Confederazione Nazionale Agraria, *Annuario Agrario 1913-14. Annuario delle associazioni agrarie italiane.* Bologna, 1914.

———. *Atti del II Congresso Agrario in Bologna, 28-29 novembre 1909.* Bologna, 1911.

———. *L'organizzazione agraria in Italia. Sviluppo, ordinamento, azione.* Bologna, 1911.

———. *Per la riforma del Consiglio Superiore del Lavoro.* Turin, 1910.

Confederazione Nazionale Sindacati Fascisti dell'Agricoltura, Unione Provinciale di Bologna. *I nostri problemi. Un anno di attività.* Bologna, 1930.

Consociazione fra Proprietari ed Affittuari del Mandamento di San Giorgio di Piano. *Relazione economico-morale del consiglio di amministrazione.* Bologna, 1907.

Consorzio Nazionale Canapicultori. *Resoconto dell'adunanza del consiglio. Relazione della presidenza.* Rome, 1930.

De Morsier, Frank. *Dalla Camera di Commercio al Consiglio Provinciale dell'Economia di Bologna.* Bologna, 1928.

Ente Nazionale Risi. *L'opera del regime fascista attraverso l'Ente Nazionale Risi.* Milan, 1938.

Federazione Provinciale Fascista degli Agricoltori. *Relazione della presidenza 1932*. Bologna, 1932.
Feletti, A. *Gli scioperi a fronte del governo e dei possidenti*. Bologna, 1902.
Fornaciari, Julo. *Attività e problemi dell'organizzazione dei bieticultori*. Bologna, 1934.
Ghigi, Giorgio. *Relazione sulle condizioni agrarie in provincia di Bologna nell'anno 1920*. Bologna, 1921.
L'Italia agricola e il suo avvenire. Rome, 1919.
Paglia, Calisto. *Donazione Pizzardi. Relazione sul modo di gestire la tenuta di Bentivoglio*. Bologna, 1923.
Poni, Vincenzo. *La tariffa doganale del 1 luglio 1921 e gli interessi dell'agricoltura*. Piacenza, 1923.
Roversi, Roberto. *Canapa ed autarchia*. Rome, 1939.
Società degli Agricoltori Italiani. *I recenti scioperi agrari in Italia e i loro effetti economici*. Rome, 1902.
Sturani, Giovanni Enrico. *Ancora del decimo sciopero di Molinella*. Bologna, 1900.
———. *Le consociazioni agrarie della provincia di Bologna. Organizzazione e programma*. Bologna, 1905.
———. *La Mutua-Scioperi. Sue basi economiche e suo ordinamento*. Bologna, 1909.
Tanari, Marchese Giuseppe. *Studi sulla questione agraria*. Bologna, 1918.
Zampieri, G. *Note sull'agitazione agraria imolese nel 1910*. Bologna, 1910.

Press

L'Assalto. 1921-24 (weekly).
Avanti! (selected issues).
L'Avvenire d'Italia (selected issues).
La Fiaccola. 1907-1909 (weekly).
Giornale dell'Emilia. 1901-1904, 1907.
Giornale di Bologna. 1904-1906.
Giornale d'Italia (selected issues).
Libertà Economica. 1918-22 (weekly).
Il Progresso. 1920-22.
Il Resto del Carlino. 1893, 1897, 1901-25.
Il Secolo (selected issues).
La Squilla. 1901-1902, 1904-1907, 1919-21.

Memoirs, Speeches, Biographies, Autobiographies

Antonelli, Lucilla. *Il santo della palude. Biografia di Giuseppe Massarenti.* Milan, 1955.

Brown, Benjamin, ed. *Sidney Sonnino. Scritti e discorsi extraparlamentari, 1870-1902.* Bari, 1972.

Carocci, Giampiero, ed. *Dalle carte di Giovanni Giolitti. Quarant'anni di politica italiana,* Vol. II, *Dieci anni al potere, 1901-1909.* Milan, 1962.

Corradini, Enrico. *Discorsi politici 1902-1923.* Florence, 1923.

Giolitti, Giovanni. *Memorie della mia vita.* Milan, 1923.

———. *Memoirs of My Life.* London, 1923.

Salandra, Antonio. *La politica nazionale e il partito liberale.* Milan, 1912.

Tanari, Marchese Giuseppe. *La mia evoluzione politica al fascismo.* Bologna, 1933.

Contemporary Books and Articles, 1900-1922

Bachi, Riccardo. *L'Italia economica nell'anno 1913. Annuario della vita commerciale, industriale, agraria, bancaria, finanziaria, e della politica economica.* Turin, 1913.

———. *L'Italia economica nell'anno 1915.* Turin, 1916.

———. *L'Italia economica nell'anno 1918.* Città di Castello, 1919.

———. *L'Italia economica nell'anno 1919.* Città di Castello, 1920.

———. *L'Italia economica nell'anno 1920.* Città di Castello, 1921.

———. *L'Italia economica nell'anno 1921.* Città di Castello, 1922.

Bertolini, Angelo. "Lo sciopero di Molinella." *Giornale degli Economisti,* Vol. XXI, 1900.

———. "Scioperi in Italia nel 1898 e 1899 e all'estero nel 1898, 1899, 1900." *Giornale degli Economisti,* Vol. XXIV, 1902.

Carli, Filippo. *L'altra guerra.* Milan, 1916.

Colajanni, Napoleone. "Il movimento agrario in Italia." *Rivista d'Italia,* 1902.

Credito Italiano. *Società Italiane per azioni, 1914.* Rome, 1915.

———. *Società Italiane per azioni, 1920,* Vols. I-III. Rome, 1921.

Lanzillo, Agostino. *Le rivoluzioni del dopoguerra.* Città di Castello, 1922.

Missiroli, Mario, *Il fascismo e la crisi italiana.* Bologna, 1921.

———. *Polemica liberale.* Bologna, 1919.

———. *La repubblica degli accatoni.* Bologna, 1916.

Morselli, Giovanni. *Le industrie chimiche italiane.* Milan, 1911.

Peglion, Vittorio. *Piante industriale. Produzione, commercio, regime doganale.* Rome, 1917.

Puglioli, Pietro. "La coltivazione del riso nei rapporti della disoccupazione operaia e della malaria nella pianura bolognese." *Bollettino Ufficiale del Ministero di Agricoltura, Industria e Commercio*, Vol. II, 1906, no. 4.

Ufficio del Lavoro della Società Umanitaria. *La disoccupazione nel basso emiliano. Inchiesta diretta nelle provincie di Ferrara, Bologna, e Ravenna.* Milan, 1904.

Valenti, G. "L'Italia agricola dal 1861 al 1911," in *Cinquanta anni di storia italiana*, Vol. II. Milan, 1911.

Zerbini, Luigi. *L'agricoltura nel bolognese. Cenni e dati statistici delle tenute Bentivoglio e San Marino.* Bologna, 1913.

———. *Illustrazione delle principali aziende agrarie nel Bolognese.* Bologna, 1913.

Contemporary Books and Articles, 1923-1939

Camera di Commercio e Industria della provincia di Bologna. *Cenno storico sulla Camera di Commercio e Industria di Bologna e caratteristiche economiche del distretto camerale.* Bologna, 1924.

Cassa di Risparmio. *La Cassa di Risparmio in Bologna nei suoi primi cento anni.* Bologna, 1937.

Chiurco, G. A. *Storia della rivoluzione fascista*, Vol. II and III. Florence, 1929.

Coletti, Francesco. *Economia rurale e politica rurale in Italia. Raccolta di studi.* Piacenza, 1926.

Consiglio Provinciale dell'Economia Corporativa. *La provincia di Bologna nell'anno decimo. Monografia statistica-economica.* Bologna, 1932.

Corbino, E. *Annali dell'economia italiana*, 5 vols. Città di Castello, 1931-36.

Einaudi, Luigi. *La condotta economica e gli effetti sociali della guerra italiana.* Bari, 1933.

Pagani, Aldo. *I braccianti della valle padana.* Rome, 1932.

———. *Rapporti fra proprietà, impresa, e mano d'opera nell'agricoltura italiana*, Vol. XIII, *Emilia*. Milan-Rome, 1932.

Passerini, Osvaldo. *Inchiesta sulla piccola proprietà coltivatrice formatasi nel dopoguerra*, Vol. VII, *Emilia e Marche*. Milan, 1932.

Perdisa, Luigi. *La bietola da zucchero nell'economia italiana.* Rome, 1938.

———. *Monografia economico-agraria dell'Emilia.* Faenza, 1937.

Pesce, G. *La marcia dei rurali.* Rome, 1929.

Pittigliani, Fausto. *The Italian Corporative State.* London, 1933.

Proni, Giovanni. *La canapicoltura italiana nell'economia corporativa.* Rome, 1938.

Riguzzi, Biagio. *Sindacalismo e riformismo nel Parmense.* Bari, 1931.

Roletto, Giorgio. "Le basi geografiche dell'economia bolognese." *Il Comune di Bologna*, 1929, no. 6-7.
Schmidt, Carl T. *The Plough and the Sword: Labor, Land and Property in Fascist Italy*. New York, 1938.
Serpieri, Arrigo. *La guerra e le classi rurali italiane*. Bari, 1930.
Sessa, Ernesto. *Della canapa e del lino in Italia*. Milan, 1930.
Tassinari, Giuseppe. *La bonifica integrale nel decennale della legge Mussolini*. Rome, 1935.
Zanolini, Carlo, Boraggine, Giuseppe, and Zucchini, Dino. *Sunto storico monografico della Società Agraria di Bologna dall'anno 1807 all'anno 1938*. Bologna, 1939.

Index

Library of Congress Cataloging in Publication Data

Cardoza, Anthony L., 1947-
Agrarian elites and Italian fascism.

Bibliography: p. Includes index.
1. Bologna (Italy : Province)—Politics and government. 2. Fascism—Italy—Bologna (Province)—History—20th century. 3. Elite (Social sciences)—Italy—Bologna (Province)—History—20th century. 4. Bologna (Italy : Province)—Rural conditions.
I. Title.
DG975.B64C37 1982 945'.41 82-47585
ISBN 0-691-05360-X